The Midshipman Culture
and Educational Reform

The Midshipman Culture and Educational Reform

The U.S. Naval Academy 1946–76

Todd A. Forney

Newark: University of Delaware Press

© 2004 by Rosemont Publishing & Printing Corp.

All rights reserved. Authorization to photocopy items for internal or personal use, or the internal or personal use of specific clients, is granted by the copyright owner, provided that a base fee of $10.00, plus eight cents per page, per copy is paid directly to the Copyright Clearance Center, 222 Rosewood Drive, Danvers, Massachusetts 01923. [0-87413-864-7/04 $10.00 + 8¢ pp, pc.]

Other than as indicated in the foregoing, this book may not be reproduced, in whole or in part, in any form (except as permitted by Sections 107 and 108 of the U.S. Copyright Law), and except for brief quotes appearing in reviews in the public press.

Associated University Presses
2010 Eastpark Boulevard
Cranbury, NJ 08512

The paper used in this publication meets the requirements of the American National Standard for Permanence of Paper for Printed Library Materials Z39.48-1984.

Library of Congress Cataloging-in-Publication Data

Forney, Todd A., 1964–
    The midshipman culture and educational reform : the U.S. Naval Academy, 1946–76 / Todd A. Forney
       p. cm.
    Includes bibliographical and references and index.
     ISBN 0-87413-864-7 (alk. paper)
    1. United States Naval Academy—History—20th century. I. Title.
V415.L1F67 2004
359′.0071′173—dc22

2003024714

PRINTED IN THE UNITED STATES OF AMERICA

Contents

Acknowledgments	7
Introduction	13
1. The Naval Academy of the 1940s: From Trade School to Naval University	38
2. The Naval Academy of the 1950s: Old Traditions Die Hard	79
3. The Early Years of the "Academic Revolution," 1959–62: Laying the Foundations for a New Academy	110
4. The "Academic Revolution" Triumphant, 1962–65: Further Gains and Controversy for the New Academy	136
5. A "Professional Revolution" at Annapolis, 1965–68: Discord for the New Academy	166
6. The Fine Line Between Athens and Sparta: The Calvert Years at Annapolis, 1968–72	203
7. Steering a Sensible Course: The New Annapolis, 1972–76	246
Conclusion	265
Tables	276
Appendix: Survey of Student Life at the U.S. Naval Academy, 1946–76	338
Notes	351
Bibliography	389
Index	405

Acknowledgments

Projects like these teach important character lessons. Few people complete their dissertations without learning about humility. However, I believe that is part of becoming a good scholar. Not only do we learn respect for the difficulties of our disciplines; it also teaches us the importance of cooperation in academic endeavors. At the beginning of the project, we know something about it but hopefully not all. If that were so, there would not be much reason for undertaking it in the first place. Along the way, we learn new skills and ways of understanding things from those who graciously work with us. In return, our insight is hopefully of benefit to them.

Authors receive most of the credit for the final product. However, most would admit others' help was crucial to even being in that position. These debts are impossible to repay. In my experience, most contributors became involved not because of any tangible reward. They lent their time and expertise because of a belief in the project's importance. And even more humbling, their efforts were a commitment to my development as a scholar *and* a person. These sacrifices are especially true of those who provided encouragement and moral support. I am profoundly grateful to everyone who has helped me through this journey. Hopefully, the final product is worthy of the faith you have shown in me.

I want to thank the members of my dissertation committee for their advice, encouragement, and patience in this whole process. They suffered through many *rough* drafts to help refine my ideas. I am deeply impressed by the high professional standards of my dissertation adviser, Dr. Allan Millett. On many occasions, it would have been easy for him to ignore slipshod ideas, especially with his busy schedule. But for as much as I questioned it at the time, his "red pen" actually showed his deep concern for this project. Dr. John Guilmartin was always a useful sounding board. His own experiences at the Air Force Academy were a valuable contrast to Annapolis. The final member of my committee, Dr. David Stebenne, was also tireless in my behalf. He challenged me to think beyond the Naval Academy in clarifying its history with other institutions. Each of them is a strong example of what I hope to be as a historian.

The staff of the Naval Academy archives was extremely supportive of my research. Oftentimes, they pointed me towards sources with which I was not familiar. My old mentor when I was a midshipman, Dr. Bill Roberts, patiently listened to my ideas. He too pointed me in directions important to the project's outcome. His efforts were crucial in putting together presentations at the Naval History Symposium and the Society for Military History. I must also thank the staffs of the Polimetrics Laboratory and the Survey Research Unit at Ohio State University. The former assisted in developing the questionnaire given to the thirty classes of academy alumni. The latter taught me how to analyze its results. Finally, Dr. Donald Mell and the University of Delaware Press were very helpful during the publication process. Being a neophyte in all these areas, their assistance was truly a godsend to me.

I would not have completed the dissertation without the unconditional support of my friends and family. My workload often stretched the boundaries of what common sense should reasonably ask of them. Yet, they were unwavering in their encouragement of the dissertation. Their faithfulness did not stem from any particular passion for military history but because of its importance to me. My good friend, Jim Bell, endured innumerable requests for computer assistance. Along the way, his support included a computer for the data entry from the questionnaire, tutorials on the intricacies of Microsoft Word, and many hours of unselfish labor correcting the inevitable formatting difficulties. He good-naturedly tells me that he did not write the dissertation. But I am not convinced its completion would have come so smoothly without his help. Another friend and former roommate, Mike Fields, designed the dust jacket cover for the book. Mike supported me when I started this project. And now, he has been of great help with its completion. I am extremely fortunate to have such supportive and creative friends.

I cannot express how important my mother, Eileen Hohenstein, has been during my years in graduate school. Without her, there were many times I would have quit out of frustration. Her life, along with many kind words, gave me the confidence to continue the battle. I have also asked much of my wife, Maureen Beytagh, more than rightfully should be expected. She has borne more than her share of our marriage's responsibilities during the dissertation. Wondering when it would be done has tested her sanity on several occasions. I do not know about other dissertations, but my family's showering of love was indispensable in completing mine.

Finally, I would like to thank my fellow alumni who participated in the survey on midshipmen life. Many of them went beyond the call providing additional material for my research. Again, their support was not because they knew me personally. First of all, it was important to them that I got the story right, a testament to their love for Annapolis. Secondly, the academy taught them well its most important lesson—whenever possible, look out for your shipmates. My hope is that what follows captures something of their "four years together by the bay."

The Midshipman Culture
and Educational Reform

Introduction

I FIRST BECAME INTERESTED IN STUDYING THE INSTITUTIONAL CULTURE at Annapolis after learning about its scandals in the early 1990s. The worst involved large numbers of midshipmen, including several prominent athletes, accused of cheating on an electrical engineering exam. Even more distressing, the academy was rumored to have to some degree swept this scandal under the rug.[1] Other smaller scandals hit alumni like shock waves in subsequent years. On a San Diego naval base, one graduate murdered two classmates, one of them his ex-girlfriend and the other a former star quarterback, and committed suicide shortly afterwards. Every few months it seemed midshipmen stood accused of antisocial behavior unthinkable in previous years, ranging from stealing cars to trafficking drugs. From a public relations standpoint, it went from being the Navy's showcase institution to its eyesore.

In retrospect, one can see that most midshipmen did everything asked of them and graduated to become productive career Navy and Marine Corps officers. At the time, it seemed as if there were endemic problems at Annapolis. Indeed, these incidents prompted the commissioning of a blue ribbon panel in 1996, headed by former CIA director and academy graduate Stansfield Turner, to determine what corrective actions were needed. Vocal alumni blamed the scandals on an overly permissive environment that taught wrong character values to midshipmen. Depending on whom you talked to, its decline dated back to a more liberal academic curriculum, the relaxation of disciplinary standards to conform to new social norms, or women's admission into the Brigade. Most of these theories were largely speculative, however, not confirmed with any sort of historical research.[2]

I was amazed by the academy's lack of formal history the further I got into the project. Most works tended to be popular histories or focused commentaries on subjects like gender integration or the honor code. But in terms of asking questions common in social and cultural history, precious little was done on it.[3] The shortage of material has nothing to do with the validity of the subject itself. Annapolis was an important institution that has produced the bulk of career officers for the Navy and the Marine Corps. Moreover, its graduates have played important roles in American history beyond fighting in its wars. They were the nation's political and business leaders, statesmen, scientists, and astronauts, to name a few accomplishments. Thus, a study of this formative institution was historically worthwhile in terms of what it taught and how it influenced these people. To borrow a concept from Samuel Huntington, Charles Moskos, and Allan Millett, I wanted to see how professional socialization took place from both the institution's and the midshipmen's perspective.[4] In other words, how were midshipmen trained to be officers? Furthermore, did the nature of officership change during this study? If it did, what caused that change, the Navy's needs or the pool from which it drew its officers?

Moreover, a study of this nature could also shed light on the military's place in American society. Did midshipmen learn and practice traditions representative of society? Or were midshipmen part of a military caste with beliefs and goals different from mainstream America? Finally, a study of the midshipmen culture might provide an interesting contrast with what Erving Goffman has called "total institutions."[5] From a sociological perspective, what was Bancroft Hall like, the place midshipmen not only called home but also the focal point for professional training and indoctrination? Did this closed society function differently than the larger one it defended? If there was a difference, what did that mean from the standpoint of American civil military relations?

I chose as my study's chronological bounds the ending of both World War II and the Vietnam War. These dates were not only major milestones for society but also the Naval Academy. Throughout the years, the culture of Bancroft Hall has been extremely resistant to change. It was quite literally the heart and soul of the Naval Academy because of its role in professional socialization. Midshipmen negotiated many hurdles, but none was more difficult or unforgiving as Bancroft Hall. The rules and obligations of that culture frequently made sense only to the Brigade. Midshipmen diligently passed down traditions to their juniors, even those that flew in the face of current regulations. The academy staff, many of them also graduates, occasionally overlooked violations necessary for preserving the spirit of that culture. Academy traditions could be a source of both pride and frustration for midshipmen however. The unbending lifestyle imposed obligations that often seemed one step removed from the times. The joke that was passed around by my peers in the late 1980s to describe this situation was "Annapolis—150 years unhampered by progress." To my surprise, I found earlier generations of midshipmen voicing similar complaints.

At the same time, midshipmen took great pride in being part of the "long blue line" of graduates; the common thread, of course, was the four-year Annapolis experience. Alumni often chided their juniors for having a softer time than they did. For example, no class would admit to having an easier plebe year to those that followed them. It would be unthinkable, however, for the older generation to admit that standards were either the same or tougher. Admitting the former confers an equivalency of status the older generation is not ready to give. Conceding the latter would take away from the accomplishments of one's youth, something that could not be redone. The actual differences seemed small, however, especially in comparison to the ties binding academy graduates together.

Amid all this continuity, there have been periods where the possibility of change was much greater than the rest. The post–World War II era was just such a turning point in academy history. Curriculum reform was an ongoing process that changed its priorities and values tremendously. For the first time, Annapolis was expected to be a center of both professional *and* academic excellence. The quest to upgrade academic standards forced it to reevaluate the essential aspects of its professional training program. Good colleges did not compromise their academic program for Bancroft Hall. Training requirements also had to be adapted because of military specialization. New warfare communities made it a marketplace of ideas and priorities with regard to professional socialization. Finally, it could not ignore the forces of democratization sweeping higher education. An ongoing challenge was reconciling institutional goals with the priorities of newer midshipmen. Fewer of them were committed to a traditional military career. Although slow at first, Annapolis also suffered a growing estrangement between it and the larger culture, an unfortunate trend common throughout the American military.

These challenges first surfaced in the aftermath of World War II. In one sense, the war was a resounding triumph for Annapolis. However, the demand for larger standing forces ended its monopoly of regular officers. To satisfy manpower needs, the Navy established NROTC as a permanent program. Although not intended that way, NROTC opened the door for criticism of Annapolis.[6] New technology developed during the war also brought its curriculum into question. There did not seem to be an alternative but to upgrade scholastic standards and take steps towards joining the larger academic community.[7] The early 1950s were also a difficult time for the academy. The intensification of the Cold War made military readiness a pressing issue. However, lingering war weariness often prevented it from securing sufficient resources for meaningful reform. The country's booming economy made it difficult to fill classes with qualified applicants. Prosperity fueled a remarkable growth in higher education, which also increased the competition for good students. Literally hundreds of midshipmen accepted Air Force commissions to avoid a restrictive assignment policy that required them to first serve onboard ships.[8]

The launching of Sputnik in 1959 raised concerns about the country's technological edge in the Cold War. Academy critics, particularly Admiral Hyman Rickover, used the crisis to demand additional reforms of the lockstep curriculum, which they claimed jeopardized national security.[9]

Within a decade, the Naval Academy enacted a flurry of reforms it dubbed "the academic revolution." By its end, midshipmen received accredited degrees and eventually earned majors. Most could expect to attend graduate school later in their careers.[10] Supporters praised the reforms for transforming the academy into a first-rate academic institution attractive to the most talented students. Critics decried that Annapolis existed for training career naval officers not professional engineers and worried about the effect of these changes on its military culture. Better students were needed to handle the tougher, new curriculum. Would these midshipmen share the same values and career aspirations as past generations?[11] How much would Bancroft Hall need to accommodate the new curriculum? Not surprisingly, upperclassmen and even officers resisted reforms that challenged their most cherished traditions, particularly in regard to plebe indoctrination.[12]

If this was not enough, Annapolis also struggled with the turmoil of Vietnam. The Brigade's morale was difficult to maintain the longer the war dragged on. Many midshipmen eventually knew classmates who were killed in combat. They were often harassed in public simply for being part of the military. Unfortunately, midshipmen had to defend themselves, their school, and the Navy from accusations that were often hurtful and unfair. This was a lot to ask of young men in their late teens and early twenties. The Naval Academy also found its lifestyle challenged by changing social values. In the early 1970s, the Supreme Court ended mandatory chapel despite its protests that it was critical in molding the midshipmen's character. Longtime restrictions on driving automobiles and consuming alcohol also seemed outdated. The academy was even ordered to follow new grooming regulations issued by Admiral Elmo Zumwalt, the maverick chief of naval operations. Academy leaders were more responsive to these concerns than they were given credit for, especially since these were no-win situations. Their reforms tried to make academy regulations more reflective of what midshipmen would find in the fleet.

Upperclassmen finally received driving privileges; first classmen could even park their cars on academy grounds. Only a small duty staff from each company was required to remain at Annapolis during a typical weekend. The rest enjoyed extended liberty privileges, including in some cases civilian clothes. Midshipmen who met Maryland's new laws could drink alcohol while on liberty. Rooms did not have to be organized exactly the same way so long as they kept up a neat and orderly appearance. Reform never came fast or far enough to please many midshipmen. They felt the academy could have done more to make its lifestyle further reflective of society. Many alumni trained under the older program were appalled by the changes however. Coupled with the academic reforms, the new academy was in their judgment inferior to the past. Newer graduates insisted that nothing essential had changed; the academy was still a rugged test of endurance that prepared them for the fleet. Traditions were important to them but not at the expense of progress.[13]

During my research, I interviewed alumni from 1946 to 1976. Some reacted harshly not only to these reforms but also my status as a recent graduate in 1986. One said he no longer wore his academy ring because he was ashamed by what it had become. Removing it was not only a symbol of protest but also his way of breaking ties with the institution. Another explained in a disparaging tone that Annapolis was so different I could not understand what it meant to him. In his mind, the community of graduates was not all-inclusive but one with barriers separating those trained under the different systems. For many older alumni, the absolute dividing line was women's admission in 1976. In their minds, this change poisoned everything the older system accomplished and the academy was forever changed as a result. It is because of perceptions like these that I ended my study in 1976 rather than include women in it. Certainly, no other event suggested such a traumatic shock to the all-male culture of Annapolis and for that reason alone demands its own study.

But for many, the roots of the academy's decline came earlier with the "academic revolution" and the social reforms of the 1960s and 1970s. Before dismissing these observations as sour grapes from a past generation, it is important to remember that their concern for Annapolis is genuine. Moreover, many of their surface observations appear correct. Much indeed has changed in the fifty or so years since World War II in terms of the curriculum and training program. If surface comparisons are the only gauge, however, then much also remains the same. Midshipmen essentially dress the same as they did fifty years ago; they participate in similar ceremonies and traditions. With the exception of gender, the Brigade that marches on Worden Field today is virtually identical. But surface comparisons are not the only observations that can be made about the midshipmen culture. Methodological tools from social and cultural history allow a more precise analysis.

For example, current midshipmen follow many of the same traditions as past classes. In some cases, traditions appear the same but have a different meaning. Conversely, with areas that seem dissimilar, continuity does exist but at a deeper level. For example, midshipmen often use slang understandable only at the academy. In the 1940s and 1950s, calling someone a "slash" was an insult, given only to midshipmen that wrecked the academic curve. Current midshipmen still use the term "slash" but to them it simply means someone who does well in their classes. On the other hand, plebe indoctrination is an area that on the surface appears incredibly different. Few plebes today experience the degree of physical hazing previous groups endured. Seen in the best light, the intent behind this abuse was to develop an ability to function under stress. That goal remains the same, the protests of older alumni notwithstanding. Teamwork and time management are just as important today in overcoming the obstacles of plebe year.[14]

Demographic studies are also useful in understanding major changes in the midshipmen culture. Although midshipmen were never clones of one another, the differences have often seemed slight. Over the long haul, even a simple demographic analysis can reveal important variations in what appears to be a relatively stable population. For example, the majority of midshipmen between 1945 and 1976 came from the middle class. After World War II, greater numbers from the working and lower classes also joined the Brigade. In looking at the reasons why midshipmen chose Annapolis, a consistent majority did so because of the career opportunities. However, over this same period, a free education also became important, especially to those from lower-income groups. Finally, a consistent majority of graduates intended upon a naval career. Yet, these numbers also declined as the priorities of that culture changed. As the quality of the academic program improved, midshipmen found themselves with a degree marketable outside the military.[15]

The goal of this project is not to determine which system was superior for the education and training of naval officers. Such intent would be inappropriate, not to mention ahistorical. Both systems had their advantages and disadvantages. Midshipmen trained under the lockstep program were well qualified for their duties as fleet division officers. The common program unified them throughout their careers. And without exception, the companies of the Brigade were the focal point of midshipmen life. Tough discipline, even with "Mickey Mouse" regulations, instilled a rigid sense of obedience to orders. Although many midshipmen were bright students, the system did not allow them to become broadly educated. Midshipmen were also at a distinct disadvantage in applying for graduate school. The curriculum was fairly inflexible to change, both in terms of technology and methods of learning. However, up through World War II, it had accomplished its mission. Annapolis graduates made up the bulk of the regular officer corps and they had never lost a war.

Post–"academic revolution" midshipmen received a far superior education, equivalent to many elite engineering schools. Their training was generally more flexible to unique requirements from the warfare communities. The program was standard enough to build esprit de corps, but it was not the "unity of suffering" experience remembered so fondly by older alumni. Different groups—majors, extracurricular activities, etc.—limited the cohesiveness of the midshipmen culture. To some extent, the post–"academic revolution" academy was also more liberal in terms of privileges allowed to midshipmen. Discipline was not as heavy-handed and instead tried to be more reflective of fleet standards. However, the environment at Annapolis was still very restrictive compared to most colleges. Finally, the character building programs of the new Bancroft Hall inculcated into midshipmen a professional demeanor virtually identical to what transpired under the lockstep program.

It is also critically important to remember the context in which these changes took place. The Naval Academy had little choice in upgrading its curriculum. The increased academic emphasis could not help but detract from Bancroft Hall. However, the overarching goal of Annapolis remained the same: to produce career officers of use to the operational forces of the Navy and Marine Corps. The academy could ill afford to ignore changes in society either. A remarkable growth of higher education dramatically increased the competition for bright students. Annapolis risked losing these kinds of applicants entirely if its lifestyle was too foreign to the times. Post–"academic revolution" midshipmen also lived in a society that was not as empathetic of the military culture. Which system produced the best officers? The easy answer but also the correct one was that both systems were appropriate for the requirements of their day. The specific hurdles may have been different but the academy has always been a rigorous challenge for midshipmen.

THE PLEBE INDOCTRINATION SYSTEM

Plebe indoctrination provided the transition from civilian to military life for most midshipmen. Within the first days at Annapolis, most found their worlds turned upside down, wondering whether it was truly for them. They went from being the pride of their families and communities to the bottom of the barrel. *The Log* expressed this frustration best: "For he wast now a Plebian. And in the days, which did follow, it did commence to occur to young Joseph, that howsoever, wast he a great hero in Podunk [a midshipman's hometown], he wast but a *jerk* in Bancroft."[16] In most cases, previous skills and accomplishments were not all that remarkable from their peers. Equally troubling, upperclassmen were rarely pleased no matter how hard they tried. Plebe year was "a life of toil, and alas they were as those forsaken of God and many were their sorrows and heavy the burden of their cross, for it was their lot to obey, and to suffer the whims of all others of the men of Bancroft."[17] Academy standards seemed unattainable, especially for individuals accustomed to success. Many were giving their best and barely making the grade.[18]

Upperclassmen were unrelenting with their indoctrination although most viewed "running plebes" as a job. In their minds as well as the minds of superiors, the Navy could not compromise on the quality of Annapolis graduates. If a plebe was screwing up, punishing him was the best and quickest way of correcting his mistakes. Personalities came into play, but the system was not designed that way. It was better to weed out misfits now rather than let them become ineffective officers. There were always some upperclassmen, however, who took perverse pleasure in plebe indoctrination. Nothing stroked the ego like humbling a plebe who did not know what he was doing. It did not matter that plebes could not possibly know everything as well as they did. The system was too large and had too many loopholes that martinets and bullies always survived. Excess was probably to be expected in a system where twenty year olds supervised and trained eighteen year olds. Nonetheless, the academy accepted this as the cost of providing leadership opportunities to upperclassmen.[19]

Although outsiders have viewed the plebe system as a cruel and unusual tradition, academy leaders and alumni have defended it as essential to its program, equivalent to the formal education it provided. The nature of its activities may have changed from 1945 to 1976, but the emphasis has remained remarkably similar. The traditional justification was that it best simulated the sort of stress found in a military career. Naval officers worked in high-tempo and frequently dangerous operating environments where decisions had to be made quickly and correctly otherwise both the mission and men could be lost.[20] If professional preparation was its explicit purpose then an implicit function was eliminating undesirables. The admissions process has never found a perfect formula for determining applicants' aptitude for military service. Academic risks were much easier to identify. Too often, failure in this area was blamed on the individual rather than the system.[21] Two problems stand out with this assumption, however. Although the worst performance cases were obvious, minimal standards were more difficult to measure. Perhaps more importantly, upperclassmen often took too much responsibility making these decisions themselves.

The evaluation process began during plebe summer, and good first impressions were always critical. Squad leaders and platoon commanders quickly determined which plebes were "squared away." Their impressions were passed to other upperclassmen after everyone returned for academic year. The microscope's glare became more intense now that plebes were outnumbered by upperclassmen. Those who started out poorly found this difficult to overcome. To claim that much of this process was up to chance would be an overstatement. But to neglect the importance played by individuals would also obscure an important part of the plebe system. Between 1945 and 1976, an overwhelming number of midshipmen claimed that indoctrination varied significantly throughout Bancroft Hall. Indeed, certain companies and battalions seem to have relished their reputation for being tough on plebes.[22]

Plebes were constantly instructed in the traditions of the naval service. Frequent repetition hammered into them the values imbedded in these customs. Few upperclassmen tolerated their plebe's failure to know the proud heritage of Annapolis. Simply learning the material culture of the Naval Academy, however, was an immense task in itself for plebes. Every building and monument had a history behind it important to remember. They were asked to recite what John Paul Jones uttered fighting the *Serapis* or David Farragut's command before entering Mobile Bay. Other bits of naval trivia, ranging from practical seamanship to navy bowl game victories, also had to be within immediate recall.[23] Many plebes considered a part of this busy work to indulge their upperclassmen. Along with developing skills in stress and time management, the academy intended these memory exercises as a way for plebes to equate its history with their own, in other words, critical to their professional socialization. Annapolis did reduce the number of plebe rates after the "academic revolution" of the 1960s. It was not that these activities were no longer valuable; the academy has always had a difficult time defining to what degree, however. Other priorities were simply becoming more important.[24]

Everyone at Annapolis fell within a distinct hierarchy of privileges and responsibilities. Plebes could not use certain stairways or walkways on academy grounds reserved for upperclassmen. They were also responsible for delivering their company's laundry, sorting its mail, and closing windows before reveille to eliminate the chill in upperclassmen's rooms. To outsiders, this might seem like forced servitude, with the lowest indulging the whims of those above them. In theory, this too reinforced a time-honored principle of naval service; certain rights *and* responsibilities came with higher rank. It also taught the importance of following orders unquestioningly, another bedrock value of the Navy.[25] But too often, the latter part of this truism was neglected in practice. Instead, the emphasis was on who enjoyed the most seniority—a habit some graduates carried with them to the fleet, obsessing where their lineal number ranked them according to their peers.

The academy routine constantly emphasized the importance of classmate unity. Annapolis prided itself on the midshipmen's distinctive military bearing, even if its standards went beyond a neat and orderly appearance. Its graduates all walked, dressed, and spoke a certain way that left little doubt about their heritage. Until the "academic revolution," midshipmen also marched to class together by company. They competed in close-order drill and intramural sports with this group. Summer at-sea training was usually on large capital ships organized by class. Each of these activities served a practical purpose, but they also reinforced a desired model of professional behavior. Team success was always more important than individual accomplishment in the naval profession. Some plebes might have found this a difficult pill to swallow. After all, individual accomplishments were what got most into the academy but now the welfare of their classmates came first.[26]

The unrelenting intensity of the plebe system made it particularly formidable. Midshipmen expressed this frustration many ways, but the meaning was always the same—cramming thirty hours of work into a twenty-four-hour day, loading more into the sack than it was designed to carry, etc. Although some handled the pressure better than others did, the stress could not be avoided. In theory, each plebe was tested to the utmost of his abilities to see if he still put forth effort after his resources were exhausted.[27] Plebe year meant just that, an endurance test that began the first summer and lasted until the climbing of Herndon Monument next June. No other system of basic training lasted as long. Indeed, opponents criticized Annapolis for exceeding what even the other academies required. Other programs were considered more intense, marine boot camp being a good example. Midshipmen maintained the duration was its greatest challenge with relief coming only if the football team beat Army or if first classmen were in a good mood near Christmas.[28]

Furthermore, no other system of basic training granted a reprieve midway through only to renew the pressure with greater intensity afterwards. Nothing was as sweet to a plebe as Christmas leave because it provided a break from indoctrination. But nothing was as bitter as returning to Annapolis afterwards, a period long known as the Dark Ages. Upperclassmen were in a foul mood with little to look forward to besides venting their frustration on them. The weather was generally at its worst, and everyone was struggling through the fall semester's final exams. The academic calendar was not changed until the end of the 1960s. The holidays were also a reminder about life outside the Naval Academy. It reinforced that their predicament was voluntary. The temptation to resign was never more real, in other words, than during the Dark Ages. In this respect, plebe year was appropriately analogous to the rigors of naval service. Occasionally, it demanded raw courage and quick thinking but that was more the exception than the rule. But perseverance through difficult situations, like overseas deployments, was a virtue every officer needed.[29]

Throughout the years, midshipmen found various reasons to value this experience. Most of them emerged from plebe year supremely confident of their abilities. It set them apart not only from friends who quit but those who had not even tried. The constant challenges had taught them essential time management and goal planning skills. All of these were essential character qualities of a good officer. No one could predict the future. Some of them might indeed face combat or become prisoners of war. Even a typical career had its routine obstacles, like overseas deployments and long periods at sea. The sense of accomplishment gave them confidence about handling those future challenges. And it unified classmates long after their graduation from Annapolis.[30]

Bancroft Hall

Few midshipmen imagined their lives after plebe year would be like a civilian college. The reason for that belief was Bancroft Hall, "lovingly" referred to as "Mother B." On the surface, Bancroft Hall was merely the home of the Brigade, the place where midshipmen slept, studied, and took their meals. It also contained their laundry, barber and tailor shops, snack bars and a store, and even a bowling alley. In that respect, it differed little from other collegiate dormitories, with the exception of the sundry services and its expanse. Annapolis boasted that it was the largest such facility in the world. The entire Brigade slept under the same roof even if it were part of eight interconnected wings.[31] With its many corridors and hidden passageways, it was an easy place to get lost, especially during plebe year. For these reasons alone, "Mother B" could be intimidating to come home to at the end of the day.

Bancroft Hall stood out for reasons other than its titanic structure, however. Most midshipmen considered it synonymous with the distinctive aspects of the academy culture. Their tolerance of it largely determined whether they stayed. No other college or commissioning source had anything like it, except perhaps the other service academies. Midshipmen learned not to expect much privacy; the doors of their rooms had locks, but they were not allowed to use them. They were always under the microscope both from the system and each other. Academy midshipmen sometimes chided NROTC for "playing Navy." Their disdain stemmed from the fact that no matter how rigorous the training, NROTC midshipmen went home after it was over. Bancroft Hall was relentless, but academy midshipmen believed it prepared them better for their careers. Life at sea was not any different—the close confines, the limited privacy, and the constant pressure. Instead of belonging to the Navy once a week, they were immersed in it all the time. Many graduates shared an odd habit of including academy years when counting their military service.[32]

Living conditions improved dramatically after plebe year, but upperclassmen also grumbled about Bancroft Hall's confines. They too endured extreme restrictions on their personal conduct. One midshipman in 1944 sarcastically described leave's importance as helping him "appreciate more the earthly paradise we have here at Navy."[33] Although standards were most exacting for plebes, upperclassmen were also frequently inspected. To make matters worse, they had more to lose if rooms or uniforms were unsatisfactory. An upperclassman's privileges might seem trivial to other undergraduates, but they meant everything at Annapolis. Punishment involved demerits, restriction, or extra duty that was worked off on weekends marching with a rifle or rowing cutters on the Severn River.[34]

Of critical importance, these hardships were endured during their college years. Midshipmen had volunteered, but that did not make the sacrifices easier to take. It was often an incredible test of willpower to choose whether to leave or stay. In some ways, the academy was a four-year test in delayed gratification. Not surprisingly, midshipmen zealously guarded the benefits thrown their way. The worst crime a junior could commit was usurping privileges he did not rate. Only first classmen could wear their academy rings or later park their cars on campus. Extra liberty, dating opportunities, and eventually stereo and television privileges made academy life more bearable. But they were also tangible reminders of their progress through the system. These privileges carried over to Bancroft Hall itself. First and second classmen alone were entitled to certain walkways and passageways and later company wardrooms. Violations of these privileges were punishable under the code of conduct, and upperclassmen did not shy from holding perpetrators accountable.

The extra benefits were small reward for everything that was expected of upperclassmen. Everyone had at least one roommate and shared a bathroom their four years at Annapolis. Classroom attendance, company drill, and intramural sports were also mandatory for the duration. Upperclassmen became more accustomed to this grueling regimen but were never excused from it. Their classes were generally more demanding, and each year they took on more leadership responsibilities. Midshipmen had little time to waste, in other words, even without plebe year's responsibilities. And the academy could easily take away the extra privileges if they were not meeting its standards.[35]

Bancroft Hall's ultimate purpose was to prepare midshipmen for naval service. Whether conscious or not, much of its routine was patterned after a warship—the close quarters, limited privacy, relentless schedules, and competing priorities. Despite these references, midshipmen interpreted their existence through another model, that of the closed institution. Ironically, instead of seeing this connection, many limited any unpleasant experiences as unique to Annapolis. The reasons why are largely unclear. Perhaps this was a way of handling their doubts about a military career. After all, most of them were not overly familiar with the operational Navy. Their professional training was the best in the Navy but it lasted only a few months each summer. The implicit message within the academy mission statement—to prepare career officers for naval service—suggested that this was a lifelong decision. The real Navy had to be different, or so they told themselves.

Although not perfectly analogous to Bancroft Hall, Erving Goffman's work on total institutions has much to say about its internal culture. Goffman studied mental asylums, but his observations ring true for other institutions, like prisons, monasteries, *and* the Naval Academy. He defined a total institution as "a place of residence and work where a large number of like-situated individuals, cut off from the wider society for an appreciable period of time, together lead an enclosed, formally administered round of life," people whom he called inmates.[36] Certainly, Annapolis was not a penitentiary or mental hospital. Unlike other inmates, midshipmen chose their situation and believed it ultimately benefited them. The frequent comparisons to these other institutions are striking, however. Midshipmen were not prison inmates or asylum patients, but they often described themselves that way.[37]

These feelings were certainly understandable. Like other closed institutions, the academy seemed isolated and controlling, all the more odd since it was supposedly college. Midshipmen took little comfort knowing it only lasted four years; a survey in the 1944 *Log* asked them what was most enjoyable about leave. The top response was additional dating opportunities, followed by being *away* from Annapolis. Leave allowed them "to expose oneself yearly to the horrors of the outside world."[38] The sarcasm in these comments was all too obvious. Midshipmen commonly believed academy walls were there not to stop intruders but to prevent their escape. "Going over the wall" violated regulations, but midshipmen admired classmates who did it.[39] In fact, at different points in the year, like before Army-Navy football, midshipmen went over the wall en masse. Officers overlooked this mass rebellion since it was done in the name of school spirit. To some extent, these activities were also a symbolic assertion of their dignity and independence.

Midshipmen had their self-esteem first challenged on their induction day. Endless lines taught them firsthand the familiar military complaint "hurry up and wait." They waited for their first haircut, which was required to be unflattering. Nearly everywhere they went, someone was prodding them for supposedly vital information. Measurements of all kinds were taken before uniforms were issued. Another physical was performed despite completing this during the appointment process. At each stop, they gathered uniforms, textbooks, and other equipment presumably useful in the future. But for now, the immense load drained them of needed energy. The volume of people caused tempers to be short; everyone was yelling at them, but it was difficult to understand why. At the end of the day, they took the oath of office, said good-bye to their families, and prepared to face

Bancroft Hall. Their separation from the outside world was abrupt and complete. It is not surprising that many felt confused, much less physically and mentally exhausted by the process.[40]

The induction experience was common to most total institutions. Although it was always disorienting, many also used it to establish control. Goffman admits that this varied by institution, both in its intent and success. Although he had not studied Annapolis, his comments are at least suggestive of its process. The goal of induction was to strip away inmates' identity leaving them vulnerable to its demands. Sharp discipline was used to teach the new environment's rules, and basic privileges were often withheld until they learned them.[41] Midshipmen were better motivated than other inmates and thus more willing to obey. Annapolis did not force them to stay either. Thus, it was not control but professional socialization that motivated the academy. The taut routine was crucial in building character. And the cornerstone was discipline, an unquestioning obedience to orders. They were taught to place others' needs above themselves and to strive for the utmost in personal and professional behavior. Nor should they have to be told twice the right way of doing things. Finally, extreme devotion to shipmates and service was always expected. Annapolis never *asked* for that kind of loyalty or those levels of performance. It demanded them.

Who would not want this as the description of their character? Obviously most people would, and the academy recognized that. The rub was that the Navy demanded these virtues in times of great emotional, mental, and physical distress. Military service called for behavior that in many ways was contrary to human nature. Many people would be less than truthful with information damaging to their careers. But military service demanded officers be accountable for their actions. In dangerous situations, the natural tendency of people is self-preservation. Military officers were called to sacrifice everything including their lives for the mission. That was why the academy imposed rules that on the surface seemed ridiculous or petty. Much of a plebe's memory work had some professional purpose such as learning weapons systems, ship types, or naval history. Admittedly, the connection between naval service and memorizing menu items or sports trivia was less clear. However, a good portion of this was also designed to frustrate plebes and to tempt them to take shortcuts. Anyone the system caught was punished severely for doing so. To be fair, the academy had its share of mean-spirited officers and upperclassmen that simply enjoyed punishing plebes. The bottom line from the academy's perspective was the same, however. Midshipmen learned to follow orders, even those they might naturally question.[42]

The enormity of this task was how Annapolis justified many of its seemingly extreme actions. Total immersion into its culture, especially early on, was the best way of making these values stick. Thus, plebes were not allowed outside contact during their first weeks, a practice common in total institutions. Visitors and phone calls only increased the temptation to resign.[43] Bizarre restrictions on their physical behavior reinforced the academy hierarchy of which they were the lowest. This too was a feature of total institutions.[44] They double-timed or "chopped" in Bancroft Hall and were limited to the center of corridors, leaving most floor space free for upperclassmen. When turning, plebes squared the corner and shouted an expression of school spirit, like "Go Navy, Beat Army." A shiny tin plate was located at hallway junctions to mark where this took place. Further complicating matters, they were at attention outside their rooms, eyes fixed forward with chins pulled into their necks, a position known as a brace.[45] Upperclassmen abused them for "taking their eyes out of the boat" even if it was to see where they were going. They had not earned full control over their bodies.[46]

The dining hall routine also reinforced their junior status. Rarely was there a chance to eat in peace or get a full meal. Meals were taken "family style" at tables reserved by company. Not even upperclassmen could miss them. Plebes waited on everyone else before they ate. The serving process required tremendous concentration and coordination since plebes were at attention throughout the meal. Upperclassmen hounded them if it was not done quickly and efficiently. Complicating matters further, they could only sit on the front three inches of their chairs.[47] The job was never really finished since drinks had to be refilled and second helpings distributed. Upperclassmen routinely quizzed them on their endless memory work too. What newspaper article had they read? What was the menu for next meal? How many days until graduation, the ring dance, or Christmas leave? God help those without the right answer or who had not served the meal correctly. Upperclassmen could provide additional "training." Plebes welcomed the bell ending the meal even if they left the table hungry. An empty stomach was a small price to pay for escaping the traps at mealtime.[48]

Finally, until the 1970s, plebes performed various odd jobs, which also conditioned them to following orders and accepting a military hierarchy. Most were standard requirements such as delivering laundry, sorting mail, and closing upperclassmen's windows before reveille. However, upperclassmen often gave them unique errands, many of which contradicted regulations. One plebe picked up his first classman's daily quart of chocolate milk from a local vendor. Others had plebes smuggle girlfriends into Bancroft Hall.[49] Plebes could not be ordered to violate the honor code, but everything else was seemingly within bounds. Obviously, these tasks took valuable time that logic told them could be better spent studying or working on other military requirements. In other words, the temptation to follow their common sense was strong, but plebes were punished severely for shirking these requests. In the military culture, only immoral orders were not to be followed; illogical was in the eyes of the beholder. Most forms of plebe servitude were eliminated during the "academic revolution." But this was done to provide additional study time for both plebes and upperclassmen. However, regulated menial service remained a part of indoctrination. The principle itself was important in teaching plebes to follow orders.

Professional Socialization at Annapolis

Professional socialization has always been at the heart of the academy's mission. Fulfilling that responsibility was the chief duty of its officers, primarily the Executive Department that ran Bancroft Hall. In most cases, Annapolis preferred line officers, those from the combat branches of the Navy and Marine Corps, because that was where the bulk of graduates served. The school's two most senior officers were its superintendent and commandant. Extensive fleet and command experience were the norm for both positions. The superintendent was usually a junior two-star admiral fresh from a minor fleet command while the commandant was a senior captain who recently commanded an air group or major surface combatant. Equally important, these assignments were not capstone tours either. They were plum positions and, if successful, a springboard to greater responsibility.[50]

The superintendent's job was similar to a university president, albeit with interesting twists. As the academy's senior officer, he also commanded the surrounding military district and served as its court-martial convening authority. Although his decisions ultimately affected midshipmen, his daily contact with them was minimal. Bancroft Hall was the commandant's responsibility and in principle its commanding officer. In a civilian college, his position would be analogous to a dean of students. Anything immediate to the Brigade—sick reports, conduct and honor offenses, academic or military aptitude problems, and resignations—filtered through his office first. Even though these areas affected the Brigade, he mostly saw midshipmen in some kind of trouble. Although neither officer dealt much with average students, their actions certainly affected the climate of Bancroft Hall.

Beneath them were officers who kept the academy running at peak efficiency. The superintendent's deputies supervised the physical plant, the naval station, the admissions and public affairs offices, and the academic departments. Staff officers headed most administrative and technical areas and rotated less frequently than the average line officer. Academic department heads were line officers who served limited tours of at most three or four years. Few of them had advanced degrees. Unlike other colleges, where department heads had equivalent credentials to the faculty, their administrative and leadership experience were considered sufficient qualifications for the job. Officers under the commandant ran the conduct, performance, and training offices. Their jobs influenced midshipmen, but daily contact was also minimal. The training officer, for example, coordinated the summer programs, but his involvement ended unless someone caused trouble on cruise.[51]

Battalion and company officers also reported to the commandant and had the greatest involvement with the Brigade. Battalion officers were commanders or lieutenant colonels straight from their first command tour. Many were also assigned important collateral duties overseeing varsity teams and extracurricular activities. Company officers were generally Navy lieutenants finishing initial sea tours or Marine captains completing company grade commands. In most cases, there was only a few years difference between them and midshipmen. Their youth was a great advantage in forging relationships. However, many were still developing their own leadership skills. On paper, their responsibilities were enormous. They spent the most time with midshipmen and essentially taught them how to be officers. Their duties frequently put them in awkward situations forcing them to switch from being mentors and counselors to supervisors and disciplinarians. As with other assignments, no special qualifications were required except for fleet experience.[52]

The Navy insisted these billets went to front-runners, officers on the fast track to advancement. Many fleet officers did not share that perception and viewed academy assignments as hurtful to their careers. Promotion boards looked at performance in operational billets—commanding troops, flying planes, or driving ships. Ironically, Annapolis was not highly viewed as a shore assignment either. The best officers went to graduate school, worked for the technical bureaus, or taught in the *operational* training pipeline. This stereotype persisted until at least the late 1960s. Officers were ordered to Annapolis. At most, it was a welcome change from sea duty. Professional socialization obviously suffered under this flawed assignment policy. Midshipmen dealt regularly with officers of questionable motivation. Many were looking for a quick transfer. Others saw sharp discipline as the best *and* quickest way of handling them. Some were even leaving the Navy. Annapolis could not fully improve the situation until the "academic revolution."[53]

A better staff was not the antidote to all of the problems between officers and midshipmen. The two groups were natural adversaries. Officers easily came across as heavy-handed with so many rules to enforce. One midshipman in the class of 1949 expressed it this way: "the Form 2 was the company officer's favorite weapon. I think they competed to see who could fry the most midshipmen." Another from the class of 1952 complained that most were "very weak officers . . . who were too tough enforcing discipline." Duty officers supposedly hid behind trees or bushes to catch them in improper uniforms or talking in ranks on their way to class.[54] Never mind that these actions violated regulations; the strictness of enforcement seemed petty. It was impossible to satisfy all of the academy's requirements. The punishment for minor infractions never seemed to fit the crime either. Conduct reports brought extra duty or restriction, which took away their limited free time.[55]

Officers always seemed to be watching them. Rooms and uniforms were constantly inspected; quite literally, their home and person were invaded on a daily basis. An officer's power was nearly absolute in these areas; judge, jury, executioner, *and* accuser were rolled into one. This too affected professional socialization. Midshipmen chose to avoid officers instead of pursuing them for training or mentoring. Unfortunately, this mindset continued in the fleet; since senior officers wielded similar power, it was also wise to steer clear of them.[56] The scrutiny continued outside Bancroft Hall. Proper liberty behavior was a source of numerous violations, most of which were conduct unbecoming a midshipman, a catchall for actions discrediting to Annapolis. Unfortunately, these often involved judgment calls. What some officers tolerated others reprimanded. Worse still, individual standards varied week to week. Midshipmen presumed the interference was to interrupt their fun. Any enforcement, legitimate or not, wound up in "Salty Sam," the anonymous gossip column of *The Log*. Whether officers were truly that bad or diligent in their duties is debatable. The reality was probably somewhere in between.[57]

The theory behind tough discipline was simple. Midshipmen were only a few years from being officers themselves. They would soon be setting standards for their sailors.[58] Furthermore, the Naval Academy was the cradle for naval traditions and values. Laziness learned now was not likely to be corrected in the fleet.[59] Unfortunately, midshipmen believed Annapolis bore little resemblance to the fleet. They frequently described its regulations as "Mickey Mouse" or "cops and robbers." The lengths to which officers monitored them were a source of recurring jokes. Stories of officers using binoculars and walkie-talkies to catch midshipmen only enhanced this atmosphere. Only so much could be done to erase these stereotypes however. From an officer's perspective, midshipmen were not likely to follow the rules without direction. Although specific rules were unpopular, midshipmen insisted they were more irritated with how officers enforced them.[60]

According to midshipmen, officers tried to get them into trouble. Many rules were so cumbersome that even a well-meaning person broke some. Conversely, many officers thought midshipmen were always looking for short cuts. Annapolis was not meant to be easy. Midshipmen could not choose which orders they followed; such attitudes had to be punished severely. True mentoring was difficult under such conditions. Officers believed that showing tolerance compromised their authority, and midshipmen felt officers were "fry-happy," satisfying their appetite for power.[61] A final example from "Salty Sam" illustrates this stereotype best. In 1946, a Steam Department instructor placed his entire thermodynamics section on report for leaving class early. What made this situation humorous was that he included students that had legitimately dropped the class. Midshipmen could not find a better example of the disciplinary system's flaws. Regulations were followed regardless of whether they made sense. Officers were either obtuse or did not care about being fair.[62]

Midshipmen reciprocated by turning many regulations into a game. For example, when officers cracked down on special request chits one year, midshipmen stretched the limits of common sense with their requests. One midshipman asked for a newspaper, "in order that I might read the funnies each morning." Another requested film "to take pictures of my girlfriend." Another midshipman wanted a bathrobe to prevent getting cold in the morning. Why act like an adult if you were treated like a child?[63] Midshipmen could not believe minor infractions were taken so seriously. It seemed inconceivable that grown men would hide behind bushes and trees or interrupt time with their family to stop them on liberty. Such examples did not inspire them to a military career. Officers should have more important things to do. Was this the immense responsibility promised them after graduation?[64]

Annapolis was so strict, midshipmen, believed, that they had to stretch the rules. No one could avoid extra duty or demerits entirely. Why not do little things that made life more bearable? Storing illegal items in your room or going over the wall was not being disobedient. It was a way of coping with the pressure. Everyone did it to some extent, including officers when they were midshipmen. In some respect, challenging the rules was an academy tradition. Midshipmen did not see an inconsistency between circumventing the rules and following orders. They described their actions as "you rate what you get away with."[65] Officers were cops looking for violations, and midshipmen were robbers daring them to try. Most of the time the game was innocent in nature. Slipping minor offenses past them boosted morale and nurtured a spirit of boldness and devil-may-care, character traits in themselves of successful officers.

However, this attitude was dangerous if taken too far; some rules mattered at Annapolis and in the Navy. Violating them endangered a midshipman's and an officer's career. Lying to escape a conduct offense was an honor violation, which resulted in dismissal from the academy. Midshipmen could be booted for other Class "A" violations including hazing, underage drinking, or driving while intoxicated. The latter two offenses also violated civil laws. The academy was usually severe with anyone who tarnished its reputation. Sometimes midshipmen continued the game after graduation. As officers, they flirted with rules not to their liking. The fleet was not as forgiving as the academy, however. Stunts that got demerits or extra duty resulted in letters of reprimand or worse, consequences that were often permanent.

Although intriguing, the Brigade's relationship with the Executive Department was not exceptional. Indeed, Erving Goffman suggests it was common in total institutions, a split he refers to as inmates and staff:

> Each grouping tends to conceive of the other in terms of narrow, hostile stereotypes, staff often seeing inmates as bitter, secretive, and untrustworthy, while inmates often see staff as condescending, highhanded, and mean. Social mobility between the two strata is grossly restricted; social distance is typically great and often formally prescribed.[66]

This definition accurately describes "cops and robbers" at Annapolis. Another characteristic of the staff-inmate relationship was the contradiction between "humane standards on one hand and institutional efficiency on the other."[67] In academy terms, the quickest way of correcting problems was to place midshipmen on report.

If this sounds harsh, officers were under incredible pressure to train midshipmen. They only had four years to turn them into competent officers. Some academic subjects could be forgotten, but fleet operations were not so forgiving. Midshipmen might one day be serving under them as junior officers; slipshod training could literally come back to haunt the Executive Department.[68] No doubt this gave greater urgency to their job. Thus, expediency was a real temptation. The best solution was invariably the quickest one. Goffman suggests this was common whenever a staff's task was beyond its resources, "having to control inmates and to defend the institution in the name of its avowed aims, the staff resort to the kind of all-embracing identification of the inmates that will make this possible. The staff problem here is to find a crime that will fit the punishment."[69]

Goffman talks about limits to the staff's control, but these ideas seem particularly relevant in large institutions like Annapolis. The staff occasionally pacifies inmates by giving them a sense of control. However, any concessions actually reinforce its authority.[70] The relationship also has a give-and-take to it, which cannot be planned. The academy periodically let midshipmen have their way; going over the wall before Army-Navy football was a good example. Nonetheless, other situations also limited its control.[71] Officers were squeezed the most by numbers and time. They could not be everywhere at once nor was watching midshipmen their only responsibility. It is also important to remember that this was shore duty, a time to be with families or further their education. Finally, company and battalion officers were only in their jobs three or four years. Experience never compensated for the lack of numbers with this kind of rotation policy. These problems only became more acute with the academy's expansion after World War II.[72]

METHODOLOGY AND SOURCES

Although the academy archives are extensive, the sources that deal explicitly with midshipmen are relatively scarce. However, in an indirect way, even these institutional sources are useful in studying its culture. For example, superintendents wrote annual reports for the Board of Visitors, one of the school's chief overseeing bodies. The Brigade and Bancroft Hall were often mentioned in their remarks. Any controversies, such as honor or hazing scandals, have usually spawned investigations. Beyond the specific incident being investigated, these inquiries indirectly show what was considered normal. Major program changes, like the "academic revolution," were always carefully studied. The new curriculum was examined in relationship to Bancroft Hall, which kinds of midshipmen were most likely to graduate, which groups had the most trouble with academy life, and so on. However, their analysis was not usually given any historical context but focused more on the immediate problem. This study hopes to give greater breadth to these subjects.[73]

Midshipmen did leave a historical record however. For example, they produced yearbooks, The *Lucky Bag,* and sports magazines, The *Splinter,* similar to student publications at other colleges. The most important source of this kind was a bimonthly magazine entitled *The Log.* It was published throughout the timeframe of this study. *The Log* contained editorials on contemporary events, articles about cultural trends, and other features appealing to young men in their late teens and early twenties. However, its greatest value was material dealing with Bancroft Hall's internal culture. Articles talked about midshipmen's interactions with officers, their perceptions of plebe indoctrination, the most onerous and exciting parts of their lives, and their career expectations. Unless otherwise noted, most of its authors were anonymous. What makes this material a rich historical source was that humor was often its primary purpose. In some ways, understanding what makes a society laugh tells a lot about its culture.

Historical research is often challenged by archival gaps, which was true with this project. Most sources on midshipmen were concentrated closest to the present. Because of this, alternative methods were needed to compare different time periods. I developed a questionnaire on academy life and the midshipmen culture that was given to 10 percent of the classes of 1946 to 1976. The database was skewed towards graduates, but there was not enough information on nongraduates to include them in the survey. The questions asked about their personal background, reasons for attending Annapolis, impressions of Bancroft Hall, and its effect on their military career. Certain classes were given specific questions on events not covered in the archival record. Post–World War II classes were asked about the war's impact on Annapolis, the defense department reorganization controversy, and the new honor system. Questions on the "academic revolution" and Vietnam were given to classes from the 1960s and 1970s. Both open and close-ended questions were coded for analysis.[74]

Of the twenty-four hundred surveys distributed, just over one thousand were returned. A 40 percent return rate in survey research is very good. Beyond the high participation rate, most respondents answered the survey as completely and accurately as possible. Many provided additional information, such as personal letters or points of contact, that they thought would help my research. Although this might seem redundant to mention, anyone familiar with survey research would agree that this should not be taken for granted. In other words, this project benefited from a survey population that responded both intelligently and responsibly to everything asked of them. At this point, I do not believe there is a more comprehensive set of data on midshipmen from this time period. It allows direct comparisons on a wide range of questions, more than any other source with which I am familiar.

The full questions are included in Appendix 1. The survey population is also somewhat skewed towards those of higher academic standing. Graduates in the upper two quartiles tend to be over represented while those nearer the bottom tend to be under represented. Fortunately, this distortion exists across all classes thus mitigating errors in comparisons done over time. How might this distribution affect the survey's results? Graduates of higher academic rank might have a more favorable perception of Annapolis. The program was likely easier for them. They also might be overzealous in crediting the academy for their career success rather than natural ability. However, most of them were very discriminating in their answers. Similar arguments could be made that they were more critical of the academy. Their expectations could have been greater. Furthermore, their own success might cause them to speculate on what could have been done better.[75]

For purposes of analysis, the thirty classes were compressed into six age-group cohorts. This was done to reduce the number of outcome variables and to combine sufficient numbers for meaningful analysis. Although the process was necessary for statistical reasons, I tried to establish cohorts with historical significance. The first included graduates from 1946 to 1949. Most of them completed an accelerated, three-year program designed to get them to the war as quickly as possible. The postwar years were a dizzying time of transition. The whole debate over officer education took place during this time. These graduates were also the first to serve with non-academy officers in peacetime.

The classes of 1950 to 1954 make up the second cohort. The atmosphere of World War II continued to permeate the academy. Many midshipmen were combat veterans and the Executive Department also included many wartime heroes. This group tended to be older and worldlier than previous classes. Perhaps it was not coincidence that they established a new honor system and were more tolerant of minorities. This time was one of profound institutional change—Defense Department reorganization, the Air Force's creation, and the Korean War. The third cohort includes the classes of 1955 to 1959. On the surface, these appear to be years of relative stability. Annapolis survived under the Holloway Plan, but it struggled to keep programs afloat in the midst of deep, post–war budget cuts. It also lost many midshipmen to the Air Force for one reason or another. And a booming economy offered lucrative career opportunities that further complicated recruiting and retention.

The fourth cohort, the classes of 1960 to 1964, entered at the start of the "academic revolution." It was a time of continual experimentation with the curriculum. Midshipmen stopped marching to class by company. They began taking electives and developing fields of concentration. In terms of national prestige, Annapolis was in its heyday. The football team produced two Heisman trophy winners and was near the top of the national rankings. Midshipmen symbolized the spirit of sacrifice President Kennedy was urging upon the nation. This group was also the first to serve in Vietnam. But at this stage, duty was seen as a career opportunity, not something to be avoided. The fifth cohort consists of the classes of 1965 to 1969. Social unrest and antiwar sentiment were in full bloom by this time. Many graduates knew shipmates killed in action and expected a combat assignment in their future. In terms of their lifestyle, they felt increasingly alienated from civilian students.

The sixth and final cohort includes the classes of 1970 to 1976. At this point, the "academic revolution" was complete. The class of 1970 was the first to complete majors and have opportunities at immediate graduate education. Others attempted very different career paths, such as becoming doctors and lawyers. In many ways, the new academic routine was little different from other elite colleges. Annapolis began allowing midshipmen to leave on weekends, drive automobiles, and drink alcohol on liberty. After the Supreme Court's decision, mandatory chapel was even eliminated. "Times had been a' changing" in American society for a while, and this reformist spirit had also come to Annapolis. This project ends with larger changes looming on the horizon. Although the Naval Academy fought it to the bitter end, women successfully petitioned for admission. Even so, the previous thirty years since World War II were also incredibly tumultuous for the academy culture.

The anthropologist Clifford Geertz once wrote that a society's culture "consists of whatever it is one has to know or believe in order to operate in a manner acceptable to its members." Almost by definition, midshipmen lived under such scrutiny every day at Annapolis. Their indoctrination never truly stopped. Rituals and traditions, some of which contradicted regulations, were used to instill the important values of the academy culture. Midshipmen were not exact replicas of one another however. They accepted some aspects of their indoctrination and resisted others depending on other formative experiences in their lives. Many either learned or had reinforced a code of behavior that has guided their actions both in and out of the Navy. At a minimum, most alumni, including those with negative memories, are extremely opinionated about the Naval Academy, even fifty years removed from the experience. There are things that they felt were done right and others that needed correction. Few colleges have this intense of a relationship with their graduates.[76]

Military institutions preserve traditions for a variety of reasons. They are used to train new members of the profession in acceptable standards of behavior. Traditions foster group unity not only among present members of the institution but also between them and previous generations. Finally, they inspire pride and a sense of duty by recalling the institution's past accomplishments. Midshipmen were continually reminded about their responsibilities as part of "the Long Blue Line."[77] The interesting thing about academy traditions is that they often have a life and power of their own. Most have a clear origin and substance to them, but occasionally subtle changes have seemingly gone undetected. For example, I was amazed by how much its mission statement had changed between 1945 and 1976. I had memorized one version as a plebe, but several others had preceded it. At the time, I assumed the current rendering had always been used. Perhaps this reflected a naiveté on my part, but it also testified to tradition's power at the Naval Academy. It was easy to assume nothing had ever changed given the importance tradition played in our daily lives.

Most graduates of Annapolis viewed it as a positive experience both personally and professionally. Only a few survey respondents would have chosen not to attend the academy again. It was a tremendous challenge, something that need not be repeated; the often-used phrase "Annapolis a great place to be from—not at" expresses these sentiments best. Bad memories did not prohibit most graduates from having an endearing loyalty to the academy. Nostalgia was a factor in their memories, but even as midshipmen, they recognized that.

And even again did the years come to pass until that which was Bancroft was but a memory—a thing of yore. And no more did they cry of terrors therein, and the trees which they did climb, and the cutters which they did once row. Nay, for pleasant now were the thoughts they kept, and fond the memories of those carefree days. For is it not that that which once had been is so oft remembered for its pleasantries and what at the time was a bitter pill becomes in late years a jest? And so did Bancroft to them become "The Years Together By The Bay" and the tongue which dids't cry the loudest there does't now the most readily recite "Now when I was a midshipman."[78]

They continued their affiliation through the alumni association or academy sponsored events, like athletic events or class reunions. The experience forged lifelong relationships. One need only look in *Shipmate,* the alumni association's monthly magazine to see the strength of these bonds. The community of Naval Academy graduates was a very real one indeed, in which members shared the important details of their lives—promotions, weddings, births, and ultimately deaths of friends and shipmates. The glue holding that community together was the shared experience of "four years together by the bay."[79]

1
The Naval Academy of the 1940s: From Trade School to Naval University

WORLD WAR II WOULD BE A DEFINING MOMENT FOR THE NAVAL ACADemy but not without complications. It basked in the glow of the country's greatest naval triumph; virtually all of the war's great naval heroes were from Annapolis. No one questioned, however, whether its monopoly on regular officers guaranteed that result anyway. Nothing demonstrated the soundness of the existing system like its graduates' performance in battle. At the same time, the war raised nagging questions about the future. New technology suggested the need for more broadly educated officers. Their education should be flexible enough to last an entire career, not one geared towards just immediate results. Larger standing forces would also be maintained than what existed before the war. Annapolis could not supply all these officers itself. Alternative commissioning sources would also be used. The task of creating a postwar academy would be difficult to put into practice however. The Navy wanted to preserve the best attributes of the existing system while accommodating its new needs.[1]

The chief question facing the academy was actually not new, but that did not make it easier to answer. It had struggled throughout its history to define the type of institution it should be. The difficulty rested in important goals that were difficult to reconcile, neither of which could be abandoned. Annapolis asked a lot of itself in what it provided in four years. Midshipmen received an undergraduate education and were trained as officers. Education and training were not incompatible, but time pressure constantly stretched its resources. Its leaders tried to do a credible job in both areas, but priorities still had to be set. Up until World War II, the Naval Academy had a reputation as being more or less a "trade school" for the Navy. Midshipmen learned what they needed to be immediately useful to the fleet; their education was generally a secondary focus. The academy was occasionally attacked for its narrow curriculum but not from voices that truly mattered.[2]

World War II disrupted its existing priorities literally over night. Within the Navy, a growing chorus of reformers began demanding substantial changes. They wanted Annapolis to expand its academic vision beyond the limited program required by a fleet division officer. The goal in mind was a true naval college, which laid the academic foundation for an officer's entire career. Training was still an important priority but not to overshadow its academic responsibilities. The Naval Academy was accredited in 1937 by the Middle States Association, albeit with strong reservations about its academic climate. Annapolis also joined the American Council on Education and the Association of American Colleges, an important olive branch to the scholastic community, which it had ignored in the past. Despite claims of becoming an "MIT on the Severn," these reforms were baby steps at best on the way to becoming a first-rate undergraduate college.[3]

The new academic climate could not help but challenge Bancroft Hall's control of the academy. For reforms to be successful, it had to tolerate new priorities in the schedule. Midshipmen had their own ideas, however, about Annapolis that did not automatically change with new policies. Bancroft Hall had generally been very resistant to change. Company officers, midshipmen stripers, and company upperclassmen occasionally blocked reforms that fell too far outside the mold. New leaders, like Admiral James Holloway, laid the groundwork for changing this culture the best they could. They attempted to codify what exactly happened in Bancroft Hall. Plebe indoctrination was no longer beyond inspection; necessary professional socialization had to be distinguished from juvenile fraternity antics. A new rewards system provided incentives for adjusting to the additional academic work. Despite their efforts, it was difficult to change this culture overnight. Remnants of older attitudes persisted even if they contradicted official policy.[4]

The war also ended the surface navy's dominance over the academy. Its efforts at professional socialization had largely been a reflection of that warfare community alone. All graduates started in the surface navy no matter what they ultimately did with their careers. With World War II, that future was no longer certain. The aircraft carrier had replaced battleships as the centerpiece of the fleet; very likely, many graduates would spend the bulk of their careers as aviators. Just like the rest of the Navy, naval aviation flexed its muscles getting its training requirements and doctrinal philosophy adopted by the academy. For the first time, the Naval Academy was split in terms of the service culture it taught to students. Midshipmen would have alternative examples of what it meant to be a professional naval officer. The dichotomy was never abrupt or total but it was real and new.[5]

The Naval Academy was not considering these decisions in a vacuum either. The war had unleashed massive social changes, which also hampered the academy from remaining true to the past. Tremendous forces of democratization were sweeping across American higher education after

World War II. Whether it was the surging postwar economy, the GI Bill, or simply increased expectations for the future, colleges and universities were opening their doors to students of vastly different backgrounds than before. Annapolis welcomed large numbers of students with previous military experience. Most of these midshipmen were generally older with substantial life experiences behind them. Many of them also came from blue-collar families, another striking departure from the past. With greater demographic diversity, the academy could no longer assume midshipmen had the same attitudes and goals in common. The task of professional socialization, in other words, would become more complicated to define.[6]

The academy was also hindered by a society incredibly weary from war. Americans were eager to end the enlarged defense budgets; they were also more skeptical of career military service. All of this made its postwar adjustments tougher to complete. Funds were notoriously slow in coming for the repair and renovation of its facilities. Midshipmen saw their salaries falling behind the cost of living with no promises of adjustment anytime soon. The depressed postwar environment produced a higher share of resignations and fewer applications than normal. The academy could not help but allow these problems to consume its attention. The consequences for not dealing with them were immediate; some of the more philosophical questions could seemingly be put off until another day. Afterwards, the academy was too drained, however, to resolve the fundamental question of what kind of institution it should be. The post–World War II reforms would be significant to the academy's future but it would take additional years before they were completed.[7]

THE PREWAR NAVAL ACADEMY: "THE TRADE SCHOOL"

The post-war academy was becoming a far cry from what it had been during the 1930s or World War II itself. The focus of that program was producing immediately useful junior officers; everything else was a second priority at best. As a result, the academic goals of the institution were extremely modest.[8] Midshipmen took courses from a standard curriculum regardless of their academic background or abilities. Students with previous college experience were intermingled with those fresh out of high school. Vice Admiral William Mack '37, superintendent in the early 1970s, described mathematics sections where "persons with high school mathematics were competing with persons who had been to MIT for three years . . . so the competition was very difficult for grades."[9] The lockstep curriculum offered few challenges to the more capable or experienced students. Midshipmen with limited academic backgrounds fought simply to survive. Courses were narrowly structured towards the Navy's technical requirements; examples were often taken verbatim from current fleet systems. Instructors gave daily quizzes that drilled into students the academy solutions to problems. Midshipmen who varied from the norm were penalized severely for their creativity. Many military instructors came fresh from the fleet with little formal education on their resume. Students often complained that their teachers seemed to be one step ahead of them, if that. Most civilian instructors were concentrated in the humanities and also relatively uninvolved in the scholarly life of their disciplines.

The weak academic culture did not provide students with incentives to work beyond the minimum for graduation. A common complaint was that the system taught midshipmen to memorize but not to think. Vice Admiral William Smedberg '26, superintendent in the mid 1950s and head of the Bureau of Naval Personnel at the start of the "academic revolution," talked about the lockstep curriculum's shortcomings: "I had six years of French before coming to the Naval Academy and I started in with 'Je suis, tu es, il est' and so forth. I never cracked a French book the whole time I was there." The academy attracted capable students but their achievements were more the result of inherent academic abilities than anything the system did for them. Most academic departments compensated for the poor instruction and rapid pace by curving their final grades. Too many midshipmen relied upon the curve instead of studying for their academic survival. Indeed, the student culture frowned upon midshipmen who took their grades too seriously. Every graduate became a naval officer regardless of his academic standing. Initial assignments were picked in a lottery so as not to penalize those at the bottom of the class. Academic merit counted little, in other words, in terms of practical consequences. Since all graduates went to sea anyway, the only difference was the type of ship and location of homeport.[10]

The limited academic emphasis led to periodic criticism, largely from civilian educators. The most serious censure of the interwar period came in 1931 from Dr. James Angell, president of Yale University and head of the 1931 Board of Visitors. He criticized the curriculum for being "devoid of any economics, of any substantial courses in government, of any biology, geography, ethics or social sciences, or of any of the literature of foreign languages, or of any of the fine arts which play so large a part in the cultural life of all peoples. These are all subjects in our day regarded as in varying degrees essential to a substantial general education and the academy can not possibly deal with them, or with any material part of them under existing conditions."[11] A disgruntled graduate from the class of 1933 also wrote an article entitled "Annapolis: A Stronghold of Mediocrity" for the annual alumni forum.[12] To be fair, Annapolis was not the only institution under such scrutiny. Questions like these were being asked throughout higher education in the 1930s.[13]

Its response to this criticism testified to the school's predominantly military priorities. Annapolis was not an ordinary college and given its unique mission should never attempt to be so. Admiral David Sellars, superintendent from 1934 to 1938, argued that its paramount responsibility was to turn out men "to whom we can entrust our naval ships," or stated another way, "officers to fight the United States Fleet."[14] Sellars did not have Dr. Angell's academic pedigree, but he did have over forty-seven years of commissioned service. From his experience, the admiral warned that "Success or failure in battle with the fleet is in no way dependent upon a knowledge of biology, geology, ethics, social sciences, the literature of foreign languages, or the fine arts."[15] The foremost priority of Annapolis was the development of "military character, including discipline, the attributes of leadership, and basic virtues" and secondly the development of a midshipman's "mental capacity, principally the ability to reason to a logical conclusion."[16]

This focus tolerated all of Bancroft Hall's high jinks, which were often excused in the name of professional training. The schedule was crowded, but the academy usually tinkered with the curriculum, not its activities, if additional time had to be found. Although physical hazing was prohibited, plebe indoctrination's boundaries were hazy at best. Every plebe was assigned to a specific first classman who was responsible for his mentoring and training. Few formal guidelines existed for defining right from wrong however. Upperclassmen often used their plebe year experiences and company culture to determine what worked best. Some first classmen and plebes developed wonderful mentoring relationships that continued throughout their professional careers. But there were other instances in which they abused their seniority, tormenting plebes beyond what regulations allowed.

Plebes were often paddled with brooms if they displeased upperclassmen. At the mess table, they could be ordered to shove out, which required them to remain in a seated position for the rest of meal without using a chair. Vice Admiral Mack described much of this as "silly," "foolishness," and "a waste of time," but something that could be handled as long as the person was in good physical shape. Plebes who were not athletic had a more difficult time finishing a meal and were more likely to be abused.[17] Hanson Baldwin '24, a well-known correspondent for the *New York Times, Saturday Evening Post,* and the *Atlantic Monthly,* remembered plebe year as varying substantially by battalion. Midshipmen were assigned to either "Spanish" or "French" battalions depending upon their choice of foreign language, which was the only option in the curriculum. Spanish battalions had a reputation for being notoriously harder on plebes: "The Spanish battalions were traditionally in those old wings fronting Bancroft Hall, which were a maze of corridors and small rooms. The plebes used to think

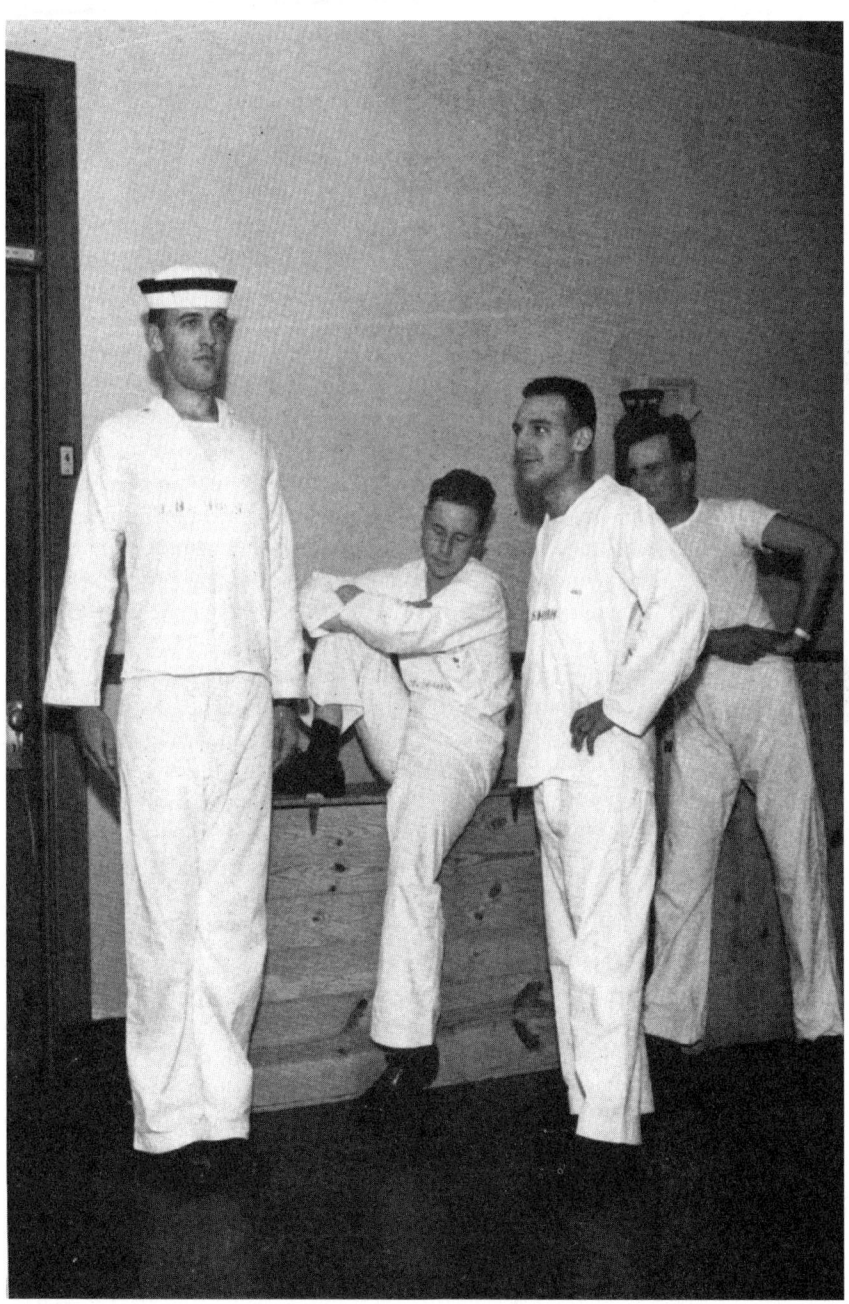

The Lucky Bag 1949. A plebe in a brace during a come around with upperclassmen.

it was worth their life to go walking down there; they would be beckoned into one of these rooms by an upperclassmen and then the torture would start!"[18]

Even in its milder forms, upperclassmen required plebes to run miscellaneous errands, including closing their windows in the morning, picking up newspapers and extra food, and delivering the laundry. Under the guise of professional training, upperclassmen assigned research projects in arcane subjects, including information for their own classes. If all of this took time away from academics, so be it. Bancroft Hall was where midshipmen became naval officers.[19] The struggle forged incredibly strong relationships that midshipmen carried with them throughout their careers. Perhaps Baldwin expressed the value of the old academy best: "I think I should stress that despite all the criticisms of the old academy; its narrowness and its limitations, I believe that it did, on the whole a superb job, in some ways superior to the job being done today. It did shape character; it did teach concentration and self-control; it helped to teach leadership, and above all it inculcated tradition, spirit, morale, and patriotism, call it what you will, and created a band of brothers, with a common dedication. I owe much, indeed, to my academy training."[20] Perhaps Admiral Sellars was not far off the mark in what his graduates found valuable about the institution.

It took a special toleration, both in American society and the Navy, to allow this sort of Naval Academy to flourish. Much of the groundwork for that older academy would be swept aside after World War II. In effect, the early business of the post–war academy was laying credible foundations for the institution's future. Before World War II, nearly all the Navy's regular officers came from the Naval Academy. Young men who wanted a naval career *had* to take the institution on its terms. The fleet never outgrew the academy's capacity to produce officers. Not every graduate of Annapolis necessarily received a commission. Thus, the school experienced little pressure from the Navy to change.[21]

The dominance of the surface navy also reinforced the status quo. Courses in steam engineering and naval gunnery were the bread and butter of the curriculum. So what if the instruction had little practical application? The fleet absorbed nearly every graduate of the institution. Midshipmen who were not physically qualified received staff corps commissions if they were available. Otherwise, they went home. The Marine Corps took a few graduates each year, but prior enlisted marines snatched up most openings.[22] Most midshipmen were generally happy with how the system worked, even with the limited choices. Career opportunities were not all that different even if they drew poorly in the selection lottery.[23] First duty assignments did not determine whether they had a successful career. Fleet performance ultimately mattered more than anything that happened at the academy.[24]

The prewar academy could also afford to ignore criticism from civilian educators. Despite its lackluster reputation, Annapolis still received enough applicants to meet its needs. Society also accepted the basic priorities of the academy. Although the majority of midshipmen came from middle-class families, the pre-war academy also included significant numbers from the upper middle class. Many in this group were "Navy juniors," midshipmen who had family members who also graduated from the Naval Academy. These families would not have considered a career for their sons other than the Navy. The survey population contained significantly less "Navy juniors" after World War II. Perhaps as American culture changed, sons from naval families were more willing to question their parent's choices. There also seemed to be an interesting change in how "Navy juniors" defined their families' economic status. Earlier groups classified their families as being upper middle class while later years viewed the Navy as more of a middle-class occupation.[25]

Families without a connection to Annapolis also believed that it was a plum opportunity. An appointment was often the only option for those who could not financially afford college. There were few aid or scholarship programs at this time, much less any that paid room and board as well as tuition. Furthermore, the military was a respectable career with reasonable pay and benefits. These circumstances were especially true during the Great Depression. Most graduates remained in the Navy for a full career of twenty to thirty years of active service. Admiral Mack talked about how word got back from midshipmen who had attempted life outside the Navy and it was not good. Within the service, "people fought to stay in—very few people left unless they were put out. It was very different in those days. So it took a person with a lot of self-confidence and abilities to leave voluntarily and very few did." The classes of 1946 to 1949 had the highest retention rate (73 percent) of any cohort in the survey group. In contrast, only 44 percent of the classes of 1970 to 1976 stayed for an entire career.[26]

World War II Mobilization

World War II would be a watershed in the academy's history although it did not appear that way at the outset. Ironically, the manpower demands of a two-ocean fleet did not change its priorities; if anything, it accelerated them. The fleet needed junior officers in a hurry, more than Annapolis could ever hope to produce itself. Although the Navy used other commissioning sources, it expected the Naval Academy to supply the cadre of its best-trained and motivated officers. The academy had never experienced a more severe emergency in its history. However, its response to the crisis did not suggest any long-term consequences for the future.[27] It turned to an accelerated, three-year program in the summer of 1940, similar to what was used during the mobilization crisis of World War I.

Under the accelerated program, midshipmen completed the bulk of their *academic* program because they attended school nearly year round. Instead of three academic terms per year, each season contained a full schedule of classes with limited breaks in between.[28] The class of 1948 had the most awkward transition with half the class finishing under the three-year regimen and the rest completing a final year after the war. Ironically, academic standing was used to divide the class in half, a decision not very popular with those who stayed the extra year. The unpopularity of this decision demonstrated the marginal position of academics in the midshipmen culture. The class of 1948B did not feel this was a valid reason to be left behind. It had never been a barometer for separating classmates before. For the first time, academic achievement, or the lack thereof, had tangible consequences beyond Annapolis. The class of 1948A would be promoted sooner; they could expect to make slightly more money than their classmates, all because they had better grades.[29]

The war was a time of constant experimentation with the curriculum, once thought to be untouchable. The impetus behind reforms was always winning the war, however, not long-term academic changes. At the same time, the curriculum was more flexible to further reform than was the case beforehand. In general, curriculum changes looked to apply combat's lessons to the classroom. The Naval Academy built trainers and mock-ups to incorporate the latest advances in fire control technology and antisubmarine warfare.[30] Midshipmen learned about the Thach weave for fighting Japanese Zeroes and new multicarrier screen formations that provided an interlocking defense for the fleet. The tone of emphasis was always pragmatic: information midshipmen needed to survive combat. Midshipmen profited from the assignment of veteran officers who drove home the consequences of failed technology, miscommunications, or inadequately conceived tactics.[31]

The war's most lasting academic change was the faculty's composition. Adequate staffing was one of the more urgent problems at the beginning of the war. The fleet's sudden expansion stripped Annapolis of most of its junior officers. Regular officers were simply too valuable to be assigned stateside, especially with active combat operations underway. Annapolis had gaping holes to fill in both its academic departments and Bancroft Hall.[32] Although civilian professors were on the staff, the balance was heavily weighted—8:2—towards military instructors at the start of the war. The academy filled vacancies using reserve and retired officers, preferably those with previous educational experience elsewhere. The few remaining regular officers were concentrated in the core professional subjects.³³

In many respects, these wartime improvisations worked out well. Midshipmen were exposed to a greater range of academic backgrounds and teaching styles. Wartime instructors introduced new pedagogical techniques in the classroom. Humanities classes especially tried to challenge midshipmen to think on their own. The mixed faculty ratio would become more balanced following World War II. One of the ways in which the postwar academy upgraded its academic reputation was to add civilians with recognized scholastic credentials. It retained many of its wartime staff as permanent civilian instructors. The transition to greater numbers of civilians was certainly made easier by the war. Annapolis learned that civilian instructors of the right background and temperament, usually veterans or reserve officers themselves, were not a threat to its military culture.³⁴

Yet, this development also started a growing dichotomy between the military and academic sides of the institution. This trend would grow most noticeably in the 1960s but the roots of that transition started here. Beforehand, the goals of the academic and executive departments were often in harmony. Indeed, many officer instructors focused on military discipline as much as they did classroom work; civilian professors understood and worked within the academy's other priorities, including Bancroft Hall. The break would never be abrupt or total but it would grow following World War II. Only 15 percent of the classes of 1946 to 1949 believed that the school's academic and military demands were unbalanced, whereas over 37 percent of the classes of 1965 to 1976 felt that way. Complicating matters further, future civilians did not have as much military experience as their predecessors.³⁵

The other major change to the academic culture was the way in which Annapolis handled struggling students. The older system tolerated turn backs, midshipmen who needed additional opportunities to pass their classes.³⁶ Turn backs received a second chance, but they paid a steep price in return. They graduated later than their peers, were promoted later, waited longer for additional privileges, and so forth. Not every academically deficient midshipman could go this route. The Academic Board decided each case individually after looking at the entirety of his record.³⁷ Normally, midshipmen who showed leadership or professional abilities were given the opportunity. However, it was also a convenient way of helping star athletes or sons of high-ranking officers who were in trouble.³⁸

Turn backs eventually completed the same requirements for graduation. Nonetheless, their existence amplifies how tightly knit and flexible a community the academy was before World War II. The process also shows the marginal place of academics within the prewar system. Promising officers were generally given greater leeway to complete the program. The crunch of wartime mobilization made it difficult to give anyone second chances. The turn back system survived World War II but just barely. Postwar expansion and academic reform made its continuance unnecessary and impractical. The new academy began admitting students with higher academic profiles and did not have to be as tolerant of academically deficient midshipmen. Elite colleges and universities did not offer such opportunities and neither could Annapolis if it wanted to join them. Like other academic changes, the war was merely a first step in forming this new academic culture.[39]

Wartime Training

The Naval Academy shortened the curriculum by reducing its normal training activities. The choice really was not all that difficult to make however. Fleet operations took priority over stateside requirements. Instead of overseas cruises, most at-sea training was limited to the eastern seaboard or the Chesapeake Bay. At first, midshipmen drilled on small craft permanently stationed at Annapolis. Shortcuts like these were the equivalent of having soldiers perform close-order drill with brooms instead of rifles. Students familiarized themselves with the content of their duties but not in ways that enhanced professional socialization.[40] Later, older surface combatants were used, which gave a slightly more realistic flavor to the training. Fuel limitations and operational restrictions still limited exercises to the Chesapeake Bay, but at least it was completed on real warships.[41] Midshipmen applauded the resumption of normal cruises after World War II. Wartime training packed only so many thrills, especially compared to the exotic ports peacetime cruises normally visited.[42]

The academy supplemented the limited training schedule with visits from newly commissioned aircraft carriers, cruisers, and submarines. In some respects, the value of these tours was more motivational than educational. They raised students' expectations that they were part of an elite, powerful Navy. Firsthand exposure certainly augmented the material covered in the trainers. Their drills were not without purpose but had definite practical application. Furthermore, these visits bolstered the seriousness of classroom study. Just like themselves, these vessels would soon be in the thick of combat.[43]

It does seem ironic that the Naval Academy made its greatest cuts in the training program. Wartime graduates completed the bulk of the academic curriculum, which was traditionally the weakest part of the academy program. Although civilian educators occasionally frowned on the heavy professional emphasis, Admiral Sellars, as well as most senior officers, believed that the academy's most important responsibility was to provide extensive, fleet specific training. Prewar midshipmen could step into any number of division officer billets and be competent in their duties. Wartime operational requirements invariably undercut these activities, but the academy had little choice in the matter. With training opportunities limited, its only choice was to spend greater time in the classroom.

Wartime midshipmen learned the basics necessary for surviving combat. Yet, the limited schedule clearly put a damper on their professional socialization.[44] Summer cruises were traditionally a welcome break from Annapolis. Midshipmen learned professional skills but they also developed lifelong friendships and reaffirmed their commitment to a naval career.[45] The wartime emergency robbed them of a crucial bonding experience that was a staple of the midshipmen culture.[46] Academy leaders understood this, but it was hard to assign a value to professional socialization. In the short term, nothing appeared to have been lost. Normal cruises also contained their fair share of drudgery and wasted time. Just as with academics, World War II provided alternatives reformers would use in arguing for changes to professional training. Academics could be improved, they said, without compromising the school's military mission. The academy might have to shed "prep school" activities, like the traditional summer cruise, if it wanted to become an elite college.[47]

The war also disrupted professional socialization efforts in Bancroft Hall. Some of its activities directly complemented classroom instruction. For example, after evening meal, companies practiced additional Morse code and flashing light drills that were a part of the color company competition.[48] Bancroft Hall's paramount function, however, was the midshipmen's character development. The military profession required exacting standards of personal discipline and accountability, a lifestyle young men did not always take to naturally. Constant oversight and exacting discipline had always been the formula for ensuring those values took root. Midshipmen learned the importance of following orders and personal accountability under extreme physical and mental stress. Company officers normally monitored Bancroft Hall to ensure no shortcuts were taken.[49]

However, most junior officers were quickly reassigned to operational billets after America entered the war. The Naval Academy never received enough replacements to maintain the normal degree of supervision over Bancroft Hall.[50] Instead of officers at both the company and battalion levels, a drastically reduced group of battalion officers, many of whom were over-age reservists, were left to train the midshipmen. In many cases, these part-time officers did not have the youth or the exuberance to handle these assignments. Compounding matters, record numbers of midshipmen were admitted throughout the war.[51] Fewer officers were supervising more

"Well — Where's your ID card?"

The Log, 1 December 1944. Executive Department "Mickey Mouse," a Duty Officer demanding the president produce his ID.

midshipmen, which forced them to spend most of their time enforcing the rules. Midshipmen griped that this was the case before the war, but the lack of officer personnel certainly exacerbated that tendency.[52] Annapolis did not have the time or the staff for professional mentoring to make it more of a priority.[53]

There was little choice but to give upperclassmen greater control over Bancroft Hall. More than a few abused the extra liberties given to them. They had always sneaked privileges or tormented plebes beyond what the rules allowed. The war, however, brought out excesses more than normal. Afterwards, many midshipmen wanted the pendulum to swing the other way. The class of 1948B issued a formal policy statement their senior year, which suggested how badly discipline needed to be restored: "We, the members of the Class of 1948B, intend to develop discipline based on mutual respect. We contend that the present inter-class relationships have lost sight of the purpose for which they were designed, namely, the indoctrination of loyalty and cooperation of all classes, with a Brigade 'esprit de corps' second to none. We intend to utilize methods which eliminate the flagrant violations of mature personal dignity. We hold that instruction by example is vital to the organization and administration of any military unit." Their statement indicated a greater commitment to disciplining themselves, strong evidence that wartime liberties were taken too far.[54]

Victory seemingly resolved most problems with the training program and Bancroft Hall. The fleet became available again to host normal summer cruises. War zone bans were removed on travel to Europe and the Far East. The personnel crunch also ended with the new peacetime routine. The Navy resumed the assignment of company officers to Annapolis.[55] Many newcomers had incredible war records under their belts. Postwar midshipmen had an unprecedented opportunity to learn from true naval heroes, officers like Captain Bush Bringle, a naval aviator and Navy Cross winner, and Commander John Bulkeley, who won the Medal of Honor for commanding the patrol boat squadron that rescued Douglas MacArthur. Midshipmen were literally rubbing elbows with combat veterans on a daily basis; moreover, these officers were still junior enough to be accessible to their questions, unlike say a Halsey or a Nimitz. The absence of high decorations was definitely the exception to the rule among officers assigned immediately after the war.[56]

However, these officers approached their duties in much the same manner as their predecessors did. Midshipmen from the classes of 1946 to 1949 and 1950 to 1954 both viewed their officers as disciplinarians first and role models second. Company officers did not console them through difficult times, nor was their primary role specific training about the fleet. Instead, they taught character lessons, usually through strict enforcement of the rules. Some survey respondents were annoyed by this emphasis, but many others thought their officers were outstanding and wanted to emulate them. These contradictions are not that unusual. Most of these midshipmen expected sharp discipline, which *toughened* them for naval service. Both they and their officers agreed this was the academy's most important responsibility and the best preparation for officership. This no-nonsense approach was what everyone believed had won World War II. Future midshipmen had different expectations of officers, but many of them were not as familiar with the traditional military culture.[57]

The Rise of Naval Aviation

Naval aviation gained the most during this whole period of academic and professional revision. Whether naval air replaced the surface line as the academy's reigning military culture is a matter of debate.[58] At the very least, aviation became the line community's preeminent rival for control of the academy in the late 1940s and early 1950s. Naval aviation wrested progressively larger control of the curriculum, the training program, and even Bancroft Hall. Eventually this warfare community would take as many graduates into its ranks as the surface navy.[59] The ascendancy of naval aviation reflected a similar trend throughout the Navy. Naval air was what won the war in the Pacific and appeared to be the Navy's future. It only made sense for the academy also to jump onto its bandwagon.

The academy had wrestled before the war with aviation's impact on the curriculum. Midshipmen took indoctrination flights in Navy training aircraft, mostly seaplanes that could be launched and recovered on the Severn River. Classes were also offered in air navigation, the fundamentals of flight, aviation gunnery, and engineering. Eventually Annapolis also constructed a new hanger to maintain and service its own aircraft. The academy stopped short, however, of training midshipmen to become full-fledged pilots.[60]

The war generated a flurry of proposals expanding the scope of aviation training at the Naval Academy. Some ideas called for too much too fast, even with the influence naval aviation wielded at the time. Numerous plans called for the construction of an airfield capable of handling fixed wing aircraft on the other side of the Severn River. Other proposals called for expanding the aviation program from orientation to the midshipmen's full qualification as pilots. Some planners wanted the academy to restrict admission to only those applicants capable of becoming pilots.[61] All these proposals eventually failed, probably because they restricted the academy's emphasis too much.

Even so, naval aviation extended its grip over the program after World War II. Aviation courses gradually took up a larger share of the already crowded curriculum. Beyond orientation work, midshipmen began taking classes similar to those offered in the operational training pipeline at Pensacola. Navy air eventually established its own academic department and sent a bright young officer, Captain Robert Pirie, to develop the curriculum further.[62] Other top officers were also assigned to solidify its hold over the academy.[63] The new department developed a slate of courses that were required of all midshipmen. Ship drivers and submariners may have grumbled, but naval aviation's star was on the rise. Postwar rumors hinted that the Navy wanted at least 40 percent of graduates to become naval aviators. Annapolis was simply following trends evident throughout the entire service.[64]

The summer training program also became more heavily oriented towards aviation requirements. Entire summers were devoted to "air cruises," something unthinkable before World War II. Within the tight summer schedule, precious time was allotted to training on aircraft carriers, at naval air stations, and at air repair facilities. All midshipmen received this training regardless of whether they were even physically qualified for aviation.[65] It might have seemed that naval aviation had captured the academy. Even if that were true, it was not anything different

The Log, 8 November 1946. Midshipmen waiting for orientation flights.

than the surface navy's dominance before the war. Line officers still wielded tremendous power despite all the changes. Much of the curriculum remained geared towards surface ships. The mandatory sea tour also remained in effect for all graduates.

Navy air expanded its control over areas not even related to aviation. For example, the genesis of new physical education requirements came from naval aviation. Midshipmen began training in contact sports, like boxing and hand-to-hand combat. They were also tested in areas of endurance and agility, with a new obstacle course and long distance swimming classes. Many new requirements had their origins in the aviation-training pipeline.[66] These changes also reflected an important shift within the service culture of the Navy. Naval aviation was determining orthodoxy service-wide, including the academy.

Its culture also penetrated Bancroft Hall. Career aviators began serving in greater numbers as company and battalion officers. Many aviators used an alternative leadership style that midshipmen found appealing. The surface navy taught midshipmen that orders were to be obeyed without question and that the line separating seniors from juniors should never be broken.[67] Naval aviation preached a less stringent vision of officership; rules were important, but performance was the bottom line. The camaraderie of flying transcended the traditional military barriers of rank and position. To midshipmen, "work hard and play hard" was not just a stereotype of aviators; it was a motto they followed on a regular basis.

It was a vision of officership that seemed youthful and vigorous, which was quite a contrast from the surface navy's traditions. Naval aviation was becoming the preferred career choice of many midshipmen. The job itself seemed glamorous and important, albeit risky, but in many ways that was also part of its appeal. Eventually it would absorb nearly as many graduates as surface line.[68] Despite the Navy's compelling need for aviators, midshipmen had to wait until 1956 before they could select Pensacola directly. Annapolis only reversed its decision on mandatory sea tours after losing too many interested midshipmen to the Air Force. Its military culture was becoming a marketplace of different ideas and values, with different groups enjoying dominance but never to the exclusion of the rest.[69]

The Challenges of a New Era

Although it had produced victory, the old academy did not survive World War II. New technology and manpower requirements would combine to make it obsolete. The Naval Academy had to feel good, however, about what it had accomplished in the war. It had adjusted effectively to the constraints of a severe mobilization crisis, and its graduates had successfully weathered the test of battle. Important changes had to be made, but the essential values of naval service remained the same. The war had not been won through new technology and operational doctrines alone. What about the spirit of duty and commitment graduates had shown in leading the service to victory? Annapolis became a showcase for accomplishments of this nature after the war. The Naval Academy welcomed into its possession all kinds of trophies of war—captured battle flags, ship's bells—won by its graduates in battle.[70] Preservation efforts honored the incredible sacrifice of graduates, but they also had an important teaching function. All were reminders of the institution's foremost purpose, the preparation of combat officers for the naval service.[71]

These efforts were invaluable to the midshipmen's professional socialization, especially as firsthand memories of the conflict began to fade. Students watched the popular documentary, *Victory at Sea,* in Smoke Hall each Friday night throughout the 1950s.[72] After a while, nothing new about the war was learned per se, but it certainly helped keep the conflict fresh in the midshipmen's memory. The Naval Academy also remembered its Medal of Honor recipients by renaming their rooms in their honor.[73] Current students learned that the Navy's greatest heroes had started out as midshipmen just like them. The school frequently welcomed back legends such as Ernest King, Bull Halsey, and Chester Nimitz to speak to midshipmen. All of them made reference to the importance the academy had played in their careers.[74] Midshipmen took summer cruises on the same ships that had won the war's major battles. No matter how naval warfare changed, it would still take dedicated and willing officers to win those battles. Perhaps, with all the other changes ahead, the academy wanted to ensure that this message rang clear to its newest midshipmen.

The Holloway Plan

World events would not allow the Navy to be reduced as much as it had been after previous wars. Instead of massive demobilization, larger standing forces would be maintained than anytime in the Navy's history. This created a severe manpower crisis that had to be solved quickly. Annapolis simply could not produce all these officers by itself. Even with major fine-tuning, it could only be counted upon for fifteen hundred regular officers a year, nowhere near the Navy's needs. Alternative commissioning programs were used during World War II, but their existence was always seen as temporary. Many of the wartime reservist officers were eager to return to civilian life. Permanent structural changes was the only way of filling this void.[75]

The Naval Academy could not help but be nervous towards some of the proposals on the table. Some plans called for the construction of a second academy on the west coast, identical to Annapolis in every respect. From the Navy's perspective, separate facilities would greatly ease the administrative and logistical burden on the existing pipeline. To be even thinking this way, Annapolis insisted, was hasty and absurd. The four-year experience had long been the glue that joined regular officers together. Two schools would cause irreparable damage to the cohesion of the officer corps, a major factor in the Navy's latest victory. Other plans called for turning over an officer's education to civilian colleges and universities, similar to reserve programs in the past. Annapolis could concentrate on making midshipmen officers and leave the educational burden to other institutions.

The Naval Academy, in other words, would become a finishing institution for students with a demonstrated willingness and aptitude for becoming career officers. This option also appeared to be fine on paper but the academy again argued that the price was too steep. Most arguments had to do with its value to professional socialization. The four-year, concentrated environment was invaluable and irreplaceable for turning young men into professional officers. It allowed few distractions from military training and character development. Immersion in the military culture was also seen as the best way of motivating students towards career service. No matter the quality of the academic program, no civilian institution could provide that degree of oversight.[76]

No other person was more influential in shaping the postwar Naval Academy than Rear Admiral James Holloway Jr. '19. Holloway's family came from deep Navy roots, leaving him with a natural tendency to protect his alma mater. But he was also a realist to the issues raised by the war and understood it had to change tradition notwithstanding. The Holloway Board of 1946 attempted to solve the Navy's problem of numbers while preserving the essence of the existing academy system. Annapolis would maintain its four-year program substantially as it was before the war and gradually expand its facilities—extra classrooms, playing fields, and new wings to Bancroft Hall—to accommodate an enlarged student body. Midshipmen would henceforth be organized into a Brigade with total numbers ranging between four and five thousand students, depending on the quality of applications.[77]

Annapolis retained its position at the pinnacle of the Navy's system of officer education, but its justification for being there was different. The Naval Academy would no longer provide the bulk of regular officers, but it would supply those trained to the highest standards of the naval profession. Holloway painted the true value of Annapolis in spiritual terms, calling it the cradle of naval values and virtues, the heart and soul of the naval profession. The change in emphasis was a watershed in its history. The academy began touting that it supplied most of the Navy's *career* officers, the implication being that its program nurtured that sense of loyalty in the first place. The question of whether career minded midshipmen were already predisposed towards Annapolis was rarely discussed. With quantity no longer available, it turned to a quality-only argument to defend its existence.[78]

However, few survey participants, only 18.6 percent overall, changed their minds about a military career while at Annapolis. Over 80 percent in each of the thirty classes followed through on their initial intentions. It would be an oversimplification to say that the academy was a neutral influence on their decisions. Annapolis obviously lived up to many people's expectations, which gave them little reason for altering their decision. Many others, however, had an erroneous understanding of what it would be like, especially Bancroft Hall. The military lifestyle was a difficult adjustment, but they survived to graduation. Those who could not make the transition left the academy. Clearly some in this group were not cut out for military life whatsoever. Yet others became disillusioned because of Bancroft Hall.[79]

These results suggest important limits to academy indoctrination. Professional socialization took place but within certain parameters. Rarely does it seem that the Naval Academy motivated someone towards a military career who was not already predisposed that way. In most cases, it seems to have reinforced attitudes and beliefs midshipmen had beforehand. The intensity of Bancroft Hall clearly tested midshipmen's convictions to their limits. That, in and of itself, was of tremendous value to an officer preparing for service in the Navy's combat branches. In other words, professional indoctrination served more of a screening purpose than it did anything else. The issue was moot so long as Annapolis recruited applicants already well versed in the military culture. However, this proposition was tested in the 1960s when fewer applicants shared these same values.

Even if he knew these results, Admiral Holloway did not have a better alternative. Other schools provided a superior education; the midshipmen's training could also be accomplished at a cheaper cost elsewhere. But no other institution offered so total an immersion into the military culture. Bancroft Hall developed midshipmen's character but it seemingly did not invent convictions that were not already there. These achievements were noteworthy even if they were not as grandiose as the academy claimed. Although the reasons were unclear, Holloway was right on one point. At least until the early 1970s, the retention rate of academy-trained officers was almost double that of other programs. If Annapolis was not doing anything specific to cause those statistics, it apparently was not hurting them either.

Perhaps an understated value of the Naval Academy was its ability to attract career-motivated applicants. Such individuals had little choice before World War II, but that was not true afterwards. Even with NROTC, they continued to flock to Annapolis. The reasons why are not totally clear. The stereotype of Annapolis being the stronghold of military professionalism and NROTC being the preserve of amateurs is a strong one yet today. The mystique and elitism of the service academies were also a powerful attraction. The very fact that it was difficult and not everyone made it was a huge enticement to many midshipmen. The cultural value of Annapolis was much more difficult to quantify however.[80]

The irony of the academy's predicament would not have been lost on its old guard, men like Admiral David Sellars. As all of this was happening, Annapolis had begun to upgrade its academic program, due largely to new technology. But academics were its weak point and a strong suit of many NROTC colleges and universities. Although needed, these reforms reflected a degree of insecurity with its new role the academy has never shed. To distinguish itself from NROTC, its leaders touted features traditionally associated with Bancroft Hall. At the same time, it was not entirely comfortable surrendering the academic baton to other institutions. The Naval Academy wanted to be both a bastion of military professionalism and a respected center of higher education. The classic academy solution was to attempt both no matter how much it stretched the institution's resources. It also reinvigorated the unresolved question of what the school's priorities should be.

Holloway's solution to the manpower crunch was to turn a wartime necessity into a virtue. To get additional officers, the Navy expanded the NROTC program, which was supposed to disappear after World War II. The genius or apostasy of his plan was to turn it into a *permanent* program. No longer would a single institution produce regular officers. Instead, the burden was distributed among fifty-two colleges and universities throughout the country. The new NROTC included two programs, contract and reserve midshipmen. The government paid the tuition of contract midshipmen as well as a small stipend for expenses. Contract midshipmen owed a limited term of active service, after which they augmented to regular status or were free to leave the Navy. Later, the plan was amended to give them regular commissions, just like academy graduates. Reserve midshipmen did not benefit financially, but they got good military training without incurring an obligation and went into a general manpower pool for emergencies. In theory, no further refinements to the pipeline were ever necessary. It could be expanded or reduced depending on the Navy's needs.[81]

Given the alternatives, the Holloway Plan was the best option for preserving the existing academy system while addressing the Navy's immediate needs. Annapolis maintained its status as a small, elite institution despite losing its monopoly of regular officers. In putting out this immediate fire, it exposed the school to future controversies about its existence. Unlike its sister service, the Navy never had to contend with Russell Weigley's "dual-army tradition." In other words, it never had a National Guard competing with it for the nation's eye or its dollars.[82] Similarly, after its creation, everyone assumed Annapolis was the sole path for a regular commission. There were no alternatives for comparison however; that relationship changed quickly after World War II. NROTC alleviated the manpower shortage but it also became a credible alternative to the academy. Simply put, Annapolis cost more and produced less than the NROTC. Its value as a repository for naval virtues and traditions was worthwhile but more difficult to measure. Yet this argument was the only one available after the Holloway Plan went into effect.

Midshipmen were not experts in officer education but they did understand what it meant to have an institutional rival. They took great pride in being a part of the Naval Academy, an attitude consciously fostered by the institution. Plebes might be the bottom of the barrel, but simply being at Annapolis made them special. Midshipmen welcomed and often expected special attention because of their status. Indeed, the public's respect was what made their sacrifices worth it, especially with financial rewards becoming so few and far between. Whether it was civilians stopping them in town to ask questions, ex-service members wanting to swap stories and buy them dinner, or parents' friends wanting to set them up on dates, midshipmen craved the attention their uniform brought them.

The Holloway Plan was yet another blow to their self-esteem, already dampened after the war. Despite the local attention, midshipmen suffered through occasional cases of mistaken identity, especially outside Annapolis. People confused their uniform with that of bellhops, railway conductors, doormen, everything but the special people they believed themselves to be. One woman replied, "Oh, I see, one of those West Point naval officers. Splendid, young man, but what do you plan to be when you grow up?"[83] Before the war, mistakes like these were taken in stride and not seen as a major threat to midshipmen's professional dignity. Midshipmen found that their stories and experiences were not that extraordinary to a society fresh out of a world war. America was full of veterans, many of them their age with actual combat experience. The triumphs of Bancroft Hall paled in comparison to those gained fighting the Germans and the Japanese. Americans still appreciated the uniform, but nothing about midshipmen per se made them stand out any more than the rest.[84]

The Holloway reforms made an already difficult situation worse. Despite the spit and polish image of Annapolis, the average person found little difference between an academy midshipman and the NROTC version. They had the same haircuts and uniforms and participated in similar activities. Academy midshipmen insisted their professional demeanor was distinctive, but they noticed the difference more than anyone else. This sort of confusion was more difficult to take than being mistaken for a run-of-the-mill bellhop. Midshipmen found themselves in a similar predicament to their institution: the uniqueness of Annapolis seemed in jeopardy. It imposed many deprivations, supposedly the price to be paid for becoming a professional officer. Their leaders claimed that there was no better preparation for naval service than Bancroft Hall. Now that the Navy had NROTC, was that necessarily true? The Holloway Plan did not silence questions about the academy; in many ways, it reinvigorated them. What made officers trained the Annapolis way worth the effort or the cost? Midshipmen understood that this was a question not easily put to rest.[85]

The New Academics

The impact of wartime technology made it impossible to dodge the question of curriculum reform any longer. The real problem was the rapid pace of technological change, which had only continued after the war. Atomic bombs, jet propulsion, and radar were only in their infancy; further changes were not a generation away but a few years at most. Officers did not need to be scientists, but they should understand how this technology worked. The fixed curriculum seemed incapable of dealing with this problem. It had always produced competent junior officers and with major overhaul could probably continue to do so. The real danger was in the future. Current graduates would likely be ineffective admirals, not only in their knowledge but also in how they made decisions. A flexible education based on theoretical principles was the best preparation for the future. Curriculum reform was a dead issue so long as it concerned just civilian educators. However, there were now compelling operational reasons why the school's priorities had to change. Most importantly, within the Navy, a growing circle of senior officers had begun to accept these ideas. Academics had to assume a more equal priority to training, including Bancroft Hall's activities.[86]

Everything took a major leap forward with Admiral Holloway's appointment as superintendent in January 1947. Holloway was the dynamo for many reforms, but he could not have acted alone. Critical to his success were sympathetic officers in key positions throughout the Navy, particularly the head of the Bureau of Naval Personnel (BUPERS). Before taking

The Log, 26 March 1947. USNA midshipman showing his disgust at an ROTC midshipman receiving the same commission as he.

the job, Holloway insisted on the assignment of top-notch officers as his academic department heads, a huge departure from past stereotypes. Their future career success helped to erase the negative perception officers had of academy duty. The support of like-minded officers was critical in allowing these reforms to permeate the institutional culture. In many institutions, not just Annapolis, reformers face an uphill battle challenging the status quo. Not only must there be compelling reasons to change but the benefits for doing so must be ironclad. The status quo might have problems with it, but in most cases it is still getting the job done. The standard of proof is also less for its supposed advantages. Holloway, in other words, needed true believers to help his ideas gain momentum.

The whole process illustrates how major reform happened at Annapolis. Friends in high places were always necessary for lasting success. As head of BUPERS in the late 1950s, Holloway assisted a protégé, William Smedberg, in initiating the next sequence of changes to the curriculum. Later during the first phase of the "academic revolution," Smedberg followed his example in helping other superintendents.[87] The other important lesson was that true reform did not happen immediately. Reformers had to overcome an institutional culture extremely resistant to change. Not all of Holloway's successors shared his convictions about the school's future. They generally did not undo reforms, but few took them further either. Midshipmen and officers blocked changes that undercut important traditions. Thus, it took repeated effort at reform for difficult changes to take root.

The Naval Academy implemented a number of academic reforms in the years immediately following World War II. Some were more substantial than others, but they all epitomized the new direction. In 1946, the academy hosted its first visit by the Middle States Association, the biggest step yet towards joining the larger academic community. The team gave the academy its preliminary accreditation, but there was much work to do before its next visit in 1956. In general, evaluators perceived a lack of coherence between the school's academic program and its larger goals. For example, it found the library to be in deplorable condition, almost as if it had never been used. If the library was not important to the midshipmen's studies, what did that say about the institution's academic priorities?[88]

The academy had been approved to confer baccalaureate degrees in the 1930s. The time lag in completing this process meant that many eligible alumni had never received their diplomas. Annapolis encouraged all graduates to apply for their degree, a situation beneficial to them and its academic credentials.[89] If its diploma was ever to mean anything scholastically, however, there was much work to do in the ten years before the Middle States group returned. In 1946, it joined the American Council on Education and the Association of American Colleges, which allowed its alumni to pursue postgraduate studies. Unlike previous years, there was not only a desire to be involved in the larger academic community but also a willingness to listen to its suggestions for improvement.[90]

These reforms were aimed more at the future, but Holloway also tried to improve the current academic environment. Wherever possible, he tinkered with the curriculum, the goal being a more flexible, theoretical emphasis. Faculty upgrades were continued, with standards tightened for both hiring and promotion. An after dinner lecture series was begun for first classmen with notable figures in government, business, popular culture, and education as guest speakers. First classmen completed additional classroom requirements, such as a public speaking course and an extended term paper based on original research. One must be careful not to overstate all of this; the lockstep curriculum was still in effect, but the emphasis of these reforms was indeed new. The commitment to broader education occurred at a time when professional expectations of Annapolis were also changing. More officers, aviators and submariners in particular, needed additional training after graduation. Certain parts of the academy training program were becoming obsolete. New requirements focused more on general skills that would be relevant throughout an officer's career.[91]

Admiral Holloway also tried to bridge the gap between academics and Bancroft Hall, just as the Middle States team recommended. Unless the new mindset was accepted there, any reform would be half-hearted at best. The genius of Holloway's leadership was that he did not ask midshipmen to do something for nothing. Greater academic expectations were being placed upon them. But the superintendent gave tangible benefits in return. Upperclassmen received additional weekends away from the academy microscope. Extra town liberty was given to all midshipmen, also to compensate for the new routine. The class of 1948B was allowed to create additional class privileges—not a big deal anywhere else but a huge plus at the academy. Not coincidentally, upperclassmen were held more accountable for unauthorized hazing; plebes also needed more time studying. With everything that could be lost, it did not make sense to test the superintendent's resolve by forcing the matter.[92]

Midshipmen appreciated everything Holloway did for them, and many liked him personally. Personal admiration rarely resulted in an altering of their culture's core values however.[93] Reforms that reflected established traditions were easily accepted; the new privileges were a good example. Deep attitudinal changes, especially towards academics and Bancroft Hall, were much tougher to accomplish. Commitment at the top was not enough, especially when many Executive Department officers opposed or were skeptical of the reforms. Compounding matters, Holloway's tenure at Annapolis, like most superintendents, was extremely short. He did not have enough time to penetrate this resistance.[94]

Holloway's reforms were a starting point, but major improvements were still required before Annapolis ever became a "MIT on the Severn." The faculty's quality remained very uneven. Most officers were still without advanced degrees, and most civilians remained concentrated in the humanities. Civilian lectures were always entertaining, but their overall influence on the academy was modest.[95] Officers continued to use the classroom to teach important "character" lessons. One example is how the Leadership Department graded a set of exams on the military justice system. Midshipmen felt the grading was trying to reinforce a lesson about the importance of precision. The exam asked a question about the maximum punishment that could be awarded at a special court-martial. Students who responded with solitary confinement not exceeding one month had their answers marked wrong; the correct response was solitary confinement not exceeding *thirty days*. "Mickey Mouse" remained a major part of the classroom just like Bancroft Hall.[96]

Most importantly, Holloway's reforms failed to change attitudes towards academics within the academy culture. Whether it was poor instruction, their own academic background, or the limited study time, midshipmen looked to the curve, not their own academic resources, for their survival.[97] Grades in their own right seemed meaningless. What difference did a high grade point average make anyway, so long as you graduated? The academy still used a lottery to pick initial assignments. Those at the top of the class could easily find themselves with undesirable orders.[98] Midshipmen continued to frown on classmates who worked too hard at their grades. "Salty Sam" mocked one slash that advised his professor that "if he made the daily class sessions harder the section would have to study harder and could therefore learn more."[99] A poem in *The Log* about the slash epitomized the low place of academics in the academy culture:

> At Severn Seminary, where the sewer meets the sea,
> a hep and happy savior cut his classmates' throats with glee.
> The boys all called him "Gish the Slash" for little Joe, you see,
> Would scratch off problem number ten while they were stuck with three.
> The chalk dust rose like snow clouds while 'Ole Gish was at the board,
> In vain his classmates talked to him, intreated and implored.
> For Gish would sneer in great disdain and calmly leave them flat,
> The next day all the buckets were a little more unsat.
> So while he led a life of ease, his classmates worked like mad.
> The things they thought of him weren't good; in fact most were quite bad.[100]

The average midshipman found ways to get even with the slash. Stealing his compass and dividers before a navigation exam was a common trick. Most survived academics by sharing information, known as the dope system. Solutions to the daily quiz were passed among classmates during meals and in the company areas. Academic integrity notwithstanding,

"What did you guys get for the last prob? I only checked the P-work twice."

The Log, 5 November 1948. For the slash midshipman, good grades came before classmate loyalty. Note the stars on his uniform. Star men at this time were reviled. By the "academic revolution," it would become a badge of distinction.

midshipmen believed they were upholding the higher principle of protecting their classmates, a lesson repeatedly emphasized in Bancroft Hall. Postwar reforms weakened many of these attitudes, but it was not until the "academic revolution" that they truly died away. But that would be a vastly different academy from the late 1940s. The necessary framework for a new academic culture would not be fully in place until the early 1960s. The demand for technically qualified officers would only increase. Future midshipmen also had greater expectations for their education. Nevertheless, Admiral Holloway's tenure as superintendent was the foundation for a modern Annapolis.[101]

Social Limits to the Holloway Reforms

Academic reform was not the academy's only problem. American society was changing rapidly after World War II and dealing with these changes often prevented the academy from concentrating on other reforms. No problem was more ominous than the declining interest among young men for military service. Not only were there not enough applications, many graduates were leaving the service at the earliest opportunity. Only so much could be done about the applicant pool, but resignations were another matter entirely. Bancroft Hall's most important function was supposedly professional motivation. According to the Holloway Plan, this was the major reason for even having an academy. Yet the current retention rate was not that much better than NROTC or OCS. The problem stemmed from many sources, none of which was easy to fix, and the magnitude would only worsen during the defense unification battles of the early 1950s. Retention figures stabilized in the late 1950s to around 70 percent, similar to what it was before World War II. At the moment, the crisis undermined the basic premises behind the Holloway Plan.[102]

Unlike during the Great Depression, postwar midshipmen had many career options that promised a good future besides the Navy. Contrary to expectations, the postwar economy was booming with no apparent end in sight. Businesses were seeking bright and ambitious young men, especially those with leadership experience, to staff its management positions.[103] War weariness also created hesitation toward a military career. Parents were still supportive of their sons attending Annapolis but counseled them to weigh their options carefully. Among survey participants, family support during the war was nearly unanimous but jumped to a 5 percent disapproval rate for the classes of 1950 to 1954. Although small, these percentages would be greater than the results for Vietnam era midshipmen. Some families hoped they could find something better and more prestigious to do, like becoming a physician or a lawyer; parents of veterans felt their sons had done enough for their country.[104]

Likewise, friends of midshipmen increasingly questioned the decision to attend Annapolis after the war. The classes of 1950 to 1954 also reported a 5 percent increase (9.4 percent overall) in the peer disapproval rate. The raw numbers are again small, making it difficult to discern precise reasons for this change. The broader social context, however, gives many possibilities. Friends, even better than families, understood the alternatives because they were making similar decisions themselves. Furthermore, many friends were also veterans with strong opinions about a military career. Perhaps the commitment of Annapolis did not seem as relevant after 1945. These numbers decreased by the middle 1950s, suggesting a new awareness of the academy's opportunities and the growing urgency of the Cold War.[105]

In addition, demobilization took its toll on midshipmen financially. Despite their admiration for the military, war weary Americans were anxious to trim defense spending to peacetime levels. Unfortunately, most people did not care whether these cuts came from servicemen's paychecks or operational expenditures. Midshipmen also felt the crunch. Then as is now, they received a salary set by Congress to take care of their expenses. They never managed their own money; the disbursing officer handled their accounts. After deducting the cost of uniforms, textbooks, haircuts, and laundry services, midshipmen received a certain portion of what remained for spending money. Traditionally, if their money was budgeted carefully, enough was left over for a nice nest egg at graduation.

It was never a considerable sum, but the money was enough to pay for additional uniforms and other items graduates needed to start their careers. This surplus disappeared after 1945; inflation left many of them in debt by graduation.[106] Superintendents repeatedly pleaded for an increase in midshipmen salaries, but little was done until 1956.[107] For the most part, cadets and midshipmen were excluded from the pay raises given to other servicemen. What made the situation worse was that other officer programs received better financial benefits than the academy.[108] More than money was at stake however; the situation undercut professional socialization. Annapolis had a much tougher time selling midshipmen on a military career. Who wanted to commit to something that penalized them financially?

Midshipmen and the academy chose an interesting way of arguing for pay increases. Besides the financial handicap, the situation undercut their professional self-esteem. Midshipmen were not being paid enough to maintain their status as officers. Annapolis repeatedly warned them about fiscal responsibility and punished those who fell into debt.[109] At the same time, their paychecks did not cover the professional lifestyle expected of them. Midshipmen had to maintain multiple sets of dress uniforms rarely worn outside a few special occasions. At hops and other social events, they were expected to entertain in a style befitting a professional officer.[110] Neither midshipmen nor the institution were willing to restructure their white-collar profession's lifestyle to the blue-collar wage they were presently paid. Whether their financial situation was truly as bleak as they portrayed was irrelevant. Indeed, many civilian students with loans probably thought the Brigade had a fairly good deal. Midshipmen were comparing themselves to an internal standard of what their peers afforded in the past. From that vantage point, the future no longer seemed as bright.

The pitiful condition of the academy's physical plant also raised concerns about the Navy's future. The last major overhaul was in the late nineteenth century when the school averaged around eight hundred students. Much had changed since then to make existing facilities obsolete but the war made this a matter of utmost necessity. Essentially, facilities had fallen into chronic overuse and disrepair during the emergency. The first postwar superintendent, Vice Admiral Aubrey Fitch, described the sever-

The Log, 24 January 1947. Midshipman lamenting the latest fashions he cannot afford.

ity of the problem: "The original buildings have served under crowded usage for 40 and more years without major renovation. Their future life and uninterrupted operation of the institution dictate the need of overhaul in the very near future."[111] Superintendents had boasted about the size of wartime classes; each year set a new record. The V-7 and V-12 programs had also been allowed to use its facilities for training. The war effort made this necessary, but it exposed holes in the physical plant faster than ever.[112] Facilities were not given much chance to recover before the Holloway Plan's expansion. The same grounds were now expected to accommodate thirty-eight hundred midshipmen.[113]

Most projects mentioned in the superintendents' annual reports were not wish-list items but necessary work to keep up with its expanded mission.[114] Physical expansion was not a dry issue but weighed heavily on the midshipmen's quality of life. Classroom space was always at a premium. The notorious Maury Hall Plan was implemented to deal with overcrowding in the academic buildings. Classrooms were to be entered using only a certain section of the building and exited vice versa. Depending on the academic period, certain classes began at one time and dismissed at another. All in all, this was a very complicated process simply to get to class. Midshipmen were placed on report for not following these cumbersome regulations to the letter. The academy's physical condition, along with everything else, weighed heavily in the declining morale of the Brigade.[115]

Bancroft Hall was also bursting at the seams despite the addition of two new wings in 1942. Upperclassmen even had multiple roommates; quite the contradiction from rank hath its privileges. Rooms were dimly lit and poorly ventilated, conditions that added to the daily strain. Sundry facilities, like the tailor shop and post office, also needed renovation. Major items on the academy's wish list were a new auditorium and a mess hall capable of seating the entire Brigade at one time. Facilities like these were crucial to professional socialization. Meals were a regular activity that companies shared each day. They were also a time to socialize with friends, to relax from the day's grind, and to train plebes if need be. Special meals were prepared to commemorate important events in the academy calendar—crab nights, one hundred days until graduation, and most importantly the Christmas banquet. Midshipmen often wore special uniforms or observed certain traditions during these events.[116]

The expansion also left Annapolis drastically short of proper athletic facilities. Midshipmen participated in either a varsity or intramural sport throughout the year. Competitive sports were also an important part of their professional socialization. Besides developing physical endurance, sports built important values of perseverance and teamwork. In particular, intramural sports gave plebes the chance to interact with upperclassmen more as equals. On the athletic field, they were generally teammates first, plebes and upperclassmen second. Good athletes also contributed to their company's prestige and standings in the color company competition. The schedule was so crowded that teams rarely had enough practice time. Breakdowns here were more than a minor inconvenience. This was essentially their leisure time, a break from the classroom and Bancroft Hall. For now, even this aspect of the day had to be closely regulated. Academy life was always potentially stifling, but these feelings became more acute with the overcrowded conditions.[117]

These problems fell on midshipmen with different backgrounds and expectations of Annapolis than past generations. The democratization of higher education also seemed to have a liberating effect on the types of individuals applying for admission. Financial limitations had never been a theoretical barrier to the Naval Academy before, but it tended to work that way in practice. The prewar academy had a prep-school reputation; midshipmen generally knew one another; many came from upper class or career naval families; classmates suffered through academics and Bancroft Hall together. In other words, Annapolis was more about the experience than anything else. In particular, it bonded classmates throughout a twenty- or thirty-year military career.

The Naval Academy became more of a middle-to-working class institution after 1945. The classes of 1946 to 1954 had well over 30 percent with prior military service; many of them were ex-Navy enlisted men.[118] A 1947 article in the alumni association's *Shipmate* reported that over 48 percent of the class of 1951 was ex-military.[119] Many new faces came from outside the academy's demographic norm of middle-class Protestants. Midshipmen from working class families jumped from only 13 percent to over 35 percent of the student body during this same time period. The academy never attracted significant numbers from the highest ranks of society, nor the lowest. Upper class numbers peaked at 5.3 percent for the World War II classes but averaged only 1.6 percent after that. Lower class midshipmen started off slow (1.8 percent of World War II midshipmen) and only averaged 3 percent.[120]

The Brigade's growing religious diversity was also evidence of Annapolis becoming a more democratic institution. Midshipmen had always been predominantly Protestant and tended towards more "High-Church" denominations. Indeed, Peter Karsten in *The Naval Aristocracy* argued that the Episcopalian Church was effectively the institutional church at Annapolis in the late nineteenth and early twentieth centuries. Karsten believed its highly liturgical and hierarchical style of worship fit in well with the school's military values.[121] Roman Catholics joined the Brigade with greater frequency after 1945. From the late 1940s through the 1950s, roughly 20-25 percent of midshipmen were Catholic. The percentage of Catholics peaked after 1960 at slightly over 35 percent. Protestants continued to dominate the Brigade from 1945 to 1976, an average of 65.6 percent for the study. However, the influence of "High-Church" denominations diminished over time. In answering this question, earlier survey participants specified that they were not merely Protestant but Episcopalian or Anglican. Those from later years were content to lump themselves together with other Protestants.[122]

Despite its Protestant traditions, the academy had little choice but to be more tolerant of those with different religious beliefs. Catholic chaplains began to be stationed at Annapolis on a regular basis. The academy also arranged for mass inside the Yard instead of forcing Catholics to find a church in town. Finally, Catholics started organizing their own clubs and choirs similar to Protestants.[123] The development of a more tolerant religious community also reflected the growing trend towards secularism in American culture. Americans still saw themselves as a religious people, but denominational differences seemed less and less important. Indeed, the country's religious heritage was often seen as a vital weapon in winning the Cold War. However, the specific tenets of American Christianity were increasingly unimportant and were perhaps best left vague. One of President Eisenhower's statements on the subject reflects this contradiction best: "Our government makes no sense unless it is founded on a deeply felt religious faith—and I do not care what it is."[124]

Demographic changes did not include racial integration however. Wesley Brown '49 was the first African American graduate, but his example did not prompt many others to follow him. For much of the 1950s and 1960s, African Americans never even bothered applying for appointments. The Naval Academy never took great pains to recruit them either, not until the government's focus on civil rights in the late 1960s. *The Log* featured cartoons that ridiculed African Americans using conventional "Sambo" images, people who were lazy, indifferent, unhelpful, certainly not worthy of the midshipmen's respect. Overt racism was rare, but African Americans were never a threat to the school's social order. Midshipmen rarely interacted with African Americans they might regard as equals. Most contact was with people who served them in some capacity: the barbers who cut their hair, the laundresses who cleaned their uniforms, or the dining hall attendants who served their food.[125]

Many newcomers had different aspirations of what they wanted from the Naval Academy. Despite the laments of alumni, they were flocking in record numbers because of the educational benefits; 13 percent of the classes of 1950 to 1954 cited this as the primary attraction, up nearly 10 percent from the war.[126] Families who could not afford college otherwise found it difficult to ignore a totally subsidized education. Survey results showed a strong correlation between midshipmen's economic status and their reasons for attending the academy. Midshipmen from poorer families tended to come for the free education or the career opportunities. Those from higher income groups cited other reasons, such as the promises of a military career or the challenges of public service. Not coincidentally, the more service-oriented responses (those mentioned by the upper and upper middle class) diminished over time while a free college education increased significantly (the top preference of working-class midshipmen).[127]

Many midshipmen continued to view Annapolis as the doorway to an exciting military career, with numerous possibilities for advancement. They always wanted to be a marine officer, to fly off aircraft carriers, or to command a ship or submarine. For those who had dreamed of becoming an admiral or general, it did not hurt that Annapolis graduates had dominated those ranks either. Some midshipmen knew what they wanted to do from their first day at the academy; others changed their minds during summer training. The popularity of different career choices fluctuated as the Navy's technology and mission focus changed. Career opportunities remained the top reason for attending Annapolis, but those numbers were declining, down over 3 percent from the war, and those numbers would plummet another 10 percent during the defense unification controversy.[128] This generation was also not as ready to commit themselves to a naval career. The drop-off in career motivation was only 3 percent for the classes of 1950 to 1954, but these numbers would tumble disastrously, another 13 percent, for the classes of 1955 to 1959.[129]

These changes did not spell disaster, but they did suggest an important break from the past. The war brought greater demographic diversity, primarily in the form of ex-veterans and working-class Americans. More midshipmen were coming for the free education; fewer of them intended on a military career. Yet, demographic trends were not working alone to produce the academy's problems. It is interesting how these changes merged with already unfavorable circumstances to make the situation worse. For example, new demographic groups were already skeptical about a naval career. Unfortunately, budgetary problems did little to convince them otherwise. The larger question was to what extent both sets of unfavorable circumstances continued. Was Annapolis ready to handle greater demographic diversity, should it continue? Had it clearly defined its post-war mission? Did it have the right resources to accomplish whatever that might be? Unfortunately it would take many years and repeated effort to answer these questions.[130]

What is amazing is that despite the many changes, the academy culture remained remarkably similar to the past. Plebe year was still a rigorous test of mental and physical endurance.[131] Formal hazing was prohibited, but it persisted in many companies anyway. The severest hazing involved various forms of physical abuse, being paddled with brooms, ordered to shove out in the mess hall, "swimming to Baltimore," and the like. Milder versions included all kinds of servitude—closing windows before reveille, delivering the company's mail, and picking up laundry.[132] The greatest struggle was often the duration of plebe year. At its end, plebes were exhausted but also confident that they could handle the challenges of a naval career. No other group had a more intimate relationship with midshipmen than their company officers. They taught a stern and unbending style of leadership, particularly in their enforcement of regulations, much of which midshipmen interpreted as Mickey Mouse. Above all else, midshipmen learned how to obey orders.[133]

The relationship between midshipmen and officers was problematic. Midshipmen fought regulations that seemed cumbersome or inane; officers diligently enforced them to the letter. For example, contraband was forbidden in their rooms. Civilian clothes, playing cards, and cigarettes detracted from a proper professional decorum. The battleground was intense as officers searched for illegal items while midshipmen hatched ingenious schemes to hide them. The whole process seemed like a game. Midshipmen expected to be punished *when* they were caught. No one got through the academy without suffering demerits and extra duty. Yet, that was all part of the fun. Midshipmen were disciplined either marching with a rifle or rowing in small boats along the Severn River.[134]

Bancroft Hall ultimately prepared midshipmen to serve on warships that spent extended months at sea. They learned to handle unrelenting discipline from their superiors, closed confines with little personal privacy, and a schedule with competing priorities. It was better to learn how to cope in that environment now. After graduation, the consequences of failure were more severe and permanent than extra duty. Bancroft Hall purposely modeled much of its routine as if it also was a ship. Instead of stairs and corridors, midshipmen used ladders and passageways. The clock sounded the daily routine through a series of bells, just like aboard ship. The frequent inspections, the limited privacy, and the taut routine were all consistent with fleet operations. It was perfectly understandable that Annapolis chose such a model. After all, the Naval Academy was in the business of preparing line officers.

These could be difficult lessons to absorb. Indeed, many midshipmen interpreted the Bancroft Hall culture through the alternative model of Erving Goffman's total institution. Instead of envisioning Bancroft Hall as a ship, midshipmen saw a penitentiary, a monastery, or an insane asylum. They viewed themselves as inmates and the Executive Department as the staff that policed them. The midshipmen culture seemingly had a code and rhythm that were all but indecipherable outside the institution. Many times, midshipmen failed to appreciate the larger model or message the academy was trying to convey. Instead, they thought their situation was unique to Annapolis and believed the fleet would be different. Perhaps that was wishful thinking to make a difficult transition easier, but it took time to assimilate this culture, even among the most perceptive or fleet-wise midshipmen.[135]

The walls of Bancroft Hall resonated with a midshipmen culture that had been many years in the making. Not even World War II could undo that way of life completely, even though substantial changes were on the horizon. The character lessons of Bancroft Hall were clearly the most important principles of the academy, and they seemed more necessary than ever. What did the Annapolis system produce first and foremost? A poem from *The Lucky Bag 1947* captured the sentiment of many midshipmen towards the Naval Academy:

> By the very nature of the restrictions imposed,
> By the long ruthless days towards one goal,
> By the inessance of drill, militarism, and bodily loneliness
> He becomes confined to the life he has chosen,
> The life of duties, orders, papers, guns, ships, and seas. Reminders become unbearable to him in the small thing, seemingly inane things,
> his attitude matches the glum, bleak winters he spends within the walls . . .
> and during this time he develops quite unbeknownst to him. . . .
> A defense . . . his sense of humor, without which he cannot survive.
> Under duress, he will ruthlessly stand by his class,
> He has no time to ally himself with violent political movements,
> He has no time for aimless collegiate relaxation,
> His time has been divided for him since his emergence from all previous life,
> But through it all he retains one thing,
> In spite of himself and the systems of conformity,
> One thing which can never be erased from his person. His individuality.
> His walk, the angle of his cap, his loves and hates, each separate and distinct.[136]

ALTERNATIVE IMAGES OF BANCROFT HALL

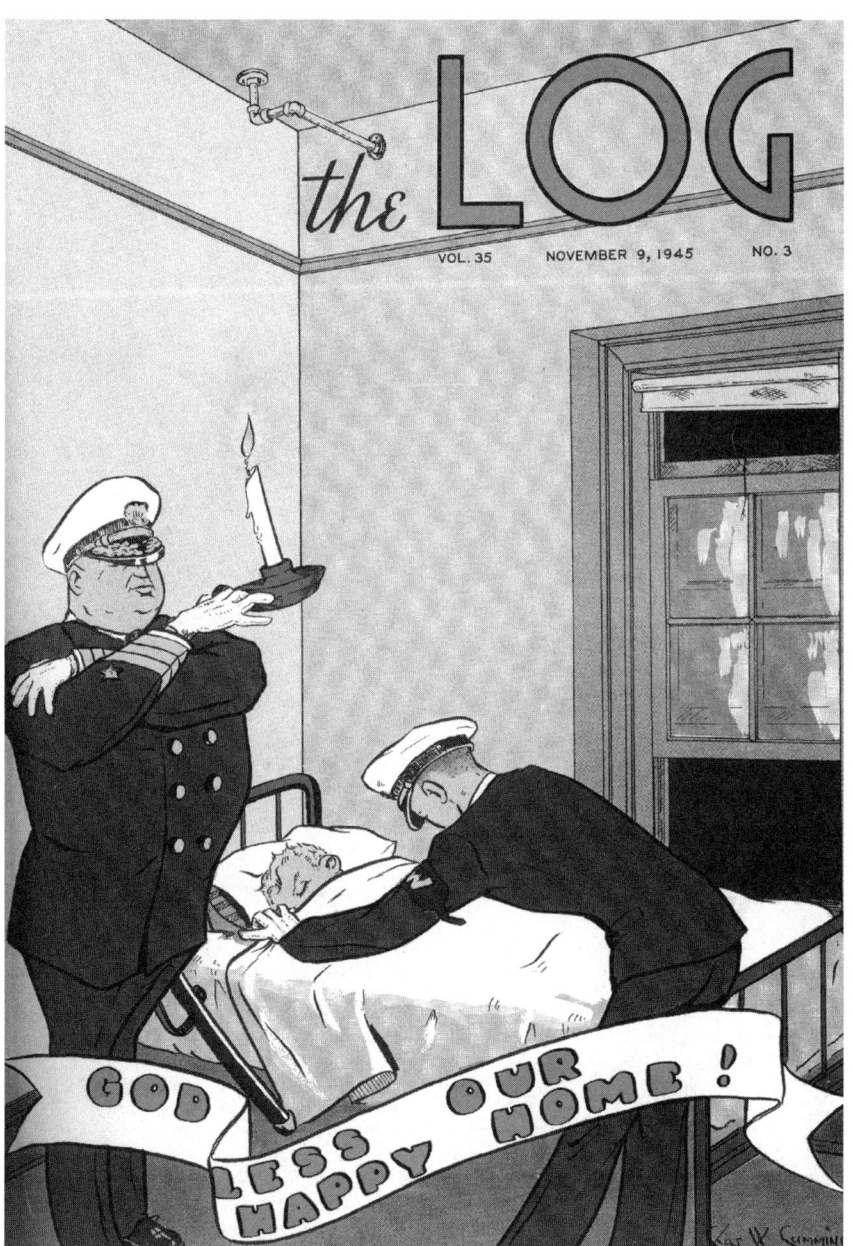

The Log, 9 November 1945. Midshipman resting comfortably in the arms of "Mother Bancroft."

The Log, 1 February 1946. USNA as penitentiary.

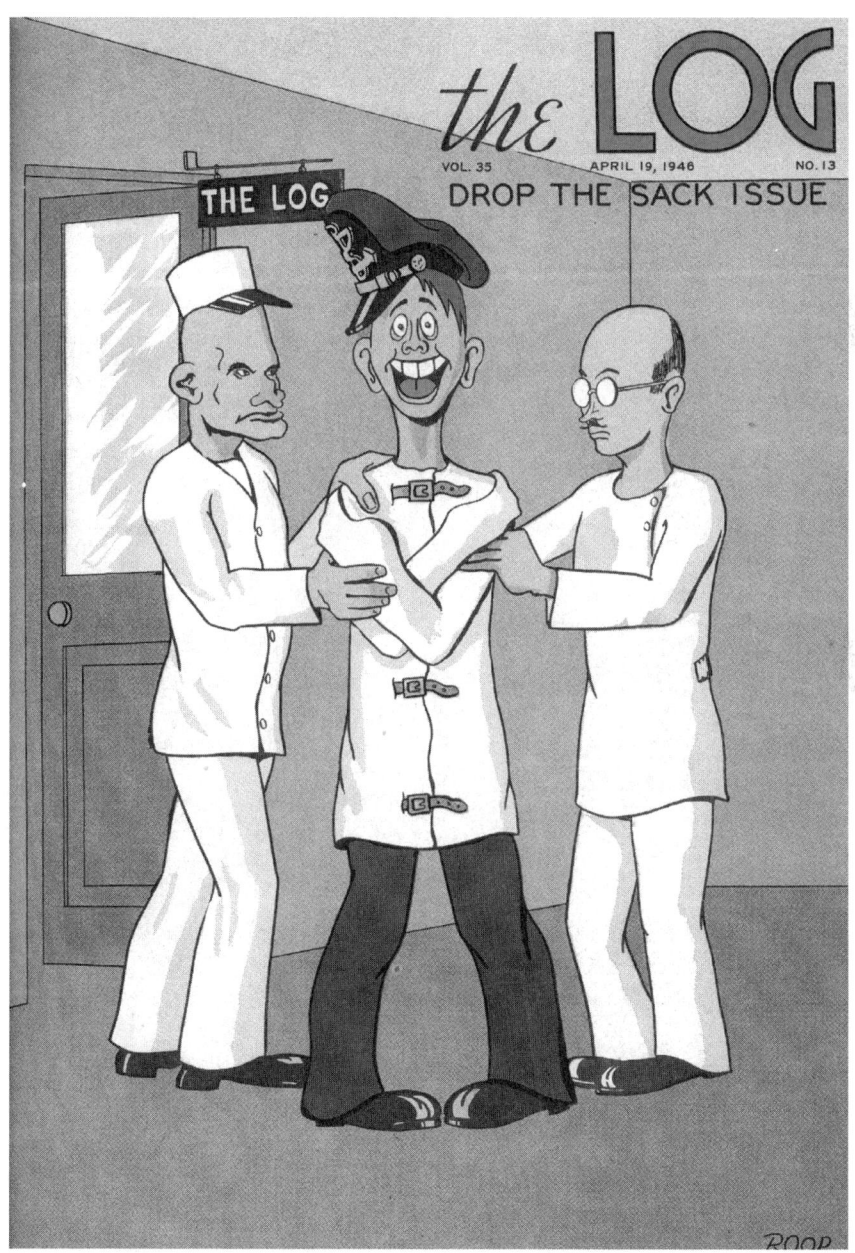

The Log, 19 April 1946. USNA as asylum.

The Log, 12 January 1951. USNA as dungeon.

2
The Naval Academy of the 1950s: Old Traditions Die Hard

WORLD WAR II HAD USHERED IN MANY REFORMS AT ANNAPOLIS. THE new Naval Academy would be a long time in coming however. Not all of Admiral Holloway's successors shared his dream of creating an "MIT on the Severn." His immediate successor, Harry Hill, did not undo any reforms, but he did not see the need for going further. Hill's emphasis was the sports program, critical to building the fighting spirit of midshipmen, ideas reminiscent of Admiral Sellars and the academy's old guard. The academy would be torn this way, choosing reform or the status quo, well into the 1950s. Reforms did not come to a standstill, but they were more steady and deliberative than before. Part of this came naturally with the periodic turnover in academy leadership. But it also reflected a genuine uncertainty about what the war had taught. Annapolis could not return to what it was beforehand, but there was little agreement beyond that. Solutions that fit its predicament after World War II were not always appropriate in the 1950s either. Although not always the best solution, the institution often marked time until better information became available.

Fiscal worries continued to consume the academy's attention. The Truman and Eisenhower administrations were both committed to lower defense budgets, no matter how badly money needed to be spent. The 1948 Manning Board was the latest blueprint for its post-war needs, but it was rarely followed in practice. Government promises to improve the midshipmen's pay also went unfulfilled until 1956.[1] Buildings and budgets were immediate problems; the energy it took to solve them could not be spent on more strategic concerns. Morale was an early casualty of government neglect, but it was not the last.[2] Declining applications and record-high resignations were also symptoms of trouble.[3] Superintendents did not stage their own "revolt of the admirals" in protest however. The academy did learn how to take matters into its own hands, the best example being the construction of Navy-Marine Corps Memorial Stadium in 1958. This project helped redefine its relationship with the federal government. Although a public institution, the school had concerns that could be at odds with its employer. It learned how to assert its interests without violating the public's trust, an important distinction in the nature of American civil-military relations.

Not coincidentally, the academy's Alumni Association became more politicized during the 1950s. The Alumni Association would become an important public relations and fund raising tool that would be put to good use in the postwar era. The association's involvement in academy affairs did not come without a price however. Almost like a CEO reporting to his stockholders, superintendents ensured that alumni were kept informed of the Naval Academy's vital business. The academy and its graduates also came to a new interpretation of the dividing line between public and private interests.[4]

A rapidly changing social environment throughout the 1950s created numerous recruiting headaches for Annapolis. The post-war economic boom had opened wide the doors of higher education. Many families were earning enough to send their children to college. New government aid programs were also making many dreams a reality. Even the Navy's other scholarship opportunities pulled applicants away from the academy. Its leaders attempted to solve these problems with a massive restructuring of the recruiting and admissions process. It launched an extensive public relations campaign, dubbed Operation Information, and began experimenting with alternative kinds of appointments, which depoliticized the admissions process.[5] College Board scores and extracurricular involvement were becoming more important than political connections in determining admission.

Recruiting woes coincided with a concerted effort to revive the winning tradition of the Navy sports program. The perception of many in the academy and the Navy was that American kids were unwilling to commit to a dud. Getting the football program back on track was critical not only for morale but for showing applicants that the Navy was still a winner. Yet, the academy found that winning and respect had its costs. It hired a highly regarded professional coach to rejuvenate the football program. The program was given considerable autonomy in managing its schedule. Football players had priority in scheduling classes and arranging watches; they had their own tables in the dining hall. The academy returned to gridiron glory, but it paid a price in terms of the Brigade's overall unit cohesion.

The Naval Academy also found itself making concessions to the new youth culture of the 1950s. College and even high school students already owned their own cars; many were not sharing rooms any longer with siblings. All of this posed new challenges for the spartan lifestyle of Bancroft Hall. Instead of civilian clothes or playing cards, midshipmen were smuggling television sets into Bancroft Hall. The academy probably had little choice but to bend with the times.[6] Current midshipmen had a greater range of social appetites than their predecessors. First classmen could eventually operate cars outside the seven-mile limit; all upperclassmen could have radios in their rooms. To older alumni, it seemed like the institution was coddling its students. This eerie refrain about the academy succumbing to materialism would be heard again from alumni in the 1960s and 1970s, much as it is today. If this process took place at all, then it began earlier in the 1950s. The larger lesson was that Annapolis occasionally adjusted its lifestyle to make it more reflective of society.

Academic reform was slow and definitely unspectacular throughout the 1950s. The overarching goal remained a strong general education midshipmen could use throughout their careers, but little effort was made to attain it.[7] The Middle States Association found little progress in 1956 beyond what was accomplished during Admiral Holloway's tenure. The academy was accomplishing its mission, but it was certainly not a center of academic achievement. Its accreditation never fell in jeopardy, but the team was not altogether pleased with what it found.[8] Annapolis became caught up in the whirlwind surrounding the deployment of the Soviet satellite Sputnik in 1959. The educational crisis fueled concerns about the mediocre academic reputation of the service academies. The controversy would be a catalyst for further reform and eventually lead to the "academic revolution."

The lackluster commitment to academic reform made it next to impossible to change Bancroft Hall. Midshipmen still depended on the dope to pass their exams and hoped for an end-of-semester curve on their final grades.[9] Study time continued to be limited regardless of seniority or academic standing.[10] The new honor system curbed the worst abuses of the dope system, but midshipmen continued to share information about their classes.[11] The academic climate took a slight upturn at the end of the 1950s. Society was more concerned about education because of the Cold War. Academic achievement was also becoming more vital to the midshipmen's careers. Classroom success opened up opportunities in the new nuclear submarine program and jet aviation. The academy also began rewarding academic achievers, with programs like the superintendent's list.

Bancroft Hall's military culture became even more competitive and harder to define in the 1950s. The surface navy and naval aviation continued to duel for the midshipmen's attention. The academy had its own defense unification scare with the Stearns-Eisenhower Board but survived nonetheless. Annapolis took its message seriously however. To be a successful officer in the future, midshipmen had to know more than just the Navy. It began sending second class midshipmen to West Point on exchange visits. Midshipmen also participated in joint training exercises with Army cadets during the summer.

The biggest shock to Bancroft Hall came from the newest military service, the Air Force. The Air Force was desperately short of junior officers and did not have its own academy to fill the void. Until this problem was rectified, up to 25 percent of any graduating class could volunteer for a commission in the Air Force. The service offered many carrots—immediate orders to flight school, sixty days leave after graduation, earlier postgraduate education opportunities—that lured many talented midshipmen away from the Navy. This threat eventually caused Annapolis to alter its practice of mandatory, initial sea duty. Midshipmen were first allowed to select Pensacola in the mid 1950s; soon afterwards, the submarine community also began accepting midshipmen directly from Annapolis.

The Doldrums of Demobilization

Demobilization wreaked havoc on the academy for much of the 1950s. The most pressing problem continued to be the deteriorating condition of the physical plant. None of the major buildings had been renovated since the turn of the nineteenth century, a time when the student body numbered around eight hundred students. Complicating matters further, the school was expanding to its postwar strength of roughly four thousand midshipmen.[12] Commandant of midshipmen, Rear Admiral Buchanan, described how the expansion had changed the Brigade: "classmates [now] know perhaps half their class by face and name."[13] Countless boards and panels had recommended extensive overhaul and expansion of its facilities but to no avail. The 1948 Manning Board laid the groundwork for a postwar academy capable of handling a Brigade this size, but its suggestions largely went ignored.[14]

The Naval Academy's predicament was symptomatic, however, of the neglect plaguing all the armed forces. With the Cold War just in its infancy, Americans were not ready to accept enlarged defense budgets. Training establishments, like Annapolis, usually took the first blows to keep the operational forces going. Recommendations meant nothing unless there was money to be spent. The academy's most urgent needs continued to be the enlargement of Bancroft Hall, the expansion of adequate outdoor and indoor athletic facilities, and the construction of the airfield. The capacity and conditions inside Bancroft Hall had been an ongoing concern since the late 1930s. Two new wings were added in 1942, but recent expansion had transformed this perennial problem into a full-blown crisis.

To make room for the extra bodies, even upperclassmen were crammed two or three to a room. Privacy was always limited, but it became nonexistent in the 1950s. Bancroft Hall managed to accommodate the extra bodies, but true improvements never came fast enough. The mess hall expansion was completed in 1952, vital to feeding the Brigade at one sitting. An executive freeze on new defense construction kept anything else from being done to dormitory space until after 1952.[15] The foundation for two additional wings was not laid until 1959 and was only finished in 1961.[16] Even now, it is hard not to view government inaction as gross negligence. It certainly did not motivate midshipmen towards a naval career.

Annapolis claimed its students suffered more than the other academies, even though its problems were similar. It cited a 1953 study that showed the allotted space per midshipman to be twenty-nine square feet compared to the 130 square feet available to each West Point cadet. Even with the proposed additions, the extra space amounted to only a total of fifty-eight square feet per man.[17] The Naval Academy was also expanding more rapidly than the Military Academy and had only limited options for improvement. Located in the heart of historic Annapolis, any modernization or renovation was more expensive than comparable work done at West Point. Midshipmen came away from their West Point exchange visits jealous of its extra space for expansion.[18] Unfortunately, summer cruises taught them to expect a similar lifestyle in the fleet. The government's unwillingness to take action dampened spirits and turned more than a few midshipmen against a military career.[19]

The Naval Academy continued to complain about the lack of playing fields and athletic facilities for its intramural and varsity teams. Using the same 1953 study as a comparison, West Point had over three times the athletic facilities even though the Corps of Cadets was only two-thirds the size of the Brigade.[20] Annapolis learned to be creative with the space it had. Practice schedules were tightly restricted to get actual competitions completed. Postponements due to inclement weather were rarely rescheduled. If needed, intramurals took a backseat to varsity team practices.[21] The situation was not ideal for anyone. But the limited free space for new construction made improvements problematic. The pre-war academy had tried for twenty years to build an all-weather field house for the indoor sports program. That goal finally came true in 1955 with the construction of Halsey Field House.[22] The space for that facility came from what had previously been Holland Field. Nothing was ever added at Annapolis without losing older facilities in return.

True expansion came only through herculean efforts. With historic Annapolis on one side and the Chesapeake Bay on the other, the best option for expansion was surprisingly enough reclamation from the sea. In the early 1950s, plans were drawn to gain an additional sixty acres by filling in the Dewey and Santee Basins. The cost of the project was not cheap; the final bill was around eight million dollars.[23] Because of the expense, the landfill project went through even more than the normal share of delays.

Work was finally begun in 1957, but it was not ready for use until 1960.[24] The Naval Academy gained just sixty acres after its completion, a meager addition compared to the space at either West Point or Colorado Springs. Its options were limited however: make do with existing facilities or work through an impossible situation for at best a modest gain. Interestingly enough, the next time a major expansion was contemplated, the academy attempted to secure land from historic Annapolis. The proposal to take over a mere seven blocks caused such uproar that the idea was dropped almost immediately. Whether it liked it or not, the school's boundaries were more or less fixed, no matter how dramatically its mission changed.[25]

The academy had long viewed the airfield's construction to be a life or death matter. The project was at the top of its wish list since World War II. With the future seemingly dependent on carrier aviation, the airfield symbolized the future lifeblood of the institution.[26] Locations were explored across the Severn River, but that was as close as it came to reality. The project permanently stalled when it came time to spend money on it. The failure to build the airfield was a huge blow. So much so that it never spoke of it again after the last attempt failed. Perhaps the project was simply too grandiose, especially with aviation training centered at NAS Pensacola. Resources were too scarce in the 1950s to allow for duplicate facilities. By the time funds became available, carrier aviation's dominance had begun to fade. Nuclear submarines were at the cutting edge of the Navy's future by the early 1960s.

What effect did this wrangling over budgets and new construction have on midshipmen during this time? The mood of the academy must have been unusually somber, more so every time a major project failed. Many midshipmen were already skeptical about the service's future anyway. More of them were choosing Annapolis for its education, not military careers. Career opportunities were the top choice of 39.6 percent of the classes of 1950 to 1954 whereas the free education drew just 13 percent. However, for the classes of 1955 to 1959, only 29.7 percent came for the career opportunities while 25 percent were motivated by the free education. Nothing at the academy changed their minds; indeed, many experiences confirmed their assumptions. All of its budgetary battles hindered the academy from concentrating on academic reform, the one solution that might have eased its manpower problems.[27]

Yet, even amidst this turmoil, midshipmen learned useful, albeit unintentional lessons in leadership. The school's actions taught them flexibility in circumstances where no perfect solution could be found. The situation also reinforced the importance of good organization and discipline in getting vital tasks completed. For example, without organization and imagination, the sports program would have floundered. The institution kept things going, often on a shoestring, but that was what naval officers did. Lastly, the experience taught an interesting lesson about the public's lackluster support for military institutions. American society was sometimes deaf to the military's needs, no matter how much they claimed to respect it. In such circumstances, military institutions had to fend for themselves, a lesson the academy put into practice with the new football stadium.[28]

Getting Navy Sports Back on Track

With everything else troubling the institution, not having a winning sports program would seem to have been the least important to fix.[29] Whether reasonable or not, making Navy teams competitive was a matter of huge importance in the 1950s.[30] Actually, the focus on athletics fit in perfectly with the institution's mood and its current struggles. Just a few years before, the Naval Academy had stood at the pinnacle of achievement; now it was on the defensive in all areas. The Holloway Plan and NROTC had stripped it of one of its primary missions. It was finding it next to impossible to get necessary funding. Applications were down, resignations were up, and to cap it all, Navy football had slipped from the ranks of the country's elite programs.[31] Nonetheless, the focus on the sports program also took energy away from academic reform, a solution that might have been more effective with students of this generation.

Restoring the athletic program, especially football, to its former greatness was seen as the solution to many problems. Nothing boosted the midshipmen's morale like having a winning team to cheer for in the fall. Dramatic victories over national powerhouses would showcase the Naval Academy across the country.[32] Everything else might be going wrong, but Navy could still field a contending team. A successful football program would be a tremendous stimulus to recruiting, it would help erase doubts about the academy's future, and it was just the ticket for reviving spirits during an incredibly difficult time.[33]

The task of rebuilding Navy football was much easier said than done however. It was easy for the service academies to field strong teams during World War II. They were the only colleges that could grant players exemptions from the draft. Top athletes no longer had the specter of military service lingering over them. Major civilian programs were the best ticket to the professional ranks for truly gifted players. Academy athletes still had to finish their obligatory service before they could even think of turning pro.[34] Complicating matters further, many civilian teams had older players on their rosters, men who were attending college after their wartime service. Navy was competing against teams whose players were older, stronger, and generally more talented.[35]

The Naval Academy Athletic Association (NAAA) learned to fight these limitations the best it could. The NAAA eventually compromised on the schedule, limiting the number of powerhouses the football team played each season. Annapolis no longer had a stockpile of players who could handle that kind of pounding an entire year.[36] Better to play schools of the same caliber and focus on a few truly big games each year than to suffer losing seasons regularly. The NAAA also worked with a private group called the Naval Academy Foundation, which helped prepare players who would not have been admitted otherwise. The Naval Academy Foundation sponsored promising applicants, many of whom were athletes, at prep schools and military high schools across the country. The additional year of academic work was crucial in their eventual admission to Annapolis.[37]

In 1950, the Naval Academy hired a top assistant coach from the San Francisco 49ers, Eddie Erdelatz, to be its head coach. At the time, Erdelatz was among the highest paid coaches in the nation. He was given strict charge to return the football program to its former glory and, regardless of what followed, proved to be an excellent coach. Within two years, the team was winning games and shortly afterwards participating in bowl games again.[38] But success came with a price, beyond the coach's hefty salary. The football team had always received certain perks for the time spent at practices and competitions. Football players, plebes and upperclassmen alike, took their meals at separate team tables. In some cases, the food was better; more importantly, plebes ate in peace, away from indoctrination from company upperclassmen. The football team also had top priority in registering for classes. They knew from the grapevine which professors to take and which ones to avoid.[39]

Erdelatz took everything one step further, all in the name of making Navy an elite program. The team arranged for tutors to accompany players to away games. He encouraged players to skip their military obligations, such as parades and lectures, while they were in season. Players needed to be focused on football and little else, regardless of the school's overall mission. The academy tolerated this up to a point, but Erdelatz eventually overstepped his bounds. At one point, he talked of sequestering the football team in its own section of Bancroft Hall. Coach Erdelatz was released in 1959 despite the overall strength of his on-the-field record. In the mind of the administration, football players were midshipmen too and had to complete the obligations expected of the rest of the Brigade.[40]

Yet, for all the eventual controversy, the academy created this monster in the first place. Granting Erdelatz autonomy was the price for returning the program to prominence. It was hard to dispel the notion that football players got special treatment; over 83 percent of the survey group felt this way. On a smaller scale, this episode was symptomatic of a problem that reoccurred during the "academic revolution." Companies were the backbone of the midshipmen culture before World War II and remained so afterwards. However, to some extent, other relationships encouraged by Annapolis became just as important to some midshipmen.[41] In this case, by making concessions, football players were separated from the Brigade. Their experiences were filtered through varsity athletics, not company activities. Their primary friendships were other team members; their most important memories were with the team; athletics, in other words, colored their professional socialization.[42]

This process was already at work with the splintering of midshipmen into prospective warfare communities. Future aviators banded together; so did the marines, submariners, and so forth. Eventually, these groups would form extracurricular activities based on common interests or career goals. Later, during the "academic revolution," academic majors would be another dividing line for the Brigade. Race and eventually gender would also separate midshipmen from one another. The dispersion of the Brigade was not too dramatic yet but it was clearly underway. To borrow an idea studied by other military historians, midshipmen were not necessarily looking to their company as the focal point of group identity and cohesion.[43] All of this would pose incredible challenges to Bancroft Hall's efforts at professional socialization. Not only were demographic differences adding new diversity to the Brigade, different experiences were separating midshipmen from one another.

Taking Matters into Its Own Hands — Navy-Marine Corps Stadium and the Naval Academy Alumni Association

The most visible commitment to restoring the prominence of Navy athletics was the construction of Navy-Marine Corps Memorial Stadium, begun in 1958. The project epitomized the academy's frustration at getting government support for needed construction. The Naval Academy had batted around a new stadium for years, but insufficient funds had always stalled the idea. The NAAA already owned land in west Annapolis that seemed an ideal location. The site supported a stadium larger than its present needs, allowed for sufficient parking space, which had been a major inconvenience, and provided easy access to the new highway system being constructed around the Baltimore-Washington area.[44] It would be the perfect venue for showcasing the academy and its winning football program in a positive light. Unfortunately, the NAAA had used the majority of its funds to buy the land; it could not build anytime soon. Given recent funding difficulties, the Naval Academy hesitated to ask the government for the needed money. Although the present facility, Thompson Stadium, was hopelessly obsolete, the request might seem like a superfluous expenditure of government funds.[45]

The completion of Navy-Marine Corps Memorial Stadium was a story of perseverance and triumph worthy itself of inclusion with the other victories commemorated on its walls. It was also an important turning point in the academy's relationship with the federal government and a reinterpretation of what it meant to be apolitical. Although a public institution, the academy recognized that it had legitimate, private concerns worthy of completion. In the future, it would be more willing to act independently to accomplish those priorities. For example, the campaigns to build Alumni Hall and the Armel-Leftwich Visitor Center in the 1980s and 1990s were financed largely through private funds. Recent superintendents have felt no compunction about asking alumni to finance critical endeavors. None of this negated the academy's status as a federally supported institution. It also did not violate the American tradition of civilian control of military institutions. In some areas, the school could venture on its own to accomplish its larger goals.

The guiding force behind the new stadium was the superintendent, Rear Admiral William Smedberg III, and the department head he placed in charge of fund-raising efforts, Commander Eugene Fluckey. Smedberg was a decorated combat veteran of both World War II and Korea who assumed command in 1956 from the surface navy. He came from a family of career military officers and was a father of several sons who had also attended the academy. Smedberg would prove to be a dynamic leader, in effect the first superintendent since Admiral Holloway committed to substantial reform. This was not altogether surprising since Holloway had handpicked him as one of his academic department heads. Smedberg's ace in the hole was Fluckey, a submarine commander who had won the Medal of Honor and four Navy Crosses fighting the Japanese. Fluckey would later go on to flag rank himself. Like his boss, Fluckey did not allow any sort of roadblock from getting this job done.[46]

Shortly after taking office, Smedberg revisited the stadium idea with the secretary of the Navy, Thomas Gates. He reiterated all of the reasons why the stadium was a critical project but could not sell Gates on the government footing the bill. Not willing to reject the idea entirely Gates proposed a near-impossible deal that placed most of the financing burden on the academy. The academy could have one million dollars in undesignated NAAA funds so long as it raised the other 2.2 million dollars through outside sources. The SECNAV thought he was calling the academy's bluff, but, to his surprise, Smedberg took the bait.[47]

The Naval Academy left no stone unturned going after the needed money. The fund-raising campaign showed the deep sentiment for Annapolis not only among its graduates but also throughout the Navy. Contributions, mainly in small dollar amounts, flooded in from a wide variety of sources. Midshipmen sold raffle tickets for a donated Cadillac, a sailboat, and a speedboat, all of which were displayed on academy grounds. Traditional academy decorum took a back seat to reaching its larger goal. Midshipmen even peddled chances for these prizes at the Pentagon, even though their actions technically violated federal regulations. Smedberg enlisted national celebrities to put their names behind the campaign. Edward R. Murrow hosted the admiral on his Person-to-Person broadcast, which put word of the project before a national audience. He also visited Hollywood to team up with film stars Burt Lancaster and Clark Gable for a short promotional movie on the new stadium shown at the halftime of Navy's home games that season.[48]

The fund-raising effort also used other nonmaterial incentives to solicit pledges. Large-dollar contributors could designate memorial chairs in the new stadium for various reasons—graduates who were killed on duty, alumni who had made a career of the service, or simply longtime supporters of the Navy. The academy was not all that fussy so long as it received the needed money. Smedberg even enlisted the support of his fellow admirals, commanding the Sixth and Seventh Fleets, to join the campaign. The Navy's two major operational commands competed with one another to see who could raise the most money for the stadium. In return, the two major entrances to the stadium, Sixth Fleet Gate and Seventh Fleet Gate, were named in their honor. Rumor had it that some sailors even enlisted the support of their Far East cathouses in the competition.[49]

In the end, the Naval Academy reached its goal, and the new stadium quickly became reality. The stadium's opening coincided with what many considered the golden age of Navy football, the years of Joe Bellino and Roger Staubach. Navy's football enthusiasts were right about the spillover effect on the academy. The stadium's construction was the catalyst for a surge in midshipmen morale and renewed public interest in Annapolis, just the right formula to shake the institution from its doldrums.[50] And the entire effort was completed without tapping into additional government funds, a useful lesson the academy would store in its memory. Besides getting their new stadium, midshipmen also learned a valuable lesson in the power of pragmatic leadership and the strength of the academy's bond with its graduates.

The alumni association adopted similar attitudes from this experience. The end result was that it became more politicized during the 1950s. Just like the academy, new ground rules were established, which included a watchdog role over the Navy's interests. *Shipmate* routinely kept tabs on Capitol Hill, serving as the eyes and ears for Annapolis and the Navy. The defense unification controversy sparked most of its interest and wrath

The Lucky Bag 1960. **Ground breaking for Navy's new football stadium, a near impossible goal the academy reached on its own.**

during the decade. Regardless of the issue, the alumni association refused to be muzzled, especially when it saw policies hostile to the academy or the Navy. All of this fell within a new definition of professional behavior; even naval officers should be heard. In effect, it began to act as a political action group that labored on the Navy's and the academy's behalf.[51]

The alumni association recognized that its voice was proportionate to the number of members on its rolls. It waged an aggressive recruiting campaign in the 1950s to expand its membership base. Older graduates, who had not been active, were encouraged to begin their affiliation. Current first classmen could enroll during their senior year. Lifetime memberships eventually became available to midshipmen at the academy. Whether they were active or not, most midshipmen graduated as members of the alumni association. Only 58.4 percent of the classes of 1946 to 1949 were alumni association members; that number jumped to 74.2 percent for the classes of 1960 to 1964.[52] The alumni association's message was not all that subtle. The camaraderie and spirit of Annapolis should not be forgotten; alumni had to do their part to preserve its traditions. Members were encouraged to be spokesmen in their communities. Their job was to persuade friends and neighbors of the Navy's continuing importance.[53]

These efforts came with at least the tacit endorsement of the Naval Academy. Annapolis ensured midshipmen heard the organization's pitch for membership. It also endorsed campaigns to enroll older graduates. There was much to gain and little to lose from the alumni association's success. Its membership roster was a ready fund-raising pool that could be used for projects like the stadium.[54] The alumni association could voice issues where Annapolis was better off remaining silent. Greater attention did have to be given to alumni concerns however. Every homecoming, it hosted an open forum to address questions of its graduates. The superintendent periodically reported on the status of major projects or policy changes in *Shipmate*.[55] All in all, the price was not too steep, however, for everything the alumni association brought to the relationship.

THE NAVAL ACADEMY'S CONTINUED RECRUITING WOES

Substandard facilities, mediocre academics, and inadequate pay all took a heavy toll on the academy's prestige, and with it recruiting. Solving these problems was even more critical with the booming economy and the democratization of higher education. It did not take a genius to tell that better opportunities lie elsewhere. The postwar academy continually suffered from a lack of qualified applicants. Oftentimes, appointments went unused, especially with the Brigade's expansion.[56] Everything else troubling the academy fed off this problem but also nurtured it in return. The lower the caliber of students, the more difficult it was to raise its academic reputation. As long as the academic program seemed inferior, it was difficult to attract top students. The fewer graduates supplied to the fleet, the less it accomplished its primary mission. The farther it fell behind meeting the Navy's needs, the less money it received for expansion, which complicated recruiting even further.[57]

The Naval Academy experimented with various solutions to boost recruiting. The admissions process gained flexibility with the passage of Public Law 586, the so-called qualified alternate rule.[58] The admissions process was hamstrung by an inequitable distribution of good candidates around the country. Some congressional districts were overstocked with quality applicants while others struggled to find one who met minimum standards. Until this point, there was no way of circumventing the traditional appointment process. Qualified applicants were lost simply because of their local competition. Critical vacancies went unfilled because some areas did not have suitable candidates.[59]

Public Law 586 gave the academy more latitude over its own admissions process. Primary nominees were still offered the first round of appointments. The remaining qualified candidates went into a qualified alternate pool from which the academy picked the best of the lot to fill remaining vacancies. Qualified alternates needed a nomination, but their eventual appointment came from the secretary of the Navy instead. Congressmen and senators could nominate several deserving candidates, an obvious boon to them politically. Everyone won under the new arrangement. The school acquired a larger manpower pool to keep it operating at full capacity. Congressmen maintained their patronage power while shifting the final tough decision onto Annapolis. Finally, qualified candidates who otherwise would have been rejected gained admittance to the academy.[60]

Critics complained that star athletes were the primary beneficiaries of these appointments. The law was a convenient tool, in other words, for keeping varsity teams competitive. While the academy did not dispute that athletes were recipients, other types of applicants also benefited. Athletic achievement had always been one of many indicators used in deciding admission.[61] More accurately, the qualified alternate appointment allowed the academy to admit the people it really wanted. To some extent, the qualified alternate rule also made the appointment process less political. Midshipmen were filling vacancies that were not tied to a geographic or political relationship. As a result, the admissions process slowly became more like that of other colleges and universities. College entrance scores, grade point averages, and extracurricular involvement became the more important factors determining admission.[62]

Before the 1950s, Annapolis did little formal recruiting to fill its classes. Information was available, but applicants were responsible for ensuring their files were completed. The athletic department was the major exception to that rule. To keep their teams competitive, coaches combed the country for promising athletes. The athletic department also tended to walk recruits through the admissions process. The applicant shortage forced the school to become more candidate friendly.[63] For the first time, it orchestrated a major public relations campaign to promote Annapolis. The catalog was revamped too; glitzy photographs and catchy slogans became key ingredients in recruiting. Copies of the documentary film, "The Annapolis Story," were distributed to naval districts around the country. Schools and other public institutions were seen as important venues for showcasing the academy. A national television corporation was hired to produce a series of half-hour segments about midshipmen life, which eventually became the popular series "Men of Annapolis."[64]

Nothing sold Annapolis better, however, than a sharply dressed, articulate, and motivated midshipman. Operation Information was launched at an auspicious time, coming on the heels of Navy's dramatic victory in the 1955 Sugar Bowl.[65] Handpicked volunteers, nearly one hundred first classmen to start, returned to their communities to be salesmen for the academy. These midshipmen completed a new public speaking course to help prepare their presentations.[66] First classmen obviously had the most to say about Annapolis. Their outlook was generally the most positive too, since they had the most privileges and were closest to graduation. Some midshipmen scoffed at the program, however, calling it Operation Propaganda, since only the top of the class could participate.[67]

The extraordinary effort was not altogether different, however, from what other colleges and universities were doing. Higher education had become a competitive marketplace with real winners and losers in the struggle for good students. The best students could choose from any number of good institutions, most of which did not have a military commitment afterwards. The Naval Academy had no choice but to take recruitment more seriously. In the years to come, an extremely sophisticated Office of Admissions and Candidate Guidance would run these programs like a fine-tuned machine. After the "academic revolution," top students were especially prized. It kept them closely appraised of their file's status and did whatever it took to get them admitted. For example, the academy became more generous with medical waivers to admit top students.

Despite these efforts, the academy continued to get the bulk of its students from the northeast and middle Atlantic states, just over 42 percent for the entire study. Midwestern states supplied the next largest group with approximately 25 percent. Southeastern states would provide noticeably fewer midshipmen after the "academic revolution," dropping from 15 percent to 8 percent of the Brigade. It is possible that stiffer academic requirements made it more difficult for this region's applicants to qualify.

The southwest and far west consistently lagged behind the other regions, just 10 percent from each region overall. The strength of the northeast and mid-Atlantic regions is not surprising, given their large population centers and proximity to Annapolis. The relative scarcity of west coast midshipmen is more remarkable, especially with the demographic changes of World War II. The immense military build-up on the west coast also did not appear to help recruitment. Even with the mass media, geographic proximity continued to be the best recruiting tool for Annapolis.[68]

The Lull in Academic Reform and the Sputnik Educational Crisis of 1959

Further academic reform was not an immediate priority for the Naval Academy until the late 1950s. Changes usually reflected immediate concerns; never were they part of a comprehensive plan of reform. For example, Harry Hill's priority was reviving the sports program, critical he felt in building mental toughness. His own experiences in the amphibious campaigns of World War II convinced him that this was the most essential aspect of Annapolis. His successor, Turner Joy, had been the chief negotiator for the United Nations in Korea. Joy's diplomatic background gave him a greater appreciation for the arts and the humanities; it was the one area in which he felt shortchanged by the academy. However, there was little impetus in the 1950s for resolving these philosophical differences. The pendulum swung back and forth depending on the leadership's preferences at the time.

The Middle States evaluators returned in 1956 hopeful that the academy was continuing in the direction set ten years ago. They were largely unimpressed and disappointed with what they found. The high hopes of creating an "MIT on the Severn" had largely gone unfulfilled, despite ten full years to make improvements. Precious little in fact had been done since the war. The biggest disappointment was the academy's failure to clarify its strategic priorities. The inspectors understood the academy was both a training and educational institution. They also realized the academy could not abandon either of those responsibilities. The team frowned upon its insistence that both priorities could be done equally well. As far as they were concerned, there was not enough time or resources for that type of commitment. To insist otherwise was simply ignoring the problem.[69]

Evaluators left no doubt of what they felt the school's foremost priority should be. No matter training's value in the short term, a sound undergraduate education had to be paramount. To do otherwise risked serious consequences for both its graduates' and the Navy's future. The greatest temptation, of course, was to emphasize objectives which paid dividends in the here and now. Training programs did prepare graduates for their initial duties. But their education was too narrow to be of much benefit later in their careers. The Middle States team thought this principle was an underpinning of the Holloway reforms. Apparently, World War II was not a severe enough crisis to make these changes permanent. Unless there was another scare, the status quo was likely to continue indefinitely.[70]

The Middle States report was certainly not a glowing evaluation of the Naval Academy: "One can not say that there is evidence of genuine academic excellence at the Naval Academy. The rigid curriculum, time pressures, and other factors limit such." At best, the Naval Academy was accomplishing its objectives, but therein was the problem. Until Annapolis resolved what its priorities should be, it would never be more than a mediocre college. "One must not let desirable academic goals be totally submerged, however, and the Naval Academy must not for a moment lose sight of its role as an educational institution. Every encouragement must be given to efforts in this direction."[71]

At no point, however, was Annapolis ever in danger of losing its accreditation. Although the overall assessment was lukewarm, evaluators found much that they respected and admired. They did not understand all the training objectives of Bancroft Hall but appreciated the magnitude of its task. The report went so far as to describe the work of the Commandant and the Executive Department as being "the *Naval Academy.*" The academy was accomplishing its objectives no matter how flawed reviewers felt they might be. Some academic departments had made steadier progress than others. While none were towers of academic achievement, no department was totally awful either. All in all, it was an average grade but that was not likely to help Annapolis with its budgetary and manpower problems.[72]

The necessary jolt for further reform came with the deployment of the Soviet satellite Sputnik in 1957. In an instant, Americans believed the balance in the Cold War to be in jeopardy. If the Soviets had the capability to put a small satellite into orbit, perhaps they had also the technology to rain nuclear missiles down onto the United States. For the first time in generations, the American homeland stood at risk from terrifying weapons of mass destruction. At the very least, the Communists could use these weapons to leverage political concessions from the United States. Americans found this predicament utterly incomprehensible. How could the Soviets have developed this technology on their own, even before the United States? The Soviet Union was a backward country. It did not seem to have either the technological or industrial resources necessary for such a project. Either the United States was slipping badly in terms of its technological advantage or the Communists had made up tremendous ground in a hurry. Neither alternative was comforting in the least to an American society that truly felt in danger.

Just like with the China fiasco in 1949, Americans were looking for someone or something to blame. For many, the leading culprit was a lackadaisical and flaccid system of education. "Progressive" education had left American minds soft by substituting vocational and "life experience" classes for instruction in basic disciplines like mathematics, the sciences, and the humanities. Mental toughness was seen as an important weapon in the Cold War, perhaps equivalent to extra divisions or squadrons at the front. Americans needed to sharpen their technological edge if they wanted to recapture the advantage over the Soviets. The Sputnik crisis fueled fears about the state of American education and led to the passage of the National Defense Education Act of 1958. Improving the quality of education had now become a matter of national security. Over the years, federal dollars would be poured into various aid programs to boost the quality of the nation's schools.[73]

The father of the American nuclear navy, Vice Admiral Hyman G. Rickover, joined the chorus decrying the pitiful state of American education. Rickover painted himself as an educational expert with important insight into the problem. He wrote a number of books and articles comparing the American system of education with those in the Soviet Union and Western Europe. According to Rickover, American institutions came up lacking in every respect.[74] The admiral testified before Congress on several occasions, lending his "expertise" to the problem. The hearings were always colorful, highly publicized affairs that enflamed people's emotions more than they did anything else. Rickover, however, was a darling of many in Congress, so he could not be ignored. In introducing him to the House Committee on Appropriations in 1959, its chairman, Clarence Cannon, lavished the admiral with praise. Cannon portrayed Rickover as a national savior: "The nation would not be safe today—if it is safe—except for the contributions of Admiral Rickover in the adaptation of nuclear power to submarines and the utilization of atomic energy in both military and civilian purposes."[75] Rickover's strong, congressional support meant that his testimony would carry great weight in any proposals to reform American higher education.

Rickover evaluated all of the military service academies negatively, but he reserved his greatest wrath for Annapolis. In his opinion, the lockstep curriculum was an utter waste of the finest minds the nation had in its fight against communism. The admiral complained that too much of a midshipman's day was taken up with nonsensical duties in the name of training, which ultimately detracted from his education. Midshipmen had too much to learn to be bothered as much as they were with Bancroft Hall. This waste of time placed Annapolis graduates approximately two years behind contemporaries educated in elite, civilian engineering schools. Coincidentally, this figure also represented his approximation of how far American students lagged behind their Soviet peers.[76]

Rickover further criticized Annapolis for perpetuating a system "that places before the talented student little challenge or opportunity for hard work. With few exceptions he takes the same courses and is encouraged to do little more than the least gifted in the class." Like other reformers, Rickover stressed that the true shortfall of the lockstep curriculum was in the future. The present system provided graduates with reasonable competence during their early careers. But as they advanced in rank, the shallowness of their education became truly apparent. More than ever, senior officers needed a broader education to solve the complex military and political problems facing the nation. The Naval Academy and the United States ignored making substantial changes only at its peril.[77]

Whatever Rickover's hand in the changes that followed, the Sputnik crisis did get the wheels of academic reform moving again.[78] The emergency crystallized the relevancy of existing reforms and gave urgency for doing more.[79] Curriculum reform became a topic of high interest not only at Annapolis but also throughout the military and federal government. What the academy chose to do or ignore was scrutinized up and down the chain of command. Complicating matters further, the other service academies were under similar scrutiny. They had never operated in lockstep, but now their differences were reviewed in agonizing detail. Not surprisingly, the schools started working closer together. Virtually all of the post-Sputnik superintendents visited West Point and Colorado Springs before assuming command. Eventually regular exchange conferences were held to discuss common matters. Total standardization was never an explicit goal; the academies did acquire a better understanding, however, of the reasons for their remaining differences.[80]

Some reforms attempted to improve the quality of the candidate pool. As of 1958, applicants had to take standardized entrance exams administered by the College Entrance Examination Board (CEEB). No longer would Annapolis have its own admissions procedures; it would use similar guidelines to other elite colleges and universities.[81] Since the exam carried tremendous weight, academic achievement became a more important qualifier for admission.[82] The academy later concluded that the original process was too restrictive and shifted to what it called a "total man" concept. Exam scores were weighted along with extracurricular involvement and leadership potential in determining admission.[83]

The academy also lowered the maximum age for entering midshipmen. No one could be more than twenty-one years old; the minimum age remained seventeen years old. The upper age limit was revised after internal studies showed a much higher attrition rate among older midshipmen. Many of them did not have the academic background to succeed; others had trouble with Bancroft Hall. Whatever the reason, it seemed pointless to admit those with so low a completion rate.[84] As a result, the Brigade's raw academic qualifications—SAT scores, grade point averages, etc.—increased in the 1960s and 1970s. At the same time, younger midshipmen did not have the same maturity or life experiences. Ironically, the overall attrition rate remained roughly the same after the "academic revolution." The sources of attrition would be significantly different however. Academic failures dropped while voluntary resignations, primarily among plebes, surged dramatically.

Other reforms attempted to improve the school's academic infrastructure. To attract better faculty, the academy offered a more generous benefits package to incoming civilian professors. The engineering and science departments especially found it difficult to attract and retain top people. Faculty began receiving the same benefits and retirement protections as other federal civil service employees. A major disadvantage was the lack of a reciprocal tuition program faculty could use on their children. Other inducements were started, such as commissary and exchange privileges, in compensation.[85] The academy copied other colleges by offering new incentives for quality research. Top scholars received sabbaticals and extended leave to keep them current in their disciplines. The reforms essentially attempted to make an academy job the same as other institutions. Talented professors should not have to sacrifice academically or financially to work at Annapolis.[86]

The Naval Academy consolidated its ten academic departments into a more efficient organization built around three academic divisions. Although most departments were doing an adequate job, the 1956 Middle States reports had highlighted a few that needed major reform.[87] A more streamlined organization would hopefully bring greater consistency to the academic program.[88] The changes supposedly facilitated future reforms as well. It would be easier to hold individual departments more accountable for implementing changes. The consolidation also reduced the number of voices on the Academic Board. In effect, the superintendent gained greater control over the academic program. The Navy wanted good command and control in place before implementing further changes.[89]

Some have viewed these changes as part of a concerted plan that culminated in the "academic revolution." Others have seen the process as being interrelated but much more haphazard in its direction. In other words, the "academic revolution" did not have a single mastermind or blueprint behind it. The evidence supports both interpretations, although it seems more ample for the latter. Whether it was by accident or design, the reforms of the late 1950s were necessary in launching the "academic revolution." The final catalyst was the convening of a Curriculum Review Board in May 1959, headed by a noted educator and friend of military education, Dr.

Richard Folsom of Rensselaer Polytechnic Institute. Folsom's group reported directly to BUPERS and the secretary of the Navy. The board did not have authority to make changes on its own, but it had the ear of those who could. It was these special circumstances that made the "academic revolution" possible.[90]

The culture of Bancroft Hall had caused problems for reformers during Admiral Holloway's tenure. Admiral Smedberg worked hard to improve attitudes towards academics in Bancroft Hall and was not averse to trying new ideas to foster change. Nor was he blind to the substantial changes in the 1950s youth culture, part of which came from being the father of boys similar in age to midshipmen. Smedberg was the first superintendent to visit the other academies before taking command. He discovered that West Point no longer held Sunday morning breakfast formations for cadets and implemented something similar at Annapolis. Midshipmen could struggle to morning meal, a relaxing break from the otherwise regimented routine, after which the first mandatory formation was for chapel. Little perks like this helped make the daily grind more bearable. Traditions were important but not if they were counterproductive to morale or recruiting. The reforms showed Smedberg's awareness of social changes and a willingness to address their impact on the academy.[91]

Alumni criticized many of these changes as being permissive and unnecessary. Smedberg reminded naysayers that most regulations remained in effect. It did not make sense, however, to hold onto obsolete traditions. For example, radios were now permitted in midshipmen rooms that could be used outside of study hour. The ban seemed ludicrous now that the academy had its own radio station. WRNV existed primarily for entertainment, but it also helped officers run Bancroft Hall. For example, the service selection lottery was conducted over its airwaves.[92] These were tricky times for the academy. Tradition and discipline had to be maintained but not to the detriment of progress and morale. The trick was to learn how and when changes should be made.

Upperclassmen received most of the new privileges, but that was how the Navy traditionally worked. Higher rank brought additional responsibilities. First classmen were expected to run the Brigade and enforce new policies. The additional privileges were also an incentive to mature behavior. Seniors would soon be junior officers; they needed to start acting as such. Smedberg revived incentives attempted by his mentor, Admiral Holloway. First classmen could own and operate cars as well as drink alcohol outside the seven-mile limit.[93] Extended weekends were also a welcome break from the new academic grind.[94]

Underclassmen received additional benefits too, which varied with their status at the academy. Everyone benefited from quality of life improvements inside Bancroft Hall. A new soda fountain and bowling alleys were installed that midshipmen could use in their free time.[95] By 1958, first classmen could even store civilian clothes in their rooms, a striking departure from past regulations.[96] Bancroft Hall was a military institution, but it was also a college dormitory. Its taut routine did not have to be entirely devoid of fun. The academy could not have picked a more opportune time to work on morale. Budgetary challenges and outside criticism continued to be a distraction to professional socialization. Furthermore, it was trying to instill higher academic standards among its students.

Most of these policies had been revolutionary during Admiral Holloway's tenure as superintendent. At this juncture, the academy was just trying to stay even with society. Midshipmen of the 1950s were part of a youth culture with different aspirations and experiences than past generations.[97] Many of them had already owned cars; their families had many modern conveniences in their homes.[98] Their friends were getting as good or better of an education without the hardships of Bancroft Hall. The Naval Academy did not buckle to changing social norms, but adjustments had to be made. Most midshipmen understood the academy lifestyle involved sacrifice and deprivation. However, standards should bear some relevance to society. Contrary to later academy critics, this had been an ongoing process and one likely to be repeated in the future.[99]

The academy targeted one final group for additional benefits, its academic achievers, through a new program called the superintendent's list. Good grades were not the only requirement for inclusion; high marks in military aptitude and physical education were also necessary. The superintendent's list clearly communicated a new message about academic achievement. Midshipmen may not have seen a reason for good grades, but the academy did. Recipients received additional privileges *beyond* the normal class system. Furthermore, a new list was issued every semester. Midshipmen had to qualify each term to keep these benefits. Unlike Bancroft Hall, the superintendent's list rewarded sustained performance, especially in the classroom, not longevity in the system.[100]

Gestures like these helped nurture a new academic climate inside Bancroft Hall. Older academic stereotypes—the slash, the dope system, etc.—did not disappear but their usage began to fade.[101] Midshipmen still joked about academics, but the tone was not as harsh as it was with the slash. Successful exams meant that the "rent had been paid" for another semester, more of a neutral attitude towards academics.[102] Alternative images were coming to the forefront that placed greater importance on academics. The superintendent's list was seen as a prerequisite for the Brigade's top leadership positions. Sketch biographies in *The Log* spotlighted top academic performers as well as star athletes. "Top Man of the Brigade," *The Log,* 20 September 1957, focused on future, two-time academy superintendent, Admiral Charles Larson, a star man as well as a gifted

The Log, 20 March 1959. New images of success were coming to the forefront. All-around success, including academics, was becoming the focus of midshipmen.

athlete and popular leader of the Brigade. "He Leads Us All," *The Log,* 24 January 1958, featured future national security advisor, Admiral John Poindexter, who was known throughout his class for his aptitude in the classroom.[103] Fewer negative stereotypes crossed its pages by the end of the 1950s. Since the superintendent's list rewarded overall achievement, classmates were less likely to shun peers with good grades.

These changes coincided with more students coming to Annapolis for academic reasons. Education was important in its own right not just a means to graduation. Within the classes of 1955 to 1959, 25 percent chose the academy for its educational opportunities, a 12 percent increase from the classes of 1950 to 1954 and a 21 percent increase from the classes of 1946 to 1949.[104] For the first time, academic standing affected opportunities after graduation. Many Air Force volunteers were attracted by the service's excellent postgraduate opportunities.[105] Only 25 percent of the class could take advantage of them. Good grades were also a prerequisite for entering nuclear power training. A new academic climate was slowly penetrating Bancroft Hall, with even greater changes looming on the horizon.

Defense Unification and the Military Culture of Bancroft Hall

World War II was the catalyst for Bancroft Hall becoming a marketplace of competing ideas and career paths, each trying to capture the midshipmen's loyalty and commitment.[106] That pattern would intensify during the 1950s. The most heated rivalry continued to be between the surface navy and naval aviation. At first glance, aviators appeared to have the upper hand. Their job seemed the most prestigious and glamorous; flying jets was risky, but it was also a lot of fun.[107] Furthermore, naval aviation appeared to have the best future.[108] Although surface line had lost some of its luster, it still exercised tremendous influence over Bancroft Hall. Most important traditions at Annapolis derived from ship operations. Naval aviation was the *wunderkind* of the moment, but the American surface fleet was still the world's largest, with the most positions for graduates to fill. It too offered a career of excitement, travel, and opportunities.[109] Finally and most importantly, Annapolis firmly believed that whatever else they might do, graduates needed to understand ships. The best way to ensure this was mandating an initial sea tour for all graduates.

The defense unification controversy was equally traumatic for Bancroft Hall even though the war hinted at this development too. Besides the aircraft carrier, an important wartime lesson had been the importance of effective interservice cooperation. The greatest battlefield victories

2: THE NAVAL ACADEMY OF THE 1950S

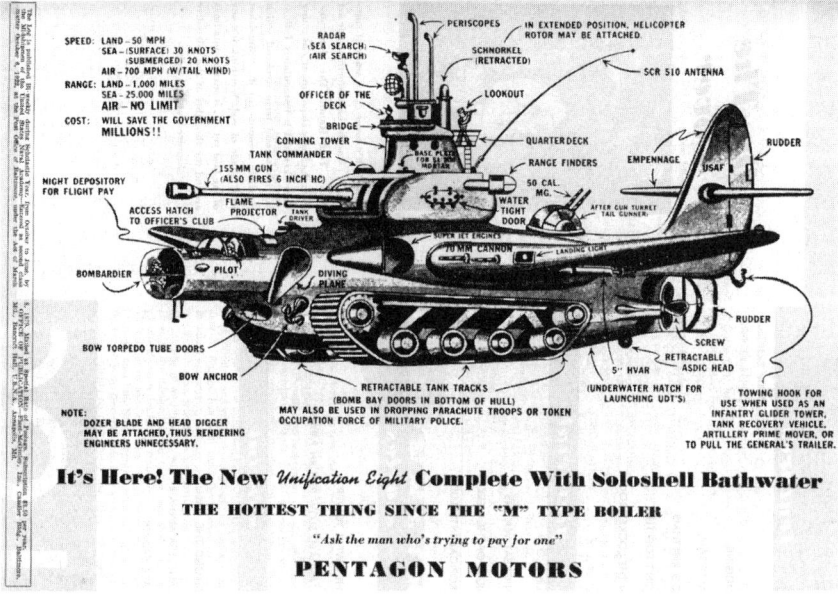

The Log, 27 April 1951. Midshipmen needed to know more than just the Navy in the new defense environment.

had come when the services cooperated in their planning and execution. Interservice bickering was a surefire recipe to disaster in the Cold War. Soviet communism posed an imminent danger to national security; the American military could not learn on the job as it had in other wars. The danger dictated an organization that could work together in the nation's defense. The Army usually urged consolidation, while the Navy favored independence as much as possible.[110] Both positions were a sincere assessment of the country's needs, albeit flavored with a heavy dose of parochialism.[111]

The service academies were not immune to the Army's penchant for unification either. The question of educational unification was the leading topic of the Stearns-Eisenhower Board, which convened in March 1949. Each armed service had representatives on the board; the Navy's was Naval Academy superintendent, Admiral James Holloway, and the Army's was the general of the Army, Dwight Eisenhower. Civilian educators completed the Board's membership, the most prominent being Dr. Robert Stearns, president of the University of Colorado and a former brigadier general in the Air Force. At first, the Stearns-Eisenhower Board appeared to be stacked in favor of unification, which was the desire of the new secretary of defense, Louis Johnson.

All of the civilian experts, along with General Eisenhower, supported a single national defense academy for officer candidates' core academic and military education. Annapolis and West Point would survive but only to provide their designees with limited, specialized training. The existing service academies were being relegated to the graveyard of World War II. Annapolis had outlived its usefulness similar to the battleship. To everyone's surprise, the board's junior member, Admiral Holloway, persuaded the group to reverse its original position. The Stearns-Eisenhower Board eventually recommended that distinctive academies be maintained, much to the dismay of Louis Johnson. The Naval Academy survived another threat to its postwar existence but just barely. At the same time, the board urged the academies to cooperate as much as possible.[112]

The unification scare was traumatic enough that the Naval Academy quickly took its warnings to heart. In the next several years, it introduced midshipmen to a wide variety of interservice training. Few were aware of the specifics of defense reorganization proposals however. Nonetheless, it was difficult to miss the message about the new demands of officership. The new program was geared towards producing broadly trained officers not just those familiar with ships. As a result, Bancroft Hall's military culture became even more jumbled than before. Midshipmen were not only exposed to the Navy's requirements; other services also competed for their attention. The Navy still dominated their professional socialization, but it no longer had a monopoly over its own academy.

The spirit of unification permeated the chain of command. Although the academies did not operate in lockstep, its superintendents communicated on a regular basis. Rather than risk unnecessary questions, exchange conferences kept everyone aware of what the others were doing. Besides submariners, aviators, and marines, the Executive Department welcomed representatives from the Air Force and Army. Not surprisingly, the other services sent their best officers to be examples to the midshipmen. The Army, for example, assigned Captains George Patton Jr. and Alexander Haig as company officers.[113] The surface navy could not be this selective since it had many more positions to fill. Some midshipmen had excellent role models; others dealt with officers who turned them against the surface navy.

Second class midshipmen traveled to West Point on weeklong exchange visits, and Annapolis hosted its cadets in return. The primary purpose of these trips was professional familiarization.[114] Midshipmen could not help but have mixed impressions of Annapolis afterwards. To many, the grass did seem greener at West Point. Unfortunately, they failed to realize that many cadets probably felt the same way. For example, midshipmen were amazed by all of West Point's unused space. Cadets did not appear to suffer from the same overcrowded and rundown facilities as midshipmen did.[115]

The summer program was also revised to include more joint training opportunities. Unfortunately, mixed messages were also sent here. Full-blown amphibious operations, involving cadets and midshipmen, consumed a huge share of the available training time. The exercises were generally well funded and attended by the chain of command.[116] In the past, the time would have been spent solely at sea, but that did not seem to be as much of a priority any more. Once again, the net result was greater difficulty motivating midshipmen towards Navy line.

The most dramatic example of cross-pollination was the adoption of a formal honor system in 1952. Honor offenses were always serious violations, punishable with immediate dismissal from the academy. Until this point, violations were administered under the normal conduct system, not through a special set of procedures. Midshipmen were expected to be honorable, but that included loyalty to their classmates as well as traditional admonitions against lying, cheating, or stealing.[117] These goals could be at cross-purposes, however, making it difficult for truly "honorable" behavior. For example, midshipmen acted honorably by hindering officers from discovering classmates who had gone over the wall.[118] Finding clandestine spots for contraband was also a normal part of "cops and robbers."[119]

The most questionable activity in which the lines between honor and classmate loyalty blurred was the dope system. The lockstep curriculum could not help but encourage suspect academic behavior. Midshipmen naturally relayed information about their classes in the company areas and at the mess tables. The lockstep curriculum, with its same courses *and* exams, was an easy temptation for abuse. The academy taught midshipmen to help and protect one another in difficult circumstances. Classmates interpreted this code to include sharing the content of quizzes and exams. Academic integrity was often an unfortunate but understandable casualty within that institutional culture.

West Point cadets also struggled with the fine line between honor and classmate loyalty. However, their honor code was more severe. Questionable behavior had to be reported, otherwise the witness risked being charged with an honor offense. The most serious academic scandal of the postwar period involved the Army football team, whose coach had developed a fiefdom similar to Eddie Erdalatz. The controversy motivated Annapolis to reform its system before anything similar happened. The fear was certainly legitimate given the similarities in the academic culture of both institutions.

The chain of events surrounding the honor system's creation is difficult to establish. The superintendent, Harry Hill, believed a formal honor program was necessary for curbing the dope system. However, he did not want midshipmen feeling that the administration was forcing these changes on them. Top leaders from the Brigade's three upper classes, including future superintendent William Lawrence '51 and billionaire industrialist Ross Perot '53, were also concerned that the dope system pushed the limits of academic integrity too far.[120]

Regardless of who deserved the credit, all parties looked at West Point to decide what to include and avoid.[121] Academy leaders and midshipmen had strong reservations about the rigidity of its honor code. Its nontoleration clause gave little leeway for resolving problems outside the formal honor system. Cadets were caught in a vicious cycle of turning in classmates, whether they believed an honor offense had been committed. If not, they risked implicating themselves, hardly a system conducive to building classmate loyalty. At the same time, Annapolis was too lackadaisical about honor, assuming midshipmen did the right thing. The new honor concept attempted to straddle a middle line.

Honor violations were serious enough to warrant their own system, but Annapolis did not force a response from midshipmen. Students decided themselves whether an honor offense had occurred. That by itself was a great responsibility, although midshipmen could incorrectly look the other way. Although never a stated purpose, the new honor concept coincided with the school's effort to upgrade its academic reputation. The dope system was probably the last image it wanted accrediting bodies to see. Many colleges had similar honor clauses in their code of academic behavior. Few of them lauded their role in developing students' character as much as the academy. If character development was truly a great strength of Annapolis, their academic behavior had to be above reproach.[122]

What was most interesting was the lack of fanfare surrounding a change of this magnitude. Admiral Hill made little mention of the new honor concept in his 1952 annual report, even though he had great responsibility in initiating it. Both the midshipmen and the academy spoke very carefully about the new honor system.[123] While praising the reforms, they quickly affirmed that midshipmen had always been honorable. The changes were not a reactionary response against possible scandal but were instead calculated reforms of a basically sound process. Midshipmen also stressed that their honor system was not an unthinking code like West Point. The honor concept was essentially a refined statement of what the Brigade was doing all along. In both cases, Annapolis thought it important not to distance itself from tradition or to embrace a system of its institutional rival.

The new honor system gives sharp insight into the Brigade's perception of honorable behavior. The worst abuses of the dope system disappeared, but midshipmen continued to pass information about their classes. Good gouge was how midshipmen got through their classes both then and today. The limits of acceptable and nonacceptable academic behavior remained hazy, however, even after the reforms. Midshipmen felt no qualms about misleading the Executive Department, especially if it protected their classmates. Classmates pulled pranks on one another, hiding or borrowing their personal property. Even though this was done without permission, it was not dishonorable since it was done in the name of fun.[124] The question of honorable behavior would be open for reinterpretation during the "academic revolution," much as it is today.

The deepest challenge to Bancroft Hall came from the nation's newest military service, the Air Force. Like the Army, the Air Force began sending officers to the Naval Academy in the early 1950s.[125] But their mission was more than familiarization; they came to recruit midshipmen.[126] The new organization desperately needed junior officers. Not until 1954 was the Air Force Academy established; even then the first graduates were not commissioned until 1958. Congress permitted the Air Force to use Annapolis and West Point to build its initial core of regular officers. From 1949 to 1963, up to 25 percent of every graduating class could select an Air Force commission.[127] The new service rarely failed to meet its quota. In the 1950s alone, 1,820 midshipmen chose it over the Navy.[128] These numbers tapered off by the early 1960s, but the damage was already done.[129]

The mass exodus of midshipmen was a bitter pill for Annapolis to swallow.[130] The academy had little choice in implementing this policy. However, the willing departure of so many graduates seemed a betrayal of everything it tried to accomplish. They had seen the best the Navy had to offer during their professional socialization—the spit and polish of its traditions, the exotic glamour of life at sea, the prestige of being an academy man.[131] Worse yet, volunteers were fleeing the Navy for the uncertainties of a new military service. Company officers and classmates were often less than gracious to Air Force volunteers. Indeed, many kept their intentions secret to avoid abuse. After service selection, hiding was no longer an option, and Air Force designees were often shunned for their choice.

Some graduates volunteered because of a family tie or longstanding interest. However, many others were attracted by opportunities not available in the Navy.[132] The Air Force promised immediate orders to flight school, making it the quickest way into a cockpit. The Navy required years of sea duty before officers could transfer to Pensacola. Volunteers also received up to sixty days leave after graduation. The Navy refused to bend from its requirement of *immediate* sea duty for *all* graduates. Finally, the Air Force was more flexible toward graduate education. Most of its officers had that opportunity after their first operational tour. Research and development programs in nuclear weapons returned some officers to the classroom immediately. These policies resonated with the increasing numbers of midshipmen concerned about their education. Although the Navy

108   THE MIDSHIPMAN CULTURE AND EDUCATIONAL REFORM

The Log, **3 March 1950. The service selection lottery now had real consequences for drawing poorly.**

was moving in this direction, it had not overcome its skepticism of advanced education. Its officers were getting graduate degrees but not as routinely as the Air Force.

To its detriment, the Naval Academy hesitated to adjust its policies to the postwar world. The old lottery method was fine when career choices were limited to ship type and homeport. Midshipmen were increasingly alienated, however, by restrictions that hindered them from pursuing other careers.[133] As a newer institution, the Air Force was not as bound by tradition as the Navy. It was probably more capable of experimentation. Annapolis would change, but the growing pains were difficult. The continual hemorrhage of graduates to the Air Force eventually prompted it into action. After 1956, physically qualified graduates could choose aviation directly. The academy had lost too many prospective pilots; better to keep them flying for the Navy than lose them to another service.[134]

These concessions did not translate into a fully open service selection policy however. Prospective submariners were still required to complete an initial shipboard tour before transfer, a policy that lasted until the early

1960s.[135] Submarine cruises were started in 1955, but nothing changed beyond that.[136] Admiral Rickover's prestige and power eventually forced concessions here too.[137] Submariners were not being lost to another service however. The policy did risk alienating them from a military career. Career motivated midshipmen in the classes of 1955 to 1959 plummeted to just 57 percent, down 14 percent from the start of the decade.[138] That trend coincided with a similar drop in those choosing the academy because of its career opportunities.[139] Fewer than 30 percent in the classes of 1955 to 1959 selected Annapolis because of the career opportunities, a 10 percent decline from what it was for the classes of 1950 to 1954.[140] Many factors accounted for this decline but its restrictive service selection policy did not help. Midshipmen would rather leave the service than be forced into something. The academy learned the hard way that its program could no longer cater to a single warfare community or military service. Just like the rest of the military, the focus changed to preparing midshipmen for the complex military environment in which they would eventually serve.

Yet, for all the changes, much of the academy remained the same, especially the ethos nurtured inside Bancroft Hall. Plebe indoctrination changed little from what it had been before World War II.[141] Midshipmen still battled with the Executive Department to test the limits of rules and regulations.[142] Getting through the Naval Academy was a test of endurance that pushed both plebes and upperclassmen to their limits.[143] Midshipmen were still skeptical about serving with NROTC officers whose training seemed substandard.[144] Midshipmen also continued to interpret professional socialization through the lens of the total institution.[145] Unlike the 1960s and 1970s, they resoundingly believed that the challenges were making them into better officers and tougher leaders.[146] The sacrifices had an underlying purpose, and the system was not in need of drastic reform. Midshipmen may not have liked Bancroft Hall, but they supported its fundamental principles.

The midshipmen ethos would face greater challenges in the 1960s however. The "academic revolution" placed greater pressure on Bancroft Hall to accommodate the classroom. Academics would finally become more of an equal priority to professional socialization. Midshipmen would continue to be exposed to additional subcultures of military service competing for their attention. The nuclear submarine program would become more dominant in the 1960s, but the new academic program would also open up opportunities in the medical corps and judge advocate general corps. Finally, the academy lifestyle would grow more out of touch with society, thanks to an unpopular war in Vietnam and the student movement protesting it. The 1950s Naval Academy had learned the costs of resisting change; it would soon discover that there were costs in accommodating it.

3

The Early Years of the "Academic Revolution," 1959–62: Laying the Foundations for a New Academy

CURRICULUM REFORM MAY HAVE BEEN DORMANT AT THE ACADEMY FOR much of the 1950s. The Sputnik educational crisis, along with the growing need for officers fluent in advanced technology, rescued this issue from the doldrums. Its priorities literally changed overnight in the early 1960s. Instead of the sports program or new construction, the foremost priority became upgrading its academic reputation. Yet, the emphasis of reform remained similar to past efforts; Annapolis was to be the educational cornerstone for an officer's entire career. The speed and completeness in which the academy pursued this goal was incredibly different from before. No stone was left unturned in becoming a modern naval college, an institution respected not only for its professional skills but also for its academic achievements.[1]

The school swept aside large chunks of the lockstep curriculum with an ease that dumbfounded traditionalists. Its replacement was a truly modern program full of academic choices. Midshipmen could validate previous coursework and pursue electives leading to minors and even majors in various fields. Top students could pursue independent study their final year under the new Trident Scholar program. Some midshipmen started working on their graduate degrees while at Annapolis. Their first assignments were occasionally delayed until they finished their programs. Taken together, these changes were a striking departure from the trade school's focus of producing immediately employable ensigns.[2]

Its academic infrastructure underwent significant reform too. Greater numbers of civilians began holding positions of real influence. A civilian dean was hired to be the superintendent's top academic advisor; eventually his authority would be analogous to the commandant's control over Bancroft Hall. The numbers of civilian faculty also ballooned; the doctoral degree became a prerequisite for hiring or at least promotion. Civilians were appointed to numerous standing committees examining school policies. Annapolis also tried to raise the scholastic credentials of military faculty; officers needed their master's degree or were at least working on it before their assignment.[3]

The Naval Academy proudly dubbed this flurry of activity its "academic revolution." On paper, the scope of changes was indeed impressive; the speed of implementation certainly bolstered the claim of being revolutionary. At the same time, the "academic revolution" did not displace the vestiges of the older academy immediately. Bancroft Hall's culture had an anti-intellectual tint that was difficult to erase. Previous reform efforts had tried to ameliorate this tendency; the "academic revolution" was certainly the most concerted and successful effort to date. Whether it had a truly revolutionary effect was more difficult to answer. At the very least, the results were not as immediate as its defenders claimed.[4]

The "academic revolution" suffered from structural limitations, which hindered its overall effectiveness. Only a portion of the Brigade was affected by the academic changes. Top students were most likely to support reforms, but they stood the best chance of benefiting from them. Midshipmen who did not validate or take electives had little stake in them or even noticed the differences. The academy also had little choice but to phase in reforms gradually. However, this strategy was not the quickest way of cracking Bancroft Hall's anti-academic attitudes. Plebes were generally the first to receive new opportunities; upperclassmen were not eligible because it delayed their graduation. Although sensible from the standpoint of efficiency, those with the most power had the least reason for seeing them succeed. Bancroft Hall changed, albeit slowly, from these reforms. But the results were not as immediate or dramatic as their title suggests.[5]

In retrospect, the "academic revolution" has spawned many fathers. Many people have claimed credit for launching the academy in this direction. Not to dismiss the work of outside contributors, military leaders have insisted that the reforms were largely self-generated. The academy reviewed problems as necessary and took corrective action on its own. Civilian experts gave useful advice, but they merely validated what the school was doing all along. Members of the Folsom Board and the Middle States team were dubious of the academy's initiative. In their eyes, the academy often had to be prodded into action. It was simply unwilling or incapable of abandoning obsolete programs. In contrast, civilian educators took the unpopular actions of appearing before Congress or circumventing the chain of command to bring Annapolis up to speed pedagogically.[6]

Neither group appreciated the difficulties of the other or the importance both played in giving birth to the "academic revolution." At the time, many proposed reforms were very controversial. Alumni wondered why the school would tamper with a proven curriculum. Military leaders almost had to be the voice of moderation under such circumstances. Academic changes would not jeopardize its fundamental mission of preparing officers. Conversely, civilian educators were generally viewed as outsiders. No matter the quality of their ideas, they had to overcome much skepticism to put them into practice. However, most of them understood the peculiar challenges of a service academy. Few of them were urging Annapolis to distance itself from its military responsibilities. They too were trying to find the right balance between training and education. Without a clear mastermind, the "academic revolution" depended on both groups for its success.[7]

Annapolis could not have picked a more auspicious time to launch the "academic revolution." The institutional mood was clearly one of revival. Public interest had rebounded from the doldrums of previous years. The early 1960s was the golden age of Navy football, and winning records and prominent bowl appearances showcased the academy in a positive light.[8] The popular television show "Men of Annapolis" was also useful in stimulating young men's interest in the academy.[9] It was a beehive of construction and activity, with the new stadium and landfill project being completed at this time. As part of its policy for getting tough on communism, the Kennedy administration was also willing to spend more money on conventional defense needs. Although he was not an academy graduate, the president also had a well-known soft spot for the Navy.[10] The Naval Academy could marshal all sorts of evidence to show that it had a bright future.

The new curriculum fit within this renewed spirit of optimism. The Navy and its academy once again had a vital role in the nation's defense. Nuclear-powered submarines, especially the Polaris program, were at the vanguard of the country's strategic nuclear deterrent.[11] More than any other program, the submarine community depended on technically qualified officers for its success. Although applicants had to weather Admiral Rickover's scrutiny, nuclear power was becoming the Navy's elite arm, a community that the best and brightest midshipmen wanted to join. Nuclear power offered extra incentives—better pay, faster promotions, the quickest route to command—similar to what the Air Force had promised in the 1950s.[12] The "academic revolution" also distinguished the Naval Academy from its sister institutions. It became the service academy of choice for those with technical aspirations and began touting the scholastic credentials—national merit semifinalists, valedictorians, and honor society members—of midshipmen like never before.[13]

Just as it appeared Annapolis had turned the corner, the United States began expanding its military commitment to South Vietnam. At first, the effect on the academy was minimal. Unlike World War II, it tried to conduct business as usual but that became increasingly difficult as the war dragged on. The Navy's commitment to Vietnam eventually overshadowed most other responsibilities, including those to the academy. The academy once again lost out to operational priorities when it came to funding, personnel requests, and cruise assignments. Unfortunately, the "academic revolution" grew to maturity during these troubled times. The academy had a mouthful to digest with the academic reforms alone. Vietnam was an untimely distraction that hindered these reforms from fully taking root.[14]

As with most revolutions, the early years of this transition, the period from 1959 to 1962, were pivotal to the new curriculum's eventual success. This was not so much for the actual changes taking place but the philosophical underpinnings that grew to support them. Academic reform had started after World War II, and the latest reforms were the next logical steps in that progression. However, the assumptions behind this wave of changes were truly groundbreaking. Most midshipmen could expect to attend graduate school sometime in their careers. The curriculum needed to accommodate that requirement. These years were also significant because it involved a "changing of the guard" at Annapolis. Its mindset was a mixture of ideas, some of which were blatantly contradictory. The "academic revolution" would eventually create a new Naval Academy, but important conflicts had to be resolved in between. The years 1959 to 1962 were a crucial turning point in which newer ideas began to triumph over old.

The Folsom Board and the Electives Program

The immediate catalyst that triggered the "academic revolution" was the convening of a special Curriculum Review Board in May 1959. The Naval Academy had "requested" the board to evaluate recent changes with the curriculum. Many civilian educators believed the evaluation would have taken place regardless of the academy's wishes. The Curriculum Review Board was an interesting example of the evolution in military education at this time. The Department of Defense was increasingly turning to civilian educators for advice on military education and training, a logical outcome of the Cold War educational crisis. The secretary of the Navy and chief of naval personnel strategically chose the board's composition, balancing the concerns and ideas of civilians against the military.

The head of the evaluating team was Dr. Richard Folsom of Rensselaer Polytechnic Institute. Folsom had a long history in military education, working with the ROTC program at RPI and the Secretary of the Navy's Board on Educational Requirements (SABER), which had also started in 1958. The military also had voices on the board, the most prominent being Rear Admiral Horatio Rivero, an alumnus with distinguished technical and academic credentials. Although the goal was an objective review of the curriculum, the Navy recognized how politically difficult that might be and did its best to ensure that all interests were fairly represented. Board members also committed themselves to an extensive review of Annapolis, stretching over many months if necessary. The Folsom Board would not be a cursory inspection of the Naval Academy, as some examinations had tended to be.[15]

The Folsom Board operated under interesting assumptions from the Navy. Unlike other inspecting groups, the board's review was to be truly independent. Folsom and the academy would work together, but his group ultimately reported to the secretary of the Navy and chief of naval personnel, leaving Annapolis somewhat out of the loop. In other words, the Naval Academy knew everything Folsom's group was doing, but it could not stop the investigation. Folsom's primary contact was another civilian educator who worked directly for the chief of naval personnel. The problem with past inspecting bodies was that their recommendations were easily ignored. Middle States inspectors had often urged the library's overhaul, for example, but their concerns were never addressed.[16] Inspecting bodies needed the ear and interest of the academy's chain of command to carry any weight. The Folsom Board was fortunate to have that firepower at its disposal.[17]

Folsom's group was also given interesting ground rules about evaluating the curriculum. It was to consider the academy only the initial phase of an officer's education. Postgraduate education would be the norm for graduates sometime in their careers. The new curriculum *had* to be flexible. No one could know technology's future direction, but the curriculum should at least accommodate it. Annapolis needed to do more than just prepare competent ensigns; graduates should have an education that would serve them well throughout their careers. It was, after all, the source of most of the Navy's admirals. Evaluators should focus on what was best for graduates' *and* the Navy's future. The logical conclusion of these guidelines was that the lockstep curriculum should end.

The Folsom Board was the catalyst for remaking the academy into a true naval college, a vision first articulated by Admiral James Holloway. The difference now was that his ideas were no longer avant-garde. Many senior officers now saw the necessity for this kind of reform.[18] The debate was rather over how drastic the changes should be. Of final importance, the board was to be brutally realistic with its recommendations. Nothing was beyond reproach. Folsom's team would look at academics, training activities, whatever was necessary for improvement. The scope of its powers suggested that even Bancroft Hall would be examined. The one variable that could not be changed was the four-year timetable to graduation. The Folsom Board searched for any unnecessary duplication of effort. Time had to be conserved to meet the twin priorities of training and education.

Annapolis understood what was coming, however, and tried to preempt its investigation. The last thing the school wanted was to be embarrassed by Folsom's review. It was better to change on its own rather than be told what to do. The challenge of dealing with the Folsom Board fell on the shoulders of new leadership. Rear Admiral Charles Melson replaced William Smedberg as superintendent in June 1958. Like Smedberg, Melson visited the other service academies before taking command, paying special focus to their academic programs. He read extensively the debate surrounding the academy curriculum—Admiral Rickover's criticism, congressional hearings, etc. By the time he took command, the new superintendent already had strong ideas about what needed to be done.

Melson admitted that he was not an educator like Admiral Holloway but felt he understood the school's recent problems. Besides his latest research, he had served as Admiral Hill's administrative aide in the early 1950s. Melson did not wait for the Folsom Board before initiating changes. He followed through on plans for standardized admissions requirements; applicants began taking the common CEEB exam shortly after his arrival. The new superintendent also consolidated his hold over the academic program with the streamlined divisional organization scheme. From Colorado Springs, Melson learned of its program of validation and electives. He implemented a similar curriculum in 1959 for the class of 1963, the first action taken by the newly restructured Academic Board.[19]

The academy's unwillingness to recognize previous coursework was easily the greatest eyesore of the lockstep curriculum. Nothing made less sense than forcing students to repeat classes completed satisfactorily elsewhere, especially with the increasingly compacted schedule. Virtually everyone familiar with the curriculum believed that this dinosaur had to go.[20] Under the new program, plebes took a battery of validation exams their first summer. A passing score freed up space in their schedule that could be used on other requirements. There were, nonetheless, a few significant bugs early on with the new program. Some plebes used the extra time to work on projects for their upperclassmen. Others were simply uncomfortable going faster than the standard curriculum. Testing out of a course did not mean they were willing or ready to tackle more difficult requirements.[21]

Yet, the logical extension of validation was electives. Electives were offered in a number of subjects, but the initial focus was the technical disciplines. The new curriculum was a boon to both current student morale and recruiting. Midshipmen near the top of their class especially wanted these opportunities. Some were motivated by the academic challenge; others understood their necessity in admission to a good graduate school.

The nuclear power program also expected applicants to have advanced courses on their resume. Annapolis could not rely on its prestigious name and history alone to attract good students either. The competition among other colleges for these individuals was too severe. A high caliber academic program demonstrated the academy's commitment to a high quality undergraduate education. Fewer young men were willing to sacrifice this to attend Annapolis.

The extra courses placed additional demands on the faculty but most welcomed the burden. Professors now had the chance to work more closely with students. Eventually their role included that of being academic advisors. The effects on professional socialization were probably not appreciated at the time. Civilian instructors became mentors to midshipmen, a role previously reserved for company officers. Electives were also a refreshing change from the monotony of the standardized curriculum. For the first time, instructors could develop courses that suited their own interests. Many were excited about the changes, and their infectious attitudes often rubbed off on their students. Upperclassmen could take electives, but the qualifications were more stringent than was the case for plebes. A minimum grade point average of 3.0 was needed, and only one elective per semester was allowed. Upperclassmen could not be derailed from graduating in four years, especially if reformers wanted their ideas accepted by the Navy's admirals.[22]

The greatest incentive of the new curriculum was the chance at an academic minor or a major. The hurdles for completing a minor were substantial, let alone a major, which remained virtually impossible. Midshipmen had to validate a considerable number of courses to even try. At that point, their schedules were overloaded each semester with the necessary extra classes. The sizable number of core hours prohibited most students from even attempting it.[23] Yet, the option itself was a significant departure from the lockstep curriculum. Each year, more students found ways of meeting these requirements. In that respect, it was invaluable in boosting a new academic climate. At this point, little else was expected of the "academic revolution." Midshipmen were better prepared for graduate school, and the school had muted objections about its academic life being stagnant. Academy leaders saw little reason, however, to equip the average midshipman with a minor, let alone a major. In their mind, all the necessary adjustments had been made.[24]

The "academic revolution" involved more than just curriculum changes however. As always, the physical plant's condition was a deep concern, but unlike before, academic priorities figured prominently in calls for repair or renovation. Proper classrooms and laboratories had become just as important as athletic fields or dormitory space in accomplishing its mission. No expense was seemingly spared in transforming Annapolis into a state-of-the-art research facility. A wind tunnel and digital computer were installed for the advanced engineering courses. Plans were even developed for construction of a noncritical nuclear reactor for familiarization training. Part of this was calculated to convince lawmakers, applicants, and midshipmen of the seriousness of the academy's change of heart. However, much more of it stemmed from its own sober realization that it had far to go in becoming a first-rate undergraduate college.[25]

Serious effort was also put into creating a new academic climate. Midshipmen began attending academic conferences at local colleges and universities. They delivered papers and put together panels, just like their civilian peers. Annapolis co-sponsored a Navy Science Symposium along with the Office of Naval Research and the Naval Research Laboratory. This effort demonstrated the academy's desire to join the scholarly community, but it was also a chance to impress outsiders with the "academic revolution." There was no denying the technical emphasis of the new program. However, attention was also paid to the liberal arts. The Naval Academy began hosting an annual Foreign Affairs Conference, which drew over 125 students from fifty colleges and universities in its initial year. Its proximity to Washington, D.C. drew prestigious speakers from the federal government and numerous foreign embassies. Annapolis did not intend to be a great, liberal arts college. However, this emphasis was not anti-intellectual. And it did not exclude the academy from being interested in other areas, especially those that enhanced its academic reputation.[26]

Officially, the Folsom Board had been convened at the academy's request. Many board members suspected it wanted the review to be perfunctory, to give academic credibility to the new curriculum. Folsom's team intended on carrying out the exhaustive review the Navy had ordered however. Unlike other groups, they investigated areas outside most normal inspections. Evaluators were not afraid to step on toes to get complete information. The Folsom Board also studied the academy longer than other teams. The Board of Visitors came each year, for example, but they were gone in a matter of days. Folsom's group started in May 1959, and its final report was not delivered until that November. Four additional trips were made beyond the initial inspection. Board members corresponded frequently and visited other training installations for comparison. No other fact-finding body had conducted as penetrating an analysis of the academy.[27]

The board's findings contained both good and bad news for Annapolis. It agreed with the school's longstanding assertion that its responsibilities must include education and training. Likewise, both groups shared similar beliefs about its primary value. The Naval Academy produced the bulk of the Navy's career officers. Its retention rate had rebounded from its post–World War II slump to a consistent 70 to 80 percent, similar to what it had been beforehand. In contrast, NROTC retention rates were horrible, only about 20 to 30 percent were staying for a career. The academy insisted that its intense four-year, character building program made the difference. Some educators wondered whether the academy simply attracted more career-motivated students anyway.[28] In retrospect, survey results from this study seem to confirm these assumptions; only 18.6 percent of participants changed their minds about a military career while at Annapolis. Regardless, the Folsom Board determined not to tamper with what the academy was apparently doing well.[29]

The Folsom Board also said significant good things about the new curriculum. It applauded the electives program and suggested ways of building upon it. Proper balance continued to be a problem; the question was whether the best use was made of the available time. The team agreed that training was important but questioned its overall effectiveness, especially with the larger student body and the greater demands of military specialization. Midshipmen seemed better educated, but that should have been the case with the quality of recent applicants. If there was not improvement, that evidence alone suggested serious problems. The greatest defect continued to be the military faculty. Top officers rarely chose Annapolis because it hindered their chances at promotion. A lack of motivation and insufficient education continued to be major problems. Without major improvements here, the success of the new curriculum would be halfhearted at best.[30]

The Folsom Board left a laundry list of recommendations, forty-two of which it knew the academy could not implement. The bar was set high to show that there was much work still to be done. Its report was essentially a working outline for the future. Ideas that were not politically or financially feasible now could be addressed at a later date. The other major task was selling the military on their validity. Many recommendations contradicted the prevailing culture of the academy and the Navy. Folsom put it this way: "the Navy has never been sold on education. The Navy has been sold on training, but not education. In this day and age, you have to have both." An essential task was "to educate the admirals on what a subsequent civilian education [was]." A new curriculum alone was not going to make the academy a top college. A new academic culture also had to be created. The Folsom Board's larger mission was to move Annapolis in that direction.[31]

Early Challenges for the "Academic Revolution"

The Naval Academy was certainly slow to implement most of the Folsom Board's recommendations. It was criticized severely, particularly by alumni, for the limited changes it had already made. Many questioned whether the greater emphasis on academics would produce the wrong kind of graduate. Academy graduates were not "technicians" or "scientific wonders." Annapolis molded "leaders of men," not those who "were familiar with machines."[32] The average alumnus pointed to the personality and career of Hyman Rickover as evidence of everything that was wrong with these reforms.[33]

The new curriculum also disrupted a vital part of professional socialization for as of yet unproven benefits. Electives eliminated the "unity of suffering" experience that was the lockstep curriculum's greatest virtue. Classmates were closer and hence more dedicated when they shared the same academic trials. Individual academic achievement or desires were not all that important anyway. Everyone began their careers as ensigns or second lieutenants.[34] Indeed, classes celebrated their last set of final exams, a ceremony known as "no more rivers." The curriculum had to be relevant to an officer's basic duties. Thus, some reform was necessary due to new technology. However, in terms of professional socialization, the curriculum was simply another obstacle classmates conquered together.[35]

The lockstep program had never challenged its military requirements either. Classmates marched together by section; courses were taken in order without exception. It was all part of the academy experience. Electives threw all of this topsy-turvy for seemingly intangible benefits. Instead of building class unity, the new curriculum scattered classmates in different directions. Electives satisfied individual desires, but at what cost to the Brigade's overall cohesion? Worse still, the new academic program disrupted the strict hierarchy of Bancroft Hall. Until this point, academic life was segregated by class the same as Bancroft Hall. Plebes and upperclassmen could now interact as peers in the classroom. Furthermore, they would be competing against one another on an equal plane.[36]

The worst scenario was a plebe outperforming an upperclassman in the classroom. Almost by definition, plebes could not do anything right while upperclassmen were supermen if for nothing else than their longevity in the system. The new academic program eliminated that glass ceiling. Upperclassmen may have been infallible in Bancroft Hall, but that was not always true in the classroom. Skeptics of the changes worried about the effect on good order and discipline. Underclassmen might be less willing to obey superiors with clear academic deficiencies. Critics wondered why these risks were being taken, especially with a proven program already in place. The lockstep program admittedly had problems, but it was a known quantity. Officers produced under this system had never lost a war. In their minds, the academy would be wise to rethink the necessity of these reforms.[37]

At the opposite end of the spectrum, Admiral Rickover and his supporters attacked the academy for not doing more. His ideas were even popular

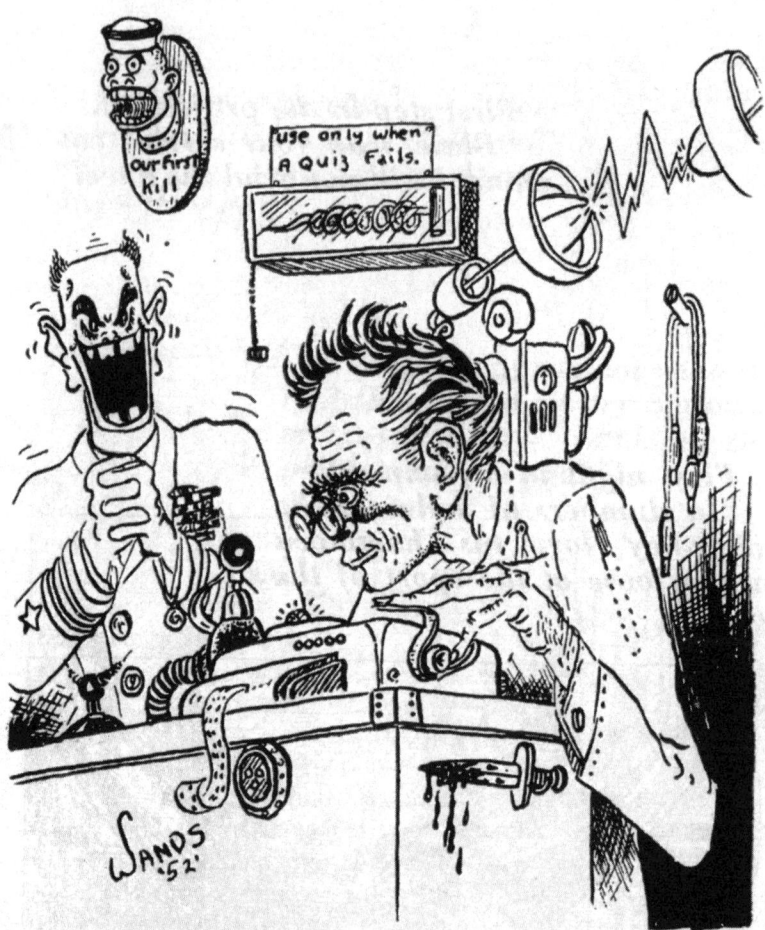

Impossible, you say. Put it on tomorrow's Quiz

The Log, 17 April 1959. The great challenge for the "academic revolution" was changing midshipmen's attitudes about their education.

with congressmen on the Board of Visitors who included them in a dissenting minority report in 1959.[38] They urged the recruitment of younger students with superior academic backgrounds and the elimination of rigid physical requirements to admit otherwise qualified candidates. Practical training should be conducted exclusively in the summer. The bulk of the traditional school year should be left free for academics. Without this, the academy would never be competitive with good civilian colleges. The system also needed greater rewards for academic achievement. Finally, additional civilians should be hired to make up for the pitiful credentials of military faculty.

Perhaps the most controversial idea was that the time spent on Bancroft Hall should also be reevaluated, despite its supposed value to professional socialization. The four-year program barely allowed time for military training much less fraternity antics. Some critics pushed for clear limits or even an end to plebe indoctrination. Most indoctrination should be conducted in the summer otherwise a midshipman's first year was a waste academically. Why recruit good students if academics were not going to be their focus? The academy had heard these ideas before, but their inclusion in an official report was particularly threatening. Its leaders were truly in a tough spot however. Traditionalists were urging them to stay the course while mavericks, like Rickover, were pressing for more drastic reforms.[39]

Admiral Rickover believed the Folsom Board gave him greater license to interfere with Annapolis. He pressured the chief of naval personnel to arrange a visit so he could see firsthand the recent changes. Rickover's acerbic personality, along with his well-known disdain for the Naval Academy, created a potentially explosive situation. Admiral Melson expected the visit to be nothing more than a short tour of the new facilities followed by a briefing on the curriculum. Rickover had higher expectations of the changes and began to criticize the academy for not doing more. Needless to say, the visit was extremely tense and short as well as accomplishing little. Academy leaders listened to him but promised nothing more than what they had already done. In their minds, the admiral would never be pleased with Annapolis. Rickover returned to Washington convinced that the academy would never be a decent center of higher learning.[40]

Rickover was a nuisance, but it seems Annapolis was more worried about critics on the other end. Admiral Melson repeatedly tried to calm fears that the changes were too revolutionary. He emphasized that the academy was "endeavoring to do less the training of the technician and more the educating of the naval leader."[41] Rapid technological change had made the flexible curriculum necessary. But the admiral was careful to point out that its primary objective remained the same: the preparation of "*well-rounded, career line officers*"[42] (his emphasis). For those fearful of the new direction, nothing more was being done than what was common in higher education. The reforms were not to compete with other elite colleges but a recognition that methods of learning had changed. Finally, the other service academies were adopting similar changes. Melson's last words were particularly helpful in calming alumni fears about an inordinate civilian influence at the academy.

The "academic revolution" sputtered along as a result. The academy preferred to move slowly rather than alienate its critics further. Severe organizational constraints also limited progress. The chronic turnover in the academy's leadership was a major problem. Just as one superintendent became comfortable with his job, he was relieved and the learning process started over again. Although it was most visible at the superintendent's level, this process repeated itself throughout the academy staff. Rarely were all levels of leadership in place—superintendent, commandant, battalion and company officers—to make reforms totally effective. Melson turned over command to Rear Admiral John Davidson in June 1960. Davidson had headed the humanities department in the 1950s so he was aware of the school's post–war problems. Like many post war superintendents, Admiral Davidson was not a great fan of the lockstep curriculum, but he was hesitant to exceed what was already done.[43]

Davidson spent most of his time consolidating Admiral Melson's reforms. The scale of the new curriculum expanded during his tenure, but its scope remained basically the same. Instead of a few scattered electives, most departments developed a variety of advanced courses. Core courses were still the bread and butter of the curriculum. However, more midshipmen were validating and taking electives each year. Minors also became more common although few midshipmen qualified for a major. Greater involvement gradually led to further changes in the academic climate. Simply put, the new curriculum developed a wider base of supporters among upperclassmen and eventually alumni. Recruiting played a significant role in this development too. More academically inclined applicants were coming to Annapolis each year and were already predisposed to the new academic direction.[44]

The "Academic Revolution" and Bancroft Hall

Alumni were correct about the growing pains the "academic revolution" would experience with Bancroft Hall. Although important, the new curriculum was actually the easiest task for reformers to accomplish. Many reforms ran counter to the existing institutional culture. The focus of midshipmen life in the early 1960s continued to be Bancroft Hall's activities. Academics were receiving greater emphasis, but many midshipmen remained unconvinced of their value. The school's primary business was producing naval officers; those who ran Bancroft Hall interpreted that to mean that its priorities came first. Company officers certainly gave that message to upperclassmen. They in turn communicated it to their subordinates. The key to producing dedicated, career-minded officers was strict discipline, rigidly enforced throughout academy life.[45]

Midshipmen essentially followed the same code of behavior their peers did in the 1940s and 1950s. Rooms and uniforms were always ready for

The Log, 17 November 1961. Bancroft Hall still kept tight control over midshipmen.

inspection, even if it took time away from academics. Duty officers prowled Bancroft Hall looking for minor violations. Punishment was swift and severe, unlike the classroom, where falling behind did not seem as dangerous. Bancroft Hall could take away weekend liberty privileges or impose extra duty. Nothing the classroom could do seemed as horrible, at least until final grades were distributed. Indeed, military instructors continued to reinforce similar priorities to Bancroft Hall. Students were placed on report for slovenly uniforms or inappropriate military conduct more so than inattention to their studies. The emphasis of the "academic revolution" may have been academics, but the classroom was still used to teach military discipline.[46]

Conversely, unlike earlier reforms, no other incentives were given for the extra academic work. The academy did not want to give ammunition to its critics and suggest that it was weakening its traditional military environment. Only first classmen were entitled to car or civilian clothes privileges; the liberty schedule also remained the same. Midshipmen continued to bend the rules over social activities common to people their age. They dared officers to catch them driving cars or wearing civilian clothes illegally. The latest gadgets, especially television sets, were smuggled inside Bancroft Hall. Officers were primarily responsible for enforcing the rules, not mentoring midshipmen. "Cops and robbers" still permeated Bancroft Hall, despite the new attitudes reformers were trying to foster.[47]

Electives did not automatically produce a new academic culture either. Remnants of older, anti-intellectual attitudes persisted. Midshipmen grumbled about "slash" classmates for working too hard on their grades and wrecking the curve. Graduation was the only important milestone anyway, the ticket to becoming naval officers.[48] First classmen joked about "pushing the coast button," the point at which minimum requirements were completed and they could relax until graduation.[49] The new curriculum softened these attitudes but did not eliminate them. The sizable core program prevented many midshipmen from even participating in the "academic revolution." Their daily lives essentially changed little. In that respect, this "revolution" was mild in tone and effect.[50]

The new curriculum also disrupted the academy's traditional military hierarchy. Upperclassmen did complain about underclassmen in their classes. Part of this was simple jealousy at not having the same opportunities available to them. Whether it made sense or not, every midshipman was supposed to follow the same path to graduation. Common academic struggles, after all, bonded graduates together.[51] Others did worry, however, about being placed in situations where subordinates could upstage them. Most first classmen understood they made mistakes. They just did not want underclassmen to know about it. Such situations compromised their authority and with it their command of the Brigade.[52]

Plebe indoctrination was also a major area of conflict, a problem that only intensified in coming years. Nothing symbolized more the dichotomy between the academy's training and academic responsibilities. Academy leaders knew that unauthorized indoctrination happened. Now more than ever it had to be got under control. Plebes had always lacked sufficient study time, many times by design. Setting priorities and functioning under stress were important training goals.[53] However, the time spent on arcane research projects and upperclassmen's errands increasingly seemed foolish with the new curriculum. Plebe indoctrination also demanded time from upperclassmen. Often it seemed that the ones most involved were those who could least afford to lose the time. For the time being, the academy preferred a soft approach in changing midshipmen's minds. By the late 1960s, more explicit steps were taken to control Bancroft Hall. The "academic revolution" could not fail, nor could it tolerate the outside criticism unauthorized activities were attracting.[54]

Complicating matters further, the Brigade's expansion made it more difficult to monitor plebe indoctrination. Upperclassmen essentially had greater leeway to determine what happened in their companies. Duty of-

3: THE EARLY YEARS OF THE "ACADEMIC REVOLUTION" 125

ficers alone roamed Bancroft Hall at night. Companies located at the far fringes of Bancroft Hall had the most freedom to do what they wanted. Additional officers would not be assigned to Bancroft Hall until the late 1960s. Plebe indoctrination became more inconsistent as a result with significant variations across the Brigade. Survey participants were asked to rank specifically how much plebe indoctrination varied by company or battalion. The grading scale ranged from no variance to slightly, moderately, or widely varied. Companies began acquiring reputations; either lenient or heavy-handed, in how they dealt with their plebes.

For the classes of 1946 to 1949, nearly 26 percent answered no variation and close to 37 percent claimed that the system was only slightly varied—a clear majority of midshipmen in that cohort. Midshipmen in the slightly varied category consisted of 34 percent of the classes of 1950 to 1954 but the no-variance group fell to only 12 percent of that cohort. These percentages changed dramatically with the "academic revolution." Only 2.3 percent of the classes of 1955 to 1959, 5.1 percent of the classes of 1960 to 1964, and 1.8 percent from the classes of 1965 to 1969, reported no variation. Nearly 42 percent of the classes of 1955 to 1959 and close to 39 percent of the classes of 1960 to 1964 and 1965 to 1969 believed plebe indoctrination varied widely by company or battalion. Midshipmen in the moderately varied category also increased significantly—making up 29 percent of the classes of 1955 to 1959, 32 percent of the classes of 1960 to 1964, and 35 percent of the classes of 1965 to 1969.[55]

Ironically, for all the fuss positively or negatively, plebe indoctrination's challenges probably remained similar. Unfortunately, alumni—officers and upperclassmen—often failed to see it that way. Survey participants were asked a question about which parts of their background prepared them best for the academy. In a roundabout way, their answers confirmed time management's importance to plebe year success. Nearly 38 percent of the classes of 1965 to 1969 and over 47 percent from the classes of 1970 to 1976 ranked competitive sports as the most essential part of their background. Conversely, midshipmen from the classes of 1946 to 1949, 1950 to 1954, and 1955 to 1959 valued a broad academic background the most by a margin of 37, 33, and 38 percent respectively. Why was past involvement with competitive sports so important during the "academic revolution?" Conversely, why was a broad academic background so valuable before it?[56]

Both groups worked under hectic schedules where time was a precious commodity. Shaving the schedule in areas of known strength put additional minutes in the day. The Naval Academy recruited midshipmen with higher academic credentials during the "academic revolution." These midshipmen were confident of their scholastic abilities but perhaps not as sure of themselves in other areas. Not that academics were not a challenge but military and physical requirements were what truly tested them. Thus, past experience in competitive sports was seen as a major advantage. Conversely, earlier midshipmen may not have had as good an academic background. But many of them had military experience or were at least familiar with the military culture. They felt confident about Bancroft Hall but the classroom was more intimidating. Both groups were responding to different hurdles but in a similar way, through organization and time management. In other words, plebe year was teaching similar skills, albeit in different ways.[57]

Yet, even at this early stage, the new curriculum was forcing significant changes to the institutional culture, none of which was more important than the question of honorable academic behavior. The new honor system was created to curb the worst abuses of the dope system. However, the dividing line between academic integrity and classmate loyalty was still difficult to resolve. High standards were expected in both areas although there was potential for conflict or confusion. Midshipmen protected one another in all cases but the classroom. Even there, cooperation was natural so long as it did not infringe on academic integrity. The major question was where healthy cooperation began and ended. Better students naturally assisted those having difficulty. Midshipmen also shared information about quizzes and exams. But when did this become unethical? The question was difficult to answer but imperative to a healthy academic culture.[58]

Just as with plebe indoctrination, the academy understood midshipmen did not necessarily come to the right answers alone. Although it insisted its students were naturally honorable, they occasionally had trouble distinguishing the subtleties of correct academic behavior. At the very least, proper scholastic conduct had to be clarified within the new academic environment. The task was certainly more difficult than the institution imagined. It struggled to define the limits of appropriate behavior within a wide range of scenarios. The goal was easy to picture but the method for getting there was not. As such, the academy tolerated a system with many loopholes. The best it could do was to lay the foundation for proper behavior and trust midshipmen would follow it.[59]

The new academic culture emphasized a mixture of values, which were sometimes contradictory. For example, academic freedom was an important principle that was difficult to put into practice. Midshipmen should feel free to talk with one another about their classes. The overarching goal was a healthy intellectual climate in which everyone benefited from the exchange of ideas. However, it was not license for swapping specific information on quizzes and exams. Much of the burden of maintaining academic integrity rested with the faculty. If they did not alter exam questions, midshipmen were naturally going to share that information with classmates. Thus, the dope system was difficult to eliminate entirely. Midshipmen could not be prohibited from communicating about their classes. Even if they could, it would have been detrimental to an open academic environment.[60]

The academy labored long and hard to create a middle ground. Midshipmen were warned about taking things too far. Classmates only hurt themselves by sharing too much information. It emphasized the importance of academic rank to their career options after graduation. Midshipmen who gave out exam answers were only placing themselves at a disadvantage. Furthermore, anyone pumping his friends for answers had overstretched the boundaries of classmate loyalty. Everyone was expected to do his own work; performance standards would not be any different in the fleet. However, the new academic climate's success depended on midshipmen using good judgment. Not surprisingly, some midshipmen abused their freedom. The worst episodes resulted in honor scandals, which tarnished the academy's reputation and cast doubt on the honor system's validity.[61]

At the time, the most controversial change to the military culture was the decision to eliminate marching to classes. Today, this decision might seem relatively insignificant. However, under the lockstep curriculum, the company was the focal point of academic life as well as Bancroft Hall. Midshipmen marched to classes in sections with company classmates. The curriculum was the same for everyone regardless of experience or ability. Although it was extremely inflexible, the lockstep curriculum was a vital part of the "unity of suffering" experience so critical to the midshipmen's professional socialization.[62]

Electives made the standard company section obsolete. With each passing year, fewer midshipmen were sharing anything close to a common schedule. Indeed, many courses contained students from all four classes. Admiral Davidson and his staff decided the time had come to allow midshipmen to straggle to class. Once again, the academy was looking for ways to save time. Section leaders were waiting for stragglers on the opposite side of Bancroft Hall before leaving for class. Students had to be dropped off at different locations, delaying the section's arrival even more. The extra fifteen minutes or so it took to form sections was a waste of time that could be better spent elsewhere.[63]

Many alumni fumed about Davidson's decision. The tradition had value beyond getting people to class. They worried about the effect of its discontinuance on military discipline. The decision symbolized the further erosion of traditional military values, largely because of the new curriculum. Marching to class reinforced unit cohesion. Midshipmen were not civilian students; everything had to be placed in a larger professional context. The primary objective of the academic program was scholastic, but it was also useful in character building. The decision to stop marching was another step away from that emphasis.[64]

However, the tradition's true value had to be separated from nostalgia. Older classes may have marched to class, but most resented it. The benefits to professional socialization, in other words, were achieved largely through negative means. Officers generated numerous conduct reports in this area. Midshipmen were put on report for talking in ranks, being out of step, or wearing their uniform improperly. Few midshipmen escaped some breach of misconduct. If academics were truly the priority, students should have been focusing on the classroom not Bancroft Hall. In retrospect, alumni may have considered marching to class invaluable, while at the academy, many saw it as nuisance they would have preferred to avoid.[65]

Critics made a valid point; they were just slightly off target in their emphasis. The crucial element being lost was not marching but time spent with the company. Over 84 percent of midshipmen ranked company classmates most important, the *lowest* percentage of any survey cohort was 82 percent. Nearly 39 percent of midshipmen ranked their company third in terms of their strongest relationships, just behind their classmates in general. Virtually every moment of a midshipman's day was spent with the company. Under the lockstep curriculum, the academic curriculum was also completed together. Bancroft Hall's activities—plebe indoctrination, the color company competition, the intramural sports program—were primarily done at the company level. Companies shared their meals family-style in the mess hall. They often went on liberty together and visited one another's home on leave.[66]

Indeed, company members' families grew close to one another during their sons' time at Annapolis. Families first met at academy-sponsored events, which became the springboard for nonofficial activities—post-game tailgate parties, Christmas and other holiday celebrations—that continued until graduation. Families who lived nearer to Annapolis routinely adopted the midshipmen who did not get home regularly. Not surprisingly then, graduation was often a group celebration. Classmates had pulled one another through all kinds of struggles to reach this ultimate goal. Given that companies did so much together, it is somewhat surprising these numbers were not higher. However, company relationships were not necessarily positive, especially with regard to plebe indoctrination. Substandard performers were harassed more in their company than they were anywhere else.[67]

The new curriculum weakened this company culture. Unlike before, large chunks of the day were now spent away from the company. Yet much more was being lost besides time. Electives brought together students with similar academic interests instead of an organizational tie. Their career pursuits were similar; these midshipmen would often study together, sometimes outside the company. These relationships would not have existed at all without the new curriculum. Eventually these relationships would become as or more important to some midshipmen. Those who did not get along with their companies also found a welcome break in the classroom. Company classmates could no longer protect one another in the classroom by maximizing the curve. The "slash" was such a hateful stereotype because his high grades came at the expense of his company. The academic program was becoming a matter of individual effort, not collective survival.[68]

Companies would certainly be important after the "academic revolution," but their influence was essentially limited to Bancroft Hall. Outside of it, midshipmen could function more independently and anonymously than before. Over time, future midshipmen would not even be aware of what was lost. They only knew the midshipmen culture that survived the "academic revolution." Since companies were still the backbone of Bancroft Hall, nothing on the surface had apparently changed, no matter what older alumni insisted. The diffusion of the old company culture was significant, however, even though the differences were slight. No longer was it as dominant as it had been in the past.

To some degree, the academy recognized the new curriculum's effect on the midshipmen culture and looked for other ways of instilling unit cohesion. As of 1959, all plebes participated in a common swearing-in ceremony their first day at Annapolis. In earlier years, the oath of office was administered more haphazardly, with plebes reporting at different times in the summer. No one was all that concerned; classmates generally became acquainted without forcing the issue. However, class sizes were much smaller before World War II. At the very least, the common academic program provided plenty of time for professional socialization to occur. The postwar expansion made it difficult to take this for granted. The new curriculum complicated matters even further. The academy consciously began working at class unity; the common swearing-in ceremony is one good example and the climbing of Herndon Monument at the end of plebe year is another.[69]

The Nuclear Navy and the Academy

The Navy's dependency on advanced technology ensured that the new curriculum was permanent. If anything, it needed to be more flexible to change, not less. Whatever the impact to training, academics had to assume a greater priority. No better evidence of this focus was the decision to concentrate core professional objectives into the summer. Academic and training goals never reached a division as distinct as Admiral Rickover would have liked. Nonetheless, the academic year focused more exclusively on the classroom.[70]

The new curriculum raised disturbing implications about the nature of officership. For generations, American naval officers had prided themselves on being jacks-of-all-trades professionally. Unlike their British counterparts, they were not experts in any single area but had a general understanding of how warships operated at sea. Academy graduates were qualified to perform a wide range of duties as fleet division officers. They had the seamanship and tactical skills to be competent officers of the deck, the technical expertise to stand basic engineering watches and enough weapons system theory to be capable gunnery officers. The Navy wanted its officers versatile, with a wide range of experiences before reaching command. Nothing prepared an officer for command than tours scattered throughout the functional areas of a ship. Without that broad-based experience, a captain would not be prepared for the contingencies that could arise while fighting his ship.[71]

In some ways, the "academic revolution" insinuated that the days of the general line officer were over. A controversial article in the June 1959 issue of *Proceedings* entitled "Is the Versatile Line Officer Obsolete?" suggested as much about the recent reforms. Its author, Captain William Brinckloe '37, had been an engineering specialist throughout much of his naval career; most recently, he had headed the marine engineering department and been secretary of the Academic Board during the Folsom review. Brinckloe had written the article to test the waters for the new curriculum and to pacify alumni concerns about the new direction. The article's tone was meant to reassure alumni that the academy's emphasis remained unchanged. Instead, it caused uproar throughout the officer corps, who feared what increased specialization might mean for their careers.[72]

Specialization was a dirty word for American naval officers, the very opposite of their professional traditions. It implied a narrowness of focus they believed was hazardous to the best principles of command at sea. It also suggested a lack of well roundedness, which contradicted the academy's overall mission. Annapolis prepared its graduates morally, mentally, and physically for the demands of officership. Now it seemed the program was being skewed too far in one direction. Most disturbing, the report seemed to indicate that naval warfare's dimensions had grown beyond an individual's ability to master. It was simply not possible for officers to be competent in everything the modern Navy required; some specialization was necessary, preferably early in an officer's career.[73]

Many officers agreed that the breadth of information was beyond the reach of formal education, especially since the academy's four-year time limit was untouchable. They insisted, however, that officers could still learn enough through on-the-job training. Either way, the consequences were severe for what it implied about the profession's future. If this assessment were true, it threw its whole conception of leadership asunder. The

Navy had long taught that command responsibility could not be delegated; commanding officers were accountable for everything. That level of responsibility was reasonable if officers could learn their command. If technology's growth no longer made that possible, command responsibility was a roll of the dice. The alternative was a diluted structure of compartmentalized leadership, which held officers responsible for the areas that they knew. No commanding officer could be master of his domain like ship's captains in the past. The academy's challenge was to incorporate the virtues of both specialization and versatility. The electives program filled the gaps created by technological advances, areas of specialty midshipmen would not hold in common. Yet it also had to provide a solid core education, the fundamentals of naval service whatever they may be, to all graduates.[74]

Many current midshipmen welcomed the opportunities provided by military specialization. This trend was first seen with the tremendous interest in naval aviation. During the aviation heyday of the 1950s, midshipmen bolted the Navy for the Air Force because of the Navy's insistence on sending all graduates first to sea. The mass exodus eventually caused the academy to eliminate that requirement but just for naval aviation only. It hesitated to deviate from its longstanding mission of producing line officers; virtually all of its educational and training requirements continued to reflect that philosophical orientation. Midshipmen hoping for alternative careers were expressing reservations about the value of Navy-specific training. Despite such pressures, the core program remained intact. Command at sea was what most graduates eventually aspired to do and the core curriculum was sufficient to meet this primary career goal.

Military specialization made it increasingly difficult to tailor the curriculum to the specific requirements of any warfare specialty. But the question of where to draw the line was difficult to resolve. The academy did not have the resources or more importantly the time to cater to every specific need. Nowhere was this predicament better seen than in its efforts to satisfy the nuclear power program and its controversial head, Admiral Hyman Rickover. Annapolis began offering submarine cruises as a training option in the mid 1950s but did not yet allow midshipmen to enter that program directly.[75] Graduates interested in submarines completed a mandatory division officer tour first before their transfer. Although interest in navy air had not waned, the submarine program's star was also on the rise, thanks to a new mode of propulsion and operational mission, both dependent on nuclear energy.

By the early 1960s if not earlier, strategic nuclear deterrence had become the military's most vital mission. Armed services that had expertise in this area had an advantage over their rivals in terms of budget dollars and service prestige. The Navy attempted to meet this mission requirement in the 1950s with its carrier attack force, which could theoretically launch nuclear strikes into the enemy heartland. Although it got the job done, the payload carried by carrier-launched aircraft was not as great as the Air Force's land-based bombers. Furthermore, to accomplish this mission, the Navy had to position carriers within dangerous range of the enemy's coastline, which also raised nagging questions about their survivability. A submarine-launched nuclear deterrent was another matter entirely. At this time, the Navy was also working on guided missiles whose payload size was devastatingly close to that carried by the Air Force. Moreover, the submarine was a weapons platform that had intrinsic advantages over land-based missile systems or intercontinental bombers. Submarines could approach and strike their targets without warning, which gave them a survivability the Air Force's platforms could not match.[76]

By the early 1960s, this mission capability had become reality with the Polaris program, which restored the Navy's bragging rights over the Air Force. Along with this, the Navy invested much effort equipping its submarines with nuclear propulsion. Instead of steam boilers or diesel batteries, nuclear reactors were the prime mover in a modern submarine's engineering plant. Nuclear propulsion had tremendous tactical advantages over conventional engineering plants. The energy generated by a nuclear reactor was virtually limitless; the fuel core could last for years depending on operational requirements and was only replaced at major overhauls. The operational radius of nuclear submarines was essentially unrestricted, the only limits being the supply requirements for its crew. Nuclear technology also made American boats much quieter than the Soviets'. With fewer moving parts than a steam-driven plant, it had an inherent noise advantage over conventional submarines, unless they were operating on batteries, which in turn limited their endurance.[77]

The difficulty in building a fleet of nuclear-powered submarines was significant but not insurmountable. The power plant was not cheap; indeed, peculiar size and operating restrictions made the Navy's reactors much more expensive than those designed for civilian applications. Nuclear-powered submarines also demanded a highly technically qualified crew to operate and maintain them. All the officers and most of the crew had to be at a minimum qualified reactor plant operators; better still for the submarine's safe operation if at least some onboard, preferably officers, had a knowledge of design and systems fundamentals.[78]

Financial limitations were the least difficult of the Navy's problems to solve, especially after Sputnik frightened Americans about their technological superiority. If the Navy's answer kept the country safe, the nation could certainly find the money for its needs. Finding the manpower resources was the more difficult problem the Navy's nuclear program had to

3: THE EARLY YEARS OF THE "ACADEMIC REVOLUTION" 133

answer. Admiral Hyman Rickover filled this void and with it resurrected his career. Rickover was a savior in the eyes of his supporters; his nuclear power program had single-handedly solidified the nation's security at a most desperate hour.[79]

The admiral used his influence to rule the nuclear power program with an iron fist; design requirements and personnel decisions were all funneled for approval through his office. Indeed, all officer applicants had to weather a personal interview with him. Given his intense dissatisfaction with the academy, its graduates often had more trouble convincing him why they should be accepted. Admiral Rickover used his perch atop nuclear power to speak out on any number of issues, including the Naval Academy's curriculum. If the admiral truly had his way, the entirety of its program would have been shaped to the nuclear navy's needs. Versatility in the curriculum, along with the majority of Bancroft Hall's activities, would have taken a backseat to what the Navy needed most, well-qualified engineers.[80] The new program of validation and electives was certainly a start in that direction, with deeper changes certainly to follow. The academy even began operating its own reactor yet further evidence of the growing weight of nuclear power.[81]

At the very least, Admiral Rickover wanted his hands on the most technically capable midshipmen, preferably before the fleet had a chance to ruin them. The growing importance of nuclear power, along with his acerbic personality, gave rise to persistent rumors about drafting midshipmen if there were insufficient volunteers. Few midshipmen were ever directly forced into nuclear power.[82] Whether midshipmen were ever subjected to more indirect coercion was a matter of debate. Nuclear power school was first made an option for the class of 1960; volunteers began an extensive six-month course in advanced mathematics, nuclear physics, and reactor engineering immediately after graduation. Formal coursework was followed by six months of practical training, with students standing watches under instruction at a shore-based reactor facility. Only after this stage of the program did nuclear-trained officers receive conventional military training in surface ships or submarines.[83]

The first volunteers had many words of advice for their shipmates about surviving the program. Not only was the curriculum technically demanding, the workload was unusually intense, requiring numerous hours of outside study to be successful. The first trainees warned interested midshipmen to improve their study skills at Annapolis; rote memorization was not sufficient to pass the advanced course at Vallejo. Prospective candidates were also encouraged to take as many electives as possible, both to expose them to higher-level course work and to condition them to work in a fast paced, concentrated academic environment. Above all, midshipmen had to realize that this program was not the academy; the same study habits that got them through Annapolis were not sufficient for the academic demands of nuclear power.[84]

Although the demands were great, nuclear power promised interesting rewards in return, at least to the caliber of students it wanted. The warning that nuclear power was not the academy was correctly intended to scare away the faint of heart. To properly motivated candidates, the same message could be an incredibly powerful attraction. Many talented midshipmen were looking for an academic challenge like nuclear power. The concentrated study environment, free from other distractions, could be a breath of fresh air compared to the academy. Nuclear trainees' sole focus was their studies—no administrative watches, no plebe indoctrination, no exercises in school spirit—nothing but academics mattered. They were still naval officers, but unlike at the academy, their studies came first. Nuclear power held out incentives the other warfare communities could not match either. It offered the quickest route to command. Only midshipmen going nuclear power could choose submarines directly; all others had to complete their fleet tours first. Eventually submarines would be restricted to officers who were nuclear trained. With a fleet of nuclear boats, the Navy did not need officers who did not have the training. Although the initial years were hard, trainees completed their engineering qualifications, the most important prerequisites to a submarine command, as rapidly as possible.[85]

The message sent by Admiral Rickover and his staff was that the nuclear community took care of its own. The program had high expectations, but it gave tangible benefits in return. Contrary to preexisting fears, the training pipeline was not a conduit to a career in specialized engineering duty. Trainees were still line officers preparing for careers that culminated in command at sea. Their specialized engineering duty was necessary to that end, and it was an experience their contemporaries would not have on their resumes. The program also worked at calming fears that nuclear-trained officers would be forced into duty aboard nuclear surface ships, primarily aircraft carriers where aviators had the inside track to command. The submarine community was growing rapidly enough that interested volunteers could be more than assured of getting that duty.[86]

Despite the hard work and heavy expectations, growing numbers of midshipmen were willing to sign up for nuclear power. The initial group, the class of 1960, had forty-three volunteers; during the second year, those numbers grew to seventy-four in the class of 1961; the third year of the program saw another increase to one hundred in the class of 1962.[87] The effect of nuclear power's popularity on Bancroft Hall's military culture was astounding. Over the next five to seven years, the numbers of midshipmen going nuclear power would swell to a total rivaling that of naval aviation and surface line. Moreover, nuclear power could truly claim that its exclusive screening process gave it the best and brightest of the Brigade. Like naval aviation in the 1940s and the Air Force in the 1950s, it organized an effective recruiting force of company and battalion officers inside Bancroft Hall. Lectures and films portrayed nuclear power as the Navy's cutting edge branch.[88]

However, the effect of nuclear power went beyond the sheer numbers in the program. The goals of nuclear power certainly reinforced the recent academic changes. Midshipmen understood their selection depended upon academic performance, not anything they did in Bancroft Hall. Simply getting by may have been good enough for Annapolis but not for Admiral Rickover and nuclear power. Midshipmen qualified by demonstrating their academic abilities, which coincidentally the new curriculum allowed them to show.

To some extent, nuclear power also swung the debate on naval officership in favor of specialization. Nuclear qualified officers were still line officers, but they were part of an elite branch nonetheless. Submarines or naval aviation had always signified a special status but not to the detriment of the line community, the traditional bread and butter of the naval service. That sense of elitism would grow as nuclear power became more important. By the end of the 1960s, only those who could not do anything else went Navy line, a telling statement to versatility's demise as a principle of officership. Both of these elite branches also required extensive, specialized training after the academy. The core program at Annapolis was still an important formative experience, both professionally and socially, but not above the training or the relationships these officers developed afterwards.[89]

By the end of 1962, the "academic revolution" was clearly underway, even though its effect on the academy's everyday routine was barely noticeable. The new program of validation and electives was a striking departure from the lockstep curriculum, despite needing time to develop. The growing numbers of midshipmen participating in the new curriculum would eventually create a new academic culture. For the time being, the most visible aspect of the new curriculum was the elimination of the company section and marching to class. Even here, roots of long-term change were developing to the detriment of the old company culture. The growing power and needs of the nuclear power program would help make the recent changes permanent. For better or worse, the "academic revolution" was at Annapolis to stay.

4
The "Academic Revolution" Triumphant, 1962–65:
Further Gains and Controversy for the New Academy

THE NEXT PHASE OF THE "ACADEMIC REVOLUTION," THE PERIOD FROM 1962 to 1965, would be equally significant and just as controversial in transforming Annapolis. The academy began experimenting with the academic program again in late 1962, just a short time after ending the lockstep curriculum. The new reforms were not a radical offshoot in another direction but the logical extension of what had already been done. The overarching goal of the "academic revolution" continued to be improving the academy's academic reputation. Like before, the stimulus for change would come, at least partially, from outside the school. If it had not been willing to go forward, its superiors would have ordered the changes. The Folsom Board's recommendations gave plenty of ammunition for further reform, many members of which were urging additional action. Admiral Rickover also continued to lurk in the shadows; his yearly visits were an unpleasant reminder of his unhappiness with Annapolis.[1]

At the same time, other critics, particularly dissatisfied alumni, fumed that too much had been done already. How did the reforms contribute to the academy's primary mission of producing combat officers? Annapolis was not a civilian college, nor should it attempt to be. The newfound emphasis came at the expense of military discipline. Both groups would remain disappointed with the "academic revolution."[2] The academy tried the best it could to straddle a middle ground. Its leaders argued that they had only made changes that enhanced its ability to produce career officers. The direction of higher education and the Navy's latest technological advances made the reforms necessary.[3] To be fair, the academy came closer to satisfying educational reformers and Admiral Rickover than it did traditionalists. The new Naval Academy was a far cry from the "trade school," both in its priorities and the institutional culture it nourished. How much different was open to debate however.[4]

4: THE "ACADEMIC REVOLUTION" TRIUMPHANT, 1962–65

The most tangible changes were those made to the school's academic infrastructure. The Navy finally implemented an assignment process to ensure military instructors were academically qualified. It was not a dumping ground for officers needing a shore billet. More civilians were hired to teach the expanded course load. Unlike earlier faculty, however, most of them lacked previous military experience. Annapolis also appointed its first academic dean, a civilian educator hired temporarily at first and later made permanent. Over time, he suggested additional curriculum changes, which solidified the "academic revolution."[5] The academy also switched to a traditional, civilian letter grade system. The change was felt to be a more realistic appraisal of midshipmen's academic progress and a way of helping their admission to graduate school.[6] The penalties for unsatisfactory academic performance became more severe. It became easier for the academy to take corrective action, either in terms of additional study requirements or eventual dismissal from Annapolis. The newer grading system also created a more competitive academic environment. Midshipmen could no longer depend on an end-of-semester curve. Academic performance, in other words, became more an individual and not a collective responsibility.[7]

Annapolis also kept busy reforming Bancroft Hall; small changes at first but ultimately they would be as or more important to the institutional culture. Some traditional activities were dropped entirely; others it continued but limited to outside the academic year. The crowded curriculum, with its higher standards, made time a more precious commodity than ever before.[8] Further limits were placed on plebe indoctrination in an effort to eliminate unauthorized activities. The academy also attempted to hold upperclassmen more accountable for their plebes. Despite the efforts, Bancroft Hall's culture would bend only so much to the new priorities. Upperclassmen and company officers occasionally took matters into their own hands, sometimes in defiance of regulations. It took time for midshipmen trained under the new system to rise to positions of responsibility. Only by hammering at new priorities repeatedly would it remold the culture of Bancroft Hall.[9]

The greatest problem continued to be the sharp increase in voluntary resignations, primarily among plebes. The brunt of new academic standards fell upon plebes first, with each class matriculating under a slightly different program. Although they were meeting academic standards, these plebes had chosen to leave because of difficulty reconciling the heavier academic expectations with Bancroft Hall.[10] Reformers used these statistics to challenge plebe indoctrination. Never were the battle lines sharper than over this controversy. The academy and alumni insisted that the plebe system was vital to its mission. Individual losses were regrettable but to be expected. Opponents countered that the new curriculum made a thorough overhaul unavoidable; some called for abolishing it altogether, if the "academic revolution" was to survive. At the very least, the controversy over the plebe system divided the academy at a crucial time when it needed to work together.[11]

The Middle States Association returned in 1966, in retrospect the midway point of the "academic revolution." Given all the recent activity, the inspection was a convenient time for reflection. Its results were crucial in determining the extent to which the "academic revolution" would continue. Evaluators commended the academy for the speed and breadth of its reforms. Most believed that academic excellence was now one of its chief institutional goals. However, for all its accomplishments, the team could not help but notice a growing schism between officers and civilians. Since many were also civilian educators, they understood how civilians could feel like outsiders. Annapolis respected their academic qualifications, but that did not translate to a willingness to involve them in its direction. On paper, the achievements of the "academic revolution" were impressive but it had not resolved the nagging dichotomy within its institutional culture. Until Athens and Sparta reached a meaningful coexistence, it would never be free from this kind of turmoil.[12]

The Korth Directive, a New Faculty, and a Civilian Academic Dean

As always, the task of expanding the "academic revolution" fell upon new leaders, both at the academy and higher up the chain of command. Looking back at this period, the 1966 Middle States report highlighted the chronic turnover in leadership as one of the academy's more significant problems, especially with many new programs in full swing. It urged the Navy to lengthen tours of duty, from the superintendent on down to the company officers. Without continuity in leadership, the academy would be challenged to sustain these reforms. Nowhere was this problem more evident than with the crisis over the appointment of the academic dean in late 1962. Although everyone was eventually satisfied with the results, the existing leadership temporarily made problems worse rather than better. A more seasoned group of leaders, accustomed to working with one another, might have settled the crisis more peacefully without all the resultant controversy.[13]

The Navy had tossed around the idea of expanded civilian influence for years, but it had never gone beyond being a topic for further discussion. Admiral Rickover and his cronies took the matter more seriously however; they viewed greater numbers of civilian educators as the key to the success of the "academic revolution." For far too long, the academy had used military instructors without graduate degrees. The Navy promised on numerous occasions to correct the problem, but its efforts were haphazard at best. Operational matters or something else always intervened; many admirals continued to believe that fleet duty was a suitable substitute for graduate school. Without this crucial first step, reformers believed Annapolis was doomed to a mediocre academic reputation. If this was the case and nothing was to be done about it, Rickover admonished Congress to consider abolishing Annapolis if not all the service academies altogether.[14]

Beyond his congressional supporters, Rickover's ideas had gained the attention of a new secretary of the Navy, Fred Korth. Korth saw a dangerous pattern in the comments about the academy faculty; everyone who had studied the issue—Rickover, most inspection teams, et al.—had noticed the same problem. Most disturbing, despite all the warnings and recommendations, the Navy had done precious little towards improving the situation. In a shocking and in some ways arguably premature announcement in May 1962, the secretary demonstrated that he would take action if the academy or the Navy would not. Over the next several years, entrance requirements were to be raised "to the maximum practicable extent." He also ordered all military instructors to be replaced with civilians; the sole exception were those in naval science courses. Finally, an academic dean would be appointed, a civilian educator responsible for overseeing the "academic revolution."[15]

The academy felt blindsided by this announcement, believing it was done to gain political attention as much to prompt it into action. The burden of following these orders fell to a new superintendent, Admiral Charles Kirkpatrick who had relieved Admiral Davidson in August 1962. The relationship between Kirkpatrick and Korth could not have started on rockier terms, with both men new to command and having a huge crisis before them. Kirkpatrick, a career submariner, had recently served as head of the Pacific Fleet's training command; earlier in his career, he had been part of the Executive Department. As such, he was not opposed to reform and in fact had significant ideas for expanding the "academic revolution." For the time being, all other priorities were postponed until this issue was resolved. Korth placed the superintendent in an awkward position. Rickover and his supporters were very happy with his decision; most officers at Annapolis, as well as alumni, were outraged by it. Regardless of his own feelings, Kirkpatrick did not want his legacy to be the turncoat alumnus who overturned the military foundations of the Naval Academy.[16]

The furor over the faculty and a civilian academic dean ignited a wave of protest from traditionalists, the largest of the "academic revolution." Opponents of the Korth directive could not help but see the proposed changes as being sudden and above all rash. His actions were not seen as a way of upgrading academic standards. Instead, they were viewed as an uninformed attempt at "civilianizing" the academy. It did not matter if the substance of these ideas were around for a while. The secretary apparently did not understand or care how long difficult transitions took at the Naval Academy. And when change did come, it usually did not take the extreme form that Secretary Korth wanted.[17]

Korth's opponents were quick to cite an extensive article by Hanson Baldwin, an Annapolis graduate and noted military columnist for the *New York Times*, about the controversy. As president of the alumni association, he fired back a strongly worded protest about the intended reforms. Not knowing much about the secretary himself, Baldwin painted Korth as falling too much under Admiral Rickover's influence, the most extreme of the academy's critics. Korth's directive literally regurgitated changes Rickover had been advocating for some time. The secretary probably did not understand, however, how exceptional Rickover was among academy alumni. Rickover's midshipman experiences had gone badly; he had not associated much with his classmates. While some of his comments had merit, their tone was often vindictive, the goal being to punish his alma mater.[18]

The greatest reason for keeping military instructors was their value to professional socialization. Secretary Korth did not appreciate the unique attributes of Annapolis jeopardized by his proposals. If implemented, midshipmen would not have an officer instructor until their junior year. The value of Annapolis had always been more than the education; the experience motivated midshipmen towards a naval career. Supporters were quick to point out the vast difference in retention rates between its officers and NROTC. While many NROTC officers had as good or superior an education, their retention rate was horrible. The Naval Academy did something special to motivate midshipmen towards lifetime service and their relationships with fleet officers were critical to their professional development. Perhaps Hanson Baldwin summed up the dangers of the Korth reforms best: "The training, the indoctrination, the tradition, the continuity with past and future, the sense of obligation, the responsibilities of leadership, the demands of honor are more important, by far, to the officer of tomorrow than an understanding of nuclear physics."[19]

Korth's opponents insisted that they were not against higher academic standards. But certainly the Navy could find a better way of doing it? They pointed to the diverse backgrounds of alumni, both active and retired, as a possible source of qualified faculty. The academy should not have to look outside its own circle for competent instructors; the right combination of experience and education could be found internally. Even here, however, defenders of the old academy had not quite understood what reformers wanted. They were making a similar assumption as BUPERS that experience and education had comparative value. Other proposals gradually recognized the importance of formal education in improving the caliber of the faculty. Perhaps the academy could establish a permanent cadre of its best officer instructors, similar to the other service academies but clearly a break from its past rotation policy. At the very least, the urgency of the Korth crisis stimulated greater discussion, even if the goal was to maintain as much of the existing system as possible.[20]

Not only did the Korth initiative weaken the professional fiber of Annapolis, its proponents could not even guarantee that it would work. Critics invoked the objections of noted military sociologist, Samuel Huntington, to raise another red flag towards the changes. Professor Huntington agreed with their concerns about the deleterious effect on the Naval Academy's military responsibilities, but he also warned about possible adverse consequences academically. The solution to incompetent military instructors was not necessarily found in greater numbers of civilians. First off, given the prevailing suspicion of many academics towards the "military mind," Huntington was skeptical that a service academy would ever attract many first-rate civilian teachers anyway. It might be better to try to improve officers' qualifications than to depend on a group that might never come to Annapolis.[21]

Huntington also worried about the effect of these changes on the academic culture. Many midshipmen were already biased towards the technical and professional courses that were the traditional backbone of the curriculum. If a related goal of the "academic revolution" was to stimulate broadened academic interests, the Korth reforms might actually produce the opposite effect. By limiting "academic" subjects to civilian instructors and "military" ones to naval officers, the institution was reinforcing existing stereotypes towards academics rather than mitigating them. The skepticism with which midshipmen viewed the humanities, for example, was well known, courses they often referred to as "bull." A more balanced faculty, or one in which qualified naval officers taught traditional academic subjects, would reinforce the universal importance of all courses in the curriculum.[22]

In defending his actions, Secretary Korth showed himself to be a more astute observer of the academy and its problems than his critics probably expected. He reiterated to alumni the ample evidence—the Folsom review, the Moreell investigation, and Board of Visitors reports—documenting the problem. The Navy and Annapolis had known about it for years; it was not just a personal whim he wanted corrected. Korth understood their concerns about civilians but did not see another way that precluded using them. Unlike the other service academies, the Navy's operational tempo made it difficult to lengthen the tours of duty for officer instructors. Furthermore, extended time away from seagoing billets hindered their chances at promotion. Naval aviators should be spending the bulk of their time flying, the same with line officers at sea, not tied to the classroom. This was certainly not the way of getting better officers to volunteer for Annapolis.[23]

The other service academies had more military instructors, but they constituted, in his opinion, nothing more than "a professional teaching corps." These officers spent the bulk of their careers in teaching not operational billets. Of course they wore a uniform, but how much value did they bring to the cadets' professional socialization? The mentoring value of military faculty stemmed from their operational experiences, not their teaching abilities per se. Their lectures should contain practical applications to a military career. Even if it were possible to create permanent instructors out of its line communities, their motivational value would diminish over time as their experiences became less relevant to current fleet operations. And with all the recent technological advancements, who knows how sharp a decline that would be? Furthermore, it would be difficult to get top-notch volunteers for such duty because of the limited promotional opportunities, especially to flag rank.[24]

Clearly, both sides had compelling arguments for why the existing system should be preserved as well as abandoned. Afterwards, the compromise that resolved the crisis appears very obvious. Reformers got their civilian academic dean to oversee the "academic revolution." The academy persuaded Secretary Korth to back down from his original ultimatum after certain concessions. Its mixed faculty of officers and civilians would continue, albeit with more stringent qualifications of both groups, enough to keep the alumni from staging an open revolt. After all was said and done, the academy jumped on the reform bandwagon too, praising the faculty improvements as a logical extension of the "academic revolution." Any memories that these reforms had been born from such controversy were quickly forgotten. The happy ending to the crisis came as much from happenstance as anything the academy or its chain of command did to achieve it.[25]

Even within his original demands, Secretary Korth was not as iconoclastic as it might have first appeared. His original statement hinted at a possible loophole: "this policy would not preclude the future assignment of officers to the Naval Academy in those instances where such officers possess the educational and teaching qualifications to be required of civilian professors." It is unclear whether Korth would have followed through on his demands, but the threat was drastic enough to prompt the academy into action. Neither side fortunately had to call the other's bluff if that ever was the intention. Efforts at compromise also benefited from friends strategically located in the chain of command. The most important happened to be the chief of naval personnel, the former superintendent William Smedberg who enjoyed a solid working relationship with both Korth and the academy.[26]

The Korth directive triggered Smedberg into action, searching for officers of the academic caliber necessary to meet his exemption. Over the

4: THE "ACADEMIC REVOLUTION" TRIUMPHANT, 1962–65

next year, BUPERS assigned fifty new officers as instructors, all of whom had at least their master's degree, along with a promise to expand this group in the future. The commitment towards officers with advanced degrees would become the general rule in making faculty assignments over the next several years. The Navy also made it easier for officers to expand their education while at Annapolis; it provided a new system of tuition reimbursement for courses taken at local colleges and universities; it also made the laboratories of naval research facilities available for the faculty's use in completing their degrees. Fortunately for the academy, it knew the right person in the right job to make all of this happen.[27]

The academy was also fortunate in the timing of the crisis. Just a few years before, the Navy did not have a reservoir of officers with advanced degrees to send to Annapolis. Unfortunately, it fell short of developing a comprehensive system to guarantee quality replacements for this first group of officers. The Naval Academy pushed for the creation of the Faculty Education Program, which identified promising officers early in their careers and linked their graduate education to future assignment at Annapolis. To the Navy, this smacked too much of the "permanent teaching corps" it wished to avoid, and so the academy depended on more of an informal promise that it would receive qualified personnel. Annapolis had learned the hard way not to place too much faith in such guarantees however. What happened when Smedberg rotated to a different job or, more importantly, when operational requirements dictated that these officers be sent elsewhere? The Navy's pledge would soon be tested with the deepening crisis in Vietnam.[28]

The Naval Academy also began upgrading the civilian faculty, an effort made mostly out of necessity but one that conveniently kept wolves like Admiral Rickover at bay. The new curriculum had created large numbers of positions, more jobs than could be filled with just military officers. Between 1962 to 1965, another eighty-five civilians were added to the faculty, a mammoth increase since the previous total was 240. Annapolis also added new enticements, both scholastically and financially, to make teaching there more attractive to top candidates. Beyond access to Navy laboratories, it offered research-oriented incentives to prospective faculty. Civilians were reimbursed for tuition costs necessary to complete their degrees. Travel stipends and research grants were expanded to keep faculty current in their disciplines. These benefits did come with higher expectations. Future faculty would need to attend conferences and perform research, just like at other elite colleges and universities.[29]

Most growth was necessary to handle the electives program; however, the additional staff allowed greater flexibility in scheduling research sabbaticals. Administrative procedures were changed to give civilians access to the midshipmen bookstore, a common privilege at other schools. Professors could buy books and other materials there at considerable discount. New financial incentives were instituted to keep Annapolis competitive with other universities. Faculty contracts were restructured; salary schedules began to be based on a standard ten-month appointment, which guaranteed them a two-month break that could be used for research or vacation. Professors who taught extra courses received additional compensation beyond their normal salary. The academy also looked into a tuition-reimbursement package for their families. The underlying goal was to minimize the differences between Annapolis and other schools all to attract top candidates.[30]

The faculty improvements would be a source of great pride in the years to come, somewhat surprising considering the stout resistance to them in the first place. In nearly every official report, Annapolis pointed to the faculty's scholastic achievements and credentials as evidence that the "academic revolution" was successful. It also touted the scholarly record of its faculty in recruiting. Academically inclined candidates not only got the chance at fine career; they also received an excellent education. The newly acquired academic pedigree did not come without a price however. The immediate addition of so many new instructors, many of them recent civilian Ph.D.s, could not help but change the academy culture. Not only were the numbers significant, it was often their first teaching job.[31]

The rapid influx created a generational divide among the faculty that was difficult to bridge. The 1966 Middle States report divided them into three camps, each of which had different goals and expectations of what they wanted to accomplish. The greatest harmony was between the military instructors and the older civilian staff, those hired before the "academic revolution." Inspectors noticed the greatest friction with newer civilians; many of them were frustrated with the institution's academic climate and expected a greater similarity between Annapolis and the colleges they attended. They had difficulty reconciling the Naval Academy's institutional goals with how it affected their classrooms. It would be this group that would be at the forefront of future controversy.[32]

It was somewhat ironic that the greatest skepticism was directed at the appointment of a civilian academic dean. The fear was that the academy was placing too much power in a civilian's hands. What if the wrong man got the job, someone who did not understand the academy's unique mission? In the end, these fears could not have been more misplaced. Annapolis could not have found a better person to be its first academic dean. Indeed, much of the credit for making the faculty overhaul as smooth as possible had to go to its new dean. To underscore the magnitude of this appointment, the search was conducted at the highest decision-making levels within the Navy. The secretary of the Navy personally wrote letters to the presidents of all colleges and universities with NROTC units, asking for their recommendations on who was the best fit for the job.[33]

4: THE "ACADEMIC REVOLUTION" TRIUMPHANT, 1962–65   145

The academy's expectations were high. The questions asked of potential candidates were exhaustive. Not only was a first-rate academic reputation required, the Naval Academy also wanted someone who understood its fundamental priorities and unique history. It believed it found the right combination of both qualities in Dr. A. Bernard Drought, who was the head of Marquette University's engineering school. Drought had been to Annapolis before, both as a V-7 midshipman during World War II and as an academic consultant at the start of the "academic revolution." As such, he quickly became the leading candidate for the job once the decision was made to put a civilian into the position.[34]

Both the academy and Dean Drought were cautious in establishing the powers of his office, which helped smooth over the transition. Even though Annapolis was ordered to create his position, Dean Drought was initially hired on a temporary basis only. For the most part, the interim appointment was a formality to ensure the compatibility of both parties before making it permanent. By structuring the language of Drought's contract this way, time was created for the huge adjustment to take hold. A temporary dean was not likely to initiate massive changes or challenge the academy's military structure. No one in the academy hierarchy expected this to be the case with Drought, but a little reassurance could not hurt calming alumni fears. This solution relieved any expectations of Drought to lead the "academic revolution," at least right away. The academy was also vague in defining where the academic dean's office fell within its chain of command.[35]

Bernard Drought understood the controversial nature of his appointment and did his best not to disrupt the academy routine. In an interview with *The Log,* the new dean explained his job to midshipmen. Drought often described himself as simply an "academic advisor" to the superintendent. His mission, he said, was "to study the entire academic routine and make suggestions for improvement." Under no circumstances could anyone have interpreted his statements as menacing to academy traditions. Dean Drought was also circumspect about recommendations for improvement and his own future at Annapolis. For the moment, he advocated no other substantive changes, while reiterating his belief in the academy's military mission, the commitment to a mixed faculty of officers and civilians, and so forth.[36]

If his position became permanent, Drought would be only one of several important voices on the Academic Board. At no point was he claiming undue authority beyond what was necessary for helping the academy. Everyone on the staff, military and civilian, worked towards the same goal: to see the academy succeed in its traditional mission of producing naval officers. At the same time, he left no doubt as to why his job was best filled with a civilian educator and hinted at an expanded role in the future. First and foremost, a civilian dean would provide continuity to the school's academic life, something that all groups who had studied Annapolis believed was lacking. To ask a military department head to remain longer than was the case already would endanger his chances for promotion. Within these simple statements, an astute observer could see that the dean's voice would not be limited for long. Longevity in office would certainly increase the value of his opinions. And with that would come more power to decide important matters independently.[37]

In retrospect, it seems ironic that some of Dean Drought's sharpest critics were among the civilian faculty, particularly the younger hires, and the more radical proponents of the "academic revolution." In their minds, Drought was either overly cautious in urging new changes or too deferential to military authorities. These judgments seem too harsh on both counts. Drought was certainly no maverick when it came to further reform, but he was not the administration's toady either. Over time, the academy's first dean would sponsor other important changes, which furthered the goals of the "academic revolution," particularly the shift away from the course-heavy core program towards a more flexible curriculum that gave midshipmen a greater opportunity for academic majors.[38]

Drought recognized that the credibility to suggest such changes did not come immediately, especially to an institution with such longstanding suspicions of civilians. Although he was technically one of them, there were understandable limits to which Drought was willing to defend the civilian faculty. The military authorities running the academy had the right to discipline their faculty; academic freedom was not a license for gross insubordination, not only at Annapolis but at any college or university. If the dean was to convince the military that they were all part of the same team, he had to be careful not to play favorites, especially in cases that furthered existing stereotypes of civilians.[39]

Continued Efforts at Reforming Bancroft Hall

The resolution of the Korth controversy allowed the Naval Academy to turn its attention to other matters equally important to the "academic revolution." For example, the admissions process underwent further overhaul to attract the top caliber students critical to its success. The new "Blue and Gold" program was launched in 1963, as a means of promoting Annapolis and screening potential applicants from around the country. The test group of thirty-three volunteer reserve officers, representing every reserve district in the country, spent two weeks of active-duty training at Annapolis learning about its program and special admissions procedures. The crash course was also useful in erasing any personal doubts about the academy, which kept them from selling it with a full heart.[40]

4: THE "ACADEMIC REVOLUTION" TRIUMPHANT, 1962–65   147

Blue and Gold officers were expected to be solid representatives of both Annapolis and the Navy; the academy also preferred people with knowledge or influence helpful to the recruiting process. Not coincidentally, many officers were high school principals, guidance counselors, and even school district superintendents, people with special access to the candidate pool it desired. Blue and Gold officers gave numerous presentations, selling the virtues of Annapolis to top students. The larger portion of their job, however, was evaluating prospective candidates, particularly in their motivation for naval service. College Board scores and grade point averages were reliable indicators of candidates' academic ability, but there was not a perfect way of determining their professional potential. The Blue and Gold program provided another input into their ability to be good naval officers.[41]

Of more immediate importance to the institutional culture were substantial changes to Bancroft Hall's activities. The new academic programs may have been the most visible part of a modern Annapolis. However, the academy's success in reforming Bancroft Hall would ultimately mean as much or more to the "academic revolution." Besides his own experiences, Admiral Kirkpatrick was assisted in this area by an extremely able commandant, Captain Charles Minter. Both men were sensitive to academy traditions and believed strongly in them. The trick for them was preserving the essence of that military culture while adjusting it enough to allow the "academic revolution" to succeed.

Minter would soon be selected for flag rank himself; in fact, despite being so junior in grade, he was handpicked to relieve Kirkpatrick in January 1964. The biggest reason for this, especially since the superintendent's job was such a plum assignment, was continuity in command with the new curriculum and an ambitious building program both underway. Kirkpatrick implicitly trusted Minter's judgment in dealing with Bancroft Hall. It was helpful that Minter was the father of a midshipman during this tumultuous time. In other words, midshipmen could not have asked for a more sympathetic ear to their new challenges.[42]

The greatest stumbling block to institutional harmony had always been the lack of time in the crowded, four-year schedule. Academic and professional goals were bound to be in conflict because there did not seem to be enough time to accomplish both. Any shift in priorities inevitably took place at the expense of others, which were equally valid if time was not an issue. With the greater emphasis on academics and the four-year timetable unchanged, the biggest quandary was what to do with Bancroft Hall. Its activities had never compromised for the academic program before. The simplest solution was to force any necessary adjustments for the new curriculum, no matter what the cost to its activities.[43]

Although simple, that option was problematic for many reasons. Most

YES, I BELIEVE YOU'LL FEEL AT HOME IN THE EXECUTIVE DEPARTMENT...

The Log, **18 January 1963. Midshipmen continued to see many rules as "Mickey Mouse."**

senior officers, including Kirkpatrick and Minter, believed in Bancroft Hall's importance. The stress and intensity of professional indoctrination was what distinguished Annapolis from other commissioning programs. It was also what many believed had helped alumni win all of the country's wars. Numerous stories existed crediting the tough atmosphere inside Bancroft Hall for their success. From a more pragmatic standpoint, the acquiescence of Bancroft Hall's leadership—upperclassmen, company officers—was crucial for the new curriculum to succeed. If the academic culture was to ever free itself from past, anti-intellectual stereotypes, like the "slash" and "surviving by the dope," a majority of them would need to be supportive of the "academic revolution."[44]

A major factor prompting Kirkpatrick and Minter to take action was the sharp increase in voluntary resignations among plebes. Throughout its history, academy attrition rates had been high, but this kind of loss was particularly disturbing. All of the effort put into the admissions process was paying dividends in terms of better-qualified candidates. It seemed a waste to lose midshipmen who had the ability but not the motivation to continue. Some in this category had come to please their parents and found that to be an insufficient reason to stay. Others were not ready to be separated from families and friends at home. Many were shocked, to some degree, by the intense military environment, especially Bancroft Hall. Their resignation letters often mentioned balance as being a major problem. The academic load was heavier, but Bancroft Hall still demanded tremendous time.[45]

To get everything completed on time, academy leaders scrambled to make the system run as efficiently as possible. A major adjustment had already been made to accommodate the electives program. The greatest time crunch for midshipmen and especially plebes was during the traditional academic year. During the first phase of the "academic revolution," the academy had reshuffled many training objectives to the summer. Cruises would primarily be used for completing professional requirements. The traditional school year would hence be devoted primarily to academics. Annapolis hoped to do something similar with plebe indoctrination, by also shifting the bulk of its requirements to the summer.[46]

Kirkpatrick and Minter did not want to start rumors that they were weakening the traditional plebe year. Reforms in this area were bound to be controversial, but certain changes had to be done. By concentrating training requirements in the summer, plebes were much more likely to survive a toughened academic year. They were better prepared to fend off upperclassmen, at a time when difficult choices between pleasing Bancroft Hall and academics had to be made. The entire system of plebe rates was introduced in the summer, the encyclopedic knowledge plebes had to know verbatim—famous sayings of great naval leaders, tactical information on naval weapons systems, academy trivia. Plebes gained additional time to master this material before the Brigade returned in the fall. The academic year had become too busy for plebes to be fumbling over rates instead of studying.[47]

Greater numbers of upperclassmen were assigned to the summer training detail. Problem cases were identified sooner, giving greater time for remedial action or early dismissal from the academy. Plebe indoctrination was not being watered down, but it was administered more efficiently. Most importantly, plebes were henceforth organized into platoons, which were transferred intact into academic year companies. Previously, everyone was scattered at the end of the summer into new companies. A final important lesson of the new plebe system was an old one: no one successfully got through plebe year alone. Midshipmen had to depend on their roommates and classmates to be successful, just like the fleet. Classmate unity was just as important as it had always been.[48]

The real key, Minter believed, was greater supervision and accountability throughout Bancroft Hall. The greatest problems were not inherent to the system but when upperclassmen took matters into their own hands. Their natural tendency was to view their experiences as inordinately more difficult. Upperclassmen compensated for any perceived softening with arbitrary measures to toughen up plebes. The commandant rewrote the current instructions to give specific ground rules on what was tolerated. Professional reports could not be a wild-goose chase; topics were limited to research that could be done in Bancroft Hall. Plebe come-arounds were restricted to certain hours so as not to interfere with study hour. Officers were instructed to work with and encourage upperclassmen in plebe indoctrination's larger principles. True leaders did not perpetuate past mistakes for tradition's sake; they worked to make the system better for their subordinates.[49]

By no means should upperclassmen interpret these changes to mean that Annapolis was now coddling plebes. However, they needed to realize how much things had changed since their plebe year. The new curriculum demanded greater study time from everyone but especially plebes. The schedule had simply become too busy to continue traditions without a clear professional application. Minter also wanted officers limiting the various errands plebes traditionally performed for upperclassmen. Company officers were also expected to conduct routine inspections of their company areas during study hour. After evening meal, the Brigade's focus needed to be academics; any violations were to be severely punished.

A balanced schedule was extremely difficult to measure however. Minter and his officers were not naïve, but it was truly hard to tell whether plebes were being coddled or mistreated. Plebes were often like children playing one parent against the other. Many of them used Bancroft Hall as an excuse for not having homework completed or being unprepared for recitation. They blamed the classroom for not finishing upperclassmen's projects on time. Upperclassmen were also clever in circumventing the rules. Many simply found less explicit ways to harass plebes. Study hour was inviolate, but it was hard to monitor whether that time was used correctly. Class work could still take a backseat to shining shoes or preparing bulletin boards if that was what upperclassmen wanted. Although Minter's improvements were important, his control over Bancroft Hall was not absolute.[50]

To make matters even more difficult, ever since the late 1950s, the job of policing the midshipmen had fallen disproportionately on a smaller group of officers. In other words, the Brigade's organizational structure had not kept pace with the slow but steady expansion of recent years. The academy was still trying to cram a student body, which now numbered between four thousand and forty-five hundred midshipmen, into the same twenty-four companies. Company officers were supervising an average of 150 midshipmen, a number that the academy recognized was far from realistic. Officers essentially had time just for disciplining troublemakers or counseling stripers; the average midshipman often fell through the cracks. Both Kirkpatrick and Minter pleaded with the Navy to assign more officers; at a minimum, the Brigade should be expanded to thirty-six companies, which would cut down their managerial responsibilities to around one hundred midshipmen in each company.[51]

Approval was received for twelve additional officers in 1964, but it was another commitment from the Navy that would prove far more important in reforming Bancroft Hall. Like Admiral Holloway and other reformers since World War II, Kirkpatrick and Minter were still fighting the stigma most officers had towards academy duty. Many promotion boards continued to frown upon such service in an officer's record, which they considered frivolous compared to more challenging assignments at sea. As such, the academy was rarely assigned the best officers, at the company and battalion levels, and those it did get were not always motivated towards their jobs. Until it erased these negative perceptions, the Executive Department was doomed to uneven performance at best.[52]

Kirkpatrick and Minter repeatedly tried to educate their peers that the academy was a demanding assignment. Annapolis was not a country club where freeloaders came to relax; training and developing midshipmen was a challenge that required topnotch officers. They worked with BUPERS to ensure that selection boards were not just fair but took a positive eye towards academy duty. To some extent, these efforts did bear fruit. Whether they were truly lasting was another matter entirely. The Navy promised to send better officers and give the academy greater say-so before final assignments were made. Like before, these promises were only good so long as everyone agreed to their importance. The Navy's mobilization for Vietnam made it difficult to keep this stringent of a rotation policy in effect.[53]

Beyond the reforms to plebe indoctrination, the Naval Academy also reevaluated aspects of its daily routine, which hindered its efforts at creating a more positive academic environment. Pre–"academic revolution" midshipmen followed a very rigid schedule in both Bancroft Hall and the classroom. The typical day was hectic and long. Midshipmen hurried from one obligation to the next with little chance to collect their thoughts in between. Classes began first thing in the morning and lasted virtually nonstop until late afternoon, with just a short break for lunch. At the end of the academic day, midshipmen rushed to sports or infantry drill depending on the season, with little free time before evening meal. Evening meal was followed by a common study time every night. Lights out was the same for all midshipmen regardless of their academic abilities or desires.[54]

Midshipmen had to budget their time wisely or risk studying after taps, which was, of course, a major violation of regulations. At some point, many of them had resorted to studying with a flashlight to get their homework done. This tight curfew was observed consistently throughout the academic year, with no exceptions for major academic deadlines, such as exams or term papers. Midshipmen could not be trusted to manage their own study time; the academy had to monitor their time closely. Otherwise, many would exhaust themselves and not be prepared for their other professional and physical requirements.[55]

The new curriculum raised questions about the validity of a common study hour. With midshipmen having different academic programs, it seemed logical that their study requirements would also be different. Many academic departments were asking for a more flexible study hour to help with electives. With all the other requirements still in place, the academy worried, however, that midshipmen would sacrifice sleep to get everything done. For this reason specifically, Minter hesitated to grant universal "late lights" privileges. Plebes especially needed their rest to handle the continued stress of indoctrination.[56] Upperclassmen were eventually allowed to determine their needs themselves. Their study time could be extended to varying degrees depending on their class rank. Sophomores and juniors had a limited number of "late lights" privileges and were required to notify the duty officer in advance to avoid a conduct violation. First classmen could stay up every night without needing permission. The absence of a curfew did not absolve them of their military responsibilities; reveille still came at 0530 regardless of how much sleep they got. The decision to cut the cord so completely was nonetheless further proof of a new academic culture; Mother Bancroft was no longer scrutinizing her children as closely as before.[57]

New social privileges were also added as a break from the hectic academic week. Upperclassmen were granted additional weekends; all midshipmen received extra liberty time. Driving inside academy grounds was still forbidden, but car privileges were also expanded. Compared to other colleges and universities, the academy lifestyle continued to be very restrictive. Indeed, the value midshipmen placed on these additional privileges probably seemed laughable to civilian students. But Annapolis was not supposed to be like other colleges, and although they complained, midshipmen generally appreciated the distinction. The rigorous lifestyle was what prepared them to be naval officers.[58]

Some alumni grumbled that Annapolis was becoming soft but these reforms were vitally important to its overall goals. Reformers like Captain Minter understood that the academy could not ignore social changes. Discipline was important, but it had to bear some resemblance to the outside world. It was unwise to think that recent trends had not rubbed off on midshipmen's expectations of the academy. The challenge was determining the restrictions essential to military discipline and the ones followed simply for tradition's sake. Midshipmen were increasingly being urged to think for themselves in the classroom. Why should not a similar emphasis be seen in Bancroft Hall? Finally, the new curriculum required

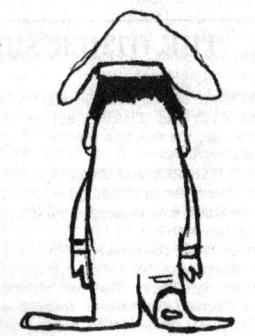

The Log, 5 October 1964. Midshipmen continued to grumble about rules that treated them like children.

greater time and effort; it seemed only fair to adjust their rewards system accordingly.[59]

The Naval Academy could not help but be proud of its progress in recent years. Many reforms were undertaken in the face of substantial opposition. The safe move would have been to stand pat with a proven program. It took a good degree of courage to implement the "academic revolution." It was no wonder then that Annapolis felt stunned and angered by the continued criticism.[60] Admiral Rickover was still the most vocal thorn in its side. Appearing before Congress in 1964, he belittled its achievements by saying, "the appearance of education is there but not the reality." Yet, to accomplish his goals, the academy would have to abandon virtually every core aspect of its program. Plebe indoctrination was a waste, the admiral testified, and should be abolished. Stripers should be selected from the bottom ranks of the class. Military duties were an inconvenience that should not be forced on the more promising students. Most of his "modest proposals" were nothing more than publicity stunts, however, to bring negative attention on Annapolis.[61]

The academy was also perturbed by a scandalous exposé of the "academic revolution" in a *Harper's* magazine article entitled "Teaching Young Sea Dogs Old Tricks." The author, David Boroff, had written a series of articles examining recent changes at Annapolis, Colorado Springs, and West Point, none of which painted a flattering picture of the service academies. The Annapolis article echoed other criticisms of the "academic revolution," all of which viewed it as window dressing for an institution that basically remained the same. The academic dean and civilian faculty had little authority to initiate changes on their own. Many classes continued to use a common textbook, which followed a prescribed course of instruction set by the military. The core program was still heavily weighted to fleet requirements, which was of little use to those going naval aviation, the Air Force, or Marines. Worst of all, Boroff believed, a strong undercurrent of anti-intellectualism still pervaded its academic life: "As long as midshipmen dismiss the humanities as 'Bull' and foreign languages by the unspeakable term 'Dago' the academy is not fulfilling its mission."[62]

The academy insisted that Boroff's conclusions were wrong or at best exaggerated. To prove its point, it published one midshipman's editorial of the Boroff article in *Shipmate*. Admiral Kirkpatrick claimed that, "Annapolis—The Rebuttal of a Young Sea Dog," was spontaneous and that its author, Midshipman First Class James DeFrancia, was a fair representative of the Brigade. Not only did he stand in the middle of his class academically and militarily, he had written it while serving restriction for going over the wall, a typical conduct offense. DeFrancia was outraged by the shallow stereotypes of the academy culture, coming after only a few days of research at Annapolis. Professional courses were geared towards the

4: THE "ACADEMIC REVOLUTION" TRIUMPHANT, 1962–65   155

Navy, but that did not mean other officers could not use them. Humanities courses were not as deep as other subjects, but most graduates went into technical billets, especially early in their careers. Furthermore, the jokes about academics were not all that different from those in college fraternities around the country.[63]

In retrospect, Boroff's article probably hit closer to home than the academy cared to admit even though it was laden with stereotypes. However, the derogatory tone guaranteed a hostile reaction. Boroff saw midshipmen as lacking in spontaneity and open-mindedness; even if that were true, he failed to appreciate the positive virtues of military discipline. He also painted the midshipmen culture in universal terms, calling it "monolithic" and "perpetually adolescent." While elements of this might have been true, DeFrancia correctly pointed out that "it is unfortunate that because we dress alike and march in step we must be accused of lacking the individuality to reason on our own." Boroff noticed aspects of the midshipmen culture framed by Goffman's "total institution," especially the "'gloomy respect' midshipman had for their rigorous existence." But he missed why midshipmen had such a love-hate relationship with Annapolis: " I can say that we might complain about having less free time than our civilian contemporaries, but given the choice we would not trade. None of us came here expecting to be free to come and go as we please. It's discipline, which is necessary in the service, and we do understand that."[64]

DeFrancia's greatest complaint was Boroff's clear lack of respect for the military culture, which the academy believed about many of its critics. Apparently, a sense of fair-mindedness and cordiality did not cross both ways. The article easily opened itself to the same charges it had leveled against the academy. Annapolis had changed greatly in recent years no matter what its detractors claimed. A military service academy would always be an easy target for critics, like Boroff, who failed to dig beneath the surface of its culture.

> Mr. Boroff cites the remark of the superintendent of a swank suburban school system, who, when asked if any of his boys entered the service academies, referred to the military life as "that kind of thing." It is indeed unfortunate that honorable service to one's country must be referred to as "that kind of thing." Men risk their lives daily on, above and under the sea so that the old saying "Sleep well, America. The Navy guards your shores tonight" might hold. It is unfortunate that these men do so only to be thought of as doing "that kind of thing." It is unfortunate that men died at Leyte Gulf, Iwo Jima, and Guadalcanal doing "that kind of thing." Yet the academy's purpose is to produce officers who will dedicate their lives to *just* "that kind of thing." Mr. Boroff concludes his article with the statement that "Annapolis gets good boys, but not the very best." And any man who died in the service of his country, be it in peacetime

while flying patrol, or in wartime on the shores of Okinawa, can without a doubt be counted among the very best.[65]

The Trident Scholar Program and the New Grading System

The next reforms of the "academic revolution" would challenge two enduring stereotypes of the older academic culture, the "slash" and the "dope system." The Trident Scholar program was the brainchild of Admiral Kirkpatrick himself, although he borrowed the idea from a similar program at Yale University. The larger question here was one that went to the core of the academy's program however. Where did the Navy get most of its top leaders? Were most of its admirals star athletes, brigade stripers, or top scholars during their time at Annapolis? In a very real way, the answer to that question, if it could be found, spoke volumes to what the institution's priorities should be. With evidence inconclusive either way, the topic had often been a matter for heated debate among alumni.

The trade-school academy often focused on midshipmen's athletic talents and leadership abilities more than their academic achievements. The prevailing myth was that a preponderant number of the academy's great leaders had been varsity athletes. Stripes were also believed to be an accurate predictor of career success. In contrast, academic achievement was not thought to be all that important of a factor. Everyone had heard stories about anchormen, those ranked last in their class academically who made admiral. Smart men also did well, but it was not essential for a successful career. Midshipmen were always said to be bright students, but that did not guarantee they would be good officers. It did not matter that the lockstep program provided little opportunity to excel academically. The ignominy of being a "slash" befell midshipmen too eager to do well in the classroom.[66]

In many ways, the Trident Scholar program epitomized the new academic culture created by the "academic revolution." Midshipmen who were able to validate and take electives had a significant advantage over their peers. They alone could qualify for a minor or a major, which affected their chances at graduate school. The nuclear power program also took a dim view of anyone with a poor academic record. Even outside nuclear power, a higher grade point average meant better choices at service selection. The Trident Scholar program was a logical extension of these priorities. The school's two recent Heisman Trophy winners were dramatic examples of midshipmen's athletic abilities. In a similar fashion, the Trident Scholars showcased the Brigade's top academic performers.

The idea for the Trident Scholars came from the Scholars of the House program at Yale University. These students had completed their undergraduate requirements early and were essentially doing independent study their senior year. During a visit, Admiral Kirkpatrick became convinced that a similar program would work at Annapolis. It would demonstrate that top midshipmen were of an academic caliber comparable to that of the nation's most prestigious schools. Kirkpatrick pushed this plan through the Academic Board in the spring of 1963, with the first six Trident Scholars selected from the class of 1964. The prerequisites for even qualifying were staggering. Candidates had to be in the top 10 percent of their class at the end of the first semester their junior year. They had to validate enough hours to pursue their research and keep themselves on track for graduation. Few midshipmen wanted to spend extra time at Annapolis. Nor did they want to fall behind their classmates either. The clause was put there to show that the program was not interfering with the academy's military responsibilities.[67]

Midshipmen were required to submit a detailed research proposal that included a project timetable and its potential value after completion. Special emphasis was placed on ideas that not only had academic value but also practical application for the Navy. Special departmental committees evaluated the proposals and gave recommendations to the Academic Board, which made the final selections. Although the hurdles were extensive, the program promised an interesting set of rewards to recipients. Trident Scholars worked with individual faculty advisors who were experts in their chosen fields of study. The academy was very flexible with their schedules to accommodate their research. They were excused from formal course requirements but could take electives that helped their research. Their course load was reduced to the minimum twelve semester hours to focus on their projects. Trident Scholars could even request research leave away from Annapolis.[68]

With the exception of the special schedule, Annapolis insisted that its Trident Scholars participated in all of the required midshipmen activities. At the same time, these privileges singled them out as exceptional. No other group, even varsity athletes, was as exempt from the everyday routine as Trident Scholars were. They essentially designed their own schedule. Many fleet officers did not have that degree of control over their day. With the exception of stripers and the Executive Department, no other group had as intimate contact with the staff as Trident Scholars did with their faculty advisers. This was a strong statement about the academy's commitment to advanced scholarship, albeit with important restrictions. Annapolis was not in the business of supporting research without immediate application to the Navy. Technology's influence could be clearly seen in the subjects chosen by the initial Trident Scholars—factors affecting submarine hull design, radiation's effect on transistors, concepts of fire-control for laser weapons in air defense systems, and counterinsurgency theories for operations in Central and South America.[69]

It was not a coincidence then that the Navy used new scientific tools, such as quantitative analysis, to settle the debate of which midshipmen made the best officers. The most in-depth study looked at career paths for the class of 1937, the most recent group to complete the standard career of twenty years active service. It searched for relationships between academic achievement, varsity sports participation, and striper rank and their eventual rates for retention and promotion. The results put to rest several preconceptions. Contrary to expectations, academic standing was extremely important. Those of higher academic rank were more likely to stay and be promoted to captain, a traditional benchmark of career success. Leadership at Annapolis was also an excellent predictor of success. Midshipmen stripers, those who were company commanders and above, had the lowest resignation rate and highest promotion rate, although they were a much smaller group numerically. Conversely, varsity letter winners had the highest resignation rate and the lowest selection rate to captain, virtually the opposite of many people's expectations.[70]

The study was a resounding affirmation of the "academic revolution," even though its sample size was limited. Indeed, the absence of other hard evidence prompted a data collection frenzy at Annapolis over the next several years. Many defense agencies were enthralled with the social sciences in the early 1960s; they had the power to yield definitive answers, or so many policymakers believed. Each of these subsequent studies showed that the academy had the best retention rate of all the Navy's commissioning programs. Not only was it producing better-educated officers, they were apparently more motivated too. To its credit, the academy was fairly objective in its analysis. It did not look for results that confirmed institutional stereotypes but wanted to know the true condition of its program. At the same time, this first study probably raised more nagging questions than it answered.

For the first time, it questioned whether resignations could be fairly attributed to Annapolis and not to what happened during an officer's initial sea tour. In other words, were there identifiable limits to professional socialization? Along with this, if love for the sea was a difficult sentiment to engender, was the academy wrong to encourage alternative career paths so long as it benefited the Navy? The academy was left wondering how many prospects had been lost to NROTC, a program with notoriously worse retention rates, because of its singular focus on producing line officers. This was radical thinking indeed to question its stated purpose for generations. Unfortunately, there were no easy answers.

The study forced the academy to examine other longstanding assumptions. Varsity athletics was apparently not the "training ground for future

4: THE "ACADEMIC REVOLUTION" TRIUMPHANT, 1962–65   159

leadership." The sports program was better justified as a stimulus for recruiting, a healthy recreational outlet, or as a boon to morale than it was a source of future admirals. A more difficult recruiting question was whether the academy had "concentrated on the top athlete who is also academically inclined, or upon the top student who is also athletically inclined."[71] The results of the "academic revolution" suggested that the academy should focus on the latter even if it had earlier concentrated on the former. If a greater emphasis on academics was better for the Navy, the academy should probably be tougher with marginal students too.

Turn backs and anchormen did not go on to great career success no matter what the stereotypes claimed. It was better for the Navy to get rid of such individuals rather than pass them along until graduation, a conviction soon put to the test with the grade-quota controversy. Finally and most disturbingly, was David Boroff right about the academy getting good boys but not the nation's best? The academy correctly recognized that the answer depended greatly on how its goals were defined. Should it focus on candidates who could handle a rigorous academic program? What about those who had outstanding records in extracurricular activities, sports, or other outside organizations? Which midshipmen made the best officers not for today's Navy but for what it would be twenty years from now? Although the "academic revolution" was the future, the academy was not trying to compete with the "Ivies," nor did it want to be. However, the question of where to draw the line between Athens and Sparta was as difficult to resolve now as it was generations ago.[72]

On the surface, the switch to a new letter grading system in 1963 was a change that seemed long overdue and thus generated little fanfare initially. Under the lockstep curriculum, each class ended with a daily quiz, which covered the previous night's homework. Grades were assigned on a 4.0 numerical system, with a 2.5 being the minimum passing score. Quiz scores were often low since the problem was picked and graded largely at the whim of the instructor. The multitude of low grades often had a numbing effect on midshipmen by the end of the semester. With many students technically "unsat" going into final exams, most departments curved their final grades to get enough passing scores. Midshipmen found it difficult to take the daily quizzes seriously under such circumstances. They were just another part of the "unity of suffering" experience at Annapolis.[73]

The Folsom Board encouraged the academy to move away from daily quizzes. It was an unnecessary disruption to the learning process that yielded little in terms of practical results. Furthermore, the wrong kind of academic culture was fostered by this approach. The time could be spent better covering new material or answering questions. The daily quiz was not that much of a stimulus to additional study; students knew it was coming and had studied whatever time they could in preparation for it. As a result, midshipmen often took a "memory dump" attitude to their classes. The emphasis was on what was needed for the day rather than placing material in its proper perspective. Ironically then, daily quizzes were probably not that reliable of an indicator of what students learned by the end of the term. The evaluators encouraged a system of fewer grades but to make them count instead of a multitude of quizzes whose scores were eventually dropped. With the curve not an option, midshipmen would be forced to take their studies more seriously.[74]

The letter grade system, common to other colleges, was the supposed remedy for these failings. Instead of trying to read the instructor's mind, midshipmen could concentrate on obtaining an overall grasp of the material. Eliminating the daily quiz was also seen as a way of encouraging academic integrity; there was simply no reason any longer to be obsessed with the dope. Under the lockstep curriculum, class sections had rotated instructors at least once in the course of the semester. The quality of instruction really did not matter since courses were taught from a common textbook and curriculum. The new system encouraged a much stronger faculty-student relationship. Instructors almost had to remain with their students the entire semester to assign their grades fairly. Midshipmen would supposedly learn more since they would not have to adjust to different styles of teaching.[75]

However, by the early 1960s, the biggest reason driving this change was the need to boost midshipmen's grade point averages. The Navy now expected academy graduates eventually to attend graduate school. Higher grade point averages were necessary if midshipmen were to compete with civilian students. The challenge facing the academy was to maintain academic standards without unduly penalizing its students. The new grading system promised to be a cure for both ills. The new grades were supposedly a better reflection of a midshipman's academic progress. It promised a healthier academic atmosphere akin to the other reforms of the "academic revolution." And hopefully the new grading system would show midshipmen in a more favorable light to their civilian peers.[76]

The new grading system was also a subtle way of increasing academic standards. Letter grades more easily identified struggling students, which allowed any remedial action to be taken quickly. Grade averages were based on a new Quality Point Ratio (QPR) in which an A was worth four points, a B three points, a C two, a D one, and a F worth zero. Midshipmen had to maintain a minimum QPR of 2.0 each semester to not be considered academically delinquent. Previously, struggling students could slide by with a D average so long as their grades improved by graduation. Occasionally, some midshipmen made it all the way to their final semester before the academy realized they would not graduate.[77]

A single D was still a passing grade under the new scale, but a D average or below resulted in academic probation. Students in this category were closely monitored until their grades improved or they were discharged from the academy. Their privileges could also be curtailed to provide more study time. Repeat offenders went before the Academic Board, which could result in their termination. A failing grade triggered immediate action by the Academic Board, even if the overall QPR was satisfactory. It was ironic then that this relatively simple change would cause so much controversy. In retrospect, such problems were probably not surprising. Unfortunately, the new grading system's benefits did not materialize as quickly as planned. Academic standards were tightened, but as a result grade point averages initially went down instead of up. The academy's reaction to this problem exposed the growing differences between its academic and military sides.[78]

The Minter Reforms and the Consolidation of The "Academic Revolution"

The newly promoted Admiral Minter relieved Admiral Kirkpatrick as superintendent in January 1964. Minter inherited an academy in the midst of significant change but also optimistic about the future. The "academic revolution" was not perfect, but it had received substantial praise from the teams that had either studied or inspected the academy. Whatever the problems, the academy would not be returning to the lockstep curriculum. The Naval Academy had also finally stopped the hemorrhage of graduates accepting commissions outside the Navy. As of 1964, the secretary of the Navy prohibited further interservice transfers, which could be overturned only under extreme circumstances, such as a family connection in the other service or a lack of naval commissions.[79]

Minter was specifically chosen for the job to provide continuity to the new building program. After much haggling with Annapolis, the academy abandoned plans to acquire the adjacent seven city blocks and chose to make do with the existing property. Although more modest in size, the scope of the project was truly expansive, surprising considering the difficulty in obtaining government funds in the past. What was most interesting about the Warnecke plan, named after the architect who designed it, was that the focus was almost exclusively on *academic* facilities. The centerpiece of new construction were two twin buildings, later to become Michelson and Chauvenet Halls, which would house the mathematics and science departments. The academy also pursued authorization for a new library and engineering facility to complete its academic renovation. Although neither facility was approved during Admiral Minter's tenure, continued efforts eventually led to the construction of Nimitz Library and Rickover Hall. As with most aspects of academy life, the "academic revolution" had become the focus of improvements to its physical plant.[80]

Although not the explicit reason for his appointment, Minter also gave stability to the "academic revolution." Over the next several years, he took Melson's and Kirkpatrick's reforms to the next level. Throughout this period, the academy came to rely more heavily on the advice of its interim dean, Dr. Drought. Largely on his recommendation, the school underwent another academic reorganization in the summer of 1964. Melson's five division directorships were abandoned in favor of a more traditional structure of twelve academic departments. A tighter organization could better coordinate the work of the academic departments and limit squabbling over the curriculum. From this point onwards, academic departments would also channel any issues through the academic dean.[81]

The decision to concentrate power into Drought's hands was a huge step for the "academic revolution." The dean was no longer just the superintendent's "academic advisor"; his decisions dramatically affected the institutional life of Annapolis. His position was made permanent in the summer of 1964. Although his temperament may have been unassuming, he had his own ideas for reform and now had the authority to act on them. The Academic Board continued to be a mixture of voices, but real power was concentrated in the hands of the superintendent, the commandant, and the academic dean. The new organization still allowed for three academic department heads, each of them Navy captains, but membership was rotated among the departments. Although the new command structure was far from absolute, the commandant was controlling Bancroft Hall and the superintendent had overall direction, but the dean was now effectively running the academic side.[82]

Although usually thought of as a bad word in higher education, greater control actually promoted the goals of the "academic revolution." Dean Drought used his authority and expertise to expand upon many reforms. The academy came away with a better academic reputation as a result. Drought established new faculty evaluation procedures with real consequences for inferior performers. Faculty also started forwarding research and leave requests through his office. The academy continued to upgrade admissions standards; the mathematics score on the CEEB exam as well as high school class standing became the two most important factors. Only under unusual circumstances did the academy admit an applicant who did not stand in the top 40 percent of his high school graduating class.[83]

The greatest change under Minter's command was further curriculum reforms, which made a minor an academic requirement for all midshipmen and a major a realistic possibility for many. Acting on the advice of Dean

4: THE "ACADEMIC REVOLUTION" TRIUMPHANT, 1962–65

Drought, Minter forwarded a radical proposal to the secretary of the Navy to restructure the curriculum once again. The largest remaining barrier to a traditional academic curriculum was the sizable number of semester hours in the core program. Midshipmen completed a mandatory 160 semester hours by graduation, a huge load in four years. Under the best of circumstances, students could validate a course or two, but rarely did anyone have enough time to concentrate in a particular discipline.[84]

The core program theoretically included only the fundamentals of naval service. Although there were suggestions that not every core course was essential, it was next to impossible to tamper with that part of the curriculum. Academic departments were like fiefdoms that jealously guarded their courses like conquered territory. Once a course was added to the core program, it was difficult to eliminate it. As much as it had encouraged reform, the Navy was also fairly dogmatic about the core program. It was difficult to say a course added no value to a midshipman's professional development. Minter understood that no matter the merits of his proposal, it would likely bump into stiff resistance.[85]

Minter's plan reduced the required course load to a total of 136 to 140 semester hours, exclusive of work done in the summer. Within this framework, midshipmen devoted approximately 30 percent of their time to a field of concentration and 70 percent to required courses. They could specialize within three broad programs, engineering or engineering science, science or naval science, and the social sciences or humanities. The hope was that the reduced course load, along with the flexible curriculum, would make it easier to qualify for minors and majors. The Navy approved of the substance of this proposal but felt that the distribution was too high in favor of electives. The new curriculum, which began in 1964 with the class of 1968, required 138 semester hours, 15 percent of which were electives and 85 percent required courses. The older program of validation and electives also remained in effect.[86]

Although it was better than nothing, the Navy's version did not produce as drastic a change as Minter and Drought had wanted. Instead of majors, they had to be content requiring minors of midshipmen. More of them began receiving majors, but the obstacles were still too great for the average student. The greatest worry with the new curriculum was an inadequate distribution of students in the three fields of concentration. Too many midshipmen might select a particular area. Annapolis did not want to coerce students into specific programs, but the Navy's needs were greatest in the technical fields. Fortuitously, the test class of 1968 had broad academic desires; nearly 90 percent of these students got their first choice out of three possible minors. Although the majors-minors ratio would be an ongoing concern, midshipmen generally received the academic program they wanted. Although limited, an even broader curriculum seemed inevitable at some point. The next step would be Admiral Calvert's majors program in 1968.[87]

The Naval Academy also moved forward with important reforms of its training program and Bancroft Hall. The underlying principle was to concentrate most professional training into the summer months. To make up for the loss of informal professional training, new naval science courses were scheduled throughout the four-year, academic program instead of the final two. The summer cruise program was also overhauled. First classmen were assigned a two-month stint with operational units in the fleet. Second classmen completed a smorgasbord of training in all of the Navy's war fighting communities. Third classmen were once again concentrated into special midshipmen training squadrons, similar to the old youngster cruise, which emphasized the fundamentals of life at sea.[88]

Emphasis was returned to practical training necessary for a division officer's initial duties. Midshipmen still did grunt work for their enlisted and officer running mates; foreign liberty ports remained the highlight of most summer cruises. Yet, none of this was guaranteed with so much training to do. Optional training opportunities were offered in lieu of summer leave. Midshipmen could apply for programs like SCUBA, airborne training, escape and evasion training, and jungle warfare school. These programs did not replace the standard training, but they were excellent opportunities for those interested in more specialized, naval careers. As with the academic program, the academy was recognizing that diversity could be a good thing, so long as it was in the best interests of the Navy.[89]

Minter was also fortunate to have an able commandant running Bancroft Hall, Captain Sheldon Kinney. Kinney continued quality of life improvements that made the Brigade's hectic routine more bearable. Berthing space was expanded to comfortably support a brigade of forty-two hundred midshipmen. Enough beds were installed so that upperclassmen would sleep at most three to a room. The renovation of the mess hall was also completed, including the installation of modern food servicing equipment, which cut down on the delays in serving the enlarged Brigade its meals. New recreational facilities—twelve new bowling lanes, ten squash courts, four billiard rooms, five television lounges, even an indoor rifle and pistol range—were added for the midshipmen's leisure time. Minter was deeply concerned that the academy should keep pace not only with "technological advances" but also "social advances," both of which he believed were important to the "academic revolution."[90]

Kinney worked towards bringing greater accountability to plebe indoctrination too. He borrowed an organizational scheme from West Point to monitor better Bancroft Hall. Instead of the older mentor relationship, in which one first classman informally supervised and trained a single plebe, a new squad system was instituted. Squads were units of ten to twelve

4: THE "ACADEMIC REVOLUTION" TRIUMPHANT, 1962–65

midshipmen, equally distributed from the four classes in the Brigade. First classmen were appointed as squad leaders, a new position within the striper organization, a minor one but a striper position nonetheless. Squad leaders supervised and coordinated the training for all members of the squad, especially the indoctrination of plebes. Plebes were supposedly no longer the prey of wandering upperclassmen; their training was limited to upperclassmen from their squad. The new system could not guarantee that these upperclassmen would not abuse their authority, nor did it necessarily stop all unauthorized activities. Nevertheless, it did bring greater order and accountability to plebe indoctrination.[91]

Admiral Minter relinquished command in June 1964, after a nearly four-year stint as commandant and superintendent, an unusually long tour at the academy. During that time, he had initiated or witnessed significant changes to virtually all aspects of its program. A new curriculum was almost fully in place, which changed its academic life for the better, Admiral Rickover's protests notwithstanding. Improved instructors, a new grading system, and more flexible courses, all headed by a civilian dean, were transforming Annapolis into a true naval college, the longstanding dream of academic reformers since World War II. Bancroft Hall had made important adjustments to these reforms too. Much of the professional training was now conducted in the summer, leaving the traditional school year free for academics. Important changes had been made to plebe indoctrination too—additional company officers, the squad system—to bring greater accountability and efficiency. New social privileges had also been added—extra liberty weekends, extended automobile privileges—to help keep the Naval Academy attractive to a changing youth culture.

Yet, this tumultuous period had also seen its share of controversy. Opinions of the changes ranged from being either too drastic or not severe enough. At the moment, however, the future looked bright. The academy believed it was well prepared for the 1966 Middle States Association accreditation and expected an enthusiastic endorsement of its reforms. No one at Annapolis could have predicted, however, all the problems brewing beneath the surface that would wrack the school with even greater controversy. In retrospect, this turmoil was not altogether surprising, especially given the magnitude of change in such a short time. The academy had not resolved the conflicting values and priorities that were tearing at its institutional culture. Indeed, many problems that would soon plague Annapolis—tensions with the faculty, the grade-quota controversy, surging numbers of plebe resignations—were all part of this clash for its institutional soul.

5

A "Professional Revolution" at Annapolis, 1965–68: Discord for the New Academy

AFTER ADMIRAL MINTER'S DEPARTURE IN MAY 1965, THE ACADEMY held off on further modifications to the curriculum. The new program may have gotten off to a rocky start, but everyone was now generally pleased with the "academic revolution." At this point, no one talked about returning to the lockstep curriculum except for a few disgruntled alumni. Annapolis especially welcomed the accolades of the academic community, which it had largely ignored in the past. The reforms spotlighted the academy as a progressive institution committed to its students' education, not just a trade school for naval officers. Even so, the school wanted time to digest everything that had happened before proceeding further.[1]

Given this conservative turn, it was surprising Annapolis would be embroiled in controversy from 1965 to 1968. The next several years it would be putting out one brushfire after another, each scandal an eyesore on the new image it worked to create. The first shock wave stemmed from the new letter grading scale. Instead of raising grade point averages, the academy resorted to grade controls to curb academic failures. Many instructors considered the measures an intrusion on their academic freedom; at the very least, they seemed more reminiscent of the trade school academy than the new Annapolis. Next, it had to survive the 1966 Middle States accreditation, the first major inspection since the "academic revolution." Although much of the report was positive, the team worried about the growing dichotomy between the military and academic sides of the institution. Their fear was the academy was developing into two camps, each with a different agenda for the institution.[2]

Finally, the academy was hit with vocal demands to end plebe indoctrination. Many civilian professors were disturbed with how plebe indoctrination interfered with the classroom. To them, Bancroft Hall's activities seemed incompatible with the "academic revolution." Admiral Minter's limited reforms were not solving the problems however. Plebes were still falling asleep in classes; they were not getting enough study time; upperclassmen were still abusing the rules and, worse, getting away with it. The most vocal reformers wanted to abolish plebe year altogether, a solution all but anathema to military officers. Unlike recent bouts with controversy, the electives program, the appointment of a civilian dean—the latest scandals became public only after attempts to solve them internally had failed. Since neither side believed they could back down, emotions were at a higher pitch, and the problems were more difficult to solve than earlier in the "academic revolution."[3]

In retrospect, these problems were probably not that unusual. Although no immediate events triggered these crises, the "academic revolution" was far from resolved. Most importantly, these episodes reflected deep divisions within the academy culture. In effect, it was operating under multiple value systems, which had yet to be reconciled with one another. Its military culture, centered in Bancroft Hall, taught that the school's primary purpose was producing combat officers, which meant its priorities took precedence. The older academic culture shared this assumption. The dope system survived because classmate loyalty was emphasized more than academic integrity. Midshipmen looked to the curve to pass their classes but they were preparing to be officers not scholars.[4]

The "academic revolution" set in motion new priorities, chief of which Annapolis was also to be an elite undergraduate college. The operational forces increasingly needed technically qualified graduates. The reforms were also needed to help recruiting. Ironically, these changes fell within its traditional mission of producing career officers. Neither the academic nor the military side of the academy appreciated how much these requirements had changed. At many points they agreed about its priorities but at critical junctures, their views were incredibly different and often opposed. The problem exposing these differences more than anything else was the lack of time in the crowded curriculum. In choosing one alternative, it was often doing so at the expense of another, equally valid concern. At best, it struggled to find less than perfect solutions. These differences made the institutional climate very tense and competitive. At the very least, it created serious misunderstandings among well-intentioned people, all of them having the academy's best interests at heart.[5]

The Naval Academy has faced problematic decisions like this before and given its unique responsibilities will do so again. No one suggested abandoning either training or education, but the relative weight given to them was another matter entirely. At the onset of the "academic revolution," many military responsibilities were shifted to the summer to make room for the new curriculum. Academic standards had to be raised, and this seemed a convenient way to do it.[6] By late 1965, there was concern that the academy had gone too far in its pursuit of academic excellence, especially if it weakened an area of established strength. Some officers and upperclassmen were calling for a "professional revolution" to rectify the imbalances of the "academic revolution." But this involved more than simply adding new professional courses to the curriculum. Midshipmen had too many privileges and too much freedom to become disciplined, duty-bound naval officers.[7] Such sentiments caused concern among younger civilian professors committed to the more open academic environment.[8]

The stakes were incredibly high, in other words, even with the absence of major changes to the curriculum. At bottom, all sides were struggling to define what the philosophical orientation of the academy should be. Not to understate what had already been done but creating the new programs was actually the easiest part of the "academic revolution" to accomplish. Now, the academy faced the more difficult struggle of integrating those reforms into its culture. The hurdles to creating a new equilibrium were difficult to overcome. If a counter-revolution to the "academic revolution" did occur, it did not bring back the trade school academy, if that even was its intent. The spirit of reform continued, albeit in less obvious ways to bring its basic premises into being.

Complicating matters further, the Navy was in the midst of mobilizing for the Vietnam War. The burden did not fall too heavily on Annapolis initially. Graduates were serving in increasing numbers in Southeast Asia. Duty fell the heaviest on those in naval aviation or the Marine Corps, but initially the war was more a curiosity than anything else. Reports of senior shipmates being killed in battle jolted midshipmen from looking at it as a good career opportunity.[9] The war's escalation could not have come at a more inopportune time for the "academic revolution." Proponents of a traditional academy would use Vietnam as evidence for a tougher military framework at Annapolis.[10] Academic reformers were challenged to rebut their arguments as the casualty lists grew inside Bancroft Hall.[11]

The war effort eventually imposed great costs on Annapolis. The Navy's focus was on operational requirements. First to go was the pledge to send only top officers as company officers and classroom instructors. The latest blueprint for physical renovation was postponed but amazingly not cancelled altogether. Training and professional socialization suffered tremendously with the cancellation of traditional cruise schedules. The school did not go to a modified routine as it did with World War II, although there was talk of bringing back a three-year, accelerated program.[12] Emergency measures were not necessary for Vietnam, but a "business as usual" mentality was not the best way to wage a major war, albeit a limited one.[13] In doing so, Annapolis deprived itself of the powerful emotions that come from responding to such a crisis. The Vietnam War never occupied its collective focus the way World War II did, the sole exception being the

The Log, 18 April 1969. Casualty boards were a constant reminder of Vietnam for midshipmen.

outpouring of sentiment at gaining the release of the nation's prisoners of war.[14]

Along with Vietnam, Annapolis wrestled with the effects of a rapidly changing youth culture. Prewar recruiting efforts had generated record numbers of qualified applicants. College Board scores of recent classes were the envy of all but the most prestigious universities. More high school valedictorians and honor society members were admitted each year, students who could pick from many fine colleges. Ever since the "academic revolution," there was a shocking reversal in attrition statistics, even though the average rate continued to be around 30 percent. Previously, the largest source was academic failures followed by voluntary resignations. These ratios switched with the new curriculum.[15] Complicating matters further, the earlier recruiting bonanza evaporated as antiwar sentiment escalated. Instead of turning away candidates, the academy fought to get its minimum numbers.[16]

Initially, academy leaders chalked up responsibility for this problem to a changed society that no longer appreciated the traditional military culture. Although these losses were unfortunate, the academy should not bend its values to society. All of that may have been true, certainly the declining interest in career service was further evidence of such trends; it was not, however, the entire reason for these problems. After much criticism and investigation, the academy accepted that it bore responsibility too. Most disheartening was evidence that plebes were most excited about the Navy during the summer, after which their motivation plummeted.[17] Most voluntary resignations occurred after upperclassmen returned in the fall.[18] Eliminating plebe year altogether was not an option, so the academy had to find a better way of managing it. The answer was not to be found in abandoning traditional military discipline however. It cracked down on the recent expansion in privileges, in hopes of distancing itself from the permissive environment on other campuses. It also held to a zero-tolerance policy in its first problem with drugs in the Brigade.[19]

THE GROWTH OF THE NEW FACULTY AND THE GRADE-CONTROL CONTROVERSY

The job of sorting out these difficult issues fell to yet another new superintendent, Rear Admiral Draper Kauffman, who took over in June 1965. Like many of his predecessors, Kauffman came from a family of Annapolis graduates and had extensive combat experience in World War II. Unlike his peers, Kauffman's experiences were more reminiscent of a Hemingway novel than a traditional Navy line officer. Poor eyesight prevented his commission after graduating from the academy in 1933. After

The Log, 25 October 1968. Midshipmen were becoming more conscious of how much they stood out in society.

war broke out in Europe, Kauffman left his civilian job to serve in the ambulance corps of the French army, whose defeat made him a prisoner of Nazi Germany. The British repatriated him, after which he volunteered his services to that country. Kauffman wound up serving the British as an explosive ordnance disposal officer until the United States entered World War II.[20]

The Americans were also interested in developing an EOD program, which gave Kauffman the commission he was denied in the 1930s. All of these experiences led to the opportunity for which he was most famous, the creation of the underwater demolition teams (UDT). Kauffman was not only the pioneer of this program; he won two Navy Crosses for leading the initial teams during the Marshall Islands campaign in the Pacific. The admiral was somewhat of a surprise choice to head the academy because, unlike other superintendents, he had not returned for duty since his own graduation. He did bring other advantages to the job: a good family name, an incredible war record, and important political connections. Most recently, Kauffman had served in the Pentagon, where he had worked closely with Alain Einthoven and other members of Robert McNamara's inner circle.[21]

Despite his relative inexperience, Kauffman had the widest possible latitude determining the priorities of his new command. After the fact, the admiral viewed this discretion to be as much the academy's complicated command structure as it was the Navy's faith in his abilities. The academy technically fell under the chief of naval personnel, but that had not stopped the chief of naval operations or the secretary of the Navy from sidestepping the chain of command, especially on volatile issues like plebe indoctrination or the academic curriculum. In other, nondescript areas, neither group took much interest in what happened at the academy. Since Kauffman was the personal choice of the CNO, Admiral David McDonald, BUPERS essentially left him alone.[22]

To his credit, Kauffman understood he was not a professional educator and worked hard to make up for any deficiencies. He read widely the recent studies of Annapolis—the Folsom report, the Harris study on plebe indoctrination—before assuming command. The prospective superintendent also visited with civilian friends of the academy, such as Father Hesburgh of Notre Dame and Dr. Sterling of Stanford University, to get their thoughts on Annapolis. At the same time, Kauffman did not abandon his own operational experiences in determining the best course for the academy. In addressing these questions for alumni, Kauffman showed himself to be a supporter of the "academic revolution" but not an ardent enthusiast of extending it.[23] At no point did he feel the academy should attempt to be a "Princeton-on-the-Severn or MIT-on-the-Severn"; whether intended or not this seemed to be a rejection of the popular phrase of academic reformers. Kauffman's ideas evoked the more traditional academy that emphasized character building and professional socialization:

> I believe that competition and the development of a will to win are vital in the training of any man who must lead his fellow men in time of war. An intensive and successful athletic program is obviously essential to that end. I believe that spiritual and moral leadership are essential ingredients in the make-up of an officer in the United States Navy and must therefore be equally essential ingredients in the life of a midshipman.[24]

Very early in his tour, Kauffman became involved in a huge crisis over grade controls that had been brewing long before he took over the academy. At the heart of this controversy were incredibly dissimilar views of academics within the academy culture. In some ways, this problem had grown worse instead of better since the "academic revolution." The chief intent of the 1962 Korth directive was improving the academic caliber of the faculty.

5: "PROFESSIONAL REVOLUTION" AT ANNAPOLIS, 1965–68

The academy had met this goal largely by hiring greater numbers of civilian instructors. The vast influx of people was a difficult transition under the best of circumstances. However, many instructors brought ideas and priorities that were disruptive to the existing institutional culture. Unlike older civilian faculty, most new hires intended on doing research and being involved in their disciplines. They also wanted the academy to be respected as a first-rate academic institution by the scholarly community.[25]

Their scholastic credentials came with a price, however. Many instructors were not afraid to speak their mind about things they disagreed with. Ironically, this was all part and parcel of Annapolis becoming a true naval college, although military authorities sometimes had difficulty appreciating it as such. Senior officers were accustomed to a traditional military culture in which the chain of command was followed at all times. They were not necessarily close-minded, but juniors followed their wishes unless there was evidence that those orders resulted in disaster. A pure academic environment traditionally promoted an open exchange of ideas, even if it brought conflict in the short-term. The academic culture valued harmony but not at the expense of members not being heard.[26]

The challenge of integrating both viewpoints at a hybrid institution, like the Naval Academy, was obvious and yet difficult to accomplish. The quest for balance would require much attention the next several years. And once found, there were no guarantees how long that equilibrium would last. The 1966 Middle States team wanted the academy to realize that no matter how unpleasant this was actually good for its long-term health. A major finding of its report said that "to fail to observe that this has led to a certain tension between the 'academic' academy and the 'military' academy would be to fail to comment on a major aspect of the Naval Academy in 1966. And to hold that this tension is entirely destructive, a sign for alarm, would be to ignore that it has as its companion a fortunate absence of complacency and a determination to discover a truly proper balance and emphasis."[27]

The growth in the civilian faculty's influence came not just from their numbers but also from concurrent problems with the military faculty. Initially the Navy had kept its promise to Secretary Korth to upgrade officers' credentials, the master's degree being a minimum requirement for assignment. It stopped short, however, of implementing the academy's more ambitious Faculty Education Program, which identified promising officers early and tied their graduate education to future assignment at Annapolis.[28]

Unfortunately a heavy operational tempo placed that commitment in jeopardy almost immediately. The deepening war in Southeast Asia made it next to impossible not to shortchange the academy from getting quality replacements. The ideal military instructor possessed enough operational experience to make his courses professionally relevant and enough formal education to make his teaching academically credible. Not surprisingly, officers of this caliber were in great demand. Stateside training institutions took whatever was left. The academy was supposedly the Navy's top priority after Vietnam, but whether that promise carried much weight was debatable. Many shore commands were claiming a connection to Vietnam to make up for the manpower shortage. The decision to fight the war with primarily active-duty forces also made this more of a transparent promise.[29]

Not only was it being shortchanged in terms of numbers, but oftentimes officers arrived too late to prepare adequately for their duties. New instructors were supposed to arrive in August for a month-long orientation before beginning their classes. Frequently, replacements arrived just in time with little opportunity to familiarize themselves with the course material. Many new instructors were not academy graduates but temporary officers commissioned from officer candidate school. Not only were they lacking in operational experience, but many of them also did not intend on a military career. These officers defied the rationale for even having military instructors, the value that their operational experiences brought to the midshipmen's professional socialization and career motivation.[30]

Under such circumstances, the academy had little choice but to rely more heavily on civilians. Many officers could not be counted on to teach more than introductory courses; the burden of the electives program truly fell on the civilian faculty. Civilians also had to shoulder many administrative and extracurricular functions. They were the midshipmen's advisors for special programs or independent research not the military faculty. In a real sense, the confluence of the "academic revolution" and Vietnam put civilians, not naval officers, in a better position to be the midshipmen's role models. Civilian instructors were teaching the more interesting and demanding courses. They were often more ambitious and dynamic than military instructors, with a clear direction for their careers.[31]

Even so, the academy hesitated to extend them any more of a leadership role. The newly reconstituted Academic Board had only one civilian voice on it, albeit a powerful one, in the academic dean. Particularly galling, all department heads were still Navy captains, chosen as much for their administrative experience as their academic abilities. The academy had received much mileage from the new faculty's academic credentials, particularly in terms of recruitment and academic standing. It was demanding a greater workload to help with the personnel crisis of Vietnam. Given their greater role, many civilian instructors believed the time had also come for a greater role in the decision-making process.[32]

The catalyst for bringing these difficult issues into the open was the grade-control controversy of 1965. The switch to a letter-grading scale in the fall of 1963 was made to help midshipmen qualify for graduate school

5: "PROFESSIONAL REVOLUTION" AT ANNAPOLIS, 1965–68

by raising their grade point averages and making them more competitive with civilian students. The first semester of the new system ended with almost double the number of midshipmen on the academically delinquent list. Obviously this was not the image the academy wanted to project of the "academic revolution." Although its response might have looked like a cover-up, Admiral Kirkpatrick was right to examine other reasons for the extraordinarily low grades. The one variable that semester was the new grading scale. Perhaps the new system had hidden flaws discovered only after it was put into practice.[33]

Although it was not a perfect solution, Admiral Kirkpatrick and Dean Drought put ceilings on the numbers of Ds and Fs that could be awarded as final grades—13 percent for plebes, 10 percent for youngsters, 6 percent for the second class, and 4 percent for the first class—to keep attrition levels similar to the past. For as much criticism as it would receive, they understood that this was not a permanent fix to the problem. Over the next two years, the academy monitored grade levels to see whether the controls were still necessary. Unfortunately progress marks were never high enough to risk lifting these constraints. For example, at the midpoint of the 1965 spring semester, nearly 26 percent of the plebe class was failing, which was almost double the preferred rate. There was simply no way it could terminate that many midshipmen; the overall attrition rate was already much too high.[34]

The biggest problem with the new grading system was setting new expectations of minimal academic performance. Under the older 4.0 scale, the minimum passing grade was a 2.5, or 62.5 percent; midshipmen also needed a passing grade in each subject to be satisfactory for the year. With the new system, a midshipman could still pass a single course with a D; however, he needed a C average to be in good standing. The academic

The Log, 17 November 1967. Midshipmen had trouble understanding the expectations of the new grading system.

culture had yet to make two critical adjustments for the new system to work. The faculty had to understand that lower grades had potentially more drastic consequences while midshipmen needed to realize that the academic bar had truly been raised, not just given another name.[35]

There was no question that grade controls were counter to an open academic climate. The warning of the 1966 Middle States team was clear in this regard: "No good college that we know permits administrators alone and directly to prescribe the distribution of grades." At the same time, the school's actions were not that unusual, especially compared to similar circumstances in its history and also that of other institutions. It was certainly not a conspiracy to hide problems with the "academic revolution." "Grading on the curve" was common at Annapolis during the lock-step curriculum. Both West Point and Colorado Springs had also used grade controls to limit attrition; even good civilian institutions worried about what to do when academic failures got too high.[36]

Many younger instructors objected to grade controls even though they recognized the academy's predicament. Their response reflected the institutional culture in which they were trained. Proscribing grades seemed too much like an intrusion on their academic freedom. Worse still, artificial constraints fostered strong, anti-academic attitudes in midshipmen. In their minds, academic progress should be determined objectively without regard to outside consequences. The sanctity of the classroom would be irreparably violated otherwise. Midshipmen were not being encouraged to take their education seriously.[37]

Despite growing faculty disapproval, Admiral Kauffman had little choice but to continue the grade controls after he took command. He did form a special committee on grade distribution and control, made up of three academic department heads, to study the problem.[38] While not attempting to minimize the situation, the committee urged everyone to keep a proper perspective. Attrition had risen in recent years but the greatest growth was from voluntary resignations not academic failures. The committee recommended a continued ceiling on Ds and Fs; all other controls were needlessly provocative. At the same time, the committee urged the academy to educate better the faculty that "the C can hardly be considered an 'average' grade. A man with a 2.0 QPR could be the anchor man for his class."[39]

Kauffman unexpectedly announced in February 1966 that all grade controls would be removed after the present semester. Progress marks had improved enough that floating the grades now seemed reasonable. Since plebes were generally the greatest source of academic attrition, forty additional plebes would be admitted the next summer to compensate for any heavier losses. At that point, the academy believed it had done everything necessary to solve the problem.[40] Although that may have been true, the ill feelings accompanying the crisis were not resolved so easily. The grade control problem became public scandal when a disgruntled faculty member, whose contract was not being renewed, took the matter to the *Washington Post* in April 1966. This professor and other faculty felt that they were ignored by the academy in its handling of the problem. His feeling was that "the academy views its civilian faculty as a commodity which it has bought like provisions for the mess hall." Other faculty members felt pressured that not complying with the grade controls could cause them to lose their jobs.[41]

Needless to say, military authorities saw things much differently. The specific episode in question involved a meeting between Admiral Kauffman and several faculty members called in to discuss the academic situation of Admiral Minter's son. Like most turn backs, Midshipman Minter was not finding academics that much easier his second go-around at the academy. His father, the ex-superintendent, had called Kauffman to see whether anything else could be done to help his son. Both parties left the meeting with widely different interpretations of the events that transpired. The faculty members who had leaked their grievances to the press believed the superintendent had threatened them to pass Minter's son or else. Kauffman insisted such stories could be nothing farther from the truth. Although he wanted to help Minter, at no point did he imply they must pass him.[42]

A conspiracy was not necessary to explain how such differences could have occurred. Misunderstandings like these were probably not unusual to an institutional culture in the midst of profound change. Civilian faculty interpreted requests for special consideration as asking for preferential treatment. Although this was a high profile case, Admiral Kauffman was not asking for anything different from what had been done in the past, not only with admirals' sons but also star athletes, Brigade stripers, or anyone else who showed promise of being a good officer. Historically, the academy bent over backwards to help these midshipmen make it to graduation either as turn backs or through reexaminations. However, these midshipmen ultimately had to meet minimal academic standards.[43]

To be fair, other institutions also looked for ways to help struggling students. The Naval Academy probably irritated the civilian faculty more by excluding them from the decision making process than from anything they were specifically asked to do. The warning of the 1966 Middle States team was not that the academy should stop helping students but only under prescribed conditions that protected its academic integrity. It had to accept the loss of such students as a cost of raising academic standards. Since 1959, the academy had been saying that better-educated officers were the key to the Navy's future. The inspecting team was simply urging the academy to follow through on those priorities.[44]

At the same time, Annapolis was irritated that its own faculty would take its dirty laundry public. It did not expect faculty to kowtow to senior officers, but they should respect the chain of command. Certainly there was room for debate during the formulation of policy, but the academy had a right to expect its staff to follow issues that were already decided. More so than ever, it could not afford an embarrassing scandal; across the country traditional institutions were under attack from radical groups.[45] The alumni association was outraged at how the scandal had needlessly tarnished the school's reputation:

> We fear much damage has been done because of normal public reaction to devour every word of a shock story (particularly if it is aimed at military authority) and to skip lightly over the prosaic truth. The Naval Academy is not all perfect; no college, no organization can claim that utopian state. Where problems existed at the academy they are known to authorities and are being corrected as rapidly as sound, mature judgment dictates. In the recent few years, the academy has undergone a tremendous evolution in both academic organization and in the curriculum. In this transition period, problems were bound to occur despite the best advanced planning and thought of outstanding naval officers and educators.[46]

The bad publicity was not a true reflection of either group however. Many officers were truly committed to academic reform, and most civilians did not intend to embarrass the institution. Unfortunately, cultural misunderstandings clouded both groups to the best intentions of the other.

THE 1966 MIDDLE STATES EVALUATION

The Naval Academy had not faced a more important inspection in recent years than the 1966 Middle States evaluation. The March inspection marked the academic community's first official visit since the "academic revolution," so tensions were bound to be high even without the recent problems. Annapolis had been preparing specifically for the visit for over a year; the Middle States team was not likely to find problems not already identified in the school's extensive self-study. Furthermore, it had tried to be as conspicuous as possible following the advice of educators since the Folsom Board. All of the changes were reforms the academic community had been urging for some time now.[47]

Even so, Annapolis was not content to rest on past accomplishments. As late as November 1965, it was implementing additional reforms to show its commitment to the "academic revolution." The Navy released unexpected funds, quite surprising given Vietnam, for the library's renovation, a sore point left over from previous inspections. Approval was also received to increase the faculty's allowance for outside research and travel stipends. Along with the alumni association, it was exploring how to fund endowed academic chairs, which would allow distinguished scholars to teach at Annapolis on a temporary basis. The necessary money was beyond the reach of federal funds so it looked to fill the gap with private funding, as it had done with the new football stadium.[48]

The Naval Academy also investigated the possibility of a new advisory group whose sole focus would be academics. It continued to upgrade recruiting efforts that were directed at top students. The formal recruiting staff and the Blue and Gold program were expanded, the latter increasing from 160 to 250 reserve officers. Athletic recruiters were instructed to search for top scholars in the schools they visited. Finally Annapolis began an expanded orientation program to high school teachers and administrators to showcase the new program. In less than a year, it had hosted fourteen groups, totaling 490 persons.[49]

Annapolis had good reason to be optimistic. The team could not have been more pleased with what it found. It highlighted just one item in its final report, the academy's progress since the "academic revolution." The reforms were not easy to make, nor would they have been for any institution. They required commitment and sacrifice, in the face of opposition and suspicion, particularly from alumni. Above all, the transition demanded a heavy dose of humility, to hear things it did not want to hear and to do things it did not necessarily want to do. The team's overall assessment was an enthusiastic endorsement of the recent changes: "the strongest and firmest impression we have is one of rapid academic growth and a well-conceived effort to strengthen the academy's academic program."[50]

All of this praise did not mean that there were not problems or areas for improvement. Annapolis had done its best to address the structural limitations of being a training and educational institution. The best advice inspectors could give was to be logical with its priorities. If preparing students for graduate school and conferring recognizable degrees were the emphases, the academy was functioning more like a traditional civilian college, albeit with a very heavy course load and training responsibilities. It should not be surprised that "the quest for academic excellence does create new demands for resources, time, and energy," all of which created tensions between its "academic" and "military" sides.[51]

As educators, the team appreciated its newfound academic emphasis but they urged the academy to be realistic with its goals. Only Annapolis could decide which programs truly fit its objectives. It was not wise to add requirements to an already crowded curriculum merely to please civilian educators. The team was duly impressed with the surface aspects of the new curriculum, course outlines, new texts, and course objectives. But in other areas, it wondered whether the academy was attempting to do too much too soon:

> We were, perhaps, skeptical that there was "delivery" or achievement of objectives in all courses. We wondered whether, with the limitations on time for study and the difficulties of using the sanction of failure, many courses did not attempt too much? We cannot be sure this is so; we only ask the faculty, in their concern about curriculum and teaching methods, to review the problem. To be too concrete would bring opprobrium where it is not intended; what we are saying is that the reading lists and assignments must be possible, the demands of the subject matter must require more than memorization, and the examinations, if they test what is attainable and feasible, must be controlling. And, if a subject is placed in the curriculum, it must be treated as an equal.[52]

The standard expectation was two hours minimum of outside study for each hour of classroom work.[53] The team felt few students were realistically approaching that goal. The academy prided itself on its heavy demands; evaluators cited a brochure that stated, "a midshipman's busy schedule leaves little time for individual contemplation." The heavy workload was certainly excellent preparation for a division officer's duties. However, it limited the scope of a midshipman's education: "Time for study has become increasingly important and has been provided. Time for contemplation, for independent investigation of a subject or idea, does not seem available." The answers to these difficult questions were not to be found in yet another reorganization of the daily schedule.[54]

More than ever, Annapolis needed firm, stable leadership with a thorough understanding of past problems and concrete ideas for the future. Evaluators were deeply concerned with the frequent turnover in academy leadership. Superintendents and commandants rarely had the opportunity to complete their reforms. Their successors finished them midstream. The team recognized that the Navy was primarily responsible for fixing this problem. Senior officers should not be penalized at promotion for staying at Annapolis. In fact, academy duty should be rewarded. Also disturbing to inspectors was the sharp increase in voluntary resignations. Given the recent efforts at recruiting and the record qualifications of entering midshipmen, attrition was still surprisingly high.[55]

Evaluators wondered how many voluntary resignations were due to these conflicting priorities. Time pressure may have been inherent to the academy's character-building program. However, it should not excuse poor management or an inability to articulate its goals. Even though it was difficult, the academy needed to clarify its priorities so midshipmen, particularly the plebes, would not be placed in an impossible situation. A case in point was substantial evidence of academic underachievement, which the team attributed to "the competition for time" more than "poor teaching, which we have not seen in evidence, poor equipment, or inadequate laboratories, which are limitations not present at the academy." Despite the recent progress, the institutional culture still nourished, inadvertently or not, values that were anti-academic. The primary intent of academic hurdles, in other words, should be their scholastic value not character development.[56]

The team was most concerned about the growing rift between the academic and military sides of the academy. If not resolved, the fear was "that the faculty may develop into two camps and that the cohesive quality so necessary if a faculty is to function as an effective force will not be achieved." Many of its substantive recommendations were aimed at improving this relationship. First of all, with all the recent changes, the academy needed more help than the Middle States Association was in a position to give. Ten years was too long between major inspections, especially with everything that was happening.[57]

The Naval Academy needed to consider strengthening the powers of the Board of Visitors. Greater numbers of professional educators should be included on the board, specifically to review the curriculum. It needed to meet more frequently, and board members should be required to attend all meetings. Annual visits were not sufficient to keep it abreast of everything that was happening. Their inspections might be more critical of Annapolis but ultimately they would benefit the institution more.[58]

The team agreed that the academy should proceed with a separate advisory body to focus solely on academic affairs. Even with the extra meetings, the Board of Visitors was too busy to give the new academic program proper attention. Members of this group needed to be senior scholars and administrators, people with outstanding academic credentials, of course, but also strong personal reputations that military officers could easily trust. The Navy would also have its representatives, senior officers chosen not only for their advanced degrees but also their operational backgrounds. In other words, the idea was to create the best possible marriage between the traditional academic and military cultures.[59]

Finally, inspectors recommended that civilians be given a greater voice in the institution's direction. Whether senior officers liked it or not, this problem was not going away, and ignoring it risked a repetition of the grade control controversy. Since the crisis, the local chapter of the American Association of University Professors (AAUP) had grown from a handful of civilian professors to over seventy members, all committed to a furtherance of the "academic revolution" and greater involvement in policymaking decisions. The academy was encouraged to follow through on plans for an Academic Council made up of military and civilian instructors, chosen by their respective departments, and a Faculty Senate, which would have substantive power over the school's academic life. Annapolis needed to be flexible to appointing civilian department heads, especially when officers lacked the basic academic qualifications for these jobs. None of these reforms was intended to subvert the chain of command. The goal was simply better communication across the academy.[60]

Even small improvements could help repair the military's relationship with civilians and vice versa. A faculty handbook was needed to train new instructors on their responsibilities and the unique history of Annapolis. Senior officers should not be surprised that younger civilians were unfamiliar with the military and the academy's place in the commissioning pipeline, much less professional indoctrination or Bancroft Hall. This publication could clarify misunderstandings before they became major disagreements. Finally, both groups needed to be more respectful of one another's responsibilities. For example, inspectors worried about "academic advising running afoul of military regulations. The academy faculty should have full responsibility for the student's academic program, with freedom to make adjustments that are important for his academic progress." In other words, faculty were the first contact for academic problems; officers needed to be involved too but primarily to counsel midshipmen about their study habits and time management.[61]

The Naval Academy quickly corrected most of the Middle States team's discrepancies, especially those that did not contradict its existing culture. The Navy worked with its congressional supporters to expand the numbers of professional educators on the Board of Visitors. With all the curriculum changes, the Board also agreed to the necessity of meeting twice a year. New standing committees were established to keep members informed on recent changes at Annapolis. The most important of these, the Committee on Educational Policy, had the academy's own Academic Dean as its secretary.[62]

Although the Board of Visitors objected to the creation of the Academic Advisory Board, the secretary of the Navy approved its establishment in July 1966. The membership of this group read like a "Who's Who of Higher Education"—Dr. Herbert Longenecker, president of Tulane University; Dr. Richard Folsom, president of Rensselaer Polytechnic Institute; Dr. Carey Croneis, chancellor of Rice University; Dr. Milton Eisenhower, president of the Johns Hopkins University, Dr. George Maslach, dean of engineering at California Berkeley, and Dr. George Schultz, dean of the Business School at the University of Chicago. As planned, the military also had its distinguished representatives, including Admiral Horatio Rivero, vice chief of naval operations and past member of the Folsom Board, and Vice Admiral William Smedberg, past superintendent and president of the alumni association. This kind of firepower made it difficult for either the academy or the academic community to ignore its recommendations. Unlike other inspecting bodies, this group visited three times a year, with little time wasted on fluff activities. Since most board members were already familiar with Annapolis, they could focus on immediate problems.[63]

The academy was surprisingly receptive to greater faculty involvement in policymaking discussions. However, military authorities saw changes here as being more advisory in nature than anything else. Like most senior officers, Admiral Kauffman did not believe in summoning juniors to ask them for complaints and suggestions. By the fall of 1966, the academy published its first faculty handbook, which laid out expectations for new instructors. Although it did not appoint any civilian professors as academic department heads, it left it open as a possibility for the future. For now, though, it was content with the existing leadership, which meant senior naval officers running the show.[64]

The most senior group advising the superintendent continued to be the Academic Council, which included the commandant, the dean, assistant deans, department heads, and senior civilian professors in the departments. Admiral Kauffman reluctantly began including younger, more vocal faculty in some policymaking discussions. In the fall of 1966, an Academic Forum was established, which in theory represented the voice and conscience of the entire faculty. Membership was based on one representative for every ten faculty; officers were appointed by the academy while the departments elected civilian representatives. The Academic Forum preempted earlier plans by younger faculty for a faculty senate.[65]

Admiral Kauffman rejected this idea because of provisions in its constitution, which made its decisions binding on the superintendent. Again, this controversy is best understood in terms of a clash between the academic and military cultures. Senior officers were not above seeking advice from civilians, but they were not about to surrender control of their academy. Conversely, many of Kauffman's faculty opponents were lukewarm about the Academic Forum. Many thought that they had been thrown a bone to quiet their protests and nothing more. Such skepticism prevented the Academic Forum from ever accomplishing anything truly substantial. Meetings were often confrontational, with all sorts of charges being lobbed back and forth between both sides.[66]

Given all of the recent controversy, it was not surprising that there was huge public speculation about the results of the Middle States evaluation. Admiral Kauffman took the unusual step of releasing a portion of the report to calm any fears about the academy. Little did he know that such actions would ignite yet another controversy. The bottom line, as far as he was concerned, was that its accreditation had been renewed. The lack of details gave suspicion that there was more to the story than Annapolis was telling. As more information surfaced, public attention focused on recommendations that were less than complimentary of the academy.[67] Sniffing a scandal, newspapers, such as the *New York Times* and the *Washing-*

ton Post, highlighted the tensions between officers and civilians, the overly congested schedule, and the growing attrition rate. What was lost was their overall consensus of rapid academic growth and praise for the new curriculum.[68]

The academy could not help but feel blindsided by these articles and felt their conclusions were often distorted. The alumni association in particular was outraged by comments that almost seemed slanderous.[69] One such article focused on the report's comments about schedule imbalances and students' supposed academic underachievement. It concluded, "midshipmen are not learning what their counterparts in civilian colleges are." To which Admiral Smedberg, the association's president, replied, "I think all Naval Academy graduates will say, 'Thank the Lord!!' . . . We know that the Naval Academy is not a university or a civilian college; it is a naval school, whose sole purpose is to produce *career* Naval and Marine Corps officers. The history of this country and of our navy shows that the Naval Academy has done a pretty good job in this respect." The differences of opinion illuminate the growing distrust between supporters of the traditional military culture and the anti-establishment groups they believed were attacking it. In a searing indictment of the condition of many Vietnam-era colleges and universities, Smedberg went on to say,

> We need not be ashamed that the midshipmen are not achieving what their counterparts in civilian colleges are; rabble-rousing on college campuses, burning their draft cards, protesting because they are told they should not use obscene language, rebelling against constituted administrative authorities, and openly reviling our country's foreign policies and spitting and trampling on her flag. As long as our academy continues to teach submergence of self in dedication to our country, integrity of character, and loyalty, both up and down, we'll have our pride in her.[70]

The Naval Academy faced a difficult time integrating the reforms of the "academic revolution" into its institutional culture. Unfortunately, these very real challenges were becoming entangled in the growing debate over the Vietnam War.

Problems with Plebe Indoctrination

The accreditation team was surprisingly mum about plebe indoctrination. It suspected some connection between the increase in voluntary resignations and the plebe system, but there was not enough hard data or time to verify any hunches. For the most part, their observations were strikingly complimentary of Admiral Minter's changes. The system seemed well supervised and administered, especially compared to previous years. The academy had finally taken serious steps to hold upperclassmen accountable for their actions. The Middle States group did recommend a formal training course for all upperclassmen supervising plebes. And to be fair, the focus of their inspection was the new curriculum, not plebe indoctrination. However, with all the concern about the crowded schedule, it was surprising that greater attention was not devoted to this critical area of academy life.[71]

Yet there were good reasons why an inspection team might be hesitant to delve too deeply into plebe indoctrination. It was difficult for outsiders to understand exactly what transpired inside Bancroft Hall. Schedule demands fell heaviest on plebes, especially during academic year. Even if they learned to budget their time wisely, there was always something important that did not get done. Beyond these surface observations, however, it was difficult to ascertain what made it so challenging or what, if anything, needed reform.[72] Only alumni understood the hassles of committing to memory all the various forms of plebe knowledge. They alone understood the terror of plebe come-arounds or the stress of mealtimes. Room and uniform standards were always applied most severely to plebes, and menial service was still expected in most companies. Adding to the frustration, plebes were responsible for many things beyond their control, the success of the football team being one good example. It was no wonder then that plebes celebrated the end of the year with such joy.[73]

Complicating matters further, reformers had to recognize that the system did not always work as planned. New ground rules tried to clarify the acceptable forms of plebe indoctrination. Minter and Kinney had developed a new organization, the squad system, to bring greater accountability to the program. Each year, the warnings were issued about hazing being a serious offense punishable with dismissal from the academy. Yet, for all efforts at reform, the academy understood that unauthorized activities still happened, even hazing.[74] Upperclassmen could be incredibly innovative at sidestepping rules they did not want to follow. New activities were invented each year or old ones were given new names to perpetuate "important" traditions. They were committed to ensuring that their plebes had a "proper" plebe year, which usually meant something similar to their own.[75] To some extent, this practice existed in all companies and battalions. However, some relished reputations for being tough on plebes. Normally upperclassmen hesitated to interfere with each other with regard to plebe indoctrination. To do so would be calling their leadership abilities into question. And if mistakes were made, that was part of the process of learning to lead.

Until recently, the Brigade's expansion had left the Executive Department undermanned. Even with extra officers in the new thirty-six company scheme, they could not be watching midshipmen all the time. Only duty officers were available at night. Not all of them were committed to enforcing the new requirements either.[76] Finally, reform efforts had to overcome the academy's natural protective tendency of the plebe system. It was, after all, the heart and soul of professional socialization. The system not only eliminated the unfit but also any who were lukewarm about a military career. It bonded classmates together and helped them succeed in combat. It did not matter that these assumptions were not fully proven. No one could conceive of Annapolis without the plebe system, they were so closely intertwined. Few supporters dared call it perfect, but the benefits outweighed any flaws. Plebes had to be trained, and upperclassmen needed practical leadership experience. Most midshipmen survived plebe year and, at least afterwards, viewed it as a positive experience.[77]

With that being said, there was growing concern, particularly among civilian faculty, that the plebe system was hampering the "academic revolution." In the fall of 1966, professors from the humanities department (English, History, and Government) spearheaded another effort at reform. Initially their goals were modest, or so they thought; most remaining requirements should be concentrated in the summer leaving the traditional school year free for academics. Formal indoctrination would essentially end when the Brigade returned in the fall. Even this "modest proposal" was too much for many officers to accept. In their mind, plebe year's greatest test was not any specific obstacle but the incredible duration. These reforms eliminated its most challenging aspect. Furthermore, a watered down version was not likely to accomplish the institution's professional goals.[78]

Many officers also resented civilian interference in an area they supposedly did not understand or belong to. The military's intransigence led to a more intensive investigation, which furthered their calls for radical reform. For the "academic revolution" to survive, the existing plebe system would have to end. The military obviously viewed these ideas as more outrageous and unacceptable as the first. Emotions on both sides grew more heated as the debate intensified, since both groups believed their actions were necessary for the school's well being. The plebe system had increasingly fallen under the microscope in recent years. In the summer of 1965, Senator Jennings Randolph launched an investigation prompted by a recent appointee supposedly "run out" of Annapolis. Beyond the details of this particular case, Randolph wanted to determine the extent of any remaining hazing in Bancroft Hall.[79]

The Randolph examination did not uncover enough evidence to warrant wholesale changes; however, its findings were not all that flattering either. Most disturbing was an interview by the Naval Investigative Service with the head of the academy's Executive Department, Captain Kenneth Brown

5: "PROFESSIONAL REVOLUTION" AT ANNAPOLIS, 1965–68

'42. To have a senior officer in that position describe plebe year as "the biggest cancer in the U.S. Navy" was a huge embarrassment for Annapolis. The system taught too many negative lessons, in his opinion, to be a useful exercise in leadership. Shortly after his remarks, Brown was unexpectedly transferred to an operational command in Vietnam. The lesson here was obvious to other potential critics. The plebe system was a sacred cow that reformers tinkered with at their peril.[80]

Coming on the heels of recent problems, the academy was in no mood for further controversy, especially from within the institution. Its leaders were challenged enough by the "academic revolution" and Vietnam; they did not need their own staff providing further ammunition to critics. However, Brown's transfer did not end the problem. Indeed, a chorus of voices began calling for major changes to the plebe system. The breadth of this opposition was what made this crisis so potentially threatening. The academy had learned to expect controversy from its Young Turks but not its normal supporters. What was interesting was how each group came to oppose it and what they hoped to accomplish.[81]

The concerns of Robert Seager, a professor in the history department, were typical of many younger instructors. Like many of his peers, Seager had come to Annapolis specifically because of the "academic revolution"; in fact, he had turned down better academic jobs to do so. No one could deny his passion for the new Naval Academy. The success of its Fulbright Scholar program, for example, resulted largely from his efforts. Seager was also committed, however, to greater civilian governance of the academy. Not only was he a pioneer member of its AAUP chapter, he also served as its first president. Seager would not be muzzled on potentially embarrassing issues either; he initiated the AAUP's decision to denounce grade controls publicly.[82]

Seager's opposition to plebe indoctrination stemmed from his commitment to the "academic revolution," which he felt it endangered. In a sharply worded letter to Admiral Kauffman, he warned that without reform, all other efforts were in vain:

> None of these things are of very much significance if there is no genuine intellectual atmosphere in our Yard. To define the role Bancroft Hall plays in the academic life of our midshipmen as merely anti-intellectual would be to praise it with faint damns. It is more than anti-intellectual. It is corrosive and destructive of everything the learning process at the college level involves. In my opinion this corrosiveness centers largely at the Company level. Not only are many of the Company Officers ill-educated themselves, they seem to have no control over, or they see fit to exercise no control over, the upperclassmen who run the Plebe System. I see no evidence that the recent reforms in the Plebe System are anything more than nice-sounding phrases committed hopefully to

paper by the Commandant's Office and committed to the wastebasket by everyone else in the Hall. The attitude there toward the entire academic program is one of muted hostility.[83]

His remarks did not win many friends among officers but they were difficult to ignore. Unlike most civilians, he had gone through a plebe system himself, both at the Citadel and the Merchant Marine Academy; his operational experiences also gave him a strong basis of what it took to be a competent line officer. Their acerbic tone guaranteed a similar response from the military. Seager pointed out the hostility of many company officers to academic opportunities, such as the Fulbright program, as evidence of what he was talking about. He cited one company officer who opposed "all this scholarship crap because it put the midshipmen behind their classmates in their service careers." Another officer informed him that his cooperation was only given "because the superintendent is pushing this nonsense this year." Most disturbing to Seager were the sentiments of a Marine officer that told him that a Fulbright candidate was "too smart for his own good and needed a little combat seasoning in Vietnam to get himself straightened out."[84]

Although Seager was among the harshest of Admiral Kauffman's critics, he was not the only faculty member to voice concerns. As the controversy grew in late 1966, even senior faculty began to speak out against plebe indoctrination. Professor E. B. Potter was one of the most respected historians, both professionally and personally, at the academy. Not known for outlandish statements, Potter got along well with officers for whom he showed genuine respect. The academy was fortunate, Potter believed, that so much of the plebe system was a mystery to outsiders; enough had gotten out however "to give the service academies a kind of silly reputation that repels many good students and teachers."[85]

Many older instructors had served alongside academy graduates as reserve officers in World War II. They too knew something of what it took to be successful in battle. While not denying the heroism of academy graduates, Potter insisted that it was premature simply to chalk that up to plebe indoctrination. "What amazes me," Potter said, "is that the alleged benefits of the system seem to be a matter of mere assumption—the sort of basis on which military men should avoid making decisions." While not linking his objections specifically to the "academic revolution," Potter was also skeptical about the plebe system's compatibility with a truly academic atmosphere:

> We are taught that education is merely living one's life, at an accelerated pace and with life problems selected and not a mere matter of chance. Therefore we teachers avoid presenting artificial problems for solution. In my opinion the

problems presented by the plebe system for solution are about as artificial as can well be contrived. Memorizing the inconsequential is no preparation for remembering the consequential. Being subjected to gross humiliation by servicemen is no way to develop pride in the service. Wasting time on nonsense is no way to learn to economize one's means. That most midshipmen come through relatively unscathed merely demonstrates the resiliency of the human spirit.[86]

Potter's comments had to sting, coming as they did from a faithful supporter of the academy, even though his remarks were given with the highest sense of personal loyalty. As opposed to Seager, at no point, did Potter hint at making his objections public. Likewise, he never crossed the bridge of directly challenging the academy to eliminate the plebe system. He expected military authorities to determine that themselves.[87]

The plebe system's detractors were not limited to the history department either. Two senior professors from the English department, coincidentally the chairmen of the Fourth and Third Class Committees overseeing the academic affairs of those classes, also objected to the present system. Professor A. S. Pitt, a faculty member for twenty-five years, had difficulty explaining to younger colleagues why plebes were not prepared for their classes. Particularly shocking to new faculty was that "midshipmen are so exhausted they cannot stay awake in class." Pitt supported the basic premises of plebe indoctrination but felt the academy was too tolerant of gross violations. Officers could not allow it to interfere with plebes' study time and sleep if their first year was to be productive academically. The bulk of indoctrination must be completed during the summer, not the academic year. Like Potter, however, Pitt advocated a milder solution than eliminating plebe year altogether.[88]

Another longtime member of the department, Professor Douglas Lacey, expressed his misgivings too. Based on his Pacific War experiences, Lacey questioned plebe year's intrinsic value in preparing midshipmen for combat. More importantly, the current system contained too much opportunity for abuse. He believed that "upperclassmen who wish to do so can and do decide whether plebes should or should not be allowed to remain at the academy. In making these decisions, they in effect veto the judgment of all those experienced educators, congressmen, instructors, and officers who taught, trusted, interviewed, and passed upon the qualifications of these plebes." Of greatest concern, Lacey felt that "the plebe system tends to be harder on validators and the intelligent plebes than those of lesser ability, and as a result we lose boys of superior ability through resignation."[89]

Most surprising to the academy was the involvement of one of its own, Captain Wayne Hoof, head of English, History, and Government. Hoof was in every way the model military faculty member. He was an academy graduate '41, had a distinguished career as an engineering duty officer, and had a solid postgraduate record capped off with an advanced engineering degree from MIT. He was also a classmate and personal friend of the commandant, Captain Sheldon Kinney. His present assignment was his second consecutive tour as a department head, the first being as head of the engineering department. There was some talk of making his position permanent to help with the turnover problems in military leadership. Ironically, Hoof was transferred into English, History, and Government because of the urgency in finding a replacement for Captain Brown. Since the engineering department primarily taught upper division courses, Hoof rarely interacted with plebes before. The heavy dose of core courses in English, History, and Government gave him greater opportunity to observe problems with plebe indoctrination and the new curriculum. What he saw led him to become a champion for reform.[90]

To be fair, Hoof also became involved because of difficulties his younger son was having that year with plebe indoctrination. After several conversations with his son and plebe friends, Hoof became convinced that the present system had gone far astray of his own indoctrination from the late 1930s. The biggest change from Hoof's perspective was the amount of time the plebe system now demanded of midshipmen. The academy had done an impressive job of curbing the unauthorized physical abuse, but upperclassmen had been ingenious in replacing it with different types of mental pressure. They were greatly stretching the definition of what proper professional knowledge entailed. Plebes were still researching obscure "professional" topics at the expense of valuable study time.[91]

Hoof also believed that the new squad system was not as beneficial as the academy had planned. The older mentoring system assigned plebes to specific first classmen, who handled their training and indoctrination but also served as their confidants and protectors. The present system did not have any of these protective features. Nor did it offer a solution in cases where the squad leader was the perpetrator of unauthorized abuse. In other words, plebes no longer had anyone running interference for them when upperclassmen were out of line. The bottom line was that these plebes were spending several hours a day on plebe responsibilities, which left little time free for academics.[92]

In retrospect, it is difficult to ascertain the extent to which Hoof's observations were true. Certainly, these plebes were having a difficult time, but Hoof's older son had also graduated from Annapolis in 1965. How much more difficult had the plebe system become in just a few years time or were the instances of abuse isolated to his younger son's company? Upperclassmen had stretched the definition of "professional knowledge" for years. The rationale was to keep plebes off balance to see how they would respond to pressure. Perhaps Hoof's natural desire to protect his son was clouding him from being objective. However, longtime faculty in his department had similar impressions that plebe year had changed since the "academic revolution." The real challenge was determining to what degree these incidents were representative of Bancroft Hall as a whole.

The plebe system had always consumed large chunks of the day, perhaps more so than Hoof remembered. Yet, it seems that the "academic revolution" may have contributed to a larger share of bizarre professional reports than normal. Many topics required hours of outside research and occasional consultation with faculty, all of which *was* prohibited. Upperclassmen joked about this in *The Log,* in effect saying let's see how much these new plebes know. Perhaps, this reflected jealousy on their part at not having the same academic opportunities available to them. Upperclassmen were well aware of their plebes' supposedly impressive academic qualifications. It may be that they overcompensated for this supposed academic imbalance with unrealistic expectations of professional knowledge.[93]

The squad system may have also contributed to the problem, but it was not its root cause. Upperclassmen could always exercise bad leadership and they could not be removed from plebe indoctrination. The organizational scheme that was in place really did not matter. The solution was not any different than the past; upperclassmen had to be properly trained and supervised. The academy also had to be willing to discipline those who were out of line. The problems were not new, but they were difficult to solve. *Attitudes* had to be changed. Upperclassmen needed to view the new squad leader position as an important responsibility and accept that plebe year meant more than dishing out what happened to them. None of this would happen unless the Executive Department supported any reforms too. Upperclassmen were probably not going to change on their own.

Yet the biggest single reason for any additional problems was the new curriculum. Most courses were now requiring two hours of outside study for every hour of classroom work. Critical adjustments were made for the new curriculum, but time balance remained a serious problem.[94] In the case of Hoof's son and his friends, none of them were getting close to the recommended study time. All of their choices were problematic: falling hopelessly behind in their classes or risking their upperclassmen's wrath for not completing their plebe duties, neither of which was a pleasant alternative. Hoof's professors reported similar conditions from plebes they questioned from other companies.[95]

Worse yet, Bancroft Hall was still intruding on time supposedly reserved for academics. Study hour violations of all kinds—upperclassmen tearing up rooms before an inspection, plebes working on spirit-related activities, like sheet posters and bulletin boards, upperclassmen barging into rooms quizzing them on their rates—persisted despite the threat of serious punishment. Most plebes risked breaking curfew, either at taps or reveille, to catch up on their impossibly busy schedule. The damage grew progressively worse over time. Losing sleep was the only option without apparent adverse consequences. Over a semester, plebes simply exhausted themselves; many were falling asleep in their classes or at a minimum doing less than their best academic work. What made this situation intolerable, according to Hoof, was that it flew in the face of regulations, and officers were overlooking gross violations. The choices in his mind were clear. If the academy was serious about the new curriculum, Bancroft Hall would have to do more to accommodate it.[96]

The great travesty here was that the academy was losing many potentially fine officers. In Hoof's opinion, most truly bad plebes had left during the summer; those who remained not only wanted to be there but had proven themselves already. Even the Naval Academy's own studies had shown that plebes were most motivated during the summer; the Brigade's return was often demoralizing because it was like leaving sheep to the wolves. Hoof questioned the benefit of continuing indoctrination into the academic year, especially with the time requirements of the new curriculum. Plebe year had essentially become a waste academically. Of those who were leaving, many wanted to become officers, but they were frustrated at not being able to do their best in the classroom.[97]

Voluntary resignations of this nature were tragic not only for the individual but also for the academy. Hoof highlighted just several cases of what midshipmen were being lost because of seemingly misguided priorities. Most discouraging personally was the loss of one of his son's friends, Midshipman Leonard Panza, a former second class hospital corpsman who won his appointment through fleet-wide examination and spent an additional year at the academy preparatory school. His quick actions during the summer had saved the life of a classmate who had fallen ill to heat exhaustion. He also possessed outstanding leadership abilities, which resulted in his selection as the fourth class regimental commander during plebe summer. Now, just halfway into his first academic term, Panza was resigning knowing it meant returning to the fleet, largely because of the plebe system. In a thoughtfully worded letter to the superintendent, Panza explained his reasons for leaving Annapolis:

> The statements that I intend to make are based primarily upon personal experiences and observations, although they do reflect in part on discussions that I have had with classmates of mine throughout the Brigade. They are widespread enough, however, that the validity of these discussions could conceivably jeopardize the mission and future of the Naval Academy. The principal faults of the plebe system, in my opinion, are as follows: violation of the fundamental concepts of leadership, lack of opportunity or encouragement to devote a reasonable amount of time to the academic program, absence of an academic environment, loss of human dignity, and injustice. The combined result of

5: "PROFESSIONAL REVOLUTION" AT ANNAPOLIS, 1965–68   193

these faults is failure to achieve motivation for a naval career, and nullification of the motivation and enthusiasm generated during plebe summer.[98]

Unfortunately Panza was not the only plebe with distinguished credentials to be leaving the academy. Midshipman Jeffrey Leppert, an enlisted marine and combat veteran of Vietnam, the only person in the class of 1970 to have such experience, had also become disillusioned with Annapolis. Leppert had also shown tremendous leadership potential during plebe summer and was the regimental sub-commander for the fourth class. Yet Leppert had also chosen to leave after only one semester knowing that it meant returning to the Marine Corps *and* possibly Vietnam. In a more bitterly worded letter than Panza's, Leppert singled out the plebe system as his primary reason for leaving the academy:

> I came to the United States Naval Academy from the ranks of the United States Marine Corps with the purpose of obtaining the finest professional military training available in the world, along with an outstanding education. Having served as a midshipman I have become convinced that though the educational opportunities are outstanding, the professional training and the standards of professional conduct set for and practiced by the Brigade are far below those I had previously been trained to expect. It is my personal preference to serve with and under men whom I respect and whose professional conduct is a source of pride and example.[99]

Although unfortunate, the academy had come to expect such losses among prior enlisted midshipmen. On the surface, prior military service would appear to have been a great advantage in adjusting to the school's "military culture." However, many former enlisted were saying that the operational forces were vastly different from Annapolis. Bancroft Hall was unique but that was not necessarily good. The age and experience of these midshipmen was a two-edged sword. It gave them the potential to be fine leaders but also made it difficult for them to stomach the immaturity found in Bancroft Hall.[100]

Finally, Professor Seager brought to Captain Hoof's attention the case of Anthony Jackson, another midshipman the academy could ill afford to lose. Seager had been so impressed with Jackson's comments and enthusiasm in class that he could not understand why this promising student started to struggle and eventually decided to resign from the academy. The culprit Seager found out was the plebe system; for reasons unbeknownst to him, Jackson's upperclassmen had determined to drive him from the academy. After the fact, Seager discovered that some of his upperclassmen had decided that Jackson did not have the right character traits to be a midshipman.[101]

Jackson, an African American from a single parent home in Washington, D.C., eventually explained to Seager his reasons for leaving the academy. He was admitted to Princeton University but had chosen Annapolis to be closer to his family. Financial considerations, especially the opportunity for a free education, had played heavily into his decision. Jackson believed that neither he nor his family could afford for him to remain at an institution where his ability to get a good education was in jeopardy. In poignant terms, Jackson described his situation:

> I may be making a tremendous mistake in having resigned if it turns out that a career as a naval officer is what I want, despite all that has transpired, but right now my primary concern is getting a good, sound college education, and I don't believe I can get it here. I guess, really, what it boils down to is that you just don't have time to do everything the way it's supposed to be done. When you know you'll have to run extra duty for not having a professional question, but nothing happens when your assignments are unprepared as long as you maintain a 2.0 QPR, there is little incentive to do any more than the minimum required academically. The system seems to say, "Do what you can get away with, nothing more," that scholarship isn't really important since you're being trained to be naval officers, not college graduates.[102]

The Naval Academy was under pressure from both Washington and the NAACP to improve its poor record with minority candidates. Here it had lost a promising student because it was not living up to the stated priorities of the "academic revolution."

It was heart-wrenching stories like these, as well as his own son's predicament, which prompted Captain Hoof to break his silence and risk his career by challenging the plebe system. The deeper he looked into the situation Hoof came to believe that drastic action was necessary to curb the mounting resignations and flagrant abuses. Hoof initially kept his concerns within the institution. He recommended that the superintendent place a moratorium on plebe indoctrination, similar to how it granted carry-on following a football victory over Army. The stopgap measure would prevent more unnecessary resignations until better information became available. Hoof's superiors had difficulty believing these problems were anything more than isolated examples. Certainly the system was not perfect, but random troublemakers did not warrant rash actions, especially to a program so vital to its interests.[103]

Unable to obtain satisfaction internally, Hoof escalated his grievances up the chain of command. The same request was made in November 1966 to the chief of naval personnel, Kauffman's immediate superior. Hoof understood the trouble his actions were causing and how difficult it was to implement his recommendations. His actions were also placing a tremendous strain on his personal relationships, especially with Captain Kinney. He was adamant, however, that his actions were worth the trouble. Hoof's bottom line was "that the Naval Academy can never achieve its present academic goals nor realize its professional potential as long as the plebe system is in existence, and as long as plebe indoctrination extends beyond plebe summer. The time consuming and wasteful practices which are involved are incompatible with any worthwhile and progressive educational program."[104]

The only other alternative was canceling the "academic revolution," which Hoof did not necessarily reject doing. At least the "trade school" academy was consistent in its priorities. So far, the new Annapolis had not truly decided what kind of institution it wanted to be. He pointed to the reservations of its critics:

> Their reasoning is that the academy exists solely for the purpose of training naval officers, and that our former curriculum, combined with the plebe system has produced outstanding officers. They believe the academy is *by, for,* and *of* the Navy and that we should not invite or worry about outside criticism. These critics may be right, but if this is really to be our policy we should put a halt to our efforts to "upgrade" our faculty and academic stature. If we are to continue to strive for a sound academic program, however, one that can not be justifiably criticized by outsiders—we must establish a suitable atmosphere.[105]

Captain Hoof took issue with the frequent comments from alumni and other officers that Annapolis should not attempt to be an "MIT on the Severn." As an alumnus of that institution too, he believed it was not the program Annapolis should try to emulate but its attitude towards academics. The difference between the two institutions, he thought, was profound: "at MIT the atmosphere is permeated with serious and scholarly efforts. Students have a goal, are working toward that goal, and moreover are proud of the academic achievement of simply being at MIT. Unfortunately we have not yet reached the point where the average midshipman is proud of his *academic* achievement upon graduation."[106]

Although his formal protest went through BUPERS, Hoof, after much agonizing about sidestepping official channels, decided to forward the same information to the secretary of the Navy. He worried that the problems were too endemic that his case would not get a fair review within the Navy. There was too much interest in perpetuating the status quo to consider such a dramatic proposal objectively.[107] The seriousness of his evidence—statements by respected faculty and eyewitness evidence from affected plebes, much less his own research—made it difficult to dismiss these claims outright. As Hoof had feared, before BUPERS did anything, it wanted specific details on these incidents. It was not that this information was unavailable, but it confirmed that the Navy's investigation was headed in the wrong place. His report was intended to show systemic problems with plebe indoctrination; the Navy was more concerned about whether the alleged events had occurred.[108]

Although not exactly a whitewash, the BUPERS inquiry was certainly less penetrating than Hoof and his faculty colleagues had hoped for. Overseeing the investigation was Commander Donald Smith, the head of the BUPERS branch on midshipmen affairs and a former company officer. Seen in the best light, Smith was the most qualified person to handle the matter; however, his own appointment letter cast doubts on the depth of his examination. Smith was directed "to limit his investigation to specific allegations and facts which may be verified, and not to inquire into the broad policy matters suggested in your letter." Furthermore, BUPERS already decided, "in no case will disciplinary action be taken as a result of information verified by Commander Smith's investigation."[109]

Given this limited focus, Smith finished his inquiry in just over a week. Most incidents had occurred just as Captain Hoof had indicated. However, Smith concluded that these were isolated instances and not part of any harmful pattern intrinsic to plebe indoctrination. The greatest discrepancies were numerous curfew violations by plebes attempting to get extra work done, professional questions beyond the scope of authorized topics, and study hour interruptions of all kinds. The new curriculum had compacted the plebes' busy schedule even more than it was before. However, it was nothing that good time management and organizational skills could not cure. Even though these were serious findings, they did not warrant as extreme an action as getting rid of plebe year entirely.[110]

Hoof and his colleagues were obviously disappointed with the findings, but it was not surprising that the Navy erred on the side of caution. Reformers believed there was enough evidence to justify extreme changes. The Navy, however, needed more information and better guarantees that drastic reforms would work. Hoof continued pressing his case through official channels, this time a letter to the other towering figure in the chain of command, the chief of naval operations. He also wrote the secretary of the Navy again, this time as a concerned parent to hedge against charges of insubordination.[111] At the same time, the crisis started to attract its share of media attention, most noticeably the same *New York Times* reporter who had "blown the lid off" the grade control scandal.[112] Although he was unsure of his stance on plebe indoctrination, at a minimum the secretary of the Navy did not want another public relations fiasco at the Naval Academy. In a surprising move announced shortly after the 1966 Army-Navy football game, Secretary Paul Nitze ordered the academy to stand down from plebe introduction until the crisis was resolved, shocking because carry-on was granted only after a Navy victory, which had not happened.[113]

All of the attention prompted the academy to take greater action to resolve the controversy. In December 1966, Admiral Kauffman convened

5: "PROFESSIONAL REVOLUTION" AT ANNAPOLIS, 1965–68   197

a special Midshipmen Time and Effort Board, made up of senior officers and senior civilian professors, to look at balance in the schedule. This group found the same problems identified earlier by Captain Hoof and Commander Smith. By this point, both groups were deeply suspicious of one another's intentions. Reformers insisted that the special board's investigation was not thorough enough—only seven plebes and four first classmen were questioned. However, the same argument could also be made towards their evidence base. Military leaders were frustrated by the reformers' impatience. No one should expect them to jettison a bedrock tradition overnight. With eliminating plebe indoctrination not an option, the board did recommend a series of striking changes that were implemented in January 1967.[114]

The revamped plebe year preserved the existing system albeit with important new restrictions, the end goal being a better balance between academics and Bancroft Hall. Company officers would closely monitor a new taps and reveille schedule, which ensured plebes a minimum of seven and a half hours of sleep each night, to keep them more alert in class. Mealtime regulations were also changed, which allowed plebes to remain in the mess hall after march-out to ensure they received a complete meal. Most importantly, new procedures were implemented to make study hour more sacrosanct than before. Plebe rates could constitute no more than thirty minutes of the day. Professional questions were limited to common source documents. Both of these changes were also to be rigorously enforced by the Executive Department. The number of rates plebes had to know verbatim was also reduced. Company administrative time was limited to the half-hour after evening meal, after which everyone was to be in their rooms studying. Alternative forms of discipline besides conduct reports and demerits were instituted to dispel any feelings that the plebe system was being diluted. However, physical exercise of any kind was forbidden as a form of punishment, which had been a way around regulations against hazing in the past.[115]

No matter how well sounding, the key to making these reforms effective was better administration and enforcement. The academy also implemented new procedures, which gave first classmen greater control and responsibility over the plebe system. The thought was that seniors were more likely to support changes they had a hand in making. Officers were personally accountable to senior leaders for the actions of their upperclassmen. On too many occasions, they had either explicitly or implicitly condoned major violations of the plebe system. At a minimum, the academy recognized that these attitudes must come to an end. To some extent, the superintendent and commandant were also personally negligent in this respect. No one could accuse Admiral Kauffman of micromanagement but perhaps that was what the system needed. In contrast, his successor, Admiral James Calvert, was more willing to excoriate officers with a poor record in this area.[116]

Hopefully this crisis resulted in a more effective plebe system because the whole episode was not without its share of unfortunate casualties. The academy lost a number of plebes who would have made fine officers, including eventually Captain Hoof's younger son. Because of his leadership in the affair, Captain Hoof chose to resign from the Navy shortly afterwards, after which he began a second career as a college administrator. It took him many years, however, to rebuild the friendships fractured as a result of this controversy. Many of Hoof's civilian colleagues, however, remember him very fondly for all he attempted to do on the academy's behalf. Robert Seager's contract was not renewed at the end of the academic year although he went on to a distinguished career in higher education.[117]

After Annapolis, he became chair of the history department at the University of Maine where he founded a Ph.D. program in military and naval history and in 1972 became dean of Washington College on the eastern shore of Maryland. Other younger faculty followed his example and left the academy disappointed with the promises of the "academic revolution." Finally, it would be fair to say that Admiral Draper Kauffman also did not emerge from this crisis unscathed. Normally, the superintendent's job was a stepping stone to a major operational command and three-star rank at a minimum. That had been the pattern for most of Kauffman's predecessors and would also be true for many of his successors. Although his rocky tenure at Annapolis was never a stated reason, Kauffman was never selected for vice admiral, nor did he go onto a major fleet command after the academy.

A "Professional Revolution"

Unfortunately these "scandals" tended to obscure the fact that within limits, the Naval Academy was still committed to academic reform. For example, in the summer of 1967, Admiral Kauffman announced the creation of the Immediate Master's Program. At first glance, this change seemed long overdue. Until this point, naval officers had to finish their first operational tour before applying for graduate school. The aviation and nuclear power communities often had a substantial backlog of officers waiting to begin their training. Rather than stashing ensigns in backwater jobs, such as being in charge of the officers' club pool, they began working on their graduate degrees immediately, even if it meant a short delay in reporting to their operational commands. Even to be thinking this way was a radical departure from the "trade school" when all officers went straight to their ships. The program's existence also said a lot about the Navy's new priorities. An officer's academic development went hand in glove with his professional development.[118]

Other improvements included a more flexible schedule to help struggling midshipmen complete their academic requirements. Instead of redoing an entire year's worth of work, delinquent students only repeated their failed courses during a special summer term. First classmen's graduation was delayed a few months until the end of that school. Logical reforms, yes, but this was quite a change from the lockstep curriculum in which everyone graduated at the same time or not at all. The training pipeline's expansion was again critical to this greater flexibility. With most warfare specialties requiring a half-year or more of follow-on training, it did not matter if a few months were gained or lost either way. A new system of academic probation was established, primarily used in courses extending over several terms. Midshipmen who failed the first half of a sequence could still pass the course if their final marks were satisfactory. In both cases, simple procedural changes allowed Annapolis to maintain high academic standards while acting compassionately towards students in academic difficulty.[119]

Conversely, the academic program was made tougher on better students. Those in the top half of the class no longer had an option at validation. To prevent coasting during a midshipman's last semester, first classmen were required to have not only a passing average but also passing grades in their final classes. Much of the credit for the eventual majors program went to Kauffman's successor, Admiral Calvert. However, the guts of that idea were tossed around earlier during this supposed period of "retrenchment." After the 1966 accreditation visit, Admiral Kauffman and Dean Drought began planning more ambitious changes to the curriculum, which further reduced the number of core hours and made majors an academic requirement for all midshipmen. By the time all of the details were worked out, it seemed logical to leave this huge task to Admiral Calvert.[120]

Kauffman was also open to suggestions that made the academic year less onerous for midshipmen. The biggest improvement was a new academic year calendar that completed the first semester before Christmas leave. Midshipmen were now free to enjoy the holiday without final exams hanging over them. June Week was pushed forward to the end of May, and Annapolis began calling the festivities Commissioning Week instead. Even so, the new schedule was more accommodating to the priorities of the academic program. Based on suggestions from the first class, the superintendent also moved graduation to the football stadium. Midshipmen were able to invite many more guests to the happy event.[121]

Most importantly, the academy launched a major overhaul of professional training and education, the so-called "professional revolution." It is tempting to view these changes as a resurgence of traditional values within the institutional culture. In other words, Annapolis retreated from the "academic revolution." While the emphasis was on improving the training program, the overhaul was not a return to the "trade school" academy. Preparing midshipmen to be career officers was still its primary mission. And therefore, a strong training program was always going to be an area of emphasis. In the zeal to upgrade academic standards, the military's nagging fear was that professional standards might have slipped. The academy did not do graduates any favors by shortchanging their professional competence any more than it did the quality of their academic degree.[122]

The growing war in Vietnam would be the catalyst for bringing these issues to the forefront. To make room for the new curriculum, the academy had removed many professional requirements from the academic year. Summer cruise was thought to be the best time for midshipmen to hone their professional skills anyway. Not surprisingly, as the operational tempo quickened, the quality of their at-sea training deteriorated. Midshipmen were soon barred from overseas cruise assignments altogether; local fleet units also had their underway time reduced to free up resources for the war. Operational units had little choice but to use their limited training opportunities on their own crews' readiness. As a result, midshipmen were constantly scrambling to make the best out of a bad situation.[123]

Vietnam left the academy with little choice but to reabsorb most of these professional responsibilities. In January 1967, Kauffman convened a special Professional Training and Education Board, made up of senior line captains, to study the problem. The board concluded that professional standards had slipped in recent years but not just because of the war. In their opinion, too many training responsibilities had been removed from the academic year to make way for the new curriculum. At the same time, the PT&E Board was not advocating a return to the "trade school" academy. In those days, academic credit was awarded for all professional courses, a practice that made the institution a laughingstock within the academic community. Professional requirements were not invisible hours in the schedule however. Somehow, they needed to show up on a midshipman's transcript.[124]

Everyone understood that these courses were unique to Annapolis but other professional schools had similar requirements. The challenge was to make professional courses academically credible. The PT&E Board's revisions went a long way towards achieving that goal. Midshipmen should be tested on this material just like other academic courses. Extensive subjects, like the military justice system or antisubmarine warfare theory, could not be left to haphazard instruction by the Executive Department either. These subjects needed formal course outlines, objectives, and exams. Instructors should have their teaching material prepared in advance. Only then would the larger academic community accept the professional curriculum as a valid part of the midshipmen's *education*.[125]

The same was true for the time midshipmen spent working on their seamanship skills on Yard Patrol craft on the Chesapeake Bay or on cruise. Other professional schools awarded classroom credit for students' lab hours but these schools' students were also tested in their proficiency. The PT&E Board found that midshipmen were not taking the training seriously since they were not receiving academic credit or being tested over it. For example, the academy provided cruise journals to midshipmen as a guide for their summer training. However, unlike fleet qualification standards, these journals were never collected much less graded, so there was little incentive to put much effort into them.

The reason behind many curriculum reforms was creating a better balance between theoretical and the practical objectives. The navigation course was lengthened to two semesters to allow time for practical skills in piloting and celestial navigation as well as classroom study in new electronic methods of navigation. Instead of duplicate lectures by the Executive Department, the academy enhanced the "history of sea power" course but limited it to a single semester taught by the academic faculty. Most weapons and engineering courses increased their focus on theoretical principles rather than current fleet systems. Overlapping education and training requirements was certainly beneficial in managing a crowded curriculum as well. If midshipmen could learn thermodynamics by studying Navy steam engineering plants, the academy wanted to take advantage of that.

Additional measures were taken to communicate the importance of professional training. Professional courses began carrying greater weight in the midshipmen's order of merit, the ranking that determined their order of service selection. Previously, the formula was weighted at 83 percent academic performance, 16 percent aptitude for service and 1 percent for physical education. The new ratio became 72 percent academic, 4 percent for physical education, 8 percent at-sea training, and 16 percent aptitude for service. To some extent, academics were de-emphasized but not radically, since the school's primary mission remained producing career officers.[126]

The years 1965 to 1968 were not easy for the academy, which was somewhat surprising since the "academic revolution" was supposedly on hold. Although no major initiatives were implemented, it still wrestled with serious contradictions in its institutional culture. The quest for balance was hard to resolve. Important progress was made but only after much controversy and heartache. These struggles were especially poignant since each of the differing groups cared deeply for the institution. Unfortunately, it was difficult to agree on what was best for the Naval Academy. And the success of one group's ideas was often seen as harmful to the other. The Vietnam War and its accompanying turmoil made its task more difficult than it had to be. The academy had to solve these issues alone since the Navy's focus was winning the war. The storm was not over for Annapolis however; it had not even reached its greatest intensity, both in the case of Vietnam and the "academic revolution."

6
The Fine Line Between Athens and Sparta: The Calvert Years at Annapolis, 1968–72

NO ONE EPITOMIZED THE SPIRIT AND IDENTITY OF THE NEW ANNAPOLIS like Admiral Kauffman's successor, Vice Admiral James Calvert '43. Like many recent superintendents, Calvert was a veteran of World War II. However, his experiences came as a junior officer fresh out of the academy, not an officer midway through his career. Indeed, in 1968 at the age of forty-seven, Calvert became the youngest admiral ever to serve as the academy's superintendent. After the war, Calvert's career was marked with a series of firsts, which placed him on the fast track to promotion and positions of greater responsibility. A submariner with nine combat patrols in the Pacific War, Calvert joined Admiral Rickover's new nuclear navy, surprising because Rickover preferred younger officers who could be easily remade in his image. In 1959, Calvert gained national attention commanding USS Skate, the first American nuclear submarine to surface at the North Pole.[1]

Besides his impressive operational credentials, Calvert was also a gifted speaker and prolific author on naval affairs. His books on the profession of officership and the polar voyage of the *Skate* made him one of the most recognizable flag officers in the Navy and American society. In a sense, his appointment could not have come at a more opportune time for the academy and for him personally. After the recent difficulties, the Navy was sending one of its best and brightest officers to take these reforms to their next level. For Calvert, this job was a stepping stone to the highest commands in the Navy, possibly including the chief of naval operations. The next few years would be critical to the hopes of both the institution and its ambitious new leader. Most pieces of the new curriculum were already in place. There was not always a compelling vision behind them however. Calvert's time at the helm would likely cement the final touches on what the new Annapolis would be.[2]

For better or worse, Calvert's name has become synonymous with the "academic revolution," surprising since its genesis occurred long before his tenure at Annapolis. He did undertake further academic reforms, most notably the majors program, which by and large forms the curriculum's basis today. However, it was his vision of the academy that established his legacy as the architect of the "academic revolution." Midway through his tour, Calvert published a landmark article in *Proceedings* entitled "The Fine Line at the Naval Academy," which laid a philosophical basis for the ongoing reforms. Much of what he said was not new, at least to those with a passing familiarity with the "academic revolution." Calvert did eloquently locate this period in academy history and show it to be the key to its future. The "academic revolution" was not an aberration but was consistent with the deepest underpinnings of the institution. Not since Admiral Holloway had a superintendent communicated such an articulate and compelling message of what the academy should be.[3]

For all his status as an academic reformer, Admiral Calvert was very much a traditional naval officer, especially when it came to professional education and military discipline. By no means should training take a backseat to education, no matter how important the midshipmen's scholarship was to the academy's reputation. Qualifying for graduate school was important, but midshipmen also needed to be ready to support to the fleet. Calvert vigorously supported Admiral Kauffman's efforts to upgrade professional education and thought those requirements should be tougher. Even here, he was more of a system builder than were his peers. Whether it was the summer at-sea programs, the curriculum's professional courses, or the character building activities of Bancroft Hall, a paramount goal had to be institutional harmony, especially with the new academic program. The time was long overdue to bring order to the "academic revolution," the lasting balance so often alluded to by past inspection teams.[4]

Admiral Calvert was also tough on standards of professional decorum. Contrary to later allegations, his reforms did not include any broad attempts at social experimentation. Indeed, Calvert attempted to hold midshipmen to a higher standard of military behavior than was currently enforced in the fleet. The Zumwalt Navy could tinker all it wanted with hairstyles and uniforms to make it more contemporary with society. Midshipmen would maintain a neat and conventional military appearance essential to good order and discipline.[5] The most dramatic example of Calvert's defense of the traditional military culture was his fight to maintain mandatory chapel. Six midshipmen challenged the legality of this tradition in a lawsuit filed in conjunction with the American Civil Liberties Union. Many of his own legal advisors and chaplains were counseling him that the practice violated the constitutional provision on separation of church and state. Nonetheless, Calvert made a symbolic stand in the courts, his motivation stemming not so much from the tradition's religious content but from what it implied about the midshipmen's character.[6]

At the same time, these reservations did not prevent him from experimenting with the academy culture in ways that advanced his vision of the new Annapolis. Like his predecessors, Calvert was concerned with the mounting voluntary resignations among plebes. He did not need a scandal, however, to prompt him to further modifications of the plebe system. With the Vietnam War winding down, the superintendent exerted his prestige to get top quality officers assigned to the academy. Unlike his peers, Calvert held these officers personally accountable for their companies and unwarranted actions by their upperclassmen.[7] Many officers, including Calvert himself, were also being detailed for longer tours of duty, which provided the continuity critical to making important changes.[8]

The trick was to make plebe year demanding while not allowing it to obscure other worthwhile goals. Their initial training was to be an intense indoctrination into military life; first classmen were handpicked for the plebes' training cadre and given specific instruction on their duties. The emphasis was always positive leadership that brought plebes into line without harassing them or demeaning their dignity. Plebe year itself was to build upon these high professional goals while allowing for the new academic program. Needless to say, violations of Calvert's revamped plebe system still occurred, but they grew less frequent over time. Part of the change was the stringency with which the new system was enforced, but it also reflected an important generational change in the Brigade. With each passing year, fewer midshipmen were familiar with the older system that had physical pressure as its top priority. As upperclassmen, they were not interested in perpetuating traditions that had no personal connection to them.[9]

The other major change during Calvert's tenure concerned the administration and organization of the Brigade, his so-called "shadow command." Oftentimes, striper functions were largely ceremonial, leaving the Executive Department running the Brigade, usually with an iron fist.[10] Calvert's shadow command tried to reverse this relationship, placing more control in midshipmen's hands, with officers providing a supporting and advisory role. The commandant and his staff also reviewed the school's regulations to eliminate those that seemed petty. Not only were striper positions expanded, but midshipmen were also handling duties previously relegated to officers. For example, company commanders were adjudicating minor conduct offenses involving their peers. They decided whether to award restriction or demerits or even dismiss the charges outright. Under this arrangement, it was not unusual for midshipmen to look at stripers as the administration's flunkies. Even so, this was a sincere attempt to place leadership opportunities in the midshipmen's hands.[11]

As part of the shadow command, midshipmen were also appointed to new standing committees created to run the academy more efficiently. They were voting members on groups looking at summer training, welfare and recreation activities, and general policy issues. Midshipmen were given sole responsibility for the planning and execution of major events like the Brigade's movement to away football games. Sometimes, the administration's trust in midshipmen's abilities and judgment backfired. But that was also part of their training to become officers.[12] For example, the editors of *The Log* took their freedom too far with features embarrassing to the academy, pushing it to the brink of censorship. Classmates also pressured striper friends to overlook minor infractions, which gave everyone reason to doubt the shadow command's integrity. Unfortunately, the Brigade of this time possessed its share of disenchanted young men who had "tuned out" traditional authority, just like their civilian counterparts. This fringe group often disparaged the attempts of class leaders to build unity although it was their behavior that was the more juvenile.[13]

Concomitant with these responsibilities, Annapolis rewarded midshipmen with more privileges, both as recognition of these new leadership roles and as an adjustment to the huge changes in the youth culture. All upperclassmen could ride in automobiles, but driving privileges remained firmly in the hands of first classmen. With many young people already owning cars, it did not make sense to restrict their availability entirely. First classmen had unlimited weekends so long as they were meeting their academic and professional responsibilities. Juniors and sophomores were not given as much freedom, but they were also awarded significant new liberty privileges. Both at the time and afterwards, critics claimed that these reforms had a negative influence on the Brigade, suggesting a connection between them and growing drug use among midshipmen for example. The lesson had always been clear about the dangers of permissiveness on good military discipline.[14]

Advocates of these policies dismissed the notion that any sort of permissive environment was ever created. Certainly disciplinary problems should not be ignored, but they had to be placed in perspective. The academy was not immune to social changes no matter how much it wanted to remain consistent with the past. Furthermore, its environment had to be relevant to the times, especially if it wanted to attract good students. Annapolis should not be surprised to see midshipmen getting into similar problems as their peers, no matter how repugnant those activities were to the institution. By and large, the Brigade stayed clear of major trouble and did the work necessary for graduation. They also remained committed to the academy's core values, especially its focus on producing career officers, which in the final analysis was probably most important to it.[15]

The greatest accomplishments of the Calvert era were also the source of its greatest irony however. Calvert's reforms completed the overarching goals of the "academic revolution" in an arguably dramatic fashion. The new academy may not have been an "MIT on the Severn," but it had become a respectable naval college nonetheless. Academic achievement, especially as measured by the scholastic community, had become an important institutional goal, at least on par with its training responsibilities. The demanding academic program provided a degree useful either in or out of the Navy. Graduate education was now the expectation for most graduates later in their careers. The research and teaching credentials of its faculty were superb; its academic facilities were also first-rate; the scholastic profile of entering students was getting better each year. All of these trends suggested that the academy had joined the ranks of the nation's elite colleges and universities.[16]

Furthermore, with the latest revisions to professional training, these goals were accomplished without sacrificing the academy's ability to produce an immediately employable ensign. Most graduates required extensive follow-on training, but that was an occupational hazard of military specialization, especially in a technologically oriented Navy. Nowhere else did midshipmen learn the fundamentals of naval service better than at Annapolis. Bancroft Hall's activities remained intact although they did not claim the limelight as much as before. The Naval Academy was also unwavering in its commitment to plebe indoctrination, which remained an incredible test of endurance, the protests of older graduates notwithstanding. If nothing else, Calvert's efforts had created a workable balance between Athens and Sparta that benefited graduates and the Navy.[17]

But for as different as the new Annapolis was from the trade school academy, the academic community had also changed immeasurably since the 1930s and 1940s. The breach may have closed academically, but the social distance between it and other institutions had widened to a chasm. And no matter what it did, that gap was not likely to close, at least not in the foreseeable future. Much of this distance had developed during the Vietnam War. Initially midshipmen were proud of the differences between them and other college students. Their sacrifices were achieving a worthwhile goal, which their countrymen respected. The academy kept telling midshipmen and their parents this message, especially as the war grew unpopular. Such exhortations rang increasingly hollow however. More and more, midshipmen felt ostracized by a society frustrated with Vietnam.[18]

By the late 1960s and early 1970s, midshipmen could not help but notice the difference between Annapolis and other colleges. Unlike earlier, that sense of distinctiveness was not always welcome by many who wanted to blend in with society. All the fuss over the academy haircut, for example, was related to this frustration over not fitting in with their peers. Academically, their experiences had become little different from students in the better engineering colleges. Socially, their lives were becoming far removed from other college students. Many midshipmen also felt that the academy had caused them to miss out on something. Even though Annapolis had trained them to be capable officers, many wondered whether they were prepared for the real world. They had never managed their own

208 THE MIDSHIPMAN CULTURE AND EDUCATIONAL REFORM

The Log, 18 April 1969. Midshipmen had difficulty squaring the dangers of Vietnam with the war's growing unpopularity.

money or done their own laundry. Many questioned how Bancroft Hall's insular lifestyle affected their ability to manage and lead sailors through the difficult issues of the day.[19]

And that was the great irony of the "academic revolution" and the new Annapolis. The title of John Lovell's book, *Neither Athens Nor Sparta?,* was a particularly appropriate description of the academy culture during this period. Midshipmen had always existed in two worlds, the military and the academic. Since 1959, Annapolis had made great strides reconciling its academic culture to the norms of higher education, a difficult process but one in which it was largely successful. Unfortunately, the focus in the early 1970s was the social gulf separating midshipmen from their peers. Current midshipmen were disappointed with reforms that did not go far enough while older graduates worried the academy had gone too far in its quest to be relevant. Yet again, the academy was finding how difficult occupying the middle ground between Athens and Sparta could be.[20]

CALVERT'S ACADEMIC REFORMS AND THE MAJORS PROGRAM

Although written halfway into his tour, Calvert's *Proceedings* article provides an interesting framework for understanding the curriculum changes he initiated. He argued that the "academic revolution" must be understood in the context of academy history and the institutional culture of the Navy.

The service, by its nature, was a conservative institution that had often been skeptical of substantive changes. Indeed, many officers had questioned the founding of Annapolis, preferring that midshipmen be trained at sea like their British counterparts. Contrary to the claims of recent critics, the academy had struggled throughout its history balancing "military professionalism and the need for sound education." Calvert also warned readers about the dangers of shortchanging either responsibility: "the graduates of the academy who contributed most are those who have best combined true military professionalism with sound learning."[21]

Again looking back at history, Calvert believed the academy was entering a unique period when its actions, or lack thereof, would be of huge importance. With the Vietnam War winding down, the country's mood indicated that "a lean period is in the offing," and "historically, the Naval Academy had played an important role for the Navy in such periods." In looking at these major downturns, Calvert found reformers in its training establishment leading the way to a renaissance in naval professionalism and sense of mission. For example, in the late 1860s, Admiral David Porter as superintendent and his commandant, Captain Stephen Luce, brought the academy out of its post–Civil War doldrums. Later, Luce would become the first president of the Naval War College. Calvert saw the academy playing a similar role in the post-Vietnam era.[22]

Like Admiral Holloway, Calvert painted the academy's value in spiritual terms. On many occasions, he described Annapolis as a naval shrine, which should be treated with special reverence. One of his biggest peeves upon taking command was its deteriorating physical condition—grounds, walkways, and even buildings in great need of repair. The Navy had approved a master plan for the academy's renovation but significant portions were uncompleted because of Vietnam. It only did itself a disservice, however, by neglecting the academy. The school's proximity to Washington guaranteed more than its share of unexpected, important visitors. More importantly, a sharp physical appearance was important to instilling esprit de corps in midshipmen.[23] Beyond the new programs, Calvert called for the academy's physical renovation; for example, consider his description of what would become Rickover Hall:

> This magnificent structure, when completed, will be perhaps the most symbolic of all the new buildings at Annapolis. It is built for, and suited to, the advances in engineering education, which have been a part of the reforms of the 1960s. It recognizes that, despite all the requirements placed on it for other academic skills, the Naval Academy must always remain, primarily an engineering school.[24]

However, at the heart of Calvert's changes was a more rational balance between the academic and training programs. It was too much to expect the academy to turn out competent junior officers and still give them an identical academic program. The sizable number of core courses made it impossible for most classes to go beyond a superficial exploration of their subject. Midshipmen needed more time with their subjects to make it a truly meaningful learning experience. In other words, it did not make sense to have electives if their content was just perfunctory in nature.[25]

Military specialization had been a major reason for the "academic revolution." The lockstep curriculum was fine when all graduates went straight to sea. However, it could not support the specific requirements of every warfare specialty. Nonetheless, it had been difficult to abandon a common program entirely. Most everyone with an interest in Annapolis—the warfare specialties, Admiral Rickover, politicians, and even the faculty—had an agenda for the curriculum. Very rarely was a core course removed from the curriculum; it was hard to prove that it was not valuable in some fashion. Calvert proposed a more flexible structuring of the curriculum. Rather than making every graduate the same, the academy should instead ask, "what must every Naval Academy class bring to the fleet."[26]

The new parameters would continue to meet fleet requirements while not overburdening the academy with programs of dubious utility. Although this would require tough decisions, Calvert did not intend it to be radical. These changes were necessary for preserving the academy's primary mission of producing career, professional officers. In concluding, the superintendent did his best to show the continuity between the old and new Annapolis:

> The contest between professionalism and academic effort is not new. The balance between Athens and Sparta must be retained, but I would point out that Annapolis became world famous as a training institution that produced effective leaders, not as an educational institution that produced renowned scholars. Both are highly important, both can exist together with benefit, but the Naval Academy will succeed or fail in the decades ahead to the degree that it produces professional officers who have the dedication and loyalty to remain with the naval service and do an excellent job.[27]

These considerations led Calvert in the spring of 1969 to launch the last major reforms of the "academic revolution." Beginning in the fall, the academy would scrap entirely the existing curriculum, in which 85 percent of the program's hours were located in core courses and 15 percent in electives. Its replacement would be an incredibly flexible curriculum, which required all midshipmen to complete an academic major. To make room for the added requirements, he boldly eliminated *all* core courses except a strengthened list of professional subjects. Midshipmen were free to pick the majority of their courses within four areas of concentration—engineering, math and sciences, the social sciences and humanities, and management. Many academic departments would offer majors within these areas of concentration, a total of twenty-four during the first year of the majors program.[28]

Calvert's plan essentially created four tracks of study. No longer would any midshipmen have the same academic program, which was quite the contrast from the lockstep curriculum. The majors program gave students tremendous latitude over their education. Best of all, however, the academy did not forego traditional requirements to offer these choices. Students continued to take a heavy dose of technical subjects no matter which program they chose. For example, all engineering, math, and science majors took at least five semesters of math. But, just as important, even humanities majors took a two-semester sequence in calculus. As Calvert intended, the academy remained primarily an engineering school even though many students were not engineering majors.[29]

The majors program was intended to solve many longstanding problems. At the very least, it addressed educators' concerns about the supposed lack of depth in the curriculum. Dr. Bernard Drought, the school's veteran dean, considered its greatest advantage to be providing a "meaningful academic experience," which allowed midshipmen to "master given material at truly advanced levels, and to be conversant with the frontiers of knowledge in his field."[30] In a sense, the challenges of military specialization had been turned inside out with the new curriculum. Since it was impossible to prepare graduates for every situation, the academy concentrated on a junior officer's essential duties along with an in-depth, albeit more narrowly focused, education. Most importantly, instead of transmitting specific knowledge, the new academy was teaching midshipmen how to learn.

Besides improving its academic environment, the academy attempted to become a leader in key academic areas. Calvert pursued certification of the engineering majors by the Engineer's Council for Professional Development (ECPD). Annapolis would not be an engineering school in name only but one that had status within the professional engineering community.[31] Ultimately he envisioned it being the academic community's leading center for naval architecture and marine engineering, the "oceanographic arts" critical to the Navy's "survival as a fighting force." The importance of naval aviation and missile technology demanded that the academy be a leader in aerospace and aeronautical engineering too. Along with its technical reputation, Calvert hoped for an eventual expertise in public policy and diplomacy. What was interesting was how broadly the academy was thinking about its graduates' responsibilities, beyond the confines of a traditional line officer.[32]

The curriculum's biggest question mark was ensuring an equitable distribution of majors. Calvert had ruled out programs that did not meet the service's needs in some fashion or another. He also stressed that no major was related to a specific naval career. A midshipman did not have to major in aeronautical engineering if he wanted to fly, for example. The primary reason for having the majors program was the educational experience it provided. Nonetheless, of the two dozen choices available, some had greater crossover value to the Navy than others. Although significant follow-on training was becoming necessary for most graduates, Annapolis hoped its academic programs would have strong application to its graduates' military careers. The worst scenario was a person reporting to the training commands and washing out of those programs.[33]

The best example of this potential problem was the academy's relationship with the nuclear power program. The target group for that training was 250 graduates each year, roughly 25 percent of each class. That figure would grow in the early 1970s as recruiting dried up on civilian campuses. The class of 1973, Calvert's last at the academy, contributed the most in a single year with 196. Midshipmen with technical majors generally handled the nuclear power curriculum the best. In a pinch, Admiral Rickover would take humanities and management majors but only if he could not get enough engineers. Their failure rate was generally higher. Rumors periodically circulated Bancroft Hall about nuclear power drafting those it wanted. This was a course of last resort that was very rarely tried however.[34]

Nuclear power obviously had the most stringent academic requirements of the academy. Its growing mission responsibilities also made its manpower needs most acute. However, each of the war fighting communities was pressuring Annapolis for as many graduates as they could get. Both naval aviation and surface line expected to draw around 30 percent of each graduating class; the Marine Corps hoped to get at least 15 percent. None of these groups preferred non-technical majors unless no one else was available. With the quality of officers from other commissioning sources increasingly uncertain, the operational forces were counting on academy graduates to perform their technical functions.[35]

However, the academy did not want to impose majors on midshipmen. Forcing the situation would be disastrous in every respect. Its own studies had shown that midshipmen performed the best in programs that suited their aptitude and interests. The majors program would further improve academic standards because it allowed students to have even greater freedom of choice. The same principle held true in the military. The most motivated officers were those who served willingly, out of love for the service. Although there might seem to be advantages in the short term, manipulating things to get the results it wanted would be extremely negative over the long haul. Not only would students' academic work likely suffer, they would also be less committed to a military career.[36]

Annapolis could not sit back and hope for the best however. The target percentages for each area of concentration were 40 percent engineering, 30 percent math-science, 20 percent social sciences-humanities, and 10 percent management. Without any constraints, the first year of the new curriculum did not come close to achieving any of these objectives. The greatest imbalance was the lack of engineering majors, just 22.9 percent overall. Math-science and humanities majors were fairly close to the academy's goals, 33.4 percent and 21.1 percent respectively. The Brigade was most top heavy in management majors, a whopping 22.6 percent of midshipmen. The ratios in each of the four classes mirrored these overall percentages.[37]

To its credit, the Naval Academy relied more on persuasive means in handling the problem. Each year during his term, Admiral Calvert wrote a personal letter to the midshipmen's parents, which addressed any recent changes. Even though many lived far away from Annapolis, most still had a significant influence over their sons. He hoped parents would encourage them to attempt the more technically demanding majors. Their sons would not have come to Annapolis unless they had wanted a challenge. Furthermore, there were many exciting opportunities available to students who did well in these programs. The same message was given to plebes during the selection process. Calvert appealed to their competitive nature to do their best academically as well as professionally. Although it might be difficult, it would benefit them in the long run.[38]

Annapolis even tried to screen possible majors during the admissions process. It was easier to weed out applicants than midshipmen if ratios appeared too distorted. However, as a last resort, ceilings were placed on the numbers of humanities and management majors, no more than 25 percent and 20 percent in a class.[39] A common curriculum was also reinstated for plebes in 1971. Majors were not picked until the end of that year to stem any hasty decisions. With Bancroft Hall and upperclassmen, plebes could easily be tempted to pick programs that demanded the least amount of time. Why force a decision where they might sell themselves short academically? There were enough core requirements to occupy that first year.[40]

Finally, the greatest drawback to getting students into the more demanding programs was the lack of fallback majors. The accredited engineering programs were the most prestigious, but they were also very difficult. Who wanted to flunk out if they were uncertain of their abilities or other alternatives were available? A critical adjustment in 1971 was the addition of two new majors, general engineering and physical science. Very rarely did midshipmen start out in either area. Although they might have lacked the luster of an elite major, midshipmen were encouraged to attempt something more difficult. Academic boards learned to take this into account with struggling students. Those who tried a difficult program and failed were more likely to receive a second chance. The majors program was never made involuntary, but it required careful monitoring well into the 1980s.[41]

Annapolis underwent another academic reorganization in 1970. The hallmark of these reforms was the opportunity for greater civilian control of the academic program. Instead of just seven academic departments, the academy established seventeen departments organized primarily along disciplinary lines. Each department would have primary responsibility for developing the academic content of majors within their area. Admiral Calvert also removed the longstanding prohibition on civilian department heads. That responsibility fell to the person most qualified *academically* in the department. Within the first year of its implementation, eleven of the seventeen chairmen were civilians, shocking considering the military's reluctance to give up such power just a few years ago.[42]

Even so, the military did not turn over control of the academic program entirely. Calvert resurrected Admiral Melson's idea of academic divisions to oversee the departments. The directorship of these five divisions was limited to senior Navy captains. Besides supervising their departments, division directors served as members on new policy and management boards as well as the Academic Board, still the senior governing body over academic affairs. The new divisions conveniently guaranteed senior officers input over the curriculum. But by no means did this reduce department chairmen to being tokens.[43]

Within their areas, department chairs were responsible for developing their curriculum; they also managed important personnel and resource issues. Division directors were occupying a watchdog role, but that was probably how it should have been. They ensured that the curriculum remained current with important fleet issues and technology. These changes clearly reflected Calvert's vision of the new academy, a true naval college, whose success depended upon "an effective blending of policy guidance and vision of senior naval officers with the expertise and experience of professional educators."[44]

Ironically, it was Admiral Calvert not the Navy that put the brake on further academic changes. The vision behind his reforms was succinct: an open academic environment that supported the academy's traditional mission of producing career line officers. The Navy wanted to expand this mission, largely because of Vietnam. Like most conflicts, the war had created a mobilization crisis. Additional officers were needed not only in the line communities but also in many staff professions. The Navy traditionally recruited doctors and lawyers straight from the professional colleges. Their military training was usually completed through officer candi-

6: THE FINE LINE BETWEEN ATHENS AND SPARTA 215

date school. The war's unpopularity had slowed recruiting to a trickle. And now the Navy was looking at Annapolis to fill this gap.[45]

Normally academy graduates were prohibited from accepting staff commissions unless they were not physically qualified for the line. The majors program inadvertently provided an opportunity for reversing this policy. Among the twenty-four new offerings was a major in the biological sciences. Rather than structuring this major to general fleet requirements, it was organized as a preparatory program to medical school. Prior to offering it, twelve medical schools reviewed the bioscience major to certify its compatibility with their admissions requirements. At this point, the academy probably thought that this would be as far this program would go. To some extent, a competitive pre-med program enhanced its growing academic reputation; it possibly attracted a few more quality applicants and gave midshipmen other career options down the road. Only in limited cases, however, would physically qualified midshipmen be able to skip duty in the line communities.[46]

Yet once the pre-med program was available, it became difficult not to allow midshipmen to apply directly for medical school. And with the critical shortage of doctors, Annapolis was hard pressed to deny this opportunity to physically qualified midshipmen. Beginning with the class of 1974, up to 2 percent of each class could apply for medical school at the Navy's expense. The only exclusion was that candidates must have completed the bioscience major. In return for its investment, individuals owed a minimum of ten years commissioned service. On the surface, the program seemed to benefit everyone. Motivated and capable midshipmen could become doctors immediately. The Navy alleviated its deficiency with doctors likely to stay for an entire career. Participants were not even eligible to resign their commissions until after fourteen years of service.[47]

Once Pandora's box was opened, it became difficult for Annapolis to say no to other opportunities. The Navy initiated the Excess Leave (Law) Program to attract any prospective lawyers in the Brigade. The shortage of lawyers was not as acute, so its terms were not nearly as generous. The Navy was not even paying tuition; indeed in order to apply, candidates had to demonstrate an ability to pay for school without resorting to outside employment. Midshipmen were not restricted to a particular academic program, nor did they have to be ineligible for line duty. As long as their grades were good enough and they were accepted into an ABA approved law school, they could apply.[48]

The program's only benefit was that officers went on extended leave to finish law school, hence the name. They did not receive pay or allowances while in school, nor did the time count against their existing service obligation. In fact, an additional year of service was accrued for each year spent in law school. The great advantage to the Navy was that it acquired lawyers at virtually no cost. Participants started their law training right away and had a guaranteed job afterwards, but at considerable personal sacrifice.[49]

The academy strongly objected to the Navy's decision, especially its inclusion of physically qualified graduates in the program. Admiral Zumwalt had removed a similar restriction from NROTC midshipmen as an incentive to keep them in the service. After that, there did not seem to be any basis for holding academy midshipmen to a different standard. Although the program applied to at most 1 percent of each class, Admiral Calvert thought an incredibly bad precedent was being set. It was one thing to make an exception for medical school because of the compelling need for doctors. In fact, the argument could be made that it was a matter of operational necessity.[50]

The situation with law school was much more ambiguous. In Calvert's opinion, the continuance of such policies would "compound attitudinal problems at the academy in terms of professional and military program and will offer a seemingly desirable alternative to fleet service."[51] By their very nature, these programs tended to drain the best and brightest students from each class. At the very least, the program should be restricted to those who had completed an initial sea tour first. The academy was ordered to comply with Admiral Zumwalt's wishes however. In retrospect, these changes probably took Annapolis too far from its traditional mission even though they appeared to benefit the "academic revolution." In the years to come, the balance would return to preparing line officers but only after the Vietnam manpower crisis had subsided.

Continuing Problems with Recruitment and Attrition

Admiral Calvert also hoped that his reforms would help with lingering problems of recruitment and attrition. The academy wanted to receive double the number of qualified candidates to those actually appointed to each class. However, over the past several years, a sharp decline in applications had forced Annapolis to accept nearly all of its qualified applicants. In 1968, for example, a total of 2,478 nominations were left unused for the class of 1972.[52] For the first time, senior officers like Calvert began talking about how transferable the academy degree was to the civilian world. The reality was that many graduates were not staying for a full career.[53] He understood the risk of such an approach but believed the academy had little choice in the matter:

> I know there are those who say the academy is now giving people educations which are so good that they will be too attractive to business and industry when their obligated service is expired. The reverse of this, however, is to argue that we should give them such a bad education that no firm will want to employ

them. I don't think any of us would seriously advocate that. There are also those who claim that today's academy upperclassmen tend to think of themselves as future mechanical engineers or oceanographers, rather than as future professional officers. I recognized this as a calculated risk of the program. It was our carefully considered opinion that we had to improve the variety and spice of our academic programs if we were to meet today's competition—both with regards to students and to faculty. The majors curriculum was the safest and most effective route to that goal but we recognized that it was not without risk.[54]

This was truly a tough predicament for Annapolis. Better students were seemingly hesitant to apply if its program was tied solely to a military career. They wanted degrees that could possibly be used in civilian jobs. The academy would not have worried about these desires in the 1930s. However, it needed students of this caliber to make the "academic revolution" successful. Calvert hoped that Bancroft Hall and the professional training programs could eventually sell them on the Navy.[55] Another difficult decision was determining what the minimum service obligation should be. Studies indicated that a longer commitment also detracted better students from considering the academy. It did not want to be unreasonable but it could only sugarcoat its requirements so much. Again, the expectation was that the summer training programs, postgraduate opportunities, or the school's growing reputation could erase any negative perceptions of military service.[56]

Besides the new academic programs, appointment procedures were also revised to help with recruiting problems. In 1968, Annapolis persuaded Congress to increase the number of nominations for each vacancy from six to ten. Some districts always seemed to have a wealth of candidates. The catalog was rewritten to erase misconceptions about the nominating process being overly political. Also that year, an important change was made to the qualified alternate rule. Previously, applicants secured their nomination from the secretary of the Navy first. Afterwards, the academy could designate qualified alternates before his final approval, in effect allowing it to make the decision. The next logical step was offering these candidates early appointments, similar to the principal nominees. The chief goal was to identify and lock in promising applicants as early as possible.[57]

The Naval Academy took over most appointment responsibilities from the Bureau of Naval Personnel in 1971. The significance of this change was that it could now interact with Congress directly in influencing nominations. A new Congressional Liaison Office was also created that year. It focused on persuading congressmen to switch to a new competitive method of nomination. Under this process, they could still designate primary and alternate nominees or allow Annapolis to rank all of the applicants from their district. The advantage of the latter was that it again gave the academy significant control over who was nominated. Although political figures were involved, the whole process was becoming less political. Admission to the academy was becoming more like any other college. College Board scores and high school academic records were essentially determining admission.[58]

Procedures were also simplified for the academy's qualifying medical exam. In the past, only limited locations across the country could administer the exam. Many good candidates were deterred from finishing their applications because of the inconvenience in completing a physical. The initial screening could now be done virtually anywhere; unqualified candidates were determined quickly without wasting much of anyone's time. Annapolis also worked with the other service academies to develop a common medical exam. It was annoying to applicants interested in all the schools to repeat the same battery of tests. Annapolis also became more flexible in the medical waivers given to otherwise qualified candidates.[59] Until 1968, tight vision requirements eliminated many good applicants each year. Everyone was required to have 20/20 vision with no refractive errors. These standards remained intact but the number of waivers was expanded dramatically, up to 20 percent of an entering class.[60]

The applicant shortage along with pressure from civil rights groups stimulated the academy to increase its efforts towards minority candidates. The Candidate Guidance Office added a new advisor for minority affairs to oversee minority recruitment and to work with congressmen who preferred nominating minority candidates. Advertisements were frequently run in black magazines and radio programs. The few African American officers and midshipmen were all involved with Operation Information. Minority recruitment was not an easy task however. Many institutions were competing for well-qualified minority students. Thus, it was often difficult to find an abundance of strong candidates.[61]

In some cases, the stiff competition from other colleges may have tempted the academy to admit marginally qualified applicants. Although slow, these efforts began bearing fruit in the early 1970s. Only thirteen African Americans were admitted to the class of 1972, Calvert's first year at Annapolis; those numbers increased slightly to 16 in the class of 1974. Over 275 minority nominations were received for the class of 1975 however, forty-two of which eventually enrolled. In Calvert's final year, these numbers climbed even further—340 nominations, eighty-seven appointments, and sixty eventual admissions to the class of 1976. Even with this growth, the percentage of African American midshipmen was nowhere close to their share of the general population.[62]

The growing number of minorities did add a new dimension to the midshipmen culture. In the past, varsity athletes and midshipmen stripers stood out from their peers because of their unique experiences. Oftentimes, average midshipmen were quick to see any differences as special treat-

The Log, 5 April 1968. Special groups, in this case athletes, were perceived to be the recipients of special treatment.

ment. To be fair, many classmates considered any perks to be a fair reward for the extra work expected of athletes and stripers. Minorities also had a difficult time maintaining a low profile. They too were seen as recipients of special treatment when it came to admission standards and cases of academic difficulty.[63]

A common stereotype among midshipmen was that the academy did everything possible to ensure that minorities graduated. The evidence supporting such allegations is shaky either way, especially since subjective determinations came into play. It is one thing to say that the academy did more to assist minorities than other midshipmen. It is quite another to say a blind eye was turned towards standards to allow them to graduate. Certainly, it is a huge overstatement that every African American needed special treatment. Annapolis was admittedly under pressure to show progress towards racial integration. However, Admiral Calvert worried about all sources of attrition, not just minorities. In situations demanding a judgment call, the temptation was strong to be lenient towards African Americans.[64]

The other side of the equation in keeping the numbers of graduates high was controlling attrition. Unfortunately the Vietnam-era academy had learned to accept a heavy loss rate of 30 percent. In the three years prior to Admiral Calvert, attrition had climbed to record levels, roughly 40 percent in the classes of 1965, 1966, and 1967. The reasons for these losses are mixed. Some dropouts had problems assimilating the military culture of Bancroft Hall. They had primarily come for academic reasons and could not adjust to the school's military regimen. To be fair, greater numbers were also leaving because of Vietnam. Most of these probably did not resign out of opposition to the war. However, the public's disfavor towards military institutions made it difficult to continue association with Annapolis.[65] Voluntary resignations were now routinely the greatest source of attrition, surprising given how much academic standards had been raised. Something had to be done soon to get this problem under control. If possible, academic failures had to be limited while identifying why so many midshipmen were choosing to leave.[66]

Although not the primary reason behind them, Calvert's reforms had actually limited academic failures even further. Recent studies had shown that midshipmen were getting much better grades in their electives. They were naturally motivated to work harder in these courses and probably had greater aptitude for them too. Many of the older core courses did not account for the varied abilities of students and were structured at too difficult a level for what most of them truly needed to know. The technical requirements of the new curriculum were more realistic. The vast majority of academy graduates were not going to be professional engineers. They needed a core program that focused on principles important to the average junior officer. Thus, all students might take a course in electrical engineering but there would be different requirements for engineering, chemistry, or history majors.[67]

Academy leaders probably did not recognize it at the time but to some extent, this multi tiered curriculum fragmented the midshipmen culture. The lockstep curriculum had been a vital part of the midshipmen's professional socialization, the "unity of suffering" experience so fondly recalled by alumni. Although it was not intended that way, the new areas of concentration were a potential dividing line. The Naval Academy subconsciously reinforced this developing hierarchy with its priorities. All majors were supposedly worthwhile to its academic breadth but some were preferable to others. It frankly preferred to get as many Group 1 engineering majors as possible. They were the ones best prepared for nuclear power and the Navy's technical fields. The academy had been scared once already when too many midshipmen wanted majors in management or the humanities.[68]

It was only natural for midshipmen to feel a bond with those in their major. The same forces were working on a smaller scale that was true with companies during the lockstep curriculum. Indeed, 11 percent of survey participants from the classes of 1970 to 1976 indicated that their strongest relationships were within their major. Formal associations, particularly in the engineering majors, developed based on these interests. Oftentimes, this attraction carried over to similar career paths. The flip side of this was a dissociation with and lack of empathy for those not in their major. The separation should not be overstated but not ignored either. The academy bond was a strong one that overshadowed most any outside the institution. Different tracks of study encouraged students to see their program as the hardest and that others were simply sliding by. Again, this was part and parcel of becoming a true naval college, not uncommon to student communities at other institutions.[69]

Curbing the number of voluntary resignations was a more complicated problem to solve however. It was easy to determine who was leaving but more difficult to pinpoint why. After careful study, the two groups who stood out the most were prior enlisted midshipmen and those with higher than average verbal scores on their SATs. The academy was already familiar with the problems of prior enlisted. Their experiences tended to fall between two extremes. Some had used their previous military service to great advantage. Already acclimated to the military culture, they were able to devote more time to academics. It was also not unusual to see them serving in top leadership positions either.[70]

Many, however, struggled at the academy and voluntarily returned to the fleet. Some simply did not have the academic background to handle the new curriculum, even after a year at the preparatory school (NAPS). They chose to resign rather than being dismissed for academic reasons. Others became disenchanted with Annapolis because of Bancroft Hall. The artificial environment irritated them after dealing with real problems in the fleet. They also tended to be older, which made it difficult to stomach juvenile behavior from upperclassmen. These losses were always disappointing because of their demonstrated professional potential. However, the range of solutions was problematic. Enough prior enlisted succeeded to warrant continuing their admission. It was also important to the cohesion of the service to have "mustangs" in the officer corps.[71]

As a result, the focus of recruiting turned even more than before towards recent high school graduates. They stood a much better chance of graduating, 85 percent of those who entered at seventeen finished the program as opposed to 45 percent who started at twenty-one.[72] Younger midshipmen tended to be better prepared academically; their youth and inexperience actually seemed to work in their favor in adjusting to Bancroft Hall. The academy also decided to be as tough as possible with prior enlisted midshipmen. During Vietnam, some fleet appointees had used the academy as a cozy place to finish their enlistment. They carefully timed their resignation to avoid any obligatory service accruing from Annapolis. Its new policy was stricter with them than with any other midshipmen; fleet dropouts were returned immediately to the fleet regardless of how much time they had left on their contract.[73]

The other leading category of voluntary resignations must have shocked the academy. A strong academic background would seem to have been a huge advantage under all circumstances. As it turned out, a strong math background was an excellent predictor of success. At first glance, the relationship between high verbal scores and voluntary resignations seemed paradoxical. However, in some ways, it did make sense. A high verbal score possibly indicated a creative personality that functioned better in a less regimented environment. It is important to remember that Annapolis was both a military *and* an engineering college. Its academic atmosphere emphasized discipline and diligence but not necessarily creativity or free thinking. It is not altogether surprising that creative personalities struggled in this environment, especially after throwing in Bancroft Hall.[74]

Again, there were no easy answers to this problem. Enough students stayed that high qualification scores could not be a reason for non-admission. Also, what did it say about the "academic revolution" if Annapolis adopted such a policy? Although it was not a strong suit of the new curriculum, it had created opportunities in tune with these students' personalities, like the Burke Scholarship Program, the annual Foreign Affairs Conference, and a new program in U.S. Government and International Studies. Given its focus, Annapolis was never going to be an elite liberal arts college. Bancroft Hall would continue to be reformed but these conflicts would not entirely disappear either. These results did cause it to look harder for ways of identifying a candidate's motivation. More attention was paid to Blue and Gold interviews and teachers' recommendations. Unfortunately, determining military aptitude was a more difficult challenge than evaluating academic potential.[75]

Professional Reforms and a New Bancroft Hall

The other side of the new Annapolis was a rejuvenated program of professional training and education. Admiral Calvert wanted to expand upon Admiral Kauffman's "professional revolution" and the 1966 Middle States recommendation that professional training and academics be administered according to similar standards. Calvert had sold his reforms on the premise that they did not compromise professional training. In fact, the flexibility of the majors program was what made further reforms in this area possible. The genius of his vision was that it permitted both sides of the academy to work in harmony: "so long as we maintain a strong professional training program at the academy, I think we have nothing to fear and much to gain from a rich and varied educational program."[76]

He followed a similar pattern to the majors program in revamping the professional curriculum. Professional education urgently needed a major administrative overhaul. Bancroft Hall had its priorities; the same was true with the military science departments and the summer programs. The overarching goals of professional training may have been clear— preparing midshipmen to effective junior officers—but the specifics were often vague. Military specialization had only complicated the task of

6: THE FINE LINE BETWEEN ATHENS AND SPARTA

defining core professional requirements. It did not have a strong organization, like the academic program with the dean and Academic Board, to manage professional education and resolve any conflicts.[77]

With this in mind, Calvert established a Professional Training Board in 1969, renamed the Professional Development Board in 1971, to oversee these programs. Chaired by the head of the department of naval science, the board was comparable in stature to the Academic Board. The Professional Development Board not only developed the content of the professional curriculum it also administered all training activities. Just like the Academic Board, it decided whether to retain or separate midshipmen not meeting professional standards. The board worked through two standing committees, the At-Sea Training Committee and the Professional Education Committee. Membership included civilian and military faculty as well as midshipmen from each of the four classes.[78]

The most immediate concern was improving the quality of the summer programs, which had deteriorated in recent years largely due to Vietnam. The cancellations and limited underway time caused the academy to reconsider the value of using operational units. A limited cruise schedule was reintroduced in 1969, similar to its program in the 1940s and 1950s. Its greatest advantage was the ability to monitor the midshipmen's training more closely. All youngsters were assigned to one of four ships, usually a large amphibious ship like a LPD or LHA, which formed a Naval Academy Training Squadron (NATRON). Overseeing these cruises were Executive Department officers and selected first classmen.[79]

NATRON provided training specifically tailored to the midshipmen's professional needs. With little time or resources to waste, the schedule avoided the mundane enlisted duties, such as chipping paint or standing boiler watches, which youngsters had traditionally performed as a rite of passage. At-sea training built upon professional courses from the academic year; any practical exercises included written examinations to reinforce core objectives. Grades factored not only into students' academic GPA but also their aptitude for service ranking, all of which went into order of merit. NATRON continued to stop at plenty of liberty ports, traditionally an important part of the cruise experience. However, Admiral Calvert's goal was to make this training efficient and predictable, two things it had not been in recent years. The key was the same routine each year, including the ships. Ultimately he hoped to create standard textbooks using examples from current fleet systems, the goal being the best possible blending of education and training.[80]

The training focus during the last two summers was professional socialization. Over time, Vietnam had undercut the academy's mission here too. It had the greatest difficulty motivating midshipmen to careers in surface line. Ships simply seemed less glamorous than nuclear submarines or naval aviation. It was also not on the cutting edge of technology like these other warfare communities either. Surface line seemed like a course of last resort for midshipmen without the class standing or aptitude to do anything else. Although these were difficult perceptions to erase, the surface navy had not helped its case with the cruises it provided. Midshipmen were most excited about cruises on small combatants, such as destroyers or frigates. Their small wardrooms and heavy operational schedule tended to give the best experiences and leadership opportunities. Unfortunately, since these ships were also most in demand, they were increasingly unavailable to the academy.[81]

Aircraft carriers or other capital ships were traditionally the least popular, especially to midshipmen *interested* in surface line. They were too large and too busy to bother with them but their size accommodated large numbers. The same problems were also true to some extent with submarines. The best cruises were attack boats, with their small crews and wide range of missions. Their heavy operating tempo made them scarce however. Ballistic submarines could hold more midshipmen, but visits were limited to familiarization tours not extended patrols. Admiral Calvert pleaded with type commanders to get midshipmen onboard their vessels. Operational constraints were understandable but type commanders only did themselves a disservice by not capitalizing on these recruiting opportunities. Again, Calvert wanted these cruises to be as much as possible part of a standard curriculum. Most operational commanders could not make that open-ended of a commitment no matter how much they supported his goals.[82]

The other side of the equation was controlling the quality of the academy's output to the fleet. Admiral Calvert understood the skepticism among fellow officers towards many of his academic reforms. Strategically, it was important for them to believe their needs still came first at Annapolis. In 1970, at the recommendation of the Professional Training Board, the academy introduced a new feedback system the Graduate Performance Evaluation System (GRAPES) to measure the fleet performance of its graduates. The system sampled commanding officers' opinions on graduates' strengths and weaknesses. GRAPES would not have been possible without the academy's growing data processing capability however. Computerized data had first been used in recent recruitment and attrition studies. Whatever the utility of this information, important political dividends were reaped from it. It sent the message that the fleet's input mattered to the type of program at Annapolis.[83]

A professional readiness exam was created in 1972 that was also part of this trend. Midshipmen did not take a bar exam to certify their competence as officers. It had always been implied in their degree. Military specialization had allowed officers to pursue widely different career paths however. Here was a way to describe the skills exactly provided by the academy. The new exam was also useful in strengthening the academy's claim to being a true naval college. Midshipmen had to demonstrate certain skills or knowledge before receiving their commissions. The overarching goal of professional preparation remained similar to what it had always been: "an officer of immediate utility to a unit of the operational forces."[84]

Every graduate needed to be able to serve as a junior officer of the deck underway, a CIC watch officer during routine operations, an officer of the deck in port, along with any number of assistant division officer duties. Each of these jobs spawned professional objectives from which exam questions were developed.[85] The initial class to take the exam was a test group to identify shortcomings in the professional curriculum. Afterwards it became a final requirement for graduation. New classes received the complete list of requirements plebe summer to guide their studies. The test was a huge weight hanging over midshipmen's heads, but it prohibited them from taking a memory dump attitude to their professional classes. With so many graduates not being initially assigned to ships, it was also a way to emphasize traditional naval skills, which might be valuable later in their careers.[86]

Supporting the fleet was also the basis for a new assignment policy for prospective aviators. Admiral Calvert was disturbed by figures that showed 80 percent of graduates reporting to shore commands for further training before their first operational assignments. Politically, this was not good for Annapolis. In a time of increased manning problems, it was not fulfilling a chief responsibility. These numbers also invalidated Calvert's claims about professional training. He believed these assignments were not in graduates' best interests either. At some point, all officers had to be familiar with ships. Better to get that knowledge now than when they were preparing for command. The academy's tough military environment was also justified upon the premise that graduates could immediately step into operational billets. Finally, they were not encouraged to take their training seriously.[87]

For all these reasons, Calvert implemented a more restrictive assignment policy beginning with the class of 1971 that required prospective aviators to complete a shipboard tour before assignment to Pensacola. He eventually hoped this policy would also apply to nuclear power and postgraduate school. Many aviators were not thrilled with the news even though the delay was only six to twelve months. The primary reason why the academy could force this change was a scheduling backlog at Pensacola. Admiral Rickover was not willing to release his officers from their training however. Even so, Calvert believed an important precedent had been set. If he totally had his way, surface line billets for twelve to twenty-four months would be the norm, with an eventual guarantee of flight school or nuclear power.[88]

Calvert's interest in professional reform also extended to plebe indoctrination and Bancroft Hall. His approach here was similar to what he attempted with the professional curriculum. Minor reforms were not sufficient if they did not conform to his vision of the new academy. Despite Captain Hoof's efforts, voluntary resignations continued to be the most serious problem with plebe indoctrination. Plebes quit for many reasons: they were not prepared for Bancroft Hall; they lacked proper motivation, losses that to some extent were unavoidable. However, many well-intentioned and capable plebes were also leaving because of continued unauthorized actions of upperclassmen. Unlike other superintendents, Calvert saw this as a personal challenge and was not above stepping on people's toes to fix it.[89]

Reform-minded superintendents had tried to fix plebe indoctrination before but their changes often died after they left Annapolis. The biggest challenge was altering attitudes in Bancroft Hall, a problem Calvert recognized: "it was passed down from class to class with surprising consistency."[90] Upperclassmen perpetuated unauthorized traditions. However, their officers were equally to blame in ignoring their actions. Greater accountability was the first step to lasting reform, which started with the officers. The slowing down of the war allowed Calvert to scrutinize more carefully officer assignments. Battalion officers were expected to have command experience and to be frontrunners for promotion. They were not only proven leaders but also had much to lose if their tours were unsuccessful. Calvert also insisted on interviewing every company officer to ensure their compatibility with the new Annapolis. They too needed to be top performers with significant operational experience. In all cases, these officers understood the superintendent was holding them personally responsible for Bancroft Hall.[91]

Better leadership among his officers allowed Calvert to concentrate on other areas, like a revamped summer training period. Second classmen took over responsibility for the plebe summer training detail, their first real leadership opportunity. They would decide how tough and rigorous to make the training so long as the administration's guidelines were followed. Volunteers were chosen after numerous interviews to ensure their compatibility with Calvert's reforms. Fifty hours of formal classes in leadership and techniques of military instruction were also required after their selection. Calvert wanted this to be as much a learning experience for them as it was for the plebes. In their case, the lesson would be that plebes did not need browbeating to be properly indoctrinated. By convincing them, he hoped these attitudes would eventually filter throughout the Brigade.[92]

The new plebe system emphasized positive leadership, skills more appropriate to what midshipmen would need to use in the fleet. Physical punishment continued to be strictly forbidden. Also removed were regulations against specific forms of harassment. Upperclassmen were not to interfere with study hour and taps; most forms of menial service were also prohibited.[93] The new concept of indoctrination was stressed the most however. At the heart of this new system was a General Responsibility Clause that stated:

> The responsibility between upperclassmen and fourth classmen must be based on the principles of regard for human dignity and respect. While it may be necessary to correct, upbraid, and reprimand new personnel so firmly that feelings are hurt and tempers grow short, it is not acceptable to humiliate or degrade them in the process.[94]

Admiral Calvert also created a special Plebe Indoctrination Board, made up of upperclassmen, to determine when violations of this ideal had occurred and what discipline to award. The key to getting their support was convincing them that plebe year remained as hard as before. New plebes were not skating out of anything. Only the activities that were humiliating and embarrassing were being removed. Each company also had a Performance Board that could discipline plebes with extra duty for poor performance. In extreme cases, plebes were sent to Battalion and Brigade Aptitude Boards for possible discharge.[95]

These concepts were refined during Calvert's tenure. Greater supervision and maturity were added to the system's administration. The training backlog allowed first classmen to take over as summer stripers and recent graduates to be assigned as assistant company officers. Indoctrination was actually toughened to further convince upperclassmen that nothing essential had changed. More time was devoted to physical conditioning as well as preparation for the validation exams. However, unlike before, these additional requirements were regulated and sanctioned by the academy. Finally, Calvert implemented reforms that increased plebes' chance of surviving a toughened indoctrination. Study skills sessions were added during the summer to prepare them for academic year. Induction day was also moved to early July to smooth the transition for high school graduates and to build classmate unity.[96]

Midshipmen were divided about the reforms, the split usually coming along the type of indoctrination they had received. Senior classes were skeptical of them and worried about their effect on tradition. One first classman from the class of 1970 expressed his misgivings to *Shipmate*. He was thankful to have gone through the old plebe year because "it helped me grow stronger and because those who did not grow stronger did not last." Many of his classmates seemed mournful that "plebe year as my class knew it or any preceding class knew it is gone." Implementing the new system had not been easy: "having experienced a physical plebe year, many firsties were at a loss to motivate plebes and withdrew from the system with a sense of frustration." Summing up the changes, he believed that "the source of frustration lies in seeing traditions die or change and in the sense of separation from other classes that results. Our mood in '70 is one of regret and a sense of loss that this year bore witness to change of some of the most treasured of navy traditions."[97]

Other upperclassmen had benefited from earlier reforms and were not sad to see some traditions abolished. They questioned their peers' reasons for holding onto the past, often attributing it to nothing more than sour grapes. One midshipman in this camp expressed his views for *The Log*:

> It seems like every time the subject "plebe system" comes up, a comparison is made between the top 2 classes and the bottom 2. I would like to know if you think that physical harassment (and that's what plebe year was) makes a better officer out of an academy graduate? If not, then why bring the topic up or better yet, why phrase it in that manner? Plebe year is bad all around. No question there. Times are changing and so is the academy and the plebe system. You were harassed, unfortunately, but when you were plebes, the system was not thought of being revised. Now that you're firsties, you have that power so necessary to do something about it. It's in your hands, no one else's. Or don't you want to change the system. Are you the type who feels, "Why, hell I got run and by gosh so is he!" That type of leadership is negative and has no place in our navy and especially here.[98]

Several comments stick out from both sides. The old system's supporters emphasized the divide between them and newer midshipmen. More recent classes insisted that nothing critical had changed; the aspects that were eliminated should have been done so long ago. Finally, there was an impetus on responsible individuals to do what they knew was right and not cling to a past that was unworthy of preserving.

Clearly, progress had been made in changing the midshipmen culture. The question was whether it was deep enough for lasting change. The observations of *The Log*'s editor seemed to echo the South's rationale for massive resistance during desegregation in this regard. He reiterated Admiral Calvert's opinion that "regardless of the support of the Executive Department of any policy involving the plebes, it must be backed by the Brigade to be effective." As far as the Brigade's breakdown, "the stripers appear to be behind the policy almost 100 percent, but the non-stripers, the majority of the Brigade, seem to be voicing the most dissent." Plebes were in the most awkward position of all. They supported the new system but did not want to be seen as crybabies. It was not easy to hear from upperclassmen that "they are worthless as plebes and will be at best, second rate officers." However, this editor wondered whether the changes were too severe and too fast and counseled moderation on both sides. Upperclassmen had to be flexible to the changes, but the academy should include greater physical challenges in the new system.[99]

Admiral Calvert also tried to get upperclassmen's support by bringing a positive leadership style to the rest of Bancroft Hall. The goal was to replace "cops and robbers" with an approach more reflective of the fleet. Officers were supposed to have a mature and professional relationship with midshipmen and then expect the same from them. First, the commandant overhauled and removed regulations that seemed outdated or petty. Next, the entire structure of discipline was reformed. Restriction was not just dead time; midshipmen would be doing something positive with those hours. Rather than marching extra duty, infractions were punished with constructive projects similar to the fleet's preventive maintenance system. The mess hall routine was also revamped. Unnecessary high jinks were eliminated to make the atmosphere more like wardrooms aboard ship.[100]

In addition, the academy revised its liberty regulations and class privileges to make them more reflective of the times. Car privileges were extended to upperclassmen any time on liberty; even plebes could ride on special occasions. First classmen were allowed to purchase their cars at the start of the academic year. Older regulations had prohibited this until after the Army-Navy football game. Seniors had unlimited weekends away from Annapolis except for their monthly duty. As much as possible, Saturday classes were also eliminated. Finally, uniform standards were changed to lighter, more comfortable materials, which were easier to maintain. Contrary to critics' claims however, the requirement for a neat and professional appearance was never abandoned.[101]

At the heart of the new Bancroft Hall was a different relationship between officers and midshipmen, Admiral Calvert's so-called shadow command. Instead of being disciplinarians, officers would theoretically concentrate on their roles as advisors, counselors, and mentors. Stripers would run the Brigade; officers would step back and intervene only as a course of last resort. The shadow command's implementation was total, from the brigade commander down to the squad leaders. Midshipmen were also included on new standing committees overseeing professional training, extracurricular activities, and general policy objectives. Much more was now expected of stripers than leading parades on Wednesdays and conducting occasional room and uniform inspections. Brigade, regimental, and battalion staffs were reorganized into distinct operations, logistics, and administrative sections, similar to a shipboard organization. Stripers were also planning actual evolutions, such as writing movement orders, evaluating menus, and running the color company competition and the intramural sports program. Finally, striper responsibilities would be rotated among three different sets to provide the experience to as many midshipmen as possible.[102]

The shadow command's greatest test was at the company level however. Stripers were also responsible for the atmosphere in their companies, including their adherence to regulations. In a bold move, Annapolis also turned over the conduct system to them. In effect, midshipmen would now be disciplining themselves, not only determining whether violations occurred but also appropriate levels of punishment. The Brigade's reaction to the new policies was mixed. On the one hand, the news generated great optimism: "one can't help but notice a more positive and constructive attitude from upperclassmen towards the academy." Not surprisingly, there was also a fair degree of skepticism. As *The Log*'s editor explained, "the Brigade still looks on the Executive Department with an attitude of fear and trepidation. This outlook can not vanish overnight." In other words, in difficult situations, would the administration truly stand aside and let midshipmen decide what to do?[103]

Stripers quickly learned firsthand how uncomfortable command could be. Although it was a good experience, they were often put in no-win situations. Regardless of whether they agreed with a policy, stripers did not want to give officers any reason to reassert their authority. Yet, Calvert and his staff expected standards to be maintained even if it meant alienating their classmates. The new tone did not mean "form-2 leadership" had totally disappeared either. Some officers still believed a conduct report was the quickest way to get things done. They heard enough statements like "I want you to start frying people until you find out who was responsible!" to have their own doubts about the shadow command.[104]

However, their classmates were also very difficult to please. Bancroft Hall was always circulating with rumors, particularly in the gossip column of "Salty Sam," about stripers letting the responsibility go to their heads. Worse still, stripers often had to overcome the Brigade's perception that they were worse martinets than officers. It did not matter whether their actions were legitimate or their classmates were simply out of line. By virtue of their position, they had forfeited their right to be just "one of the boys" and had become "the symbol of authority, the 'tax collector' of the establishment."[105]

Ironically, many midshipmen envisioned a more limited role for the striper organization. Stripers should be their advocates with the administration. Furthermore, they should be willing to lose their stripes, if necessary, to maintain their trust. Their time should be spent fighting for increased privileges and running interference for their classmates.[106] If they were not willing to do this, they were too interested in pleasing officers. One critic expressed a common doubt: "most of us realize by this time that it is a popularity contest at best, and a complete farce at worst."[107] In a stinging article, "It's That Time Again: Gold Stripe Fever," even *The Log*, however, attacked the motivation of would be stripers:

> In early stages, the disease may make itself known by an oily smile for everyone from its victim, and other well known symptoms of the greasus-smackus

complex. Many of its victims find numerous trips to the company officer's office necessary. At this point, the afflicted individual starts seeing thin gold stripes before his eyes. The victim feels a driving compulsion to say "yes, sir" to any and all statements directed to him from those with more and larger gold bands. The victim seems to get a fiendish glee from "searching out and reporting" others for the same things he used to do until the mysterious gold bands appeared on his sleeve.[108]

Other midshipmen did urge classmates to be more supportive—"he must enforce the will of the Executive Department in order to retain his job while maintaining a working relationship with those he must command." Standards would be maintained regardless of who enforced them. "Is this guy the mortal enemy of the underclass? On the contrary, he is one of their best friends. He is doing his job so the officers won't do it for him." Furthermore, by being tough on little things, stripers were gaining officers' respect on issues that truly mattered. "First class now sit on many boards that have to do with life at the academy. The same first class that bugged you about wearing a spiffy to class is working to make this place better for you." Midshipmen showed maturity by disciplining themselves. All of the finger pointing makes it difficult to discern exactly how much of this was true. Some stripers were tyrants using the situation for their own gain. Oftentimes, however, classmates knowingly challenged the regulations, forcing them to take action.[109]

The New Midshipmen Culture

Whatever its failings, the new Annapolis was a far cry from the trade school academy. The academic opportunities were significantly greater. Military specialization had created greater career options after graduation. Bancroft Hall was even different; its primary mission remained the midshipmen's character development, accomplished through strict military discipline. However the method did not have to be "cops and robbers." As much as it had changed, the cultural gap between Annapolis and other colleges had grown. Midshipmen were exposed to a greater range of social experiences, which made many regulations appear outdated and even unreasonable. Never before had the distance between mainstream and traditional military values seemed greater. That being said, a "hippie" lifestyle did not take over the academy. It would not have allowed it, *nor* would most midshipmen. Most of them were still very conservative compared to other college students. By and large, they accepted the academy's taut routine as part of the professional socialization process.

Yet, many of them did seem more willing to question the status quo. The reasons why were various. They often had a rough time dealing with civilian students. It was tough hearing from peers that their institution and its traditions were odd. They had always heard how much alumni had been respected by society. Current midshipmen understood the social turmoil but desired something similar from their generation. Instead, many felt ostracized and even ridiculed beyond the walls of the academy. Midshipmen reacted by speaking out on many issues they felt should be changed. Only rarely, however, did anyone challenge the chain of command. They simply wanted to know why certain traditions remained relevant. And if not, the academy should not allow them to stand in the way of progress.[110]

However, most questioning was due to the outcry over Vietnam. Few midshipmen questioned the government's handling of the war and most of them understood assignment there was a risk of their profession. But it was difficult to accept why their countrymen would protest the war. They saw themselves giving up things "that our civilian counterparts take for granted" and stood ready "to take the place of the other academy graduates who had died in Vietnam." Rarely were the specific causes of the war discussed however. Participation was linked to the higher goals of freedom and democracy. It had never been American military policy to be the aggressor. Vietnam service was honorable because it was in defense of the weak. Initially midshipmen dismissed any criticism as groups just wanting to cause trouble: "a lot of people can say a lot of things about a lot of subjects and come up with nothing bigger than a mole hill."[111]

The Naval Academy never had to contend with large numbers of critics of the war. Midshipmen were increasingly challenged, however, to support the government without reservation. They saw themselves as being in a unique situation, which gave them a greater ability to see things differently from their peers. While not conceding the correctness of the anti-war movement, they gradually developed a greater understanding for their opinions. A good example of these feelings was the reflections of one first classmen shortly before his graduation in 1967. Looking back at his four years, he candidly observed:

> The thing that amazes me the most about my experience at the academy was my tremendous impressionability. It is frightening to look back on exactly how vivid were the first impressions of summer squad leaders, company officers, or senior officers. And, very frankly, the entire four years have been a series of profound impressions in a world with which I am still very unfamiliar. This time in my life has been one of a fiercely intense need to prove my capability, find my place, plan my future. Paradoxically, all this must be accomplished in a world of imposed conformity. Sometimes, I think one of the best examples of being overly content with the atmosphere within the walls is the ease with which we slip into a language and set of standards peculiar to the academy. For instance, it is difficult for us to *understand* the reasoning behind much of the anti-Vietnam action merely because we have not been exposed to it.[112]

6: THE FINE LINE BETWEEN ATHENS AND SPARTA

Fewer aspects of the war drew unanimous support the longer it went along. The ones midshipmen unilaterally defended related to the integrity of the naval profession. Like most officers, midshipmen were repulsed by the actions of American troops at My Lai. The massacre of innocent civilians seemed like the worst possible breakdown of the chain of command. To midshipmen, it showed the dangers of ignoring the moral responsibilities of their job. William Calley's platoon was "an example of men who either follow blindly or are not capable of accepting moral responsibilities. In an officer corps both characteristics are appalling and detestable." The lesson was clear that an officer has "the moral obligation from the beginning of his commission to be prepared for the occasion."[113]

Midshipmen were also emotionally committed to the fate of American prisoners of war. Indeed, the class of 1972 spearheaded a letter writing campaign to families, friends, communities, and schools, urging that these men not be forgotten. At Annapolis itself, numerous bulletin boards and displays were built calling attention to the situation. The issue united students from all the military service academies. It was not an attempt at some grandiose political statement however. Midshipmen were simply trying to gain the release of shipmates whose families were missing their husbands, sons, and fathers.[114]

Although they were training to be military officers, midshipmen found themselves concerned with similar issues as other college students. It

Prisoner-of-war memorial display board erected by the midshipmen in Bancroft Hall

POW CAMPAIGN IN BANCROFT HALL

***Shipmate,* July 1971. The class of 1972 spearheaded a letter-writing campaign on behalf of American POWs.**

The Lucky Bag 1972. **Poster inside Bancroft Hall encouraging midshipmen to write letters for the POWs.**

should not be surprising to see such a high degree of social awareness. Military service after all was a strong indicator of public commitment. Interest in such issues was also healthy for the midshipmen culture, probably more than the administration realized—a sign that midshipmen were not too isolated from society. Like many of their peers, midshipmen were interested in preserving the environment. Compared to the present day, not much was known in terms of possible solutions. There was a growing sense, however, that the country's resources were not limitless. And to do nothing was to condemn their generation to a bleak future.[115]

All midshipmen became eligible to vote after the legal age was lowered to eighteen. The ramifications of this decision were far different from those on other campuses however. As future officers, midshipmen had to be concerned with the subtleties of appropriate political behavior. Their political opinions could not overshadow a professional demeanor that was essentially nonpartisan. This was a fine line to ask of eighteen-year-old college students, especially in a politically volatile time.[116] Finally, midshipmen saw their generation coming of age in events like Woodstock. While not condoning everything that happened there, midshipmen urged their classmates to maintain a spirit of toleration: "it is quite true that the 400,000 people at Woodstock were peace-loving. We're going to have to keep a foot in Woodstock and a foot in Annapolis. We can conform to professionalism and learn the methods of conflict and deterrence without losing sight of who we must eventually serve."[117]

Midshipmen continued to voice their opinions on such matters in *The Log*. The magazine's tone had changed greatly by the early 1970s however. Although humor was still an important goal, writers also wanted to speak out on pertinent issues. No subject was taboo in its quest to be relevant, including the plebe system, the shadow command, the chapel case, and the aforementioned social concerns. What was surprising was not only the willingness to explore contentious issues, but also the wide range of opinions on these subjects. As was the case with plebe indoctrination, these differences occasionally revealed sharp divisions between the four classes. The magazine's coming of age placed the academy in a tough situation however. Although written primarily for midshipmen, the magazine enjoyed a wide readership outside the academy, primarily friends and relatives but occasionally Washington politicos as well. At the very least, many issues were sensitive to Annapolis; at worst they could be considered outright embarrassing.[118]

On occasions in the past, Annapolis had censored material that was considered too scandalous. In comparison, the present staff had tremendous editorial freedom. However, several issues in 1970 were so shocking, including those on Woodstock, that the administration felt it had little choice but to intervene. Its officer representative was relieved and the staff was counseled about the limits of appropriate behavior. It did not want to stifle their creativity but could not risk *The Log*'s outside readership taking these opinions as reflective of the Brigade. What was surprising was that *The Log*'s staff did not retreat from this challenge. One third classman wrote his senator protesting the incursions on free speech. The positions taken by the administration and the magazine's staff are highly revealing of the new midshipmen culture. Never before would it have agonized as much about putting the clamps on a student publication. Likewise, midshipmen seldom would have challenged the academy in so direct a manner as taking their case to Congress.[119]

Yet, the most direct challenge to the academy's authority was the court case over mandatory chapel. In retrospect, it seems the academy was always on dubious constitutional ground with this tradition. It was likely to be struck down the first time a midshipman dared to fight it. Several things stand out about this episode that bears relevance to the larger midshipmen culture however. Mandatory chapel was defended on its value to good order and discipline. It primarily served a secular purpose, in other words, not a religious one. Church services were vital in preparing midshipmen for "the moral responsibilities of command." Midshipmen were not being converted to any specific belief; it was making them into better officers. In his testimony before the court, Admiral Calvert conceded that "an officer has a privilege not to believe," but that did not relieve him from attending to his men's spiritual needs. The Navy's mission placed it in situations where spiritual matters became important; not all circumstances was a chaplain going to be available. The court would reject the validity of these assumptions in ending mandatory chapel.[120]

The whole affair was very divisive for the Brigade. Few midshipmen, however, defended mandatory chapel on the academy's terms. Those who supported the administration were upset that the academy was being put in an unfavorable light. Too often the press painted the plaintiffs' feelings as representative of the Brigade. "Salty Sam" for one did not want to be included with the chapel six:

> I can best sum up my attitude towards this unfortunate circumstance by mentioning that one of the six principals had first semester grades of 2 D's and 3 F's. It's no wonder that our image might begin to slip when people like that are depicted as representing the views of the Brigade. I have never made any pretense of agreeing with everything we put up with as midshipmen, but neither have I ever felt the necessity of going outside the wall of the academy to express my discontent.[121]

The editor of *The Log* also felt the suit was needlessly tarnishing the academy's reputation. He did not feel it was fair that a "tiny fraction" could decide the fate of a tradition that many midshipmen felt was worthwhile.

Although midshipmen grumbled about it, he could imagine "thousands of things we could have marched to which would have been more unpleasant." Of greater importance, he worried about the case's effect on the reformist spirit at Annapolis. Many things had recently changed for the better—greater privileges and responsibilities. This did not seem to be the right way to repay the administration's actions. At bottom, the plaintiffs were being selfish, like so many of their generation:

> Our generation has long advocated breaking away from the establishment, finding ourselves and doing our own thing. But it's beginning to appear that many of this generation are much too content with going no further than discovering themselves. But to be really effective, to be a good leader, or serve one's country, a person must dedicate and devote his efforts towards something that is beyond and greater than himself.[122]

Other groups believed the time had come to eliminate mandatory chapel. One midshipman implored *The Log* to get its facts straight before publicly condemning six classmates. The plaintiffs had tried to settle the issue privately but were rejected by the academy: "a little research would reveal that, in the past few years, many official channels have been tried and found unopened, clogged by unreasoning tradition." Traditions were important but he failed to see "how an unwilling, tired, and uninterested midshipman is improving his morals by sitting benumbed in chapel every Sunday." Quite ironically, some chaplains felt the same way. Like the administration, *The Log* was mistakenly "equating chapel attendance with morality." Midshipmen should be able to choose where and if to worship, "we all realize the military is not a democracy, but I believe the right to worship as one pleases is a basic American freedom, for all Americans, even midshipmen."[123]

Midshipmen questioned other longstanding academy traditions, including grooming regulations. Admiral Calvert considered a short haircut essential to good military bearing. However, many of his midshipmen wanted regulations changed to conform to newer styles in society. Personal responsibility was often how they argued for greater control over their haircut. Midshipmen had often complained about being treated like children but there was more to this recent dirge than that. It has become almost cliché to talk about the military culture's estrangement from American youth in the late 1960s. Like any young person, peer approval was desperately important to midshipmen. Rather than standing out, they were anxious to blend in with society or, at a minimum, not to be ostracized by their peers. And that was what short hair did; it identified them as being part of the establishment. The haircut was more of a problem than their uniform because they could not hide it. Some of them tried to disguise their appearance by wearing wigs, laughable now but it shows the lengths

The Log, **20 February 1970. The chapel case divided midshipmen. Many wanted the tradition to continue.**

6: THE FINE LINE BETWEEN ATHENS AND SPARTA

The Log, **13 March 1970. Other midshipmen believed the suit's plaintiffs were being vilified for challenging a dubious tradition.**

midshipmen would go to distance themselves from the military and the academy.[124]

Wearing wigs was only a temporary answer; the better solution was to allow midshipmen to grow their hair longer. What made the situation particularly galling was that the rest of the Navy had revised its grooming standards. For all the criticism it received later on, the Zumwalt Navy was at least attempting to bridge the distance between the military and civilian cultures. Admiral Calvert refused to budge from traditional standards however. His argument was that training institutions had a greater need for a neat and uniform military appearance. Also, because of its high visibility, the academy could not tolerate deviation from traditional standards. The chief of naval operations would only accept these arguments so much. Beginning in 1971, Annapolis was *forced* to conform to the fleet, with the exception of beards, mustaches, and sideburns, which continued to be forbidden.[125]

The question of hair length generated as much controversy as mandatory chapel. Midshipmen understood they represented the academy wher-

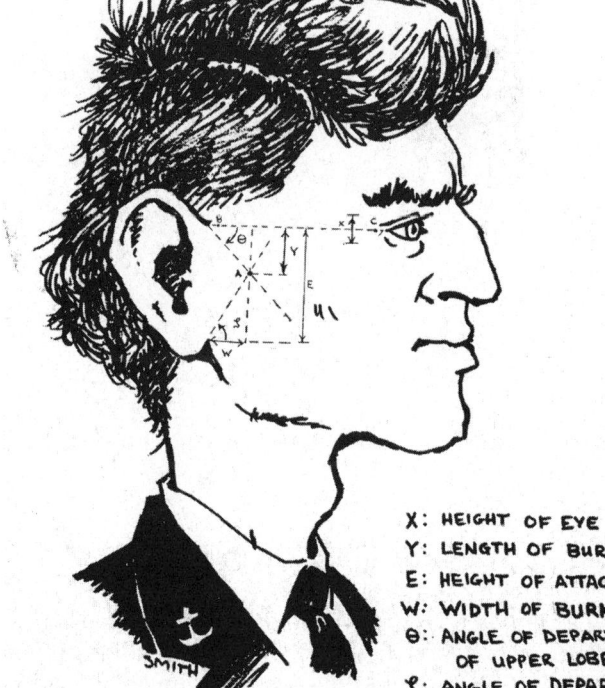

The Log, 30 January 1970. Midshipmen continually tested academy regulations on hair length to conform to the changing styles of society, in this case long sideburns.

ever they went. To do so, they recognized the need for "a badge to identify us in the outside world. A badge, yes; a disgrace, no." Its unwillingness to compromise neglected how much standards of appearance had changed before: "any picture of Albert Michelson will show, the naval uniform is not incompatible with longer hair and sideburns."[126] One midshipman implored the academy to recognize that "midshipmen are representatives of American youth, not outcasts from it." Another argued that since he was paying for the haircuts, he should have the right to determine the type of cut: "Does not accountability imply responsibility? Why should eighteen to twenty-two year old men not be afforded the opportunity for the haircut they desire, and then take their chances at inspection?" The biggest complaint, however, was how much the regulation haircut made them stick out from their peers: "I now get to take my long weekend to see my girl back home. The only thing which looks worse than a totally bald head is one on which remain two inches on the top—and bald sides."[127]

Some midshipmen attempted to see both sides of the issue in arguing for change. The best example talked about the subject's importance to both groups:

> One of the preoccupations of the Brigade is the length of hair. Indeed Friday inspections have come to mean not an outstanding military appearance but a Thursday haircut. From the viewpoint of the administration the problem is mainly one of discipline. A midshipman should be willing to sacrifice something to contribute to the appearance of the Brigade. From the viewpoint of the Brigade, it is extremely hard for us to realize the validity for this regulation. Is it unreasonable for us to have hair the length of cadets at the Air Force Academy or the length of both our naval superiors and subordinates? The Commandant wishes to maintain an outstanding Brigade appearance. The Midshipmen want this as well but also desire to maintain an identity with their civilian peers, and hair is the major block to that goal. Is this wish for longer hair just a selfish desire? Perhaps, but it is the fundamental desire of human nature—the desire to be accepted by one's peers. And that is important.[128]

To show that this was more than a fashion statement, it is important to see how much midshipmen saw themselves alienated from their peers. Beginning in late 1967, *The Log* regularly began publishing the "Dear John" letters of midshipmen. Included in parentheses were their reactions, often dripping with sarcasm, to their girlfriends dumping them. Much of this was done for humor's sake, a way of easing the blow. Many failed relationships were simply part of the adolescent dating process; enough letters had a social content to them that makes their inclusion historically worthwhile. The best example was one girl who broke up with a midshipman because he was "too much God, mother, and country and rather sickening about the whole business." Others could not wait until their midshipmen were free from the academy's restrictions. Regardless of the reasons, their willingness to air such news was evidence of how much they felt abandoned by society.[129]

Hair regulations were demoralizing enough to midshipmen. Yet, there were other concerns that hinted at future retention problems among graduates. Midshipmen were not ignorant of the difficulties of a military career after a major war; demobilization was hard enough let alone after Vietnam. To make matters worse, the American economy was also showing signs of slowing down. For those who stayed in the Navy, inflation was already stretching an officer's paycheck thinner than before. *The Log* broke down an ensign's sample monthly budget, which showed virtually everything taken up in the necessities of life. After rent, car payment, et cetera, the typical ensign had a total of $7.16 left each month for recreation. This was a more frugal leisure life than what most had enjoyed as midshipmen. For those thinking about starting a family, the situation was even bleaker.[130]

No wonder retention rates for the classes of 1970 to 1976 dropped precipitously during this time; only 44 percent of survey respondents intended upon a military career, the lowest among the thirty classes of graduates in the study.[131] In response to these trends, the administration wrote an article for *The Log,* "Is the Grass Greener?," which tried to show the pitfalls of civilian life. The article emphasized the difficulties of finding a stable civilian career, the problems with inflation there as well, and the lack of comparable benefits and camaraderie in most civilian jobs. Although many observations were true, they rang hollow to midshipmen already frustrated with the military culture.[132]

The more disturbing problem was a growing level of apathy in the Brigade. Whatever else its failings, very rarely had it suffered from a lack of motivation. Indeed, excess zeal was often the reason for problems in areas like plebe indoctrination. Retention problems drew more attention, but its symptoms were also easier to spot. This group did everything asked of them but little else beyond that. They were not very happy at Annapolis but there was not much talk of leaving either. Of greatest concern, they preferred to take a "wait and see" attitude to professional socialization. It was easier to mock class leaders' attempts at building unity than joining them. This was more of a lingering crisis but equally as dangerous to the academy's primary mission. Lukewarm midshipmen frequently became lukewarm officers, doing little to inspire sailors during their limited time in the Navy. The class president from 1973 implored his fellow midshipmen to shake off their doldrums and get involved:

> The class of 1973 is very quiet, and very apathetic right now, and this present attitude can only be described as a 'cop-out' on the part of our class. It is wrong to adopt the attitude that nothing will ever be changed, and therefore, we should

stop trying. If for no other reason, we owe it to ourselves, and our self-pride to continue to make the effort to extract change from the system. The matter of attitude and apathy is very significant in a military system. Apathy, in any form, is unprofessional and a totally useless quality.[133]

Perhaps feelings of malaise had begun to cloud over Annapolis just like the rest of society. The academy found this a difficult problem to cure, especially with the growing gap between it and the larger culture. The handmaiden of apathy was cynicism, which this group of midshipmen also possessed in abundance. Respondents from the classes of 1970 to 1976 would also have the least favorable rankings of the academy and among the highest percentages choosing another college if they could make the decision again.[134] One midshipman expressed his reservations of the academy this way:

I have heard the academy referred to as the only place where they take away your rights and give them back to you as privileges. Well, I have always treasured my rights and if there were any effective purpose for putting this yoke around my neck for four years I would have no objections. But right now I feel as though I don't have any identity or any independence. As usual, I got out of the rack at 0615 this morning so I would not get fried for sleeping in. Of course, discipline and accountability are important but doesn't it take just as much discipline to have to make that decision whether or not it is necessary to wake up at 0615 to get one's work done? I am only twenty and maybe I fail to grasp the objectives of a lot of practices around here. But if it is true that NROTC officers are becoming as competent and respected officers as their academy counterparts then maybe "things" around here should be reevaluated.[135]

The Naval Academy and its midshipmen faced trying times in the late 1960s and early 1970s. Much of its struggles were not without a fair share of irony. Annapolis had changed immeasurably with the "academic revolution." It had been a struggle, but the Calvert reforms appeared to be the optimum balance between training and education. The new program seemed ready to meet the needs of a modern Navy while satisfying the academic goals of higher education. Any equilibrium was short lived however. The Vietnam era was the catalyst for a growing gap between the military culture and society. The new academy was probably surprised by the number of frustrated midshipmen in its midst. But there was only so much it could do to appease them. Institutionally, the tension between Athens and Sparta appeared to be satisfactorily resolved. Socially and culturally, however, different groups in the institution continued to be at war. A poem from the 1970 *Lucky Bag* expressed many of these contradictions best:

The Log, 19 December 1973. The growing cynicism of midshipmen is very apparent here. The cartoon warns that attending the academy is hazardous to one's sanity. Furthermore, its lifestyle is not for anyone.

> Different? Sure we're different but we have to be.
> Not only do we subject ourselves voluntarily,
> To four years of personal and outer discipline here at the academy;
> A degree of discipline and self-sacrifice incomprehensible to outsiders
> But we also devote a major portion of our lives to the protection
> And maintenance of a governmental system that enables a disproportionate

6: THE FINE LINE BETWEEN ATHENS AND SPARTA

> Remainder of the nation's population to enjoy or abuse
> As they see fit, the privileges of our heritage.
> But still, we have our differences.
> In a period of time characterized by apathy, disunity, and a search for identity,
> We stand 4,000 firm involved within ourselves, each other and our country,
> And yet, 4,000 individuals, 4,000 united, yet individuals and different.
> The eagle scouts, the class presidents, the football stars, the kid next door,
> The bright ones, and the not so bright, the good ones and the not so good,
> 4,000 individuals . . . and still united.
> How simple life becomes when categorized and stereotyped;
> When good is distinguished from bad by the color of the hat,
> The color of the skin or whether he wears a uniform.
> *But life's not that simple and neither are we.*
> The nation watches us constantly or so we're told.
> And judges not only us but the entire naval service by our actions,
> As they observe us, we watch them. Why not, we pay taxes too.
> Four years is a long time, in many ways, perhaps just as long as the next twenty.[136]

The academy curriculum and culture had changed immeasurably since the "academic revolution." However, Annapolis had not kept pace with the change in American society and it could not do so without abandoning many of its traditional values. Unfortunately, midshipmen often bore the brunt of any tensions between the institution and society. Midshipmen were more observant and reflective of these changes than outsiders gave them credit for. These challenges certainly made it difficult for midshipmen to support the academy culture wholeheartedly. Not surprisingly, some midshipmen challenged regulations that fell too far outside social norms. However, a closer reading of this poem shows that these midshipmen continued to hold onto the core values of Annapolis, especially their appreciation for the value of military service and their commitment to one another.

7
Steering a Sensible Course: The New Annapolis, 1972–76

ANNAPOLIS WAS READY FOR PEACE AFTER THE TURBULENCE OF THE LAST decade. Much of its excitement came from the adjustments of the "academic revolution." However, Vietnam complicated this difficult transition even more. The academy had to resolve most issues on its own since the Navy's focus was winning the war.[1] Society's frustration with the conflict led to a questioning of military institutions, including the academy. Midshipmen were often ridiculed as a result for their school's traditions and lifestyle. Although they defended Annapolis, the outside criticism raised doubts about their professional socialization. Morale could not help but suffer under such circumstances. The academy was more sensitive to these concerns than anyone probably expected. Tradition was not thrown out the window, but Bancroft Hall's culture was not sacrosanct by any means. Academy leaders did their best to eliminate obsolete regulations or show the relevance of those that remained in place.[2]

Admiral Calvert had been one of the truly maverick superintendents in academy history. His administration had been a time of endless reform, most notably the majors program and the revamped plebe system. The job that fell to his successor was that of consolidation, a task inherently less glamorous but certainly not easier to do. Reformers steal the limelight because of the brilliance of their ideas, but it is those who come after who often give breadth and longevity to their changes. After the pattern of recent years, Vice Admiral William Mack '37 was an unusual appointment as superintendent. Mack came to Annapolis in 1972 with three stars already; in fact, before this assignment, he led the Seventh Fleet, the Navy's primary operational command in Vietnam. In other words, he had already achieved everything a successful academy tour accomplished for a superintendent.[3]

Mack had been a strategic choice of the chief of Naval Operations, Admiral Elmo Zumwalt, for several reasons. Both his seniority and personality were seen as a calming influence at Annapolis. Mack's stature guaranteed that he would not be overeager for drastic changes simply to pad his chances at promotion either. He could more calmly evaluate what, if anything, needed to be done next. For the same reasons, his appointment would bring extra respectability at the academy and in the Navy. No one could question Admiral Calvert's zeal, but with it came a tendency to step on people's toes. His tongue in cheek nickname from subordinates was "Lord Jim." For an officer of his rank, Admiral Mack had one of the more easygoing personalities in the Navy. Any changes on his watch would only come after thoughtful deliberation. No one was likely to feel that Admiral Mack had rammed his personal preferences down their throat.[4]

Zumwalt tried to alleviate Mack's concerns that this junior position might be damaging to his career. In no way should he interpret these orders as a hindrance to making full admiral. Indeed, Mack took the job under the assumption that it would last at most a year. Afterward, Zumwalt promised to find a suitable four-star position, a contingency that ironically never took place. For the time being, Mack was needed in Annapolis to smooth over recent events. Although Calvert's accomplishments were legendary, Mack was not afraid of walking in his shadow. Besides his operational credentials, Mack had commanded the academy preparatory school and been a deputy assistant secretary of defense for manpower and reserve affairs. In other words, Mack had plenty of administrative and educational experience to handle the school at this delicate time.[5]

Admiral Mack expressed his philosophy of command several ways, all of which essentially meant the same thing. His job was "to steer a sensible course." Annapolis was headed in the right direction; all it needed were minor adjustments. He also described his policies as more "evolutionary than revolutionary in nature." In either case, Mack was not standing still admiring the work of his predecessors. "What has been good has been left alone, what has needed change for improvement has been dealt with quietly and without fanfare—all for the purpose of producing better officers and for keeping the academy abreast of the changing times in the country." This tone could not have been more different from past years. Significant attention did not have to be drawn to every improvement. Preserving the institution's dignity was also an important part of the superintendent's job. Recent reforms had attracted much publicity but a side effect was also unwanted controversy.[6]

However, an implicit assumption was that there was still significant work to be done. Many reforms had improved things, but in some cases the academy had gone too far. Annapolis did not have to apologize for any unique priorities; foremost was preparing midshipmen to be military officers. In pursuing the "academic revolution," past leaders had often assumed that reform happened in only one direction. Mack had different ideas. The "academic revolution" was not inconsistent if midshipmen could not become doctors or lawyers. A good academic program did not have to offer unlimited choices either. Moving in the opposite direction was not the same as retrenchment; reform could still occur albeit in different ways. That was all part of steering a sensible course. Slight corrections were inherently necessary to keep the school headed in the right direction.[7]

The academy's task only grew more difficult in the aftermath of Vietnam. It struggled to keep programs afloat in the wake of deep budget cuts. The Navy heaped additional responsibilities on it as other commissioning programs shut down. Recruiting continued to be abysmal. Midshipmen remained unhappy with what they perceived as unnecessary restrictions. Annapolis was also the focus of several "impartial" investigations, most notably a GAO study on all the service academies. Many investigators had a specific agenda for what they wanted changed however. Anything that differed from social norms—the honor code and the plebe system—were fair game for outside scrutiny. Mack was not paying lip service, in other words, keeping the academy current with the times. Showing the relevance of its culture was necessary to restoring the public's trust and maintaining its autonomy, much less boosting the midshipmen's morale. Annapolis faced difficult choices the next several years remaining true to the "academic revolution."[8]

Keeping the Curriculum and Professional Training on Track

Academically, Admiral Mack agreed wholeheartedly with the thrust of the new curriculum. Although he graduated near the top of his class, Mack knew full well how limited his education had been in the 1930s.[9] The academy may have been too zealous, however, in expanding the curriculum. The school's academic reputation must not come at the expense of serving the fleet. A good example was the premed program. Many academy officers felt it was not the best answer to the Navy's pressing need for doctors. The numbers had been too few to justify the expense or divisiveness of the program. Traditionally, Annapolis produced line officers with limited exceptions for medical disqualification. Both Calvert and Mack believed midshipmen would see these programs as an alternative to the hardships of fleet duty. The Navy and the academy chose to eliminate this program in 1974 after only a few years of attempting to make it work.[10]

The academy ran into similar problems with graduate school. The question here, however, was largely one of timing. Advanced education was an underlying reason for the "academic revolution," but the balance had apparently swung too far. With more midshipmen starting their graduate work at Annapolis, fewer of them were reaching the fleet in a timely manner. Coupled with their extensive follow-on training, some officers were delayed several years before reaching an operational command. A growing perception was that the academy was not supporting the fleet. Some graduates did see it as an easy way of shortening their minimum service obligation. The academy rectified this in 1974 by eliminating most of these programs; the only exceptions were prestigious civilian scholarships like the Rhodes Scholar program or the Fulbright fellowships. Graduate school was important but not until officers established themselves in a warfare specialty.[11]

The biggest problem with the curriculum continued to be a proper distribution of majors. Admiral Calvert first dealt with this issue by imposing a ceiling of 75 percent technical majors and 25 percent nontechnical majors. Several years later, the academy was still struggling to achieve the right balance. The current ratio also seemed too generous in the number of nontechnical majors. Admiral Rickover was clamoring for additional graduates to compensate for the recruiting problems on civilian campuses. His target goal of 250 graduates had been tough enough to reach; Rickover now wanted three hundred even though he continued to reject most nontechnical volunteers. Ironically, he was also pushing a return to a core curriculum, heavy in engineering subjects however. In his mind, midshipmen should not be free to pursue programs, no matter how reputable, that did not prepare them for nuclear power.[12]

Annapolis was left with solutions that did not please anyone entirely. Unless technical majors were drafted, it would never get these numbers. Rickover was probably correct to reject those with a slim chance of graduating, but the academy could bend only so much to him without shortchanging other responsibilities. It was fine to be selective, but the school did not exist solely for nuclear power.[13] At the same time, programs with little crossover value had to be limited. With this in mind, Mack redrew the balance between technical and non-technical majors at 80-20 instead of 75-25. Some students would just not get their first choice if there were too many in that program. Ironically, problems with NROTC probably helped the academy take this tougher line. With units being eliminated, Annapolis had less competition for those who truly wanted to be officers.[14]

Whether these changes retreated from the "academic revolution" is debatable. Certainly the motives behind them were not. Other reforms showed the same commitment to academics. The admissions process continued to be made less political. The emphasis remained on making as many early appointments as possible. To do this, a new way of evaluating candidates was developed known as "prospective nominees." The files of promising applicants were treated as if they already had a nomination. Once the nomination was awarded, the actual appointment followed soon after. This idea was also extended to the nominating process. Congressmen and senators could request the files of "prospective nominees." Politicians retained their nominating power, but in effect the academy was telling them whom it preferred. The academy's assumption, of course, was that they would honor its wishes.[15]

Much effort was also put into restoring the candidate pool after Vietnam. Vision waivers were further expanded to 30 percent of each entering class. Exemptions were given primarily to those with good grades, however.[16] The academy also focused on its academic programs in recruiting. It began hosting a weeklong engineering and science seminar in 1974 for high school juniors. Applicants were selected based on their science and math scores on the pre-SAT. Most of their time was spent in state of the art laboratories and engineering halls. The academy was hoping to lure these students based on its academic opportunities. Afterwards, it could sell them on its military environment and the Navy.[17]

To limit attrition, an orientation day was begun in 1975 for entering students. Appointees met with the superintendent and commandant as well as other officers. They were briefed on the academic program *and* Bancroft Hall, more than was possible during the admissions process. The underlying goal was to ease the shock of plebe summer and Bancroft Hall. The first year of the program was a remarkable success. Of the 427 candidates who participated, 423 showed up for induction and 408 of them made it through plebe summer; their attrition rate of 3.5 percent was well below the expected rate of 6 percent.[18]

Mack intensified the focus on minority recruiting, but the challenges remained difficult to overcome. Acknowledging past problems in this area, he promised an approach that walked "a very fine path between no discrimination and no patronization."[19] Yet the academy's problems were not unlike other selective colleges; it did not help itself or these students by compromising standards. The head of Candidate Guidance described these problems best: "There can be no 'easy track,' no perfunctory course of studies at the Naval Academy. The Admissions Board must continue to ask itself 'Can this young man succeed in the academic program *and graduate?*' not the question many civilian institutions are free to ask, 'Should we give him a chance?'"[20] Even though this was a visible issue, effort alone would not fix things immediately, especially since it was ignored for so many years. The head of Candidate Guidance also described these challenges:

> It must be understood that improvement in recruiting in a poor area is essentially a "bootstrap" operation. You don't do well in a particular geographic area where few young men are aware of the Naval Academy or know of the opportunity. To date one of the reasons we have not been as effective in our black recruiting is because there were so few black midshipmen to send out to talk to other blacks.[21]

Mack's efforts eventually bore fruit, however. A key turning point was the addition of a second minority affairs officer. One officer could now focus on recruiting while the other concentrated on limiting attrition. Advertisements started to run monthly in prominent black magazines like *Ebony* and *Black Enterprises*. Operation Information stepped up its efforts in primarily black high schools, and the admissions office tried to identify congressmen who preferred to nominate minorities. The extraordinary effort was not done for whites, but Admiral Mack felt it was fair compensation for past inattention. He could not have been more pleased with the results. For the first time, minorities were a significant part of the Brigade. The class of 1978 set the record with ninety African Americans followed by a dip to fifty-five in the class of 1979. Even so, at the end of his tour in 1975, Annapolis had a total of 380 minorities compared to the one hundred when he assumed command. Even more encouraging, projections had this growth continuing in the future.[22]

Admiral Mack also believed that future academic or professional reforms depended on a better relationship with the chain of command. The academy had generally reported to the Bureau of Naval Personnel since 1945. Occasionally this created problems because BUPERS approached matters from a service-wide perspective rather than what was important to Annapolis. For example, the academy had constantly fought BUPERS over officer faculty assignments. Other elite colleges did not suffer such constraints. Admiral Zumwalt changed the reporting structure in 1972, but his reforms actually made the situation worse instead of better. All training and educational commands—the Naval War College, Pensacola, NROTC—reported to a new vice-chief, the Chief of Naval Education and Training. In theory, since all commands did the same thing, CNET would be best suited to manage them.[23]

Although there were similarities, the Navy continued to blur the important distinctions between training and education. Training centers generally covered the same material regardless of the number of students. Their curriculum was usually limited to certain skills, which made them more flexible to change and centralization. In contrast, educational institutions required greater autonomy to establish continuity in their curriculum. It was not so much specific skills but their philosophy of learning that was important. As a result, the dust from any significant changes generally took a long time to clear. NROTC's mission was probably most similar to Annapolis. However, the college or university host was responsible for its midshipmen's education; the Navy was essentially just handling training. Senior institutions like the Naval War College also had a restricted curriculum, which mitigated their need for independence.

Despite Zumwalt's changes, the Naval Academy continued to fight for special status within the chain of command. It was, after all, the undergraduate college of the Navy. The aftermath of Vietnam had exposed serious shortcomings with these reforms. Budget cuts had fallen heaviest on training and educational commands. It seemed logical that CNET would administer this burden equally. The Naval Academy was hard pressed absorbing its fair share however. Congress determined many of its responsibilities independently, the size of the Brigade being the best example. Demobilization left it in a tough predicament. The budget was shrinking yet it had to supervise roughly the same number of midshipmen.[24]

Zumwalt's successor, Admiral James Holloway III, ironically the son of the Navy's great educational reformer, agreed that because of its unique responsibilities Annapolis deserved special treatment. Beginning in November 1975, the superintendent would report to the chief of naval operations. His deputies would continue managing the academy on most day-to-day affairs. However, on broad policy issues, Annapolis would deal directly with the Navy's top command.[25] In essence, this change gave the academy the functional autonomy it had long requested. Holloway's reasons for making this change echoed many of his father's ideas about Annapolis:

> I consider the educational and professional tone set at the academy to be the bellwether for professionalism within the entire officer corps of the Navy and the quality of the graduates to be the bedrock for future fleet readiness. The Naval Academy must be responsive to the basic missions of the Navy and Marine Corps. This dictates a requirement for systematic review of and continuing improvement in prescribed policies and practices to ensure that the academy retains its proper stature and prestige. This excellence, then, must be excellence along the lines that best serve the naval profession. Not all academic disciplines are well suited for the central role in this regard.[26]

Mack also intended on further reforms to professional training but felt that Calvert's changes were basically sound. The Academic Advisory Board, the new group evaluating the curriculum, agreed. Students' attitudes towards professional training had dramatically improved. Most now believed that their professional development was "for real," their slang for an emphasis on practical fleet applications.[27] The ending of Vietnam was a double-edged sword. Many problems in the summer schedule were alleviated. As expected, the resumption of overseas cruises boosted the quality of training and the midshipmen's morale. A less hectic operational schedule also allowed greater time for warfare familiarization. Demobilization created its share of headaches however. Professional goals were a challenge with shrinking budgets and limited underway time. Yet, to some extent, these were known quantities. The academy dealt with similar problems after World War II.[28]

Calvert's smaller core curriculum had indeed been the savior of professional training. Fewer academic requirements had enabled the academy to accomplish both its professional *and* academic goals. Yet, the philosophy of the "academic revolution" was what contributed the most to making professional training "real"; all parts of the curriculum were now administered under similar standards. Professional syllabi listed concrete objectives; students were tested in them at the course's conclusion. Summer training concentrated on practical applications; theoretical principles were emphasized during the academic year. However, Mack also wanted the professional curriculum to address contemporary social concerns. The Navy increasingly needed its officers to be effective managers as well as war fighters. Various social and economic pressures had exposed serious shortcomings in this area. The new Human Goals Program was created to tackle these challenges.[29]

Racial tensions, for example, were a growing threat to good order and discipline throughout the Navy. Drug and alcohol abuse increasingly threatened operational readiness as well. Accidents at sea or in the field were always a possibility, much more so if sailors or marines took drugs. The Navy's problems were not just limited to its enlisted men either. Officers too were abusing alcohol or drugs either for social experimentation or as means of coping with their jobs. The military was certainly not the only institution in the 1970s to be struggling with these problems. However, the consequences of ignoring them were much worse than in society. At the very least, they undermined unit cohesion and morale; at worst, they could cause the loss of countless lives and material.[30]

At first, Bancroft Hall was responsible for instructing midshipmen on these difficult issues. Company officers casually talked with midshipmen about how they handled these situations in the fleet. Not coincidentally, the academy found this a way of encouraging proper behavior from the Brigade. Occasionally videos were used to reinforce subjects gone over by the Executive Department. To its credit, Annapolis soon realized that this training was too haphazard to accomplish the Navy's objectives. Their seriousness required a formal curriculum, similar to the rest of professional training.[31]

Eventually these topics were incorporated into a formal course, "the Professional Officer and the Human Person," which spanned the four years at Annapolis. Rear Admiral John O'Connor, head of the Navy Chaplain Corps, wrote a special, multivolume text for the course. Most topics were supported with multimedia presentations that enlivened their discussion. Company officers continued to be the primary instructors, but regular faculty supplemented them when it was appropriate. Here again the academy held firm to the philosophy of learning established during the "academic revolution." Anything important to the midshipmen's education had to conform to a similar organization and pedagogy.[32]

Preparing midshipmen for fleet service had long been the focus of professional training. The problem was that since World War II, fewer midshipmen were choosing careers in service line. Those who had the physical or mental ability preferred naval aviation or nuclear submarines, either for the pay, the excitement, or the prestige. Although these other warfare communities were growing, the surface navy still had large numbers of billets to fill. By the early 1970s, this perennial problem had escalated into a full-blown crisis. Both the academy and the Navy were desperate to restore the reputation of surface line. Admiral Mack exerted his considerable prestige to get the Navy to renew its pledge to send only the best officers in that community to Annapolis. Cruise schedules would once again be screened carefully to showcase surface warfare in the best possible light.[33]

Surface warfare was established in 1973 as a distinct combat specialty like submarines and aviation. Officers could now qualify for a new uniform device similar to aviator's wings or submariner's dolphins. It had its own advanced schools, similar to the other warfare communities, and prospective captains completed special command qualifications like their counterparts. The Navy's message was unmistakable. Surface warfare was not for the dregs; it required special training and abilities.[34] How much of this was done for image's sake is difficult to say. Shipboard systems—propulsion, weapons, navigation, and communications—had become more complicated. Surface warfare officers had to master new tactical and operational skills to function in the multithreat environments of the day. If part of this was done to bolster egos, there was ample operational evidence to show it was needed too.

Neither the Naval Academy nor NROTC were capable of training surface warfare officers in all their duties however. SWOS, the Surface Warfare Officer's School, was created to ensure a common foundation for these officers. SWOS could not help but undercut the academy's position in the Navy's system of officer education. SWOS became an alternative to the Naval Academy just like NROTC had been in the 1940s. These latest reforms were also necessary, but they too rekindled the debate over of a four-year service academy. SWOS raised difficult questions about the cost effectiveness of Annapolis. If the academy was doing its job, why did its graduates need SWOS?[35]

It was no wonder then that academy leaders looked upon SWOS with suspicion. Direct attacks were limited, but no one was an ardent supporter either. Some graduates could, of course, benefit from remedial work. However, most were fully prepared without the additional time or expense. The debate was extremely awkward for the Navy to resolve. SWOS was eager to show its value and claimed that its program exceeded the academy, which was probably true. However, it was a dedicated training center so that should have been the case. At the same time, Annapolis argued that its professional curriculum was sufficient preparation for a junior officer's essential duties. Complicating matters further, both institutions insisted on their own standards to decide the issue. SWOS insisted academy graduates take its competency exam. Annapolis was almost ready to make Calvert's professional readiness exam a mandatory requirement for graduation.[36]

Admiral Mack negotiated a deal with SWOS to end the controversy. Midshipmen would immediately begin taking the SWOS exam. Those who passed the test skipped SWOS and reported directly to the fleet. Mack understood that this was a temporary arrangement however. Eventually, all academy graduates entering surface line were required to complete SWOS. Although there was duplication of effort, the academy could not match the depth of training at SWOS. Its curriculum was also the foundation for the new surface warfare designation. Annapolis would be equally embarrassed if graduates were not getting their pins. Just like with NROTC, it wanted to show that its program was self-sufficient. Its graduates could make an *immediate* contribution, if need be, without SWOS.

Two final reforms show the ambiguous nature of what it meant to steer Mack's "sensible course." Beginning in 1976, the rules for class standing were revised, which gave greater weight to professional training. Admiral Kauffman had experimented with this once before, but Mack felt that professional training was still not getting sufficient credit. Instead of lumping professional training into academic order of merit, a separate Professional Military Order of Merit (PMOOM) was created. Academic Order of Merit would still count for 70 percent of class standing but PMOOM would contribute the final 30 percent. The PMOOM figure would include grades for military aptitude, conduct, and physical education, as well as the professional curriculum. Academic success still meant the most at the new Annapolis, but good grades should not hide students who were likely to be marginal officers.[37]

However, Mack also looked at reducing the school's minimum service obligation from five years to three. In fact, it was a chief goal of his administration. Along with this, he explored ways to release athletes from their active duty commitment if a professional team drafted them. The Navy would still get service from them but mainly in the form of reserve time that did not hinder their athletic careers. How did this fit within the school's underlying purpose of producing career officers? Mack, above all, was a realist. He understood many graduates were not staying for a twenty-year career and that a longer obligation deterred good candidates from even applying to the academy. The concession to athletes was a way of keeping varsity teams competitive and modernizing the academy's image.[38]

A New Bancroft Hall

Mack also appeared more pragmatic than his predecessor in how he managed Bancroft Hall. Admiral Calvert had attempted to maintain traditional standards of discipline, even when it contradicted current fleet practices. Part of this reflected his personal beliefs about professional indoctrination; there was nothing wrong with holding midshipmen to a higher standard since they would eventually be setting the bar in fleet. However, he was not interested in reforms that could inhibit the "academic revolution." The new curriculum was his foremost priority, and there was already enough skepticism to it. Mack questioned how much of this dogmatism was wise or even necessary at this point. His preferred tone with Bancroft Hall was summed up by an often-used phrase, "a realistic military environment."[39]

High standards were one thing, but graduates risked a mutiny if they enforced some of the rules they followed as midshipmen. It was this line of behavior, after all, which contributed to past stereotypes of graduates being martinets. That was the one thing the Navy needed to avoid in the early 1970s. Perhaps a part of Mack's flexibility came from his experiences commanding the Seventh Fleet during Vietnam. He knew full well the struggles officers had leading sailors, given the growing gap between the Navy and society. Moreover, Mack understood how these problems affected operational readiness. Senior officers did not need to support enthusiastically all the changes in American society. They had to know which adjustments were necessary to accomplishing the Navy's larger mission.

Mack's first challenge was implementing the Supreme Court's decision ending mandatory chapel in January 1973. Unlike his predecessor, Mack was not totally averse to seeing this tradition eliminated. He agreed with the academy's chaplains that an attendance requirement was not the best way to run chapel services. Although turnout dropped dramatically after the regulation was lifted, Mack insisted that the number of true worshippers remained the same. In other words, the midshipmen who wanted to attend did so while the others slept, relaxed, or did what they preferred with the time.[40]

Remembering back to his own days at Annapolis, Mack believed this was better than the spectacle of midshipmen falling asleep in their pews. At the same time, the academy continued to be involved in the Brigade's moral development. Although services were no longer compulsory, Mack advised midshipmen "to worship according to the dictates of your conscience" and urged them to remember the peculiar challenges of a military career. A strong moral code was vital, he believed, in making decisions and leading subordinates. One could argue that lifting the requirement actually improved the academy's character building program. With the freedom to decide such issues themselves, midshipmen were likely to develop stronger convictions of what they truly believed.[41]

Mack was also more receptive to the Navy's revised grooming requirements, which Admiral Calvert had fought tooth and nail. Midshipmen had been frustrated by the academy's insistence on going beyond fleet standards with their haircut. The standard crew cut frequently made them a laughingstock on liberty or in situations with their peers. Even their officers were not asked to make such a sacrifice. Admiral Zumwalt would have insisted on greater conformity to the Navy's standards if Mack had resisted further.[42] When the Brigade returned in autumn 1972, they were pleasantly surprised by new regulations implemented during the summer. Contrary to later stereotypes, the requirement for a neat military appearance never disappeared. Maximum hair length was not to exceed four inches, a drastic improvement over the old crew cut. Most importantly, sideburns were not prohibited. Annapolis did not totally adopt the fleet's more relaxed standards. Nonetheless, midshipmen appreciated something being done to make them less open to ridicule. Beards and mustaches were still forbidden even though the fleet *and* NROTC allowed them.[43]

Many midshipmen thought these regulations should have been loosened even more, at least to what the fleet permitted. They stretched the new standards to their limits, hoping to slip by officers' weekly personnel inspections. Even if they were caught, a few conduct reports seemed a small price to pay for greater social acceptance. They were outraged that academy barbershops did not give them any control over their haircut. The most defiant cut their own hair even though this violated regulations. In part, these midshipmen were playing the classic game of "cops and robbers." Even here, Admiral Mack and his commandants saw useful lessons in character development. They had honestly attempted to eliminate obsolete requirements. However, those that remained must be obeyed. Regulations were inherent to military life and midshipmen had to understand the consequences of not following them. That was all part of what "a realistic military environment" was about.[44]

Annapolis also revised its regulations concerning alcohol. Again, the stimulus for change came from outside the institution. Previous regulations had followed Maryland law, which prohibited drinking within seven miles of the capitol dome.[45] Midshipmen of otherwise legal drinking age considered this a nuisance, but it did not stop them from drinking. In fact, all the law did was to cause them to drink irresponsibly. Other aspects of academy policy also seemed counterproductive to good behavior. The regulations were not in effect at certain functions, like away football games, which simply encouraged midshipmen to drink to excess. The school was often embarrassed by a range of boorish behavior, including stumbling onto buses or getting sick in public and starting fights with civilians. The Executive Department always disciplined the offenders harshly. However, the academy often failed to recognize its responsibility in encouraging such behavior.[46]

The more serious problem, however, was midshipmen drinking outside the seven-mile limit on weekend liberty. Since drinking was forbidden in Annapolis, midshipmen simply went elsewhere to do it. All this did, however, was to promote drinking *and* driving. Moreover, the restrictive lifestyle encouraged binge drinking on weekends. In essence, midshipmen tried to cram a normal college social life into a few liberty hours on Saturday and Sunday. Heavy drinking usually left them rushed to get back to Bancroft Hall before liberty expired. Although accidents were possible, many believed it could never happen to them. In some ways, midshipmen were not all that different from other young men their age. Besides, any thrills were a way of coping with their everyday pressures.[47]

Admiral Mack recognized this as a serious problem shortly after taking command. Although midshipmen were ultimately responsible for their actions, the academy lifestyle might somehow encourage such behavior. He changed the regulations in June 1973 after the Maryland legislature repealed the seven-mile limit. Drinking became permissible for upperclassmen inside Annapolis during normal liberty hours. Compared to other students, their freedom was still very limited. However, the reforms encouraged more mature behavior. Midshipmen could spread out their drinking over a greater period of time. At a minimum, it removed the temptation for drinking and driving. Irresponsible drinking was not totally eliminated but the academy was certainly justified in ruthlessly punishing such behavior.[48]

Besides the new liberty regulations, Annapolis created opportunities for drinking in the Yard. First classmen could consume alcohol if they were dining with officers or faculty on academy grounds. Furthermore, they could become members of the Officers' Club, which entitled them to use its bar while on yard liberty. Second and third classmen were not permitted to join but could use its facilities during their free time. In part, these changes were done to stir up business for the club, which was losing money to bars in town. However, it was also a sincere attempt to foster "a realistic military environment." Midshipmen were only under the academy's supervision for four years, after which they would make these decisions independently. Despite the hard-drinking reputation of naval officers, the academy recognized this tradition was in need of reform. At the very least, it did not need to foster bad habits in an area increasingly troublesome for the Navy.[49]

These reforms alone were significant in changing the atmosphere of Bancroft Hall. However, the academy also pursued internal initiatives towards "a realistic military environment." Mack was assisted by two able commandants, Captains Max Morris '48 and Donald Forbes '50, both of them naval aviators and on the fast track to promotion. Morris, in fact, had his Ph.D. in international relations from the Fletcher School. Unlike earlier periods in its history, all echelons of academy leadership understood the "academic revolution" and were committed to reforms that enhanced it. The commandant and his staff reviewed regulations and purged those that seemed outdated. Stripers were also involved to get their opinion of what was "Mickey Mouse." Afterwards, the group rewrote all of Bancroft Hall's regulations to better fit the environment of the new Annapolis.[50]

Many alumni complained that the academy had become foolish and overly permissive. Traditional military discipline was being abandoned to conform to society. However, these values were not what prepared officers to win wars. Supporters of these reforms insisted that nothing was farther from the truth. The changes were overdue to bring continuity between Annapolis and the fleet. Instilling discipline was important but graduates had to be prepared to lead today's sailors. Furthermore, traditional arguments assumed that rigid discipline was the best preparation for combat. However, as younger alumni pointed out, this was the equivalent of believing that mandatory chapel made midshipmen moral.[51]

What was interesting was that this debate reflected a growing generational divide between academy graduates. For classes before the "academic revolution," the prevailing belief was that discipline, no matter how onerous, was valuable. "Mickey Mouse" regulations taught midshipmen perseverance in the midst of adversity. No virtue was more important in an officer's character development. Younger graduates questioned the necessity of such a rigid and thoughtless system. Officers needed discipline, but they also should be able to think their way through difficult situations. Midshipmen would not have the gouge telling them what to do after the academy. Furthermore, cumbersome policies only encouraged midshipmen to break them. Was it not better to have midshipmen obey rules that truly mattered than to nourish an attitude of "you rate what you get away with?"[52]

The scope of the changes was exhaustive. Midshipmen were given additional privileges that better reflected the times. The most welcome were new car regulations. For the first time upperclassmen could drive within the seven-mile limit. Historically, the prohibition on cars was because of the insufficient parking space on academy grounds. Although that had not changed, it did not make sense to forbid the use of cars entirely. First classmen received car privileges, including the ability to park inside the Yard, their entire senior year. There was not enough room even to consider this for other upperclassmen. However, the academy permitted them at least to drive on the weekends.[53]

In addition, new liberty policies more closely matched the fleet. Midshipmen did not gain many additional hours, but they were given greater freedom to plan and hence enjoy their weekends. Upperclassmen were excused from most meal formations and other military obligations. They could also wear civilian clothes during certain types of liberty, which made the break from Bancroft Hall more real and satisfying. The new tone was what was most important, however. Midshipmen were technically always on duty, but weekend liberty should signify the time when they were essentially released from military obligations.[54]

Yet, more was happening than simply new privileges. Although midshipmen will probably always find a portion of Bancroft Hall "Mickey Mouse," these reforms sincerely attempted to create a more professional atmosphere. For example, the new room standards treated midshipmen more like adults. Instead of specifying exactly how everything was to be organized, midshipmen were responsible for keeping their rooms neat and orderly. Military discipline did not have to be "cops and robbers" with officers scrutinizing where well meaning midshipmen inadvertently went wrong. For those who looked to challenge the rules, discipline was swift and severe, which is what graduates should expect in the fleet. In essence, there appears to have been a growing convergence between the academic and military cultures of the academy. That had not been the case in the early stages of the "academic revolution" according to the 1966 Middle States team. Annapolis was now placing greater responsibility on midshipmen in both areas. Midshipmen reaped the consequences of their choices in the academic program; the same was also becoming true in Bancroft Hall.[55]

The most explicit attempt at creating "a realistic military environment" were reforms to Admiral Calvert's "shadow command." Further responsibility for running the Brigade was put in the hands of midshipmen stripers. Company and battalion officers were there to advise but midshipmen were entrusted with the truly difficult decisions. Stripers were even expected to discipline their classmates. Given this role, it was not unusual for stripers to be viewed as toadies for the administration. But disciplinary action was a part of what real officers did, even in the fleet. To its credit, Admiral Mack's administration truly placed the success or failure of the "shadow command" in the hands of midshipmen.[56]

In an interview done with *The Log,* Captain Morris talked about this new philosophy of command. He had constantly heard the demands of midshipmen for more responsibility, especially policing one another. That was fine, according to the commandant, but the *enforcement* must truly be in place. In other words, standards were not going to be compromised simply because stripers were now in charge. Captain Forbes agreed wholeheartedly with this approach. He too believed in "leadership by example." Contrary to past stereotypes of the Executive Department, Forbes did not intend to change his leadership style just because he was at the Naval Academy. At the same time, positive leadership meant that stripers had a real job to perform. If midshipmen wanted their input taken seriously, then they had to show the maturity that these roles demanded.[57]

Colonel Bruce Ogden '53 was assigned as the Third Battalion Officer during the implementation of these policies. In a letter to *Shipmate,* he talked to fellow alumni about the growing pains of the "shadow command." For all the difficulties, Ogden believed this was the right approach to teach midshipmen fleet leadership:

> Despite mixed emotions and some natural misgivings, we decided to test the Shadow Command Concept in the extreme sense. Accordingly we convened the battalion and company commanders and informed them that it was our intention that they would command their respective organizations in the fullest sense; the Third Battalion was theirs to make or break. The Commandant was sometimes heard to refer to our roles as "high risk" and not without some justification. The mistakes by the mids were our mistakes, by the same token, their triumphs were shared fully by their somewhat impatient and sometimes long-suffering "advisers." The major lessons learned embraced the basic concept of the "Annapolis Experience," to prepare young men for command through real life experiences. Only the mids themselves can know to what degree they absorbed the objectives of the course, but their advisers know for their part that no apologies to the mids or the alumni are required.[58]

By and large, most stripers appeared to have taken their new responsibilities seriously. In his last report to the Board of Visitors in July 1975, Admiral Mack noted that the average number of demerits, the number of midshipmen on conduct probation, and the number of major conduct offenses had all risen considerably. Although these figures were disturbing, Mack did not believe the Brigade was getting into significantly greater trouble than it had before. In his mind, the increase indicated that standards were being more rigorously enforced after stripers had assumed their disciplinary responsibilities and Bancroft Hall had been purged of its sillier regulations.[59] *The Log* interviewed the two Brigade commanders that year to get their thoughts on the new policies. Both men talked about the importance of first class leadership even if it alienated other midshipmen.

Midshipman Captain Jim Fitzsimonds reminded classmates that he was not their arbitrator with the administration, nor was his role getting "good deals" for them. His job was commanding the Brigade. Fitzsimonds also noticed the recent surge in conduct violations, in his mind, the reason for any increase was a better sense of accountability among the first class. More violations were being reported instead of hidden from the Executive Department. Midshipmen Captain Jim Adams echoed many of these sentiments. Standards would be enforced whether it was officers or midshipmen doing the job. It was his idea, for example, to assign gate watches and rover watches to monitor the Brigade's behavior on liberty. Once midshipmen proved that they were responsible, these watches would be removed. Adams was not averse to asking for additional privileges. However, he was not going to rubber stamp harebrained ideas simply because his peers wanted them. Statements like these were not always popular with other midshipmen. Nonetheless, the "shadow command" made the academy more of a leadership laboratory than it was before.[60]

The 1976 Middle States Evaluation

The report of the 1976 Middle States Association was a fitting epitaph to the reforms of the "academic revolution." Just thirty years before, this group first visited Annapolis to inspect changes made in the wake of World War II. Although they were pleased with what they found, Annapolis had much work to do before it could be considered a first-rate college. Over the years, the Middle States Association found reasons to be both happy and disappointed with its progress. After its visit in 1956, evaluators wondered about the academy's commitment to undergraduate education. The 1966 inspection came at the midway point of the "academic revolution." Although there was much chaos, the inspecting team was delighted by its energy and commitment to reform. For the first time, Annapolis seemed genuinely interested in balancing its responsibilities to training and education. The 1976 visit would be the first after all the major reforms were completed.[61]

The 1976 team was impressed with how much the academy had followed through on its previous recommendations. Unlike earlier disappointments, it had not wavered from its stated priorities in 1966. Overall, it was a glowing endorsement of the new Annapolis:

> The team has been greatly impressed with the great advances the academy has made on many fronts in recent years. In general, the institution is strong and solid in academic terms. Specifically, it has a superior student body, a capable faculty, a remarkable physical plan, and fine educational support arrangements. It is characterized by high spirit and much devotion on the part of faculty, midshipmen and support staff. Its mission—uniformly understood and subscribed to—is clear, and it is clearly fulfilling its mission. It is significant that

all the officer faculty members interviewed felt that the academy is significantly better as an educational training ground for Naval and Marine Corps officers than when they were midshipmen.[62]

Although evaluators found opportunities for improvement, the tone of their remarks could not have been more different than past reports. In no sense were they talking down to the academy as if their institutions were superior. These were only suggestions from its *colleagues* in higher education. In other words, the academy had accomplished the goal first articulated by Admiral Holloway in 1946, a naval college recognized for *both* its academic and professional excellence. Many team members could not help but be jealous of the new physical facilities, which placed Annapolis "among the finest undergraduate engineering schools in the country." There was similar praise for its new library: "Nimitz Library is one of the more successful undergraduate buildings erected in this generation—generous in space and seating, functional, inviting, comfortable, and well planned for growth and future technology." For many years, the library's dilapidated condition was an eyesore to its academic pretensions. Very few midshipmen even used the older facility. Although it had taken many years, the library was now the envy of other colleges.[63]

Step by step, inspectors found substantial improvements in areas of past deficiency. They were pleased to find civilian chairmen in eleven of the nineteen academic departments; scholastic qualifications were the rule in making these assignments. Civilian leadership had brought greater continuity to the school's academic climate. Past problems in academic counseling also seemed to have been corrected. The academic side was now responsible for all issues affecting the Brigade's academic life with Bancroft Hall providing an important supporting role. Inspectors praised the availability and dedication of both civilian and military faculty "to a degree very unusual on the civilian undergraduate campus." Two areas that had caused so much controversy in 1966—grade quotas and turn backs—had also been fixed. Unlike before, remedial students repeated work in clearly defined programs that upheld academic standards. The demanding curriculum caused the loss of some students with the potential to be fine officers. However, this was not an excuse for compromising academic integrity. In terms of grading practices, the academy was now at the forefront of tougher standards. Evaluators found no evidence of the "grade creep" problem plaguing other institutions.[64]

The Navy had also become more supportive of the "academic revolution." Both commandants and superintendents were being assigned to longer tours of duty, which was a necessary prerequisite to reform. At the same time, the team worried about the Navy's rotation policy with regard to military instructors. In their minds, this continued to be the academy's single biggest problem. The Navy had yet to ensure that all of these instructors had advanced degrees. The double standards in terms of faculty qualifications were unequivocal. For civilians, the Ph.D. was the norm; for officers, the master's degree was truly an advanced degree. However, promotion boards continued to frown upon officers with academy service in their records. Until these problems were erased, the future of the new Annapolis was still clouded. The skepticism many naval officers had towards higher education was also a difficult attitude to erase. Yet for all the complaints about officers at Annapolis, there were likely hundreds more in the fleet whose attitudes were worse.

The Middle States Association had also become more familiar with Bancroft Hall. The team was truly appreciative of the efforts to keep its time pressures more manageable. Training and indoctrination were important, but the commitment to an inviolate study hour was a major improvement. At the same time, inspectors had some interesting observations about the midshipmen culture. The academy expected a lot from itself and midshipmen in four short years. To get everything done, midshipmen lived in an environment that was in many ways foreign to the outside world. Team members found that "the academy's sharply focused professional objectives lead to a program that in some respects is considerably more stressful that that on a civilian campus, but in other respects it is very protective."[65]

The academy fostered a "pattern of development that places the midshipmen ahead of civilian students in some ways and behind them in others." Evaluators could not say whether this was right or wrong, but it was noticeable. Unfortunately this dilemma was probably unavoidable. Annapolis primarily existed to turn civilians into military officers; professional socialization took time and it had to happen. At the same time, graduates had to be comfortable with the outside world to lead sailors through the difficult issues of the day. It was not enough that they had been trained to be capable mariners. Officers needed new social and managerial skills in the 1970s to be successful. Even after so much had changed, the tensions in the midshipmen culture were eerily the same and just as difficult to answer. The Middle States team summed up this dilemma best: "What the midshipmen do question is how much of their academy career should be so tightly controlled at the expense of opportunities to learn to manage freedom responsibly before they suddenly emerge into the freedoms and opportunities of their professional career."[66]

Conclusion

THE NAVAL ACADEMY HAS JUGGLED COMPETING PRIORITIES THROUGHout its history. It could never be just Athens or Sparta, nor did it want to be. The schedule at Annapolis has always been intense. The midshipmen's training and education had to be completed within four years to support the Navy's operational needs. That timetable was difficult enough to meet, even without Bancroft Hall. Reform was difficult to say the least under such constraints. Many colleges have offered a better education, and many of the Navy's training commands have operated more efficiently than Annapolis. Bancroft Hall's activities have caused the loss of midshipmen who had the potential to be fine officers. Furthermore, any equilibrium in the curriculum was bound to be temporary at best. Changes in technology or mission requirements periodically altered the Navy's expectations of Annapolis. Both groups accepted these circumstances as the cost of the academy's existence however.

The bottom line, which Annapolis defined as its ability to produce warwinning, career officers, outweighed any disadvantages of the academy system. Over time, these convictions have become dogma regardless of the evidence behind them. The plebe system, for example, was undeniably the best test of a midshipman's fitness for combat. Training and education could be done equally well regardless of the strains it placed on the institution. For all these reasons, the academy culture has generally been resistant to change. Unless there were compelling reasons otherwise, it has simply been easier to stick with tradition. With that being said, the academy culture was not reactionary by any means. Neither Annapolis nor the Navy was foolish enough to continue a system that had outlived its usefulness. However, reforms had the onus of proving their utility, not vice versa. If not, the tendency was to follow that familiar military maxim, "if it ain't broke, don't fix it."

Given its purpose, it is not surprising that tradition was the lifeblood of the academy culture. Professional socialization was never the sole justification for its existence. However, many academy leaders and graduates have considered it to be its greatest responsibility. Tradition provided the roadmap for how it produced its officers, especially their indoctrination into the values and mindset of the naval profession. Although never a formal part of its mission statement, an unstated assumption was that combat leadership was the most important quality developed at the academy. This has never been an exact science however. For all the graduates who have shined in battle, there were others who barely got by or even failed in their duties. Nonetheless, certain principles of officership have seemed obvious. Among these, any environment replicating that kind of stress was valuable in time of war. Part of the academy's tight schedule was unavoidable. However, a good portion was by design. Time demands taught midshipmen how to function under pressure. For that reason alone, the academy has never retreated from the importance of Bancroft Hall.

Not surprisingly then, outside groups have often had to be the catalyst for significant changes to the academy system. Annapolis could be suspicious of suggestions that fell too far outside its existing paradigm. Outsiders had to overcome its skepticism that they did not understand the academy's business. How could they recommend solutions when they did not grasp the difficulty of its problems? Anyone who cooperated from within the institution risked being ostracized if they tinkered with sacred cows, like Bancroft Hall or the plebe system. The examples of Admiral Hyman Rickover and Captain Wayne Hoof, both graduates of Annapolis, illustrate this problem the best. Rickover always had a volatile relationship with the academy even though many of his ideas for reforming the curriculum and Bancroft Hall had merit. Oftentimes, they were made publicly with an acerbic tone that embarrassed the institution, which guaranteed a defensive response.

In contrast, Hoof initially voiced his concerns within the institution. When he was ignored, he escalated them through official channels to the chief of naval operations and the secretary of the navy. Only reluctantly, however, did he voice any criticisms of the academy in public. Unfortunately, the quixotic challenge he took up for reform was the plebe system. Few at Annapolis could imagine the institution without it even though that was not what Hoof was initially demanding. The context of this crisis was unusual insofar as it took place during the Vietnam War. Military institutions like Annapolis felt under attack for anything they did, so it is not surprising that the academy was less tolerant of a differing opinion than it should have been. This is not to excuse how Captain Hoof and his compatriots were treated, but it does make it more understandable. To its credit, Annapolis has demonstrated a spirit of open-mindedness on countless other occasions.

Inspection teams, like the Folsom Board and the Middle State Association, generally found an open ear after they demonstrated their empathy for the academy's problems. It did not hurt, however, that these groups had a sympathetic ear among the academy's superiors. As much as possible, their ideas were considerate of the academy's priorities, especially its commitments to the fleet. Whatever it decided, teams urged Annapolis to be logical with its priorities. Wishful thinking was not going to solve some of its more severe problems; choices had to be made as to what was most important. The difficulty for everyone was determining these priorities, when they changed, and what adjustments should be made. In other words, timing could be everything in how reform happened at Annapolis. Reform-minded superintendents, like Admirals Holloway and Calvert, were more than willing to make drastic changes to preserve the essence of the academy system.

Holloway and Calvert were unusual, however. Not only did they understand the pertinent issues, they also enjoyed the clout and, more importantly, the time to deal with them. Unfortunately, most superintendents were not given that luxury. The average assignment lasted at most a few years, which was never long enough to grasp the problem *and* do something about it. The fleet's operational schedule, along with the skepticism many senior officers had towards academy duty, made it difficult to alter this rotation policy. The other challenge superintendents faced was persuading the Navy to listen to them. Most flag officers were focused on operational issues, not conditions in the training establishment. Only when it impacted readiness or they received significant heat from Washington was attention given to Annapolis. This was certainly true during the Cold War educational crisis. Rickover's congressional cronies, along with tough-minded Secretary of the Navy Fred Korth, put the Navy on its heels: either help make the academy's new curriculum successful, with better officers and resources, or suffer the consequences, including the removal of military instructors from Annapolis. The ultimatum worked until more pressing operational priorities intervened with the Navy's mobilization for Vietnam.

The final variable in understanding the culture of Annapolis was the midshipmen themselves. They too were active participants in their professional socialization. Bancroft Hall was the focal point of indoctrination and upperclassmen were often the primary teachers. The mindset of the midshipmen culture was shaped primarily at a grassroots level, in the company areas, mess hall, and athletic fields. Upperclassmen often relied upon their own experiences to tell them what was right. However, the Brigade's expansion after 1945 introduced significant variations in this process. In particular, some companies developed reputations for being tough on plebe indoctrination. In theory, Executive Department officers oversaw the Brigade's character development programs, bringing the fleet's values to Bancroft Hall. However, this group was not always the best motivated and was frequently undermanned. Their relationship with midshipmen was also intrinsically adversarial, a characteristic of life in what sociologists have called "total institutions." Officers were seen as martinets who used discipline not as a teaching tool but as means of control. And instead of seeing their experiences as analogous to the fleet, midshipmen compared Annapolis to a penitentiary, a monastery, or an insane asylum.

The companies of the Brigade were like families to midshipmen. Most stayed with the same company their entire time at Annapolis. Companies often occupied the same rooms in Bancroft Hall; they took their meals together in the mess hall. Individuals who did not get along with their companies struggled to get through Annapolis. Midshipmen learned military discipline in the scrutiny paid to rooms and uniforms during company inspections. Competitions on the parade ground and athletic field reinforced the importance of teamwork. Until the "academic revolution," companies also attended class together. Sharing the same trials was vital to the "unity of suffering experience" that bonded classmates together through their military careers and beyond. Companies became less important after the "academic revolution" however. Class schedules were no longer the same; midshipmen often studied outside the company with those in their major. A greater range of extracurricular activities also became available. The time spent at meetings and practices or at team and activity dining tables came at the expense of company activities.

That being said, companies remained the nucleus for the midshipmen's most important relationships and experiences. Upperclassmen continued to set the tone for company activities despite the Executive Department's efforts at greater supervision. Most officers went home at the end of the day, which was ironically the greatest free time in the midshipmen's schedule. The limited staff on duty could not be everywhere at once leaving upperclassmen in the best position to determine the "rules" of the institution. This situation obviously complicated any efforts at reform. New policies were important but not sufficient by themselves in changing the academy culture. To ultimately be successful, academy leaders depended on officers to enforce their reforms. Upperclassmen also had to be willing to follow them when no one else was watching. In most cases, midshipmen accepted changes without much trouble. They either supported what was being done or felt the cost of challenging the academy was too severe. However, with reforms that undercut their most cherished traditions, midshipmen could resist the academy's efforts tooth and nail.

The biggest problem was with plebe indoctrination. For years, the academy tolerated activities that went beyond official guidelines, including physical hazing. Unfortunately, discussion of the subject was often taboo, which also made reform difficult. No one— senior officers, the Executive Department, upperclassmen—wanted to be labeled as soft on plebe indoctrination, but it was difficult to define what was excessive. Plebes had to be trained, and it was supposed to be difficult. Upperclassmen could not be removed from the process either; mistakes were natural as they learned how to lead. Some of them absorbed a dangerous lesson from this that got them into trouble after graduation. Haphazard enforcement of the rules was interpreted to mean "you rate what you get away with," in other words, you were only guilty if you got caught. Some graduates played this game in the fleet where rules generally mattered. Thus, reforms in this area were not likely to be immediate. To be effective, strong leadership was also required at all levels. Upperclassmen had at least to tolerate reforms and finally time was needed for overall attitudes to change.

Midshipmen also tended to resist efforts at academic reform. For years, the academy culture had taught that academics were a secondary priority to Bancroft Hall. The experience was what turned them into officers, not anything from the classroom. Although study hour was technically inviolate, midshipmen frequently used the time for everything other than the books. Upperclassmen assigned plebes research projects that had to be completed by the next meal. Sometimes uniforms and rooms had to be prepared for inspection. The consequences of not meeting military obligations were immediate and severe. Classroom demands could seemingly be put off until another day. The jam-packed schedule rewarded cramming more than it did the actual retention of classroom material.

And perhaps most dangerous, midshipmen twisted Bancroft Hall's lesson about classmate loyalty to their own purposes in the classroom. The academy expected midshipmen to be honorable in all circumstances. But that meant more than simply not lying, cheating, or stealing. Bancroft Hall taught that the highest form of honor involved classmates watching out for one another. That was the only way to get through the difficult hurdles of a naval career. Too often, this principle was misapplied in the classroom. Midshipmen shared information about their classes, including specific material from quizzes and exams. Although the dope system clearly violated the school's academic integrity, midshipmen believed they were following the higher principle of classmate loyalty.

World War II had been the Naval Academy's greatest triumph. Virtually all of the war's great naval heroes were its graduates. At the same time, the conflict raised nagging questions about the future. The Navy's postwar commitments demanded a larger officer corps than the academy could supply itself. NROTC became a permanent program that commissioned the bulk of the service's officers. Annapolis survived, but its new justification was that it provided a majority of its career officers. NROTC also raised lingering doubts about the necessity of the four-year academy program. More officers were obtained from NROTC at only a fraction of the expense. Although Annapolis graduates were better trained, NROTC midshipmen often had the better education. In other words, academy officers had greater short-term advantages, but the long haul was more difficult to judge.

World War II also accelerated the Navy's trend towards occupational specialization. More officers wanted to be lifelong aviators and submariners, the combat specialties that had seemingly done more to win the war and thus had a brighter future than the surface navy. Military specialization also made it more difficult for Annapolis to define its core training requirements. Prewar training was geared to the surface navy alone, including exact systems from the fleet. The new warfare communities agitated for their training requirements to be added to the curriculum. Furthermore, Bancroft Hall's culture had also reflected the traditions and discipline of the fleet. Line officers were the only role models midshipmen had in the old Executive Department; aviators and submariners began serving in these capacities after the war. Oftentimes, their leadership styles and experiences were more popular with midshipmen than the drab surface navy. At the very least, midshipmen had alternative visions to ponder when it came to professional socialization.

Finally, the war would shatter the foundations of the academy's academic program. Technology was changing so rapidly that its fixed curriculum was hopelessly obsolete. Midshipmen could be prepared for their duties as junior officers, but their education was too shallow to last a twenty-year career. More officers were expected to attend graduate school to keep pace with the degree of technological change. Academy graduates were at a distinct disadvantage in competing for these opportunities. As such, academic reform was one of the leading topics for the postwar academy. The emphasis turned to a broader-based education that would better serve midshipmen throughout their careers. Tougher academic programs would also be helpful in preparing them for graduate school.

For the first time, Annapolis seemed genuinely interested in conforming to the standards of the larger academic community. It sought outside accreditation and took steps to confer recognizable degrees. At the same time, it was not interested in becoming a liberal arts college. Fleet requirements dictated the limits of the new curriculum. Bancroft Hall was also skeptical of the new academic programs. Midshipmen failed out for academic reasons, but Bancroft Hall was the more immediate challenge to their existence. Midshipmen continued to rely on the curve and the dope system to pass their classes. The "slash" was still a hated stereotype in the Brigade. Academic standing had little practical consequences to them anyway, especially since initial assignments were still chosen through a lottery.

However, there was little energy or interest for pursuing academic reform in the 1950s. Many academy leaders believed that all of the necessary changes had already been completed. Most of their attention was focused on the deteriorating condition of its physical plant. The Brigade had expanded rapidly to accommodate a permanently enlarged fleet. Yet postwar budget cuts made it difficult to secure funds for renovation let alone expansion. The newest military service, the Air Force, was also a huge thorn in the academy's side. For much of the decade, the Air Force could tap into 25 percent of its graduates for its cadre of regular officers. Annapolis never ran short of volunteers since the Air Force promised immediate flight school and graduate education. The Navy also came out on the losing side to the Air Force in the defense reorganization scheme. Strategic deterrence drew most of the defense dollars and the Air Force had a stranglehold on that mission.

The 1950s Naval Academy also struggled to make itself attractive to American youth. The booming economy offered plenty of opportunities besides a military career. Prosperity also made college more affordable to working and middle class families. New government aid programs likewise fueled the explosion of higher education. None of these opportunities required a military commitment afterwards, especially in a dead end service like the Navy. Although it could offer more appointments, the Naval Academy never filled up its classes. The democratization of higher education also affected the demographics of the Brigade. More midshipmen started to come from middle and working class, Catholic or Lower Church Protestant families. Fewer of them had a family connection to Annapolis, i.e., "Navy juniors," compared to prewar classes. Their reasons for choosing the academy were also strikingly different. Career opportunities in the Navy were important, but the educational programs were a growing attraction. For the most part, the trend towards demographic diversity did not include African Americans or other minorities however.

The launching of the Soviet satellite Sputnik revived the academy's interest in academic reform. Americans worried that their education system was falling behind the Soviet Union and with it their technological edge in the Cold War. Admiral Hyman Rickover used the crisis to renew his attacks on its lockstep curriculum, which was putting the nation's security in danger. Yet reform was also critical to the success of his nuclear navy. Its officers received extensive engineering training after Annapolis; however, a sound undergraduate foundation was an essential prerequisite for success. The program wielded tremendous influence in the late 1950s and early 1960s. Submarines put the Navy into the mission of strategic deterrence, a role that it arguably performed better than the Air Force. It was also attracting the best and brightest officers, men who would one day be the Navy's future leaders. Academic reform would have happened without nuclear submarines however. Although its share of graduates was increasing, the bulk of midshipmen did not complete the training. Yet the mindset of the nuclear community was crucial to reform. Education was paramount to the nuclear navy's success and those attitudes filtered over to the academy's priorities.

The Navy's rivalry with the Air Force was also useful in stimulating reform. The hemorrhage of midshipmen bolting the service ended with the Air Force Academy's first graduation in 1960. However, Colorado Springs took pride in being the academic pioneer among the nation's service academies. Its curriculum was more flexible with greater opportunities at advanced education; its leaders were also very creative at adapting its military routine to academic requirements. For bright students considering an academy, the best option seemed to be Colorado Springs. Just like the Navy, Annapolis wanted to regain its reputation as the most academically prestigious school. The Air Force Academy provided examples for how to structure its curriculum. It also became more difficult for the academies to defend their eccentricities from an educationally conscious public. Although programs were never identical, each institution tried to minimize any differences.

Yet the immediate catalyst for the "academic revolution" was the Folsom Board of 1959. Unlike other inspecting bodies, its authority came from outside the academy's normal chain of command. Although a majority of members were civilian educators, most were familiar with military education and the service academies. Annapolis tried to preempt its investigation with limited reforms, but Folsom's superiors wanted a more penetrating analysis of the curriculum. Many recommendations went beyond what the academy and the Navy could do at the time but they did serve as a blueprint for future changes. Despite its name, Annapolis moved cautiously with the "academic revolution." Faculty credentials were improved by hiring greater numbers of civilian Ph.D.s. However, military department heads still controlled most of the academic program. Most reforms were phased in gradually. Midshipmen could take electives but only by testing out of required courses. The bulk of the core program was also retained, which made it difficult to qualify for a minor or major.

Caution clearly limited the effectiveness and impact of the "academic revolution." Since many older requirements remained intact, the reforms effectively applied to only the top midshipmen in each class. Plebes were generally the only ones eligible for the newest changes. Upperclassmen could not be derailed from graduating on time, but this gave them little incentive for understanding the changes let alone seeing them succeed. Many officers outside the academic departments were also skeptical of the "academic revolution." Although they were academy graduates, many of them were not top fleet performers. The only way they knew to run Bancroft Hall was the "cops and robbers" mentality they had experienced. Whenever reforms were made, the academy heard howls from alumni that they were weakening the school's military culture. Alumni could not be ignored since they were increasingly counted on to fund nonappropriated projects, like the new football stadium.

Annapolis had little choice but to expand the "academic revolution" in the 1960s. Civilian leaders, like Secretary Korth, threatened more drastic changes if the academy did not act. However, progressive superintendents, like Admirals Kirkpatrick and Minter, already intended on doing more. They searched for ways to better align the curriculum with good civilian colleges. Kirkpatrick borrowed the idea for the Trident Scholar program from Yale University and implemented a traditional letter grading scale to help midshipmen's opportunities for graduate school. Minter reduced the core curriculum's hours to make a minor feasible for all midshipmen. Both as commandant and superintendent, he encouraged greater toleration of the new curriculum in Bancroft Hall. Study hour and plebe indoctrination were monitored more closely to allow extra time for studying. Finally, the rewards system was adjusted to favor the new emphasis on academics. Midshipmen no longer marched to class; they could study after taps without risking curfew violations. Additional liberty privileges were given to those doing well in their classes.

None of these changes came easy for Annapolis. The reforms inadvertently unleashed a battle for the institutional culture of the academy. Ironically, all sides in this contest had its best interests at heart but disagreed about what that entailed. The administration and the civilian faculty came to blows on several occasions. The new marking scale escalated into a very public crisis over grade controls. Faculty interpreted the administration's efforts at limiting attrition as an intrusion on its academic freedom. The administration was equally hostile to the formation of groups, like the AAUP and Faculty Senate, interested in faculty government. To the military, it seemed like civilians wanted to take over its academy. Unfortunately, these crises often seemed like scandals by the time they became public. At worst, they usually involved serious misunderstandings. Whether it was for good copy or their own desire for more drastic changes, columnists were eager to report the latest controversy at Annapolis. Like most military institutions of the Vietnam era, the Naval Academy was probably more sensitive than normal to any such attacks.

Annapolis overhauled its recruiting and admissions process to solve problems from the 1950s. Operation Information was a program that returned midshipmen to their communities to sell the institution's virtues. It also cooperated in the production of the popular television show, "Men of Annapolis." The new Blue and Gold program used reserve officers, preferably those who were teachers or school administrators, to search for good candidates. The emphasis of recruiting grew markedly different after the "academic revolution" however. New tools of quantitative analysis allowed the academy to study the career demographics of its graduates.

Contrary to legend, class anchormen did not generally make admiral; most successful career officers were at the top of their graduating class. As a result, the admissions process was restructured to meet academic requirements first. Scores on College Board exams became a critical determinant for admission. For the first time, it awarded eye waivers but primarily to those who were good students. Rarely were applicants from the lower half of their high school class admitted anymore, even if they were promising athletes. The whole nominating process also became less political. New procedures, like the Qualified Alternate Rule, allowed the academy to pursue the candidates it truly wanted.

The new academic programs helped produce record numbers of applications to the Naval Academy. Not only was it providing exciting career opportunities, but students were now receiving an excellent college education too. Graduate school opportunities were on the rise, and alternative career paths, particularly in the medical and legal communities, were also becoming available. However, attrition rates remained roughly what they had always been, around 30 percent. Although similar numbers were leaving, the sources of attrition were shockingly different. Before the reforms, academic failures were the largest source of attrition followed by voluntary resignations. Now, despite tougher standards, academic failures had dropped dramatically while voluntary resignations were rising. Many who left did so because of Bancroft Hall, primarily during their plebe year. The headaches and harassment were not worth it when a good or better education was available elsewhere.

The greatest tension was during the middle years of the "academic revolution." Upperclassmen trained under the older system were reluctant to abandon it. Many officers shared their opinion that a tough, physical plebe year was indispensable preparation for combat. These opinions were especially difficult to disprove during Vietnam. Although the demands were different, plebe year remained incredibly rigorous, but these groups could not see that. Tradition blinded them to how much the academy had already changed. In some cases, petty desires motivated them to inflict similar treatment on their subordinates. The worst problems with plebe indoctrination resulted in yet another scandal. Civilian professors from the humanities department, along with their military department head, petitioned for major reforms to the plebe system. Some of them wanted it eliminated entirely. However, the academy selected a more moderate course with stricter limits on upperclassmen's actions and holding the Executive Department more accountable for any infractions.

Eventually the "academic revolution" gave birth to a new institutional culture at Annapolis. Academic reform achieved its greatest accomplishments during Admiral Calvert's tenure as superintendent. Further curriculum reforms eliminated virtually all core courses except a strengthened list of professional subjects. This bold approach allowed all midshipmen to complete majors while not undercutting their professional training. The balance between Athens and Sparta seesawed well into the 1970s and 1980s. However, there was never a possibility of Annapolis returning to its focus from the 1930s, the days of the trade school academy. It did not waver from the new goal of providing the best possible education while meeting the requirements of the fleet. Bancroft Hall still wielded tremendous influence at the academy. Somehow the system needed a way of weeding out midshipmen who would not be good officers. However, the onus was now on it to show which aspects were necessary. Training would always be an important component of the academy program. Fraternity antics were not an acceptable way of accomplishing this.

Finally, academy leaders struggled to understand how a new youth culture affected the Brigade. New midshipmen seemed to have vastly different expectations of Annapolis. Many did not intend upon a military career; they had chosen the academy because of its national reputation and academic programs. They understood the school was not a civilian college but were not above questioning regulations that appeared irrelevant to their professional socialization. In their minds, academy restrictions should show some appreciation for the larger culture. Annapolis wisely avoided being overly dogmatic on these issues while preserving its essential traditions. Some accommodation was unavoidable, however, given the growing gap between social and military values. Midshipmen had too many options for the academy to rule with an iron fist. Ironically, any changes to professional socialization appeared to engender similar attributes in midshipmen. Most considered the experience to be a rigorous test of their abilities. The effort built a sense of confidence and teamwork among classmates that lasted long after graduation. The many demands gave them valuable skills in organization and time management, much less an ability to function under stress. Excellence was the institutional standard in both academics and matters of military bearing. Finally, midshipmen emerged from the experience with a deep loyalty and affection for one another and the institution. For better or worse, they would always remember their "four years together by the bay."

Table 1. How did you receive your appointment?

		1946-49	1950-54	1955-59	1960-64	1965-69	1970-76	Total
Congressional nomination	Count	75	100	113	100	105	144	637
	% Cohort	66.40%	58.80%	65.30%	56.20%	62.50%	75.80%	64.20%
Presidential or vice-presidential nomination	Count	3	6	10	19	21	19	78
	% Cohort	2.70%	3.50%	5.80%	10.70%	12.50%	10.00%	7.90%
Prior enlisted service	Count	33	58	32	31	22	7	183
	% Cohort	29.20%	34.10%	18.50%	17.40%	13.10%	3.70%	18.40%
Other	Count	2	6	18	28	20	20	94
	% Cohort	1.80%	3.50%	10.40%	15.70%	11.90%	10.50%	9.50%
Total	Count	113	170	173	178	168	190	992
	% Cohort	100%	100%	100%	100%	100%	100%	100%

Chi-Square Tests	Value	df	Asymp. Sig. (2-sided)
Pearson Chi-Square	100.87a	15	0
Likelihood Ratio	111.676	15	0
Linear-by-Linear Association	0.489	1	0.485
N of Valid Cases	992		

a. 0 cells (0%) have expected count less than 5. The minimum expected count is 8.89.

Table 2. What region did you consider home before entering the academy?

		1946-49	1950-54	1955-59	1960-64	1965-69	1970-76	Total
Northeast or Middle Atlantic	Count	41	71	60	90	78	78	418
	% Cohort	36.30%	41.80%	34.70%	50.60%	46.20%	41.10%	42.10%
Middle West	Count	35	41	44	36	36	52	244
	% Cohort	31.00%	24.10%	25.40%	20.20%	21.30%	27.40%	24.60%
Southeast	Count	16	26	26	26	14	21	129
	% Cohort	14.20%	15.30%	15.00%	14.60%	8.30%	11.10%	13.00%
Southwest	Count	6	11	12	9	10	19	67
	% Cohort	5.30%	6.50%	6.90%	5.10%	5.90%	10.00%	6.70%
Far West	Count	14	20	30	17	27	19	127
	% Cohort	12.40%	11.80%	17.30%	9.60%	16%	10%	12.80%
Other	Count	1	1	1		4	1	8
	% Cohort	0.90%	0.60%	0.60%		2.40%	0.50%	0.80%
Total	Count	113	170	173	178	169	190	993
	% Cohort	100%	100%	100%	100%	100%	100%	100%

Chi-Square Tests	Value	df	Asymp. Sig. (2-sided)
Pearson Chi-Square	34.873a	25	0.091
Likelihood Ratio	34.482	25	0.098
Linear-by-Linear Association	0.441	1	0.507
N of Valid Cases	993		

a. 6 cells (16.7%) have expected count less than 5. The minimum expected count is .91.

Table 3. What was your primary reason for accepting an appointment?

		1946-49	1950-54	1955-59	1960-64	1965-69	1970-76	Total
Free college education	Count	4	22	43	35	33	33	170
	% Cohort	3.60%	13.00%	25.00%	19.70%	19.50%	17.50%	17.20%
Career opportunities in naval service	Count	47	67	51	59	52	46	322
	% Cohort	42.30%	39.60%	29.70%	33.10%	30.80%	24.30%	32.60%
Patriotic or public service motivation	Count	26	24	20	21	23	35	149
	% Cohort	23.40%	14.20%	11.60%	11.80%	13.60%	18.50%	15.10%
Prestige of the Naval Academy	Count	25	39	47	49	53	56	269
	% Cohort	22.50%	23.10%	27.30%	27.50%	31.40%	29.60%	27.20%
Other	Count	9	17	11	14	8	19	76
	% Cohort	8.10%	10.10%	6.40%	7.9 %	4.70%	10.10%	7.90%
Total	Count	111	169	172	178	169	189	988
	% Cohort	100%	100%	100%	100%	100%	100%	100%

Chi-Square Tests	Value	df	Asymp. Sig. (2-sided)
Pearson Chi-Square	49.063a	20	0
Likelihood Ratio	53.788	20	0
Linear-by-Linear Association	0.139	1	0.709
N of Valid Cases	988		

a. 0 cells (0%) have expected count less than 5. The minimum expected count is 8.76.

Table 4. Which least affected your decision to come to the academy?

		1946-49	1950-54	1955-59	1960-64	1965-69	1970-76	Total
Free college education	Count	67	81	68	83	66	74	439
	% Cohort	61.50%	50.00%	40.00%	47.20%	39.50%	40.00%	45.30%
Career opportunities in naval service	Count	13	26	40	38	50	59	226
	% Cohort	11.90%	16.00%	23.50%	21.60%	29.90%	31.90%	23.30%
Patriotic or public service motivation	Count	17	38	48	46	35	21	205
	% Cohort	15.60%	23.50%	28.20%	26.10%	21.00%	11.40%	21.20%
Prestige of the Naval Academy	Count	10	16	14	7	16	30	93
	% Cohort	9.20%	9.90%	8.20%	4.00%	9.60%	16.20%	9.60%
Other	Count	2	1		2		1	6
	% Cohort	1.80%	0.60%		1.10%		0.50%	0.60%
Total	Count	109	162	170	176	167	185	969
	% Cohort	100%	100%	100%	100%	100%	100%	100%

Chi-Square Tests	Value	df	Asymp. Sig. (2-sided)
Pearson Chi-Square	66.143a	20	0
Likelihood Ratio	69.137	20	0
Linear-by-Linear Association	2.935	1	0.087
N of Valid Cases	969		

a. 6 cells (20%) have expected count less than 5. The minimum expected count is .67.

Table 5. Did your immediate family support your decision to come to the academy?

		1946-49	1950-54	1955-59	1960-64	1965-69	1970-76	Total
Yes	Count	112	162	167	172	165	184	962
	% Cohort	99.10%	95.30%	96.50%	96.60%	97.60%	96.80%	96.90%
No	Count	1	8	6	6	4	6	31
	% Cohort	0.90%	4.70%	3.50%	3.40%	2.40%	3.20%	3.10%
Total	Count	113	170	173	178	169	190	993
	% Cohort	100%	100%	100%	100%	100%	100%	100%

Chi-Square Tests	Value	df	Asymp. Sig. (2-sided)
Pearson Chi-Square	3.704a	5	0.593
Likelihood Ratio	4.266	5	0.512
Linear-by-Linear Association	0.003	1	0.96
N of Valid Cases	993		

a. 1 cell (8.3%) has expected count less than 5. The minimum expected count is 3.53.

Table 6. Did your closest friends and peers support your decision?

		1946-49	1950-54	1955-59	1960-64	1965-69	1970-76	Total
Yes	Count	108	154	164	166	160	159	911
	% Cohort	95.60%	90.60%	94.80%	93.30%	94.70%	83.70%	91.70%
No	Count	5	16	9	12	9	31	82
	% Cohort	4.40%	9.40%	5.20%	6.70%	5.30%	16.30%	8.30%
Total	Count	113	170	173	178	169	190	993
	% Cohort	100%	100%	100%	100%	100%	100%	100%

Chi-Square Tests	Value	df	Asymp. Sig. (2-sided)
Pearson Chi-Square	23.365a	5	0
Likelihood Ratio	21.049	5	0.001
Linear-by-Linear Association	7.804	1	0.005
N of Valid Cases	993		

a. 0 cells (0%) have expected count less than 5. The minimum expected count is 9.33.

Table 7. What was your religious preference when you entered the academy?

		1946-49	1950-54	1955-59	1960-64	1965-69	1970-76	Total
Protestant	Count	75	121	126	113	105	111	651
	% Cohort	66.40%	71.20%	73.30%	63.50%	62.10%	58.40%	65.60%
Catholic	Count	30	36	40	63	52	67	288
	% Cohort	26.50%	21.20%	23.30%	35.40%	30.80%	35.30%	29.00%
Jewish	Count		5			1	2	8
	% Cohort		2.90%			0.60%	1.10%	0.80%
No religious preference	Count	7	7	2	2	8	7	33
	% Cohort	6.20%	4.10%	1.20%	1.10%	4.70%	3.70%	3.30%
Other	Count	1	1	4		3	3	12
	% Cohort	0.90%	0.60%	2.30%		1.80%	1.60%	1.20%
Total	Count	113	170	172	178	169	190	992
	% Cohort	100%	100%	100%	100%	100%	100%	100%

Chi-Square Tests	Value	df	Asymp. Sig. (2-sided)
Pearson Chi-Square	43.320a	20	0.002
Likelihood Ratio	46.157	20	0.001
Linear-by-Linear Association	2.665	1	0.103
N of Valid Cases	992		

a. 13 cells (43.3%) have expected count less than 5. The minimum expected count is .91.

Table 8. Did your religious preference change while at the academy?

		1946-49	1950-54	1955-59	1960-64	1965-69	1970-76	Total
No change	Count	108	161	155	165	157	164	910
	% Cohort	95.60%	94.70%	91.20%	92.70%	92.90%	86.30%	91.90%
Protestant	Count	1	2	3	2	1	1	10
	% Cohort	0.90%	1.20%	1.80%	1.10%	0.60%	0.50%	1.00%
Catholic	Count		4	4	2		3	13
	% Cohort		2.40%	2.40%	1.10%		1.60%	1.30%
Changed to no religious preference	Count	4	2	7	7	10	19	49
	% Cohort	3.50%	1.20%	4.10%	3.90%	5.90%	10.00%	4.90%
Other	Count		1	1	2	1	3	8
	% Cohort		0.60%	0.60%	1.10%	0.60%	1.60%	0.80%
Total	Count	113	170	170	178	169	190	990
	% Cohort	100%	100%	100%	100%	100%	100%	100%

Chi-Square Tests	Value	df	Asymp. Sig. (2-sided)
Pearson Chi-Square	28.323a	20	0.102
Likelihood Ratio	32.083	20	0.042
Linear-by-Linear Association	12.665	1	0
N of Valid Cases	990		

a. 18 cells (60.0%) have expected count less than 5. The minimum expected count is .91.

Table 9. What did you consider your family's economic background to be?

		1946-49	1950-54	1955-59	1960-64	1965-69	1970-76	Total
Lower class	Count	2	2	4	7	8	7	30
	% Cohort	1.80%	1.20%	2.30%	3.90%	4.70%	3.70%	3.00%
Working class	Count	15	60	59	56	46	59	295
	% Cohort	13.30%	35.30%	34.30%	31.50%	27.20%	31.10%	29.70%
Middle class	Count	67	77	79	81	81	94	479
	% Cohort	59.30%	45.30%	45.90%	45.50%	47.90%	49.50%	48.30%
Upper-middle class	Count	23	31	25	32	33	28	172
	% Cohort	20.40%	18.20%	14.50%	18.00%	19.50%	14.70%	17.30%
Upper class	Count	6		5	2	1	2	16
	% Cohort	5.30%		2.90%	1.10%	0.60%	1.10%	1.60%
Total	Count	113	170	172	178	169	190	992
	% Cohort	100%	100%	100%	100%	100%	100%	100%

Chi-Square Tests	Value	df	Asymp. Sig. (2-sided)
Pearson Chi-Square	41.318a	20	0.003
Likelihood Ratio	43.345	20	0.002
Linear-by-Linear Association	6.425	1	0.011
N of Valid Cases	992		

a. 7 cells (23.3%) have expected count less than 5. The minimum expected count is 1.82.

Table 10. What race do you consider yourself?

		1946-49	1950-54	1955-59	1960-64	1965-69	1970-76	Total
White	Count	112	170	167	177	167	185	978
	% Cohort	100.00%	100.00%	97.70%	99.40%	99.40%	97.40%	98.90%
Black	Count			1		1	2	4
	% Cohort			0.60%		0.60%	1.10%	0.40%
Hispanic	Count			1				1
	% Cohort			0.60%				0.10%
Asian	Count			1			1	2
	% Cohort			0.60%			0.50%	0.20%
Other	Count			1	1		2	4
	% Cohort			0.60%	0.60%		1.10%	0.40%
Total	Count	112	170	171	178	168	190	989
	% Cohort	100%	100%	100%	100%	100%	100%	100%

Chi-Square Tests

	Value	df	Asymp. Sig. (2-sided)
Pearson Chi-Square	16.557a	20	0.682
Likelihood Ratio	18.22	20	0.573
Linear-by-Linear Association	2.663	1	0.103
N of Valid Cases	989		

a. 24 cells (80.0%) have expected count less than 5. The minimum expected count is .11.

Table 11. Did you intend upon a military career before you entered the academy?

		1946-49	1950-54	1955-59	1960-64	1965-69	1970-76	Total
Yes	Count	82	120	99	115	94	83	593
	% Cohort	72.60%	70.60%	57.20%	64.60%	55.60%	43.70%	59.70%
No	Count	31	50	74	63	75	107	400
	% Cohort	27.40%	29.40%	42.80%	35.40%	44.40%	56.30%	40.30%
Total	Count	113	170	173	178	169	190	993
	% Cohort	100%	100%	100%	100%	100%	100%	100%

Chi-Square Tests	Value	df	Asymp. Sig. (2-sided)
Pearson Chi-Square	39.805a	5	0
Likelihood Ratio	40.039	5	0
Linear-by-Linear Association	31.841	1	0
N of Valid Cases	993		

a. 0 cells (0%) have expected count less than 5. The minimum expected count is 45.52.

Table 12. Did this decision change while you were at the academy?

		1946-49	1950-54	1955-59	1960-64	1965-69	1970-76	Total
Yes	Count	20	27	40	41	21	36	185
	% Cohort	17.70%	15.90%	23.10%	23.00%	12.40%	18.90%	18.60%
No	Count	93	143	133	137	148	154	808
	% Cohort	82.30%	84.10%	76.90%	77.00%	87.60%	81.10%	81.40%
Total	Count	113	170	173	178	169	190	993
	% Cohort	100%	100%	100%	100%	100%	100%	100%

Chi-Square Tests	Value	df	Asymp. Sig. (2-sided)
Pearson Chi-Square	9.794a	5	0.081
Likelihood Ratio	10.029	5	0.074
Linear-by-Linear Association	0.05	1	0.822
N of Valid Cases	993		

a. 0 cells (0%) have expected count less than 5. The minimum expected count is 21.05.

Table 13. What part of your pre-academy background prepared you best for plebe year?

		1946-49	1950-54	1955-59	1960-64	1965-69	1970-76	Total
Competitive sports	Count	10	27	21	43	64	90	255
	% Cohort	8.80%	15.90%	12.20%	24.30%	37.90%	47.40%	25.70%
School clubs or organizations	Count	4	7	13	12	10	14	60
	% Cohort	3.50%	4.10%	7.60%	6.80%	5.90%	7.40%	6.10%
Broad academic background	Count	42	56	66	51	47	34	296
	% Cohort	37.20%	32.90%	38.40%	28.80%	27.80%	17.90%	29.90%
JROTC participation	Count	15	11	17	13	4	7	67
	% Cohort	13.30%	6.50%	9.90%	7.30%	2.40%	3.70%	6.80%
Other	Count	42	69	55	58	44	45	313
	% Cohort	37.20%	40.60%	32.00%	32.80%	26.00%	23.70%	31.60%
Total	Count	113	170	172	177	169	190	991
	% Cohort	100%	100%	100%	100%	100%	100%	100%

Chi-Square Tests	Value	df	Asymp. Sig. (2-sided)
Pearson Chi-Square	123.391a	20	0
Likelihood Ratio	125.112	20	0
Linear-by-Linear Association	70.037	1	0
N of Valid Cases	991		

a. 0 cells (0%) have expected count less than 5. The minimum expected count is 6.84.

Table 14. Did information supplied by the academy adequately communicate the demands of plebe year?

		1946-49	1950-54	1955-59	1960-64	1965-69	1970-76	Total
Yes	Count	46	84	63	56	45	64	358
	% Cohort	40.70%	49.40%	36.40%	31.50%	26.60%	33.70%	36.10%
No	Count	67	86	110	122	124	126	635
	% Cohort	59.30%	50.60%	63.60%	68.50%	73.40%	66.30%	63.90%
Total	Count	113	170	173	178	169	190	993
	% Cohort	100%	100%	100%	100%	100%	100%	100%

Chi-Square Tests	Value	df	Asymp. Sig. (2-sided)
Pearson Chi-Square	22.834a	5	0
Likelihood Ratio	22.655	5	0
Linear-by-Linear Association	12.052	1	0.001
N of Valid Cases	993		

a. 0 cells (0%) have expected count less than 5. The minimum expected count is 40.74.

Table 15. To what degree did plebe indoctrination vary by company or battalion?

		1946-49	1950-54	1955-59	1960-64	1965-69	1970-76	Total
Not at all	Count	28	20	4	9	3	5	69
	% Cohort	25.70%	11.80%	2.30%	5.10%	1.80%	2.60%	7.00%
Slightly varied	Count	40	57	46	43	42	57	285
	% Cohort	36.70%	33.70%	26.60%	24.30%	24.90%	30.00%	28.90%
Moderately varied	Count	22	46	50	56	59	67	300
	% Cohort	20.20%	27.20%	28.90%	31.60%	34.90%	35.30%	30.40%
Widely varied	Count	17	43	72	68	65	60	325
	% Cohort	15.60%	25.40%	41.60%	38.40%	38.50%	31.60%	32.90%
Other	Count	2	3	1	1		1	8
	% Cohort	1.80%	1.80%	0.60%	0.60%		0.50%	0.80%
Total	Count	109	169	173	177	169	190	987
	% Cohort	100%	100%	100%	100%	100%	100%	100%

Chi-Square Tests	Value	df	Asymp. Sig. (2-sided)
Pearson Chi-Square	116.947a	20	0
Likelihood Ratio	103.086	20	0
Linear-by-Linear Association	32.633	1	0
N of Valid Cases	987		

a. 6 cells (20%) have expected count less than 5. The minimum expected count is .88.

Table 16. What accounted most for any variations in the plebe system?

		1946-49	1950-54	1955-59	1960-64	1965-69	1970-76	Total
Attitudes of company upperclassmen	Count	74	129	150	140	146	163	802
	% Cohort	91.40%	88.40%	89.30%	83.80%	88.50%	88.10%	87.90%
Personality of company officer	Count	2	7	8	5	8	5	35
	% Cohort	2.50%	4.80%	4.80%	3.00%	4.80%	2.70%	3.80%
Company location in Bancroft Hall	Count	1	4	6	7	5	2	25
	% Cohort	1.20%	2.70%	3.60%	4.20%	3.00%	1.10%	2.70%
Other	Count	4	6	4	15	6	15	50
	% Cohort	4.90%	4.10%	2.40%	9	3.60%	8.10%	5.50%
Total	Count	81	146	168	167	165	185	912
	% Cohort	100%	100%	100%	100%	100%	100%	100%

Chi-Square Tests	Value	df	Asymp. Sig. (2-sided)
Pearson Chi-Square	17.820a	15	0.272
Likelihood Ratio	18.488	15	0.238
Linear-by-Linear Association	1.257	1	0.262
N of Valid Cases	912		

a. 7 cells (29.2%) have expected count less than 5. The minimum expected count is 2.22.

Table 17. Did a midshipman's plebe year reputation stay with them throughout their time at the academy?

		1946-49	1950-54	1955-59	1960-64	1965-69	1970-76	Total
Significant carryover (1)	Count	19	34	34	31	27	47	192
	% Cohort	16.80%	20.00%	19.70%	17.40%	16.00%	24.70%	19.30%
2	Count	28	59	70	72	87	81	397
	% Cohort	24.80%	34.70%	40.50%	40.40%	51.50%	42.60%	40.00%
3	Count	36	40	34	40	28	31	209
	% Cohort	31.90%	23.50%	19.70%	22.50%	16.60%	16.30%	21.00%
4	Count	14	23	23	30	21	21	132
	% Cohort	12.40%	13.50%	13.30%	16.90%	12.40%	11.10%	13.30%
No carryover (5)	Count	13	9	7	4	5	4	42
	% Cohort	11.50%	5.30%	4.00%	2.20%	3%	2%	4.20%
Other	Count	3	5	5	1	1	6	21
	% Cohort	2.70%	2.90%	2.90%	0.60%	0.60%	3.20%	2.10%
Total	Count	113	170	173	178	169	190	993
	% Cohort	100%	100%	100%	100%	100%	100%	100%

Chi-Square Tests	Value	df	Asymp. Sig. (2-sided)
Pearson Chi-Square	56.586a	25	0
Likelihood Ratio	54.015	25	0
Linear-by-Linear Association	12.815	1	0
N of Valid Cases	993		

a. 7 cells (19.4%) have expected count less than 5. The minimum expected count is 2.39.

Table 18. Did the academy strike an appropriate balance between academics and Bancroft Hall?

		1946-49	1950-54	1955-59	1960-64	1965-69	1970-76	Total
Yes	Count	96	141	136	131	106	120	730
	% Cohort	85.00%	82.90%	78.60%	73.60%	62.70%	63.20%	73.50%
No	Count	17	29	37	47	63	70	263
	% Cohort	15.00%	17.10%	21.40%	26.40%	37.30%	36.80%	26.50%
Total	Count	113	170	173	178	169	190	993
	% Cohort	100%	100%	100%	100%	100%	100%	100%

Chi-Square Tests	Value	df	Asymp. Sig. (2-sided)
Pearson Chi-Square	38.243a	5	0
Likelihood Ratio	38.638	5	0
Linear-by-Linear Association	35.711	1	0
N of Valid Cases	993		

a. 0 cells (0%) have expected count less than 5. The minimum expected count is 29.93.

Table 19. Strongest relationships at the academy- company classmates.

		1946-49	1950-54	1955-59	1960-64	1965-69	1970-76	Total
Strongest (1)	Count	101	139	146	154	138	158	836
	% Cohort	89.40%	81.80%	84.40%	86.50%	81.70%	83.20%	84.20%
2	Count	4	16	12	18	22	19	91
	% Cohort	3.50%	9.40%	6.90%	10.10%	13.00%	10.00%	9.20%
3	Count	5	10	8	4	5	6	38
	% Cohort	4.40%	5.90%	4.60%	2.20%	3.00%	3.20%	3.80%
4	Count		2	5	1	2	5	15
	% Cohort		1.20%	2.90%	0.60%	1.20%	2.60%	1.50%
Weakest (5)	Count			2	1	2	2	7
	% Cohort			1.20%	0.60%	1%	1%	0.70%
Other	Count	3	3					6
	% Cohort	2.70%	1.80%					0.60%
Total	Count	113	170	173	178	169	190	993
	% Cohort	100%	100%	100%	100%	100%	100%	100%

Chi-Square Tests	Value	df	Asymp. Sig. (2-sided)
Pearson Chi-Square	38.779a	25	0.039
Likelihood Ratio	42.147	25	0.017
Linear-by-Linear Association	3.342	1	0.068
N of Valid Cases	993		

a. 19 cells (52.8%) have expected count less than 5. The minimum expected count is .68.

Table 20. Strongest relationships at the academy- classmates in general.

		1946-49	1950-54	1955-59	1960-64	1965-69	1970-76	Total
Strongest (1)	Count	13	17	14	10	9	13	76
	% Cohort	11.50%	10.00%	8.10%	5.60%	5.30%	6.80%	7.70%
2	Count	51	82	86	90	95	99	503
	% Cohort	45.10%	48.20%	49.70%	50.60%	56.20%	52.10%	50.70%
3	Count	28	43	50	52	51	53	277
	% Cohort	24.80%	25.30%	28.90%	29.20%	30.20%	27.90%	27.90%
4	Count	11	16	15	18	10	20	90
	% Cohort	9.70%	9.40%	8.70%	10.10%	5.90%	10.50%	9.10%
Weakest (5)	Count	5	7	5	8	4	5	34
	% Cohort	4.40%	4.10%	2.90%	4.50%	2%	3%	3.40%
Other	Count	5	5	3				13
	% Cohort	4.40%	2.90%	1.70%				1.30%
Total	Count	113	170	173	178	169	190	993
	% Cohort	100%	100%	100%	100%	100%	100%	100%

Chi-Square Tests	Value	df	Asymp. Sig. (2-sided)
Pearson Chi-Square	33.026a	25	0.13
Likelihood Ratio	35.973	25	0.072
Linear-by-Linear Association	1.769	1	0.184
N of Valid Cases	993		

a. 7 cells (19.4%) have expected count less than 5. The minimum expected count is 1.48.

Table 21. Strongest relationships at the academy - midshipmen in the same company.

		1946-49	1950-54	1955-59	1960-64	1965-69	1970-76	Total
Strongest (1)	Count	2	7	5	3	1	3	21
	% Cohort	1.80%	4.10%	2.90%	1.70%	0.60%	1.60%	2.10%
2	Count	28	45	33	29	29	38	202
	% Cohort	24.80%	26.50%	19.10%	16.30%	17.20%	20.00%	20.30%
3	Count	45	68	71	68	56	77	385
	% Cohort	39.80%	40.00%	41.00%	38.20%	33.10%	40.50%	38.80%
4	Count	26	34	43	54	59	55	271
	% Cohort	23.00%	20.00%	24.90%	30.30%	34.90%	28.90%	27.30%
Weakest (5)	Count	6	10	19	24	24	17	100
	% Cohort	5.30%	5.90%	11.00%	13.50%	14%	9%	10.10%
Other	Count	5	6	2				13
	% Cohort	4.40%	3.50%	1.20%				1.30%
Total	Count	113	170	173	178	169	190	993
	% Cohort	100%	100%	100%	100%	100%	100%	100%

Chi-Square Tests	Value	df	Asymp. Sig. (2-sided)
Pearson Chi-Square	63.856a	30	0
Likelihood Ratio	62.678	30	0
Linear-by-Linear Association	7.661	1	0.006
N of Valid Cases	993		

table 22. Strongest relationships at the academy- sports teammates.

		1946-49	1950-54	1955-59	1960-64	1965-69	1970-76	Total
Strongest (1)	Count	16	27	30	22	26	29	150
	% Cohort	14.20%	15.90%	17.30%	12.40%	15.40%	15.30%	15.10%
2	Count	22	42	37	51	37	47	236
	% Cohort	19.50%	24.70%	21.40%	28.70%	21.90%	24.70%	23.80%
3	Count	30	43	46	48	56	51	274
	% Cohort	26.50%	25.30%	26.60%	27.00%	33.10%	26.80%	27.60%
4	Count	25	38	41	40	30	44	218
	% Cohort	22.10%	22.40%	23.70%	22.50%	17.80%	23.20%	22.00%
Weakest (5)	Count	14	17	16	17	20	19	103
	% Cohort	12.40%	10.00%	9.20%	9.60%	12%	10%	10.40%
Other	Count	6	3	3				12
	% Cohort	5.30%	1.80%	1.70%				1.20%
Total	Count	113	170	173	178	169	190	993
	% Cohort	100%	100%	100%	100%	100%	100%	100%

Chi-Square Tests	Value	df	Asymp. Sig. (2-sided)
Pearson Chi-Square	33.428a	25	0.121
Likelihood Ratio	32.535	25	0.143
Linear-by-Linear Association	0.496	1	0.481
N of Valid Cases	993		

a. 6 cells (16.7%) have expected count less than 5. The minimum expected count is 1.37.

Table 23. Strongest relationships at the academy- clubs or activities.

		1946-49	1950-54	1955-59	1960-64	1965-69	1970-76	Total
Strongest (1)	Count	3	9	6	7	6	6	37
	% Cohort	2.70%	5.30%	3.50%	3.90%	3.60%	3.20%	3.70%
2	Count	9	30	27	20	24	18	128
	% Cohort	8.00%	17.60%	15.60%	11.20%	14.20%	9.50%	12.90%
3	Count	25	29	45	40	38	53	230
	% Cohort	22.30%	17.10%	26.00%	22.50%	22.50%	27.90%	23.20%
4	Count	27	33	46	48	39	48	241
	% Cohort	24.10%	19.40%	26.60%	27.00%	23.10%	25.30%	24.30%
Weakest (5)	Count	42	65	45	61	61	63	337
	% Cohort	37.50%	38.20%	26.00%	34.30%	36%	33%	34.00%
Other	Count	6	4	4	2	1	2	19
	% Cohort	5.40%	2.40%	2.30%	1.1	0.60%	1.00%	1.80%
Total	Count	112	170	173	178	169	190	992
	% Cohort	100%	100%	100%	100%	100%	100%	100%

Chi-Square Tests	Value	df	Asymp. Sig. (2-sided)
Pearson Chi-Square	38.925a	30	0.127
Likelihood Ratio	37.065	30	0.175
Linear-by-Linear Association	1.672	1	0.196
N of Valid Cases	992		

a. 13 cells (31.0%) have expected count less than 5. The minimum expected count is .11.

Table 24. Unity building activities- intramural sports program.

		1946-49	1950-54	1955-59	1960-64	1965-69	1970-76	Total
Strongest (1)	Count	20	35	38	44	57	59	253
	% Cohort	17.70%	20.60%	22.00%	24.70%	33.70%	31.10%	25.50%
2	Count	32	57	67	64	69	72	361
	% Cohort	28.30%	33.50%	38.70%	36.00%	40.80%	37.90%	36.40%
3	Count	45	54	49	44	24	38	254
	% Cohort	39.80%	31.80%	28.30%	24.70%	14.20%	20.00%	25.60%
4	Count	10	13	14	17	11	14	79
	% Cohort	8.80%	7.60%	8.10%	9.60%	6.50%	7.40%	8.00%
Weakest (5)	Count	2	6	4	5	7	4	28
	% Cohort	1.80%	3.50%	2.30%	2.80%	4%	2%	2.80%
Other	Count	4	5	1	4	1	3	18
	% Cohort	3.50%	2.90%	0.60%	2.3	0.60%	1.60%	1.70%
Total	Count	113	170	173	178	169	190	993
	% Cohort	100%	100%	100%	100%	100%	100%	100%

Chi-Square Tests	Value	df	Asymp. Sig. (2-sided)
Pearson Chi-Square	53.004a	30	0.006
Likelihood Ratio	52.269	30	0.007
Linear-by-Linear Association	11.268	1	0.001
N of Valid Cases	993		

a. 16 cells (38.1%) have expected count less than 5. The minimum expected count is .11.

Table 25: Unity building activities- Color Company competition.

		1946-49	1950-54	1955-59	1960-64	1965-69	1970-76	Total
Strongest (1)	Count	20	24	32	27	11	9	123
	% Cohort	17.70%	14.10%	18.50%	15.30%	6.50%	4.80%	12.40%
2	Count	15	28	35	33	21	27	159
	% Cohort	13.30%	16.50%	20.20%	18.60%	12.40%	14.30%	16.00%
3	Count	20	40	52	45	47	38	242
	% Cohort	17.70%	23.50%	30.10%	25.40%	27.80%	20.10%	24.40%
4	Count	23	39	28	42	41	58	231
	% Cohort	20.40%	22.90%	16.20%	23.70%	24.30%	30.70%	23.30%
Weakest (5)	Count	21	31	25	26	44	55	202
	% Cohort	18.60%	18.20%	14.50%	14.70%	26%	29%	20.40%
Other	Count	14	8	1	4	5	2	34
	% Cohort	12.40%	4.70%	0.60%	2.3	3.00%	1.10%	3.30%
Total	Count	113	170	173	177	169	189	991
	% Cohort	100%	100%	100%	100%	100%	100%	100%

Chi-Square Tests	Value	df	Asymp. Sig. (2-sided)
Pearson Chi-Square	99.853a	30	0
Likelihood Ratio	92.716	30	0
Linear-by-Linear Association	37.889	1	0
N of Valid Cases	991		

a. 7 cells (16.7%) have expected count less than 5. The minimum expected count is .11.

Table 26. Unity building activities- company dining tables.

		1946-49	1950-54	1955-59	1960-64	1965-69	1970-76	Total
Strongest (1)	Count	38	64	70	66	69	54	361
	% Cohort	33.60%	37.60%	40.50%	37.10%	40.80%	28.40%	36.40%
2	Count	47	54	55	71	51	79	357
	% Cohort	41.60%	31.80%	31.80%	39.90%	30.20%	41.60%	36.00%
3	Count	18	38	33	32	38	40	199
	% Cohort	15.90%	22.40%	19.10%	18.00%	22.50%	21.10%	20.00%
4	Count	1	9	8	9	7	11	45
	% Cohort	0.90%	5.30%	4.60%	5.10%	4.10%	5.80%	4.50%
Weakest (5)	Count	2	1	6		3	3	15
	% Cohort	1.80%	0.60%	3.50%		2%	2%	1.50%
Other	Count	7	4	1		1	3	16
	% Cohort	6.20%	2.40%	0.60%		0.60%	1.60%	1.60%
Total	Count	113	170	173	178	169	190	993
	% Cohort	100%	100%	100%	100%	100%	100%	100%

Chi-Square Tests

	Value	df	Asymp. Sig. (2-sided)
Pearson Chi-Square	47.448a	25	0.004
Likelihood Ratio	48.376	25	0.003
Linear-by-Linear Association	4.156	1	0.041
N of Valid Cases	993		

a. 12 cells (33.3%) have expected count less than 5. The minimum expected count is 1.71.

Table 27. Unity building activities- common classes.

		1946-49	1950-54	1955-59	1960-64	1965-69	1970-76	Total
Strongest (1)	Count	30	33	40	34	10	9	156
	% Cohort	26.80%	19.40%	23.50%	19.30%	6.10%	4.80%	15.90%
2	Count	27	57	52	66	31	41	274
	% Cohort	24.10%	33.50%	30.60%	37.50%	18.90%	21.90%	28.00%
3	Count	22	46	42	44	55	55	264
	% Cohort	19.60%	27.10%	24.70%	25.00%	33.50%	29.40%	27.00%
4	Count	4	15	17	12	26	38	112
	% Cohort	3.60%	8.80%	10.00%	6.80%	15.90%	20.30%	11.40%
Weakest (5)	Count	7	5	4	6	20	19	61
	% Cohort	6.30%	2.90%	2.40%	3.40%	12%	10%	6.20%
Other	Count	22	14	15	14	22	25	112
	% Cohort	19.60%	8.20%	8.80%	8%	13.40%	13.40%	11.40%
Total	Count	112	170	170	176	164	187	979
	% Cohort	100%	100%	100%	100%	100%	100%	100%

Chi-Square Tests	Value	df	Asymp. Sig. (2-sided)
Pearson Chi-Square	124.990a	25	0
Likelihood Ratio	130.524	25	0
Linear-by-Linear Association	42.318	1	0
N of Valid Cases	979		

a. 0 cells (0%) have expected count less than 5. The minimum expected count is 6.98.

Table 28. Unity building activities- professional development programs.

		1946-49	1950-54	1955-59	1960-64	1965-69	1970-76	Total
Strongest (1)	Count	3	5	8	5	1	4	26
	% Cohort	2.70%	2.90%	4.70%	2.80%	0.60%	2.10%	2.60%
2	Count	12	25	19	23	19	21	119
	% Cohort	10.60%	14.70%	11.00%	13.00%	11.20%	11.10%	12.00%
3	Count	21	43	46	53	46	66	275
	% Cohort	18.60%	25.30%	26.70%	29.90%	27.20%	34.90%	27.80%
4	Count	32	43	53	56	58	55	297
	% Cohort	28.30%	25.30%	30.80%	31.60%	34.30%	29.10%	30.00%
Weakest (5)	Count	23	34	33	29	40	41	200
	% Cohort	20.40%	20.00%	19.20%	16.40%	24%	22%	20.20%
Other	Count	22	20	13	11	5	2	73
	% Cohort	19.50%	11.80%	7.60%	6.2 %	3.00%	1.10%	7.40%
Total	Count	113	170	172	177	169	189	990
	% Cohort	100%	100%	100%	100%	100%	100%	100%

Chi-Square Tests	Value	df	Asymp. Sig. (2-sided)
Pearson Chi-Square	62.122a	25	0
Likelihood Ratio	62.562	25	0
Linear-by-Linear Association	22.665	1	0
N of Valid Cases	990		

a. 6 cells (16.7%) have expected count less than 5. The minimum expected count is 2.97.

Table 29. Unity building activities - social activities.

		1946-49	1950-54	1955-59	1960-64	1965-69	1970-76	Total
Strongest (1)	Count	2	6	14	4	23	29	78
	% Cohort	1.80%	3.60%	8.10%	2.20%	13.60%	15.30%	7.90%
2	Count	10	23	24	29	24	35	145
	% Cohort	8.90%	13.60%	13.90%	16.30%	14.20%	18.40%	14.60%
3	Count	12	22	36	29	34	48	181
	% Cohort	10.70%	13.00%	20.80%	16.30%	20.10%	25.30%	18.30%
4	Count	25	41	39	37	33	31	206
	% Cohort	22.30%	24.30%	22.50%	20.80%	19.50%	16.30%	20.80%
Weakest (5)	Count	37	63	49	62	47	39	297
	% Cohort	33.00%	37.30%	28.30%	34.80%	28%	21%	30.00%
Other	Count	26	14	11	17	8	8	84
	% Cohort	23.20%	8.30%	6.40%	9.60%	4.70%	4.20%	8.50%
Total	Count	112	169	173	178	169	190	991
	% Cohort	100%	100%	100%	100%	100%	100%	100%

Chi-Square Tests	Value	df	Asymp. Sig. (2-sided)
Pearson Chi-Square	104.950a	25	0
Likelihood Ratio	100.433	25	0
Linear-by-Linear Association	3.773	1	0.052
N of Valid Cases	991		

a. 0 cells (0%) have expected count less than 5. The minimum expected count is 8.82.

Table 30. Did certain companies develop reputations in the Brigade?

		1946-49	1950-54	1955-59	1960-64	1965-69	1970-76	Total
Yes	Count	60	108	138	155	156	169	786
	% Cohort	53.10%	63.50%	79.80%	87.10%	92.30%	88.90%	79.20%
No	Count	53	62	35	23	13	21	207
	% Cohort	46.90%	36.50%	20.20%	12.90%	7.70%	11.10%	20.80%
Total	Count	113	170	173	178	169	190	993
	% Cohort	100%	100%	100%	100%	100%	100%	100%

Chi-Square Tests	Value	df	Asymp. Sig. (2-sided)
Pearson Chi-Square	107.228a	5	0
Likelihood Ratio	102.347	5	0
Linear-by-Linear Association	89.331	1	0
N of Valid Cases	993		

a. 0 cells (0%) have expected count less than 5. The minimum expected count is 23.56.

Table 31. Who controlled the Brigade on a day-to-day basis?

		1946-49	1950-54	1955-59	1960-64	1965-69	1970-76	Total
Executive Department and company officers	Count	48	70	58	41	43	33	293
	% Cohort	43.20%	41.70%	33.90%	23.00%	25.90%	17.60%	29.90%
Midshipmen stripers	Count	12	22	22	37	33	42	168
	% Cohort	10.80%	13.10%	12.90%	20.80%	19.90%	22.50%	17.10%
Company upperclassmen	Count	51	75	90	97	88	109	510
	% Cohort	45.90%	44.60%	52.60%	54.50%	53.00%	58.30%	52.00%
Other	Count		1	1	3	2	3	10
	% Cohort		0.60%	0.60%	1.70%	1.20%	1.60%	1.00%
Total	Count	111	168	171	178	166	187	981
	% Cohort	100%	100%	100%	100%	100%	100%	100%

Chi-Square Tests	Value	df	Asymp. Sig. (2-sided)
Pearson Chi-Square	47.068a	15	0
Likelihood Ratio	48.632	15	0
Linear-by-Linear Association	24.437	1	0
N of Valid Cases	981		

a. 6 cells (25.0%) have expected count less than 5. The minimum expected count is 1.13.

Table 32. What functions did company officers perform best?

		1946-49	1950-54	1955-59	1960-64	1965-69	1970-76	Total
Positive role model	Count	31	42	68	56	59	86	342
	% Cohort	28.40%	25.10%	39.30%	31.60%	35.30%	45.70%	34.90%
Practical leadership training	Count	9	22	16	10	12	11	80
	% Cohort	8.30%	13.20%	9.20%	5.60%	7.20%	5.90%	8.20%
Maintained good order and discipline	Count	43	71	58	59	58	45	334
	% Cohort	39.40%	42.50%	33.50%	33.30%	34.70%	23.90%	34.00%
Encourage high morale	Count	2	2	8	8	6	3	29
	% Cohort	1.80%	1.20%	4.60%	4.50%	3.60%	1.60%	3.00%
Other	Count	24	30	23	44	32	43	196
	% Cohort	22.00%	18.00%	13.30%	24.90%	19.20%	22.90%	20.00%
Total	Count	109	167	173	177	167	188	981
	% Cohort	100%	100%	100%	100%	100%	100%	100%

Chi-Square Tests	Value	df	Asymp. Sig. (2-sided)
Pearson Chi-Square	46.161a	20	0.001
Likelihood Ratio	46.675	20	0.001
Linear-by-Linear Association	1.75	1	0
N of Valid Cases	981		

a. 3 cells (10.0%) have expected count less than 5. The minimum expected count is 3.22.

Table 33. Was the Executive Department unduly harsh in enforcing academy regulations?

		1946-49	1950-54	1955-59	1960-64	1965-69	1970-76	Total
Yes	Count	17	23	28	29	44	52	193
	% Cohort	15.00%	13.50%	16.20%	16.30%	26.00%	27.40%	19.40%
No	Count	96	147	145	149	125	138	800
	% Cohort	85.00%	86.50%	83.80%	83.70%	74.00%	72.60%	80.60%
Total	Count	113	170	173	178	169	190	993
	% Cohort	100%	100%	100%	100%	100%	100%	100%

Chi-Square Tests	Value	df	Asymp. Sig. (2-sided)
Pearson Chi-Square	19.807a	5	0.001
Likelihood Ratio	19.362	5	0.002
Linear-by-Linear Association	15.808	1	0
N of Valid Cases	993		

a. 0 cells (0%) have expected count less than 5. The minimum expected count is 21.96.

Table 34. Regulation enforcement- uniform appearance.

		1946-49	1950-54	1955-59	1960-64	1965-69	1970-76	Total
Unduly harsh (1)	Count	1	4	4	1	8	6	24
	% Cohort	0.90%	2.40%	2.30%	0.60%	4.70%	3.20%	2.40%
2	Count	8	9	8	7	10	15	57
	% Cohort	7.10%	5.30%	4.60%	4.00%	5.90%	7.90%	5.80%
3	Count	2	5	4	9	9	9	38
	% Cohort	1.80%	3.00%	2.30%	5.10%	5.30%	4.70%	3.80%
4	Count	4	4	5	5	10	15	43
	% Cohort	3.50%	2.40%	2.90%	2.80%	5.90%	7.90%	4.30%
Appropriate discipline (5)	Count	5	4	9	10	9	11	48
	% Cohort	4.40%	2.40%	5.20%	5.60%	5.30%	5.80%	4.80%
Other	Count	93	143	143	145	123	134	781
	% Cohort	82.30%	84.60%	82.70%	81.90%	72.80%	70.50%	78.80%
Total	Count	113	169	173	177	169	190	991
	% Cohort	100%	100%	100%	100%	100%	100%	100%

Chi-Square Tests	Value	df	Asymp. Sig. (2-sided)
Pearson Chi-Square	32.563a	25	0.142
Likelihood Ratio	33.381	25	0.122
Linear-by-Linear Association	12.403	1	0
N of Valid Cases	991		

a. 8 cells (22.2%) have expected count less than 5. The minimum expected count is 2.74.

Table 35. Regulation enforcement- room appearance.

		1946-49	1950-54	1955-59	1960-64	1965-69	1970-76	Total
Unduly harsh (1)	Count	2	7	4	4	8	6	31
	% Cohort	1.80%	4.10%	2.30%	2.20%	4.70%	3.20%	3.10%
2	Count	4	8	6	7	16	14	55
	% Cohort	3.50%	4.70%	3.50%	3.90%	9.50%	7.40%	5.50%
3	Count	7	5	9	11	8	12	52
	% Cohort	6.20%	3.00%	5.20%	6.20%	4.70%	7.90%	4.50%
4	Count	6	4	8	4	8	15	45
	% Cohort	5.30%	2.40%	4.60%	2.20%	4.70%	7.90%	4.50%
Appropriate discipline (5)	Count	1	2	3	6	6	10	28
	% Cohort	0.90%	1.20%	1.70%	3.40%	3.60%	5.30%	2.80%
Other	Count	93	143	143	146	123	133	781
	% Cohort	82.30%	84.60%	82.70%	82.00%	72.80%	70.00%	78.70%
Total	Count	113	169	173	178	169	190	992
	% Cohort	100%	100%	100%	100%	100%	100%	100%

Chi-Square Tests	Value	df	Asymp. Sig. (2-sided)
Pearson Chi-Square	36.299a	25	0.067
Likelihood Ratio	36.339	25	0.067
Linear-by-Linear Association	15.817	1	0
N of Valid Cases	992		

a. 5 cells (13.9%) have expected count less than 5. The minimum expected count is 3.19.

Table 36. Regulation enforcement- grooming standards.

		1946-49	1950-54	1955-59	1960-64	1965-69	1970-76	Total
Unduly harsh (1)	Count	1	4	4		7	8	24
	% Cohort	0.90%	2.40%	2.30%		4.10%	4.20%	2.40%
2	Count	4	7	5	5	9	17	47
	% Cohort	3.50%	4.10%	2.90%	2.80%	5.30%	8.90%	4.70%
3	Count	6	7	6	12	10	12	53
	% Cohort	5.30%	4.10%	3.50%	6.70%	5.90%	6.30%	5.30%
4	Count	5	5	7	8	10	13	48
	% Cohort	4.40%	2.90%	4.00%	4.50%	5.90%	6.80%	4.80%
Appropriate discipline (5)	Count	4	3	8	7	9	7	38
	% Cohort	3.50%	1.80%	4.60%	3.90%	5.30%	3.70%	3.80%
Other	Count	93	144	143	146	124	133	783
	% Cohort	82.30%	84.70%	82.70%	82.00%	73.40%	70.00%	78.90%
Total	Count	113	170	173	178	169	190	993
	% Cohort	100%	100%	100%	100%	100%	100%	100%

Chi-Square Tests	Value	df	Asymp. Sig. (2-sided)
Pearson Chi-Square	33.848a	25	0.111
Likelihood Ratio	37.211	25	0.055
Linear-by-Linear Association	9.178	1	0.001
N of Valid Cases	993		

a. 7 cells (19.4%) have expected count less than 5. The minimum expected count is 2.73.

Table 37. Regulation enforcement- liberty infractions.

		1946-49	1950-54	1955-59	1960-64	1965-69	1970-76	Total
Unduly harsh (1)	Count	5	4	8	7	16	17	57
	% Cohort	4.40%	2.40%	4.60%	3.90%	9.50%	8.90%	5.70%
2	Count	3	8	11	9	11	9	51
	% Cohort	2.70%	4.70%	6.40%	5.10%	6.50%	4.70%	5.10%
3	Count	2	5	6	7	8	9	37
	% Cohort	1.80%	2.90%	3.50%	3.90%	4.70%	4.70%	3.70%
4	Count	6	3	2	1	10	12	34
	% Cohort	5.30%	1.80%	1.20%	0.60%	5.90%	6.30%	3.40%
Appropriate discipline (5)	Count	4	5	3	8	1	9	30
	% Cohort	3.50%	2.90%	1.70%	4.50%	0.60%	4.70%	3.00%
Other	Count	93	145	143	146	123	134	784
	% Cohort	82.30%	85.30%	82.70%	82.00%	72.80%	70.50%	79.00%
Total	Count	113	170	173	178	169	190	993
	% Cohort	100%	100%	100%	100%	100%	100%	100%

Chi-Square Tests	Value	df	Asymp. Sig. (2-sided)
Pearson Chi-Square	46.351a	25	0.006
Likelihood Ratio	50.068	25	0.002
Linear-by-Linear Association	8.274	1	0.004
N of Valid Cases	993		

a. 3 cells (8.3%) have expected count less than 5. The minimum expected count is 3.41.

Table 38. Regulation enforcement- classroom discipline.

		1946-49	1950-54	1955-59	1960-64	1965-69	1970-76	Total
Unduly harsh (1)	Count		2	1		2	2	7
	% Cohort		1.20%	0.60%		1.20%	1.10%	0.70%
2	Count	3	3	1	2	1	6	13
	% Cohort	2.70%	1.80%	0.60%	1.10%	0.60%	3.20%	1.30%
3	Count		2	6	5	6	12	34
	% Cohort		1.20%	3.50%	2.80%	3.60%	6.30%	3.40%
4	Count	6	6	7	7	12	10	48
	% Cohort	5.30%	3.50%	4.00%	3.90%	7.10%	5.30%	4.80%
Appropriate discipline (5)	Count	9	10	14	16	25	25	99
	% Cohort	8.00%	5.90%	8.10%	9.00%	14.80%	13.20%	10.00%
Other	Count	95	147	144	148	123	135	792
	% Cohort	84.10%	86.50%	83.20%	83.10%	72.80%	71.10%	79.80%
Total	Count	113	170	173	178	169	190	993
	% Cohort	100%	100%	100%	100%	100%	100%	100%

Chi-Square Tests	Value	df	Asymp. Sig. (2-sided)
Pearson Chi-Square	36.767a	25	0.061
Likelihood Ratio	38.754	25	0.039
Linear-by-Linear Association	15.059	1	0
N of Valid Cases	993		

a. 13 cells (36.1%) have expected count less than 5. The minimum expected count is .80.

Table 39. Did varsity athletes get preferential treatment at the academy?

		1946-49	1950-54	1955-59	1960-64	1965-69	1970-76	Total
Yes	Count	90	137	147	156	134	162	826
	% Cohort	79.60%	80.60%	85.00%	87.60%	79.30%	85.30%	83.20%
No	Count	23	33	26	22	35	28	167
	% Cohort	20.40%	19.40%	15.00%	12.40%	20.70%	14.70%	16.80%
Total	Count	113	170	173	178	169	190	993
	% Cohort	100%	100%	100%	100%	100%	100%	100%

Chi-Square Tests	Value	df	Asymp. Sig. (2-sided)
Pearson Chi-Square	7.171a	5	0.208
Likelihood Ratio	7.229	5	0.204
Linear-by-Linear Association	0.957	1	0.328
N of Valid Cases	993		

a. 0 cells (0%) have expected count less than 5. The minimum expected count is 19.00.

Table 40. Did minority midshipmen get preferential treatment at the academy?

		1946-49	1950-54	1955-59	1960-64	1965-69	1970-76	Total
Yes	Count	7	4	5	4	8	49	77
	% Cohort	6.20%	2.40%	2.90%	2.20%	4.70%	25.80%	7.80%
No	Count	106	166	168	174	161	141	916
	% Cohort	93.80%	97.60%	97.10%	97.80%	95.30%	74.20%	92.20%
Total	Count	113	170	173	178	169	190	993
	% Cohort	100%	100%	100%	100%	100%	100%	100%

Chi-Square Tests

	Value	df	Asymp. Sig. (2-sided)
Pearson Chi-Square	109.142a	5	0
Likelihood Ratio	86.327	5	0
Linear-by-Linear Association	47.057	1	0
N of Valid Cases	993		

a. 0 cells (0%) have expected count less than 5. The minimum expected count is 8.76.

Table 41. Did midshipmen stripers get preferential treatment?

		1946-49	1950-54	1955-59	1960-64	1965-69	1970-76	Total
Yes	Count	28	38	43	46	59	63	277
	% Cohort	24.80%	22.40%	24.90%	25.80%	34.90%	33.20%	27.90%
No	Count	85	132	130	132	110	127	716
	% Cohort	75.20%	77.60%	75.10%	74.20%	65.10%	66.80%	72.10%
Total	Count	113	170	173	178	169	190	993
	% Cohort	100%	100%	100%	100%	100%	100%	100%

Chi-Square Tests	Value	df	Asymp. Sig. (2-sided)
Pearson Chi-Square	11.062a	5	0.05
Likelihood Ratio	10.946	5	0.052
Linear-by-Linear Association	8.121	1	0.004
N of Valid Cases	993		

a. 0 cells (0%) have expected count less than 5. The minimum expected count is 31.52.

Table 42. Scholastic ability of academic faculty.

		1946-49	1950-54	1955-59	1960-64	1965-69	1970-76	Total
Most favorable (1)	Count	22	45	40	39	48	66	260
	% Cohort	19.50%	26.50%	23.10%	21.90%	28.40%	34.70%	26.20%
2	Count	41	64	83	77	77	99	441
	% Cohort	36.30%	37.60%	48.00%	43.30%	45.60%	52.10%	44.40%
3	Count	38	44	42	47	31	20	222
	% Cohort	33.60%	25.90%	24.30%	26.40%	18.30%	10.50%	22.40%
4	Count	7	9	6	10	9	2	43
	% Cohort	6.20%	5.30%	3.50%	5.60%	5.30%	1.10%	4.30%
Least Favorable (5)	Count	2	3	1	2	1	2	11
	% Cohort	1.80%	1.80%	0.60%	1.10%	0.60%	1.10%	1.10%
Other	Count	3	5	1	3	3	1	16
	% Cohort	2.70%	2.90%	0.60%	1.70%	1.80%	0.50%	1.60%
Total	Count	113	170	173	178	169	190	993
	% Cohort	100%	100%	100%	100%	100%	100%	100%

Chi-Square Tests	Value	df	Asymp. Sig. (2-sided)
Pearson Chi-Square	52.580a	25	0.001
Likelihood Ratio	56.714	25	0
Linear-by-Linear Association	18.007	1	0
N of Valid Cases	993		

a. 13 cells (36.1%) have expected count less than 5. The minimum expected count is 1.25.

Table 43. Teaching ability of academic faculty.

		1946-49	1950-54	1955-59	1960-64	1965-69	1970-76	Total
Most favorable (1)	Count	16	35	27	34	25	36	173
	% Cohort	14.20%	20.60%	15.60%	19.10%	14.80%	18.90%	17.40%
2	Count	38	64	88	76	88	105	459
	% Cohort	33.60%	37.60%	50.90%	42.70%	52.10%	55.30%	46.20%
3	Count	39	49	49	50	42	39	268
	% Cohort	34.50%	28.80%	28.30%	28.10%	24.90%	20.50%	27.00%
4	Count	12	16	8	11	11	7	65
	% Cohort	10.60%	9.40%	4.60%	6.20%	6.50%	3.70%	6.50%
Least Favorable (5)	Count	5	2		4		3	14
	% Cohort	4.40%	1.20%		2.20%		1.60%	1.40%
Other	Count	3	4	1	3	3		14
	% Cohort	2.70%	2.40%	0.60%	1.70%	1.80%		1.40%
Total	Count	113	170	173	178	169	190	993
	% Cohort	100%	100%	100%	100%	100%	100%	100%

Chi-Square Tests	Value	df	Asymp. Sig. (2-sided)
Pearson Chi-Square	49.271a	25	0.003
Likelihood Ratio	54.044	25	0.001
Linear-by-Linear Association	7.981	1	0.005
N of Valid Cases	993		

a. 12 cells (33.3%) have expected count less than 5. The minimum expected count is 1.59.

Table 44. Academic faculty's availability for extra instruction.

		1946-49	1950-54	1955-59	1960-64	1965-69	1970-76	Total
Most favorable (1)	Count	8	36	38	37	51	86	256
	% Cohort	7.10%	21.20%	22.00%	20.80%	30.20%	45.30%	25.80%
2	Count	12	42	35	44	47	58	238
	% Cohort	10.60%	24.70%	20.20%	24.70%	27.80%	30.50%	24.00%
3	Count	28	36	49	36	37	32	218
	% Cohort	24.80%	21.20%	28.30%	20.20%	21.90%	16.80%	22.00%
4	Count	19	17	33	37	22	9	137
	% Cohort	16.80%	10.00%	19.10%	20.80%	13.00%	4.70%	13.80%
Least Favorable (5)	Count	35	30	11	15	8	4	103
	% Cohort	31.00%	17.60%	6.40%	8.40%	4.70%	2.10%	10.40%
Other	Count	11	9	7	9	4	1	41
	% Cohort	9.70%	5.30%	4.00%	5.10%	2.40%	0.50%	4.10%
Total	Count	113	170	173	178	169	190	993
	% Cohort	100%	100%	100%	100%	100%	100%	100%

Chi-Square Tests	Value	df	Asymp. Sig. (2-sided)
Pearson Chi-Square	185.183a	25	0
Likelihood Ratio	182.686	25	0
Linear-by-Linear Association	68.563	1	0
N of Valid Cases	993		

a. 1 cell (2.8%) has expected count less than 5. The minimum expected count is 4.67.

Table 45. Empathy of academic faculty for midshipmen's time demands.

		1946-49	1950-54	1955-59	1960-64	1965-69	1970-76	Total
Most favorable (1)	Count	18	37	33	28	39	38	193
	% Cohort	15.90%	21.80%	19.20%	15.70%	23.10%	20.00%	19.50%
2	Count	29	45	61	62	58	71	326
	% Cohort	25.70%	26.50%	35.50%	34.80%	34.30%	37.40%	32.90%
3	Count	35	49	46	49	42	45	266
	% Cohort	31.00%	28.80%	26.70%	27.50%	24.90%	23.70%	26.80%
4	Count	11	19	21	25	20	29	125
	% Cohort	9.70%	11.20%	12.20%	14.00%	11.80%	15.30%	12.60%
Least Favorable (5)	Count	10	10	9	11	7	7	54
	% Cohort	8.80%	5.90%	5.20%	6.20%	4.10%	3.70%	5.40%
Other	Count	10	10	2	3	3		28
	% Cohort	8.80%	5.90%	1.20%	1.70%	1.80%		2.80%
Total	Count	113	170	172	178	169	190	992
	% Cohort	100%	100%	100%	100%	100%	100%	100%

Chi-Square Tests	Value	df	Asymp. Sig. (2-sided)
Pearson Chi-Square	46.766a	25	0.005
Likelihood Ratio	46.259	25	0.006
Linear-by-Linear Association	0.065	1	0.799
N of Valid Cases	992		

a 4 cells (11.1%) have expected count less than 5. The minimum expected count is 3.19.

Table 46. Did summer training adequately expose you to the fleet?

		1946-49	1950-54	1955-59	1960-64	1965-69	1970-76	Total
Yes	Count	86	145	146	161	136	159	833
	% Cohort	76.10%	85.30%	84.40%	90.40%	80.50%	83.70%	83.90%
No	Count	27	25	27	17	33	31	160
	% Cohort	23.90%	14.70%	15.60%	9.60%	19.50%	16.30%	16.10%
Total	Count	113	170	173	178	169	190	993
	% Cohort	100%	100%	100%	100%	100%	100%	100%

Chi-Square Tests	Value	df	Asymp. Sig. (2-sided)
Pearson Chi-Square	12.477a	5	0.029
Likelihood Ratio	12.679	5	0.027
Linear-by-Linear Association	0.549	1	0.459
N of Valid Cases	993		

a. 0 cells (0%) have expected count less than 5. The minimum expected count is 18.21.

Table 47. *Did you notice a large difference between the academy's professional preparation and other commissioning sources?*

		1946-49	1950-54	1955-59	1960-64	1965-69	1970-76	Total
Yes	Count	82	130	141	148	124	155	780
	% Cohort	72.60%	76.50%	81.50%	83.10%	73.40%	81.60%	78.50%
No	Count	31	40	32	30	45	35	213
	% Cohort	27.40%	23.50%	18.50%	16.90%	26.60%	18.40%	21.50%
Total	Count	113	170	173	178	169	190	993
	% Cohort	100%	100%	100%	100%	100%	100%	100%

Chi-Square Tests	Value	df	Asymp. Sig. (2-sided)
Pearson Chi-Square	9.687a	5	0.085
Likelihood Ratio	9.6	5	0.087
Linear-by-Linear Association	1.37	1	0.242
N of Valid Cases	993		

a. 0 cells (0%) have expected count less than 5. The minimum expected count is 24.24.

Table 48. Class rank- top 25% of class.

		1946-49	1950-54	1955-59	1960-64	1965-69	1970-76	Total
Yes	Count	49	57	66	58	60	72	362
	% Cohort	43.40%	33.50%	38.20%	32.60%	35.50%	37.90%	36.50%
No	Count	64	113	107	120	109	118	631
	% Cohort	56.60%	66.50%	61.80%	67.40%	64.50%	62.10%	63.50%
Total	Count	113	170	173	178	169	190	993
	% Cohort	100%	100%	100%	100%	100%	100%	100%

Chi-Square Tests	Value	df	Asymp. Sig. (2-sided)
Pearson Chi-Square	4.558a	5	0.472
Likelihood Ratio	4.53	5	0.476
Linear-by-Linear Association	0.251	1	0.617
N of Valid Cases	993		

a. 0 cells (0%) have expected count less than 5. The minimum expected count is 41.19.

Table 49. Class rank- middle 25-50% of class.

		1946-49	1950-54	1955-59	1960-64	1965-69	1970-76	Total
Yes	Count	28	44	53	52	49	58	284
	% Cohort	24.80%	25.90%	30.60%	29.20%	29.00%	30.50%	28.60%
No	Count	85	126	120	126	120	132	709
	% Cohort	75.20%	74.10%	69.40%	70.80%	71.00%	69.50%	71.40%
Total	Count	113	170	173	178	169	190	993
	% Cohort	100%	100%	100%	100%	100%	100%	100%

Chi-Square Tests	Value	df	Asymp. Sig. (2-sided)
Pearson Chi-Square	2.165a	5	0.826
Likelihood Ratio	2.191	5	0.822
Linear-by-Linear Association	1.285	1	0.257
N of Valid Cases	993		

a. 0 cells (0%) have expected count less than 5. The minimum expected count is 32.32.

Table 50. Class rank- Lower 50- bottom 25% of class.

		1946-49	1950-54	1955-59	1960-64	1965-69	1970-76	Total
Yes	Count	24	36	32	40	34	34	200
	% Cohort	21.20%	21.20%	18.50%	22.50%	20.10%	17.90%	20.10%
No	Count	89	134	141	138	135	156	793
	% Cohort	78.80%	78.80%	81.50%	77.50%	79.90%	82.10%	79.90%
Total	Count	113	170	173	178	169	190	993
	% Cohort	100%	100%	100%	100%	100%	100%	100%

Chi-Square Tests	Value	df	Asymp. Sig. (2-sided)
Pearson Chi-Square	1.686a	5	0.891
Likelihood Ratio	1.691	5	0.89
Linear-by-Linear Association	0.386	1	0.534
N of Valid Cases	993		

a. 0 cells (0%) have expected count less than 5. The minimum expected count is 22.76.

Table 51. Class rank- bottom 25% of class.

		1946-49	1950-54	1955-59	1960-64	1965-69	1970-76	Total
Yes	Count	12	32	21	28	26	26	145
	% Cohort	10.60%	18.80%	12.10%	15.70%	15.40%	13.70%	14.60%
No	Count	101	138	152	150	143	164	848
	% Cohort	89.40%	81.20%	87.90%	84.30%	84.60%	86.30%	85.40%
Total	Count	113	170	173	178	169	190	993
	% Cohort	100%	100%	100%	100%	100%	100%	100%

Chi-Square Tests	Value	df	Asymp. Sig. (2-sided)
Pearson Chi-Square	5.102a	5	0.404
Likelihood Ratio	5.1	5	0.404
Linear-by-Linear Association	0.005	1	0.946
N of Valid Cases	993		

a. 0 cells (0%) have expected count less than 5. The minimum expected count is 16.5.

Table 52. Alumni affiliation- joined academy alumni association.

		1946-49	1950-54	1955-59	1960-64	1965-69	1970-76	Total
Yes	Count	66	100	105	132	110	129	642
	% Cohort	58.40%	58.80%	60.70%	74.20%	65.10%	67.90%	64.70%
No	Count	47	70	68	46	59	61	351
	% Cohort	41.60%	41.20%	39.30%	25.80%	34.90%	32.10%	35.30%
Total	Count	113	170	173	178	169	190	993
	% Cohort	100%	100%	100%	100%	100%	100%	100%

Chi-Square Tests	Value	df	Asymp. Sig. (2-sided)
Pearson Chi-Square	13.567a	5	0.019
Likelihood Ratio	13.822	5	0.017
Linear-by-Linear Association	5.99	1	0.014
N of Valid Cases	993		

a. 0 cells (0%) have expected count less than 5. The minimum expected count is 39.94.

Table 53. Alumni affiliation - returned for homecoming or class reunion.

		1946-49	1950-54	1955-59	1960-64	1965-69	1970-76	Total
Yes	Count	22	48	59	72	48	80	329
	% Cohort	19.50%	28.20%	34.10%	40.40%	28.40%	42.10%	33.10%
No	Count	91	122	114	106	121	110	664
	% Cohort	80.50%	71.80%	65.90%	59.60%	71.60%	57.90%	66.90%
Total	Count	113	170	173	178	169	190	993
	% Cohort	100%	100%	100%	100%	100%	100%	100%

Chi-Square Tests	Value	df	Asymp. Sig. (2-sided)
Pearson Chi-Square	24.349a	5	0
Likelihood Ratio	24.973	5	0
Linear-by-Linear Association	12.723	1	0
N of Valid Cases	993		

a. 0 cells (0%) have expected count less than 5. The minimum expected count is 37.44.

Table 54. Alumni affiliation- attended academy sporting event.

		1946-49	1950-54	1955-59	1960-64	1965-69	1970-76	Total
Yes	Count	61	85	87	102	78	105	518
	% Cohort	54.00%	50.00%	50.30%	57.30%	46.20%	55.30%	52.20%
No	Count	52	85	86	76	91	85	475
	% Cohort	46.00%	50.00%	49.70%	42.70%	53.80%	44.70%	47.80%
Total	Count	113	170	173	178	169	190	993
	% Cohort	100%	100%	100%	100%	100%	100%	100%

Chi-Square Tests	Value	df	Asymp. Sig. (2-sided)
Pearson Chi-Square	5.774a	5	0.329
Likelihood Ratio	5.782	5	0.328
Linear-by-Linear Association	0.054	1	0.816
N of Valid Cases	993		

a. 0 cells (0%) have expected count less than 5. The minimum expected count is 54.05.

Table 55. Alumni affiliation- attended alumni association chapter function.

		1946-49	1950-54	1955-59	1960-64	1965-69	1970-76	Total
Yes	Count	9	23	14	16	9	14	85
	% Cohort	8.00%	13.50%	8.10%	9.00%	5.30%	7.40%	8.60%
No	Count	104	147	159	162	160	176	908
	% Cohort	92.00%	86.50%	91.90%	91.00%	94.70%	92.60%	91.40%
Total	Count	113	170	173	178	169	190	993
	% Cohort	100%	100%	100%	100%	100%	100%	100%

Chi-Square Tests	Value	df	Asymp. Sig. (2-sided)
Pearson Chi-Square	8.108a	5	0.15
Likelihood Ratio	7.713	5	0.173
Linear-by-Linear Association	2.731	1	0.098
N of Valid Cases	993		

a. 0 cells (0%) have expected count less than 5. The minimum expected count is 9.67.

Table 56. Date of first affiliation- 5-10 years after graduation.

		1946-49	1950-54	1955-59	1960-64	1965-69	1970-76	Total
Yes	Count	15	30	16	19	12	22	114
	% Cohort	13.30%	17.60%	9.20%	10.70%	7.10%	11.60%	11.50%
No	Count	98	140	157	159	157	168	879
	% Cohort	86.70%	82.40%	90.80%	89.30%	92.90%	88.40%	88.50%
Total	Count	113	170	173	178	169	190	993
	% Cohort	100%	100%	100%	100%	100%	100%	100%

Chi-Square Tests	Value	df	Asymp. Sig. (2-sided)
Pearson Chi-Square	10.873a	5	0.054
Likelihood Ratio	10.572	5	0.061
Linear-by-Linear Association	3.316	1	0.069
N of Valid Cases	993		

a. 0 cells (0%) have expected count less than 5. The minimum expected count is 12.97.

Table 57. Date of first affiliation- 10-20 years after graduation.

		1946-49	1950-54	1955-59	1960-64	1965-69	1970-76	Total
Yes	Count	19	18	24	19	38	29	147
	% Cohort	16.80%	10.60%	13.90%	10.70%	22.50%	15.30%	14.80%
No	Count	94	152	149	159	131	161	846
	% Cohort	83.20%	89.40%	86.10%	89.30%	77.50%	84.70%	85.20%
Total	Count	113	170	173	178	169	190	993
	% Cohort	100%	100%	100%	100%	100%	100%	100%

Chi-Square Tests	Value	df	Asymp. Sig. (2-sided)
Pearson Chi-Square	13.221a	5	0.021
Likelihood Ratio	12.753	5	0.026
Linear-by-Linear Association	1.665	1	0.197
N of Valid Cases	993		

a. 0 cells (0%) have expected count less than 5. The minimum expected count is 16.73.

Table 58. Date of first affiliation- More than 20 years after graduation.

		1946-49	1950-54	1955-59	1960-64	1965-69	1970-76	Total
Yes	Count	16	27	22	15	11	6	97
	% Cohort	14.20%	15.90%	12.70%	8.40%	6.50%	3.20%	9.80%
No	Count	97	143	151	163	158	184	896
	% Cohort	85.80%	84.10%	87.30%	91.60%	93.50%	96.80%	90.20%
Total	Count	113	170	173	178	169	190	993
	% Cohort	100%	100%	100%	100%	100%	100%	100%

Chi-Square Tests	Value	df	Asymp. Sig. (2-sided)
Pearson Chi-Square	23.208a	5	0
Likelihood Ratio	25.083	5	0
Linear-by-Linear Association	21.349	1	0
N of Valid Cases	993		

a. 0 cells (0%) have expected count less than 5. The minimum expected count is 11.04.

Table 59. Date of first affiliation- never established any relationship.

		1946-49	1950-54	1955-59	1960-64	1965-69	1970-76	Total
Yes	Count	6	15	17	10	10	9	67
	% Cohort	5.30%	8.80%	9.80%	5.60%	5.90%	4.70%	6.70%
No	Count	107	155	156	168	159	181	926
	% Cohort	94.70%	91.20%	90.20%	94.40%	94.10%	95.30%	93.30%
Total	Count	113	170	173	178	169	190	993
	% Cohort	100%	100%	100%	100%	100%	100%	100%

Chi-Square Tests	Value	df	Asymp. Sig. (2-sided)
Pearson Chi-Square	5.909a	5	0.315
Likelihood Ratio	5.7	5	0.336
Linear-by-Linear Association	1.608	1	0.205
N of Valid Cases	993		

a. 0 cells (0%) have expected count less than 5. The minimum expected count is 7.62.

Table 60. Overall ranking of Naval Academy experience.

		1946-49	1950-54	1955-59	1960-64	1965-69	1970-76	Total
Most favorable (1)	Count	63	97	91	101	75	79	506
	% Cohort	56.30%	57.10%	52.60%	56.70%	44.40%	41.60%	51.00%
2	Count	37	50	65	50	67	72	341
	% Cohort	33.00%	29.40%	37.60%	28.10%	39.60%	37.90%	34.40%
3	Count	9	12	9	15	14	21	80
	% Cohort	8.00%	7.10%	5.20%	8.40%	8.30%	11.10%	8.10%
4	Count	1	4	4	7	6	9	31
	% Cohort	0.90%	2.40%	2.30%	3.90%	3.60%	4.70%	3.10%
Least favorable (5)	Count		2	2	3	3	9	19
	% Cohort		1.20%	1.20%	1.70%	1.80%	4.70%	1.90%
Other	Count	2	5	2	2	4		15
	% Cohort	1.80%	2.90%	1.20%	1.10%	2.40%		1.50%
Total	Count	112	170	173	178	169	190	992
	% Cohort	100%	100%	100%	100%	100%	100%	100%

Chi-Square Tests	Value	df	Asymp. Sig. (2-sided)
Pearson Chi-Square	39.827a	25	0.03
Likelihood Ratio	42.952	25	0.014
Linear-by-Linear Association	22.705	1	0
N of Valid Cases	992		

a. 13 cells (36.1%) have expected count less than 5. The minimum expected count is 1.69.

Table 61. Would you have attended another undergraduate institution?

		1946-49	1950-54	1955-59	1960-64	1965-69	1970-76	Total
Yes	Count	20	24	33	41	43	47	208
	% Cohort	17.70%	14.10%	19.10%	23.00%	25.40%	24.70%	20.90%
No	Count	93	146	140	137	126	143	785
	% Cohort	82.30%	85.90%	80.90%	77.00%	74.60%	75.30%	79.10%
Total	Count	113	170	173	178	169	190	993
	% Cohort	100%	100%	100%	100%	100%	100%	100%

Chi-Square Tests	Value	df	Asymp. Sig. (2-sided)
Pearson Chi-Square	10.054a	5	0.074
Likelihood Ratio	10.385	5	0.065
Linear-by-Linear Association	7.883	1	0.005
N of Valid Cases	993		

a. 0 cells have expected count less than 5. The minimum expected count is 23.67.

Table 62. Appointment motivation vs. economic class

		Family Economic Background					
		Lower class	Working class	Middle class	Upper Middle class	Upper class	Total
Free college education	Count	9	89	62	9		169
	% class	30.00%	30.30%	13.00%	5.30%		17.10%
Career Opportunities	Count	4	93	150	69	6	322
	% class	13.30%	31.60%	31.50%	40.40%	37.50%	32.60%
Patriotic or public service obligation	Count	4	31	79	31	4	149
	% class	13.30%	10.50%	16.60%	18.10%	25.00%	15.10%
Prestige of academy	Count	11	65	141	49	3	269
	% class	36.70%	22.10%	29.60%	28.70%	18.80%	27.30%
Other	Count	2	16	44	13	3	78
	% class	6.70%	5.40%	9.20%	7.60%	18.80%	7.90%
Total	Count	30	294	476	171	16	987
	% class	100%	100%	100%	100%	100%	100%

Chi-Square Tests	Value	df	Asymp. Sig. (2-sided)
Pearson Chi-Square	79.025a	16	0
Likelihood Ratio	82.029	16	0
Linear-by-Linear Association	22.062	1	0
N of Valid Cases	987		

a. 6 cells (24.0%) have expected count less than 5. The minimum expected count is 1.26.

Appendix: Survey of Student Life at the U.S. Naval Academy 1946–76

Dear Sir:

I am a Ph.D. student in military history at Ohio State University and a graduate of the Naval Academy (class of 1986). The questionnaire you received seeks information about your experiences and perceptions of the United States Naval Academy during your time there as a midshipman. The information gathered from it will be used in a doctoral dissertation about the post–World War II Naval Academy. During my studies at Ohio State, I noticed that this period in the Naval Academy's history has largely been overlooked by historians, something I considered unfortunate. The post–World War II era was an incredibly important period for the Naval Academy and its graduates. First of all, the school itself underwent many substantive changes during this time period. Secondly, academy alumni also figured prominently in many key events of the nation's history. Thus, it is important for historians to understand more about what was happening at the Naval Academy during this time frame.

During my research, I have found many sources that have described these changes from the perspective of the institution. I have also spoken with former faculty members, administration officials, and superintendents to get their view of the period. But I believe it is also important to look at these questions from the standpoint of the midshipmen themselves. Unfortunately, there are not as many sources available to understand what life was like within the Brigade of Midshipmen. Therefore, your participation plays a critical part in my research. My project examines the Naval Academy from the end of World War II through the Vietnam War. I have randomly distributed questionnaires to 3,000 graduates from the classes of 1946–76, each class being represented proportionately. The format of the questionnaire covers your entire experience at the Naval Academy from plebe year to graduation. I have also included questions about your reasons for coming to Annapolis and how your experiences at the Academy eventually affected your early naval career.

The questionnaire includes a mixture of close-ended and open-ended questions. Close-ended questions ask you to choose from a predetermined list of options. Such questions provide the easiest way of correlating information among a large survey population such as this. Open-ended questions provide more leeway for you to answer freely about your experiences. I have included those questions I considered most relevant but I would certainly not claim this questionnaire to be exhaustive. Thus, I encourage you to include any additional comments or information that you believe would be relevant to my research. In order to ensure your privacy, this questionnaire can be completed and returned anonymously. Each questionnaire does have a number on the first page. It is there simply to track the number of questionnaires sent out to particular classes not specific individuals. I have left a spot at the end of the questionnaire, however, for your name and address if you have important additional information. I want to thank you for your participation in this project. Although I stand to benefit personally from your involvement, your participation serves a larger goal of enriching our history of an important national institution.

Sincerely,
Todd Forney

Survey of Naval Academy Graduates from 1946–76

This survey inquires into the experiences and perceptions of life at the United States Naval Academy 1946–76 from the vantage point of midshipmen who graduated during this time. As part of this study, would you please fill out this short questionnaire pertaining to your experiences there. Thank you.

(Please circle one code number for each question unless otherwise specified.)

Section I.—This section asks several questions about your family background and your reasons for coming to the Naval Academy.

1) Which Naval Academy class did you graduate with? _____

2) How did you receive your appointment to the Naval Academy?

a) Congressional nomination
b) Presidential or Vice-Presidential nomination
c) Prior enlisted member of the armed forces
d) Father was Medal of Honor winner
e) other (please explain) _____

3) What region of the country did you consider home before coming to the Naval Academy?

a) Northeast/Middle Atlantic
b) Middle West
c) Southeast
d) Southwest
e) Far West
f) other (please explain) _____

4) What was your primary reason for accepting an appointment to the Naval Academy?

a) free college education
b) career opportunities in the naval service
c) patriotic/public service motivation
d) prestige of the Naval Academy as an institution
e) other (please explain) _____

5) Of the choices listed above, which least affected your decision to come to the Naval Academy? _____

6) Did your immediate family support your decision to enter the Naval Academy?

a) Yes
b) No (please explain) _____

7) Did your closest friends and peers support your decision?

a) Yes
b) No (please explain) _____

8) What was your religious preference, if any when you entered the Naval Academy?

a) Protestant
b) Catholic
c) Jewish
d) No religious preference
e) other (please explain) _____

9) Did your religious preference change during your time at the Naval Academy? If so, what did it become?

a) No
b) Protestant
c) Catholic
d) Jewish
e) No religious preference
f) other (please explain) _____

10) What did you consider your family's economic background to be?

a) lower class
b) working class
c) middle class
d) upper middle class
e) upper class

11) What race do you consider yourself? Are you . . .

a) White
b) Black
c) Hispanic
d) Asian
e) Something else (Specify) _____

12) Did you intend upon a military career (active service of twenty years or more) before you entered the Naval Academy?

a) Yes
b) No

13) Did this decision change during your time at the academy? If yes, please explain briefly what factors affected your decision.

a) Yes _____
b) No

Section II—The following questions have to deal with your experiences and attitudes towards the fourth class or plebe indoctrination system at the Naval Academy.

14) What part of your pre-Academy background prepared you best for the demands of plebe year?

a) competitive sports
b) involvement or leadership in school clubs or organizations
c) broad academic preparation
d) participation in JROTC or other para-military organizations
e) other _____

14a) How did these activities prepare you for the demands of plebe year?

15) Did information supplied by the Naval Academy adequately communicate what the nature and the demands of plebe year would be?

a) Yes
b) No

16) If you answered no to question 15, what do you believe surprised you the most about the plebe system? _____

17) What did you consider the most challenging aspect of the plebe indoctrination system to be?

18) What aspects, if any, of plebe indoctrination did you feel were counterproductive?

19) In what ways, if any, did plebe indoctrination prepare you for your service with the fleet?

20) To what degree, did the plebe system vary depending on the company or battalion a midshipman was assigned to?

a) Not at all
b) Slightly varied but basic nature still the same
c) Moderately varied with minor variations among companies or battalions
d) Widely varied with major variations between companies or battalions
e) Other (please explain) _____

21) If you chose (b), (c), (d), or (e), what do you believe accounted most for any inconsistencies? Please feel free to expand your answer in the space given below the four choices.

a) attitudes and experiences of upperclassman in the company
b) personality of the company officer
c) location of the company in Bancroft Hall
d) other _____

22) Please answer the following question using a scale of one to five, with one indicating no carry-over and five indicating the highest carry-over. To what degree did the reputation a midshipman acquired in his plebe year stick with him throughout his Academy career?

No carryover				Significant carryover
1	2	3	4	5

23) Did the academy strike an appropriate balance between the military demands seen in Bancroft Hall and the academic demands in the classroom?

a) Yes
b) No (Please explain how things could have been improved)
_____

Section III—**The following section includes a variety of general questions about life at the Academy, your relationship with classmates, members of the faculty and the Executive Department, etc.**

In which groups did you tend to forge the strongest relationships? Please rank the following groups from 1 to 5, with 1 being the strongest relationship and 5 being the weakest.

	strongest				weakest
classmates within your company	1	2	3	4	5
classmates in general	1	2	3	4	5
other midshipmen in your company	1	2	3	4	5
teammates on intramural/varsity sports	1	2	3	4	5
midshipmen in clubs or activities	1	2	3	4	5

24a) Were there any other groups in which midshipmen formed strong relationships?

25) Using a similar scale from 1 to 5, with 1 being the strongest and 5 being the weakest, please rank the following activities in forging unity among the members of your company?

	strongest				weakest
intramural sports program	1	2	3	4	5
Color Company competition	1	2	3	4	5
company tables in dining hall	1	2	3	4	5
common classes (if applicable)	1	2	3	4	5
professional development programs	1	2	3	4	5
tailgates/other social activities	1	2	3	4	5

25a) Were there any other activities that were important in forging unity within your company?

26) Did certain companies acquire distinct reputations within the Brigade?

a) Yes
b) No

26a) If yes, how did midshipmen throughout the Brigade become aware of these reputations?

27) Who tended to exercise the most day-to-day control over the Brigade of Midshipmen?

a) the Executive Department and Company Officers
b) the midshipmen striper organization
c) upperclassmen in the various companies
d) other (please explain) _____

28) What functions did company officers perform the best?

a) positive role model of what a professional junior officer should be
b) practical leadership and military training
c) maintaining good order and discipline within the company
d) encouraged high morale within the company
e) other (please explain) _____

29) What could the Executive Department (Bancroft Hall) and its officers have done to improve its relationship with the Brigade?

30) Did you feel the Executive Department was unduly harsh in enforcing academy regulations?

a) Yes (please answer question 31)
b) No (please go on to question 32)

31) Please rank the Executive Department's enforcement of regulations in the following areas (with 1 being excessively harsh and 5 being an appropriate level of discipline).

	unduly harsh				appropriate discipline
uniform appearance	1	2	3	4	5
room appearance	1	2	3	4	5
grooming standards	1	2	3	4	5
liberty infractions	1	2	3	4	5
discipline in the classroom	1	2	3	4	5

31a) Were there any other areas in which midshipmen tended to have an adversarial relationship with the Executive Department?

32) In what ways, if any, did your relationship with the Executive Department affect your outlook on the fleet and your naval career?

33) Please check which groups, if any, received preferential treatment while at the academy?

_____ members of varsity athletic teams
_____ members of certain minority groups
_____ midshipmen striper organization
_____ other (please explain)

33a) If yes, in what ways did members in that group receive special treatment?

34) Please rank the academic faculty in the following areas using a scale of 1 to 5, with 1 being the most favorable evaluation and 5 being the least favorable evaluation.

	most favorable				least favorable
scholastic ability	1	2	3	4	5
teaching ability	1	2	3	4	5
availability for extra instruction	1	2	3	4	5
appreciated demands in midshipmen's schedule	1	2	3	4	5

35) In what areas, could the academy have improved the education given to midshipmen?

36) Did your summer training adequately expose you to what life would be like in the fleet?

a) Yes
b) No

37) In what ways, if any, could the academy have prepared you better for your duties after graduation?

38) Did you perceive a large difference in the professional preparation you received at the academy with shipmates from other commissioning sources?

a) Yes
b) No

39) In what areas, did the Naval Academy provide you with a better professional background than contemporaries from other commissioning sources?

39a) In what areas, were these other officers just as adequately prepared as Naval Academy graduates?

40) Please rank the following factors that might have affected your choice of service selection from 1 to 5, with 1 being most important and 5 being least important.

	most				least
career opportunities after graduation	1	2	3	4	5
warfare specialty of your company officer	1	2	3	4	5
experience on summer training cruises	1	2	3	4	5
family history in particular warfare community	1	2	3	4	5
recruitment program sponsored by particular warfare community	1	2	3	4	5

40a) Were there any other factors that affected your choice of service selection?

40b) Did any specialty have a particularly good or bad reputation in the Brigade?

41) Did the academy attempt to direct midshipmen to any warfare community above the rest?

a) Yes
b) No

41a) If yes, how were those efforts received by you and your classmates?

APPENDIX 347

42) Which warfare community did you select at service selection? Please also indicate to the side whether that community was your preferred choice.

_____ surface warfare (unrestricted line)
_____ submarine
_____ surface warfare (nuclear)
_____ Navy pilot
_____ Naval Flight Officer
_____ Marine Corps
_____ Restricted line
_____ Other (Please specify)

43) Which academy traditions mattered the most to you?

43a) Which traditions mattered the least?

44) Please indicate where your order of merit placed you in your class?

_____ top 25% of your class
_____ middle 25–50% of your class
_____ between lower 50%–bottom 25% of your class
_____ bottom 25% of your class

45) Please indicate which of the following activities you participated in during your first five years after graduation?

_____ joined Academy Alumni Association
_____ returned to the Naval Academy for homecoming or class reunion
_____ attended Naval Academy sporting event
_____ attended Alumni Association chapter function in the area you were living

46) If you did not have any contact during those years, when did you first begin contact with either the Academy or organizations like the Alumni Association?

_____ 5–10 years after graduation
_____ 10–20 years after graduation
_____ more than 20 years after graduation
_____ never established any sort of relationship

47) On a scale from one to five, with 1 being the highest ranking and 5 the lowest, please rank your overall experience at the Naval Academy.

        1   2   3   4   5

48) Given what you know now, would you have considered a different institution for your undergraduate education?

a) No
b) Yes (Please explain) _____

This completes the general portion of the questionnaire. What follows are two short sections broken down by different groups of graduating classes. Answer the section applicable to your graduating class.

Section IV—This section asks specific questions for classes graduating between 1946–58. If you graduated between 1959–76, please begin with question 56 at the bottom of page 11.

49) Were most midshipmen aware of the controversy surrounding defense department reorganization? If so, how did it affect decisions about their Naval Academy career?

50) In what ways did the Navy's experience in World War II filter over into the Naval Academy?

51) How did the Academy try to make midshipmen aware of the Navy's contributions in World War II?

52) Did you perceive an unusual emphasis placed on naval aviation in your training and professional development at the Naval Academy?

a) No
b) Yes (please explain)

53) What factors led to the creation of the Honor Concept? How successful was its initial implementation?

54) In what ways, was the Air Force viewed as an attractive career choice by either you or your classmates?

55) How were you received or treated by society in your status as a midshipman?

Section V—This section asks specific questions for classes graduating between 1959–76.

56) How were academic reforms (i.e. validation program, majors program, Trident Scholar program) received by the Brigade of Midshipmen? Did they view these reforms as moving the academy in a positive or negative direction?

57) Do you feel the academic and professional demands were properly balanced at this time? Did professional demands impinge upon your ability to do your best work in the classroom?

58) In what ways did the Vietnam War affect life at the Naval Academy?

59) How did midshipmen respond to the criticism of the Naval Academy during the 1960s and 1970s?

60) In what ways, did you perceive a difference between yourself and friends attending civilian colleges?

61) Do you believe programs, like Admiral Calvert's "shadow command" system, increased the level of responsibility to the Brigade of Midshipmen?

62) The academy loosened many regulations (grooming standards, ending of mandatory chapel, more privileges, etc.) during Admiral Calvert's and Admiral

Mack's tenure as superintendent? In what ways were these reforms a positive experience for the Naval Academy? In what ways were these a negative experience?

63) How were you treated or received by society in your status as a midshipman?

This completes the formal portion of the questionnaire. I want to thank you again for your participation. Please feel free to use the remainder of the questionnaire for any additional comments or suggestions you might have.

Name (Optional): _____
Address/PhoneNumber: _____
(Optional)

Notes

INTRODUCTION

1. United States General Accounting Office Report to Congressional Committees, "DOD Service Academies—Comparison of Honor and Conduct Adjudicatory Processes," April 1995.

2. Criticism of the Naval Academy comes in various forms. Alumni have sometimes used their association's magazine, *Shipmate,* as a sounding board for changes they oppose at Annapolis. Debate of this kind has also spilled over into the Naval Institute's *Proceedings.* Occasionally, the Naval Academy has been the subject of fictional novels whose tone has criticized some direction the institution has taken. Perhaps the best example of this was 1968 alumnus James Webb's *A Sense of Honor.*

3. The best popular history of the Naval Academy is Jack Sweetman and Thomas Cutler, *The United States Naval Academy: An Illustrated History* (Annapolis: Naval Institute Press, 1995). J. Arthur Heise's *The Brass Factories: A Frank Appraisal of West Point, Annapolis, and the Air Force Academy* (Washington, D.C.: Public Affairs Press, 1969), and David Boroff's series on the service academies that appeared in *Harper's Magazine* (the article on Annapolis appeared in the January 1963 edition entitled "Teaching Young Sea Dogs Old Tricks") are within this vein of more narrowly focused commentary—in this case focused on the "academic revolution" of the 1960s.

4. For an overview of military professionalization see Samuel Huntington, *The Soldier and the State* (Cambridge: Harvard University Press, 1957); Allan Millett, *Military Professionalism and Officership in America* (Columbus: Mershon Center, 1977); and Charles Moskos, *The American Enlisted Man: The Rank and File in Today's Military* (New York: Russell Sage Foundation, 1970), and *Public Opinion and the Military Establishment* (Beverly Hills: Sage Publications, 1971).

5. Erving Goffman, *Asylums: Essays on the Social Situation of Mental Patients and Other Inmates* (Chicago: Aldine University Press, 1961).

6. Rear Admiral Holloway's analysis of the Holloway Plan can be found in "The Holloway Plan—A Summary View and Commentary," in *Report of the Board of Visitors of the United States Naval Academy, 1948.* All of the reports from the Board of Visitors can be found at the Naval Academy Archives, Nimitz Library, Annapolis, Maryland.

7. Todd Forney, "Charting Institutional Change: The United States Naval Academy during the 1960s," in *New Interpretations in Naval History: Selected Papers from the Thirteenth Naval History Symposium,* (Annapolis: Naval Institute Press, 1998).

8. For insight into the relationship between regular and reserve officers during World War II, see "Why Not a Navy Gray Line?," *Shipmate,* January 1946; and "A Reserve Looks at Regulars," *Shipmate,* July 1946.

9. The best overview of the Sputnik education crisis is Barbara Barksdale Clowse, *Brainpower for the Cold War: The Sputnik Crisis and National Defense Education Act of*

1958 (Westport, CT: Greenwood Press, 1981). For criticism of the academy's educational program, see Admiral Hyman Rickover's report to Congress in U.S. Congress, House, Committee on Appropriations, *Educational System at the Service Academies,* 18 August 1959 (Washington, D.C.: Government Printing Office, 1959).

10. For an overview of events leading up to the "academic revolution," see Charles Sheppard, "An Analysis of Curriculum Changes at the United States Naval Academy during the Period 1959 through 1974" (Ph.D. diss., George Washington University, 1974).

11. For an analysis of the issues regarding the structure of officer education and the role of the service academies during this period, see William Simons, *Liberal Education in the Service Academies* (New York: Teacher's College, Columbia University, 1965); John Masland and Lawrence Radway, *Soldiers and Scholars: Military Education and National Policy* (Princeton: Princeton University Press, 1957); and Allan Millett, *The American Political System and Civilian Control of the Military: A Historical Perspective* (Columbus: Mershon Center, 1979).

12. John Lovell's *Neither Athens Nor Sparta?* (Bloomington: Indiana University Press, 1979) provides a comparative analysis of the development of the service academies and the problems each faced during the 1960s and 1970s.

13. James Webb's *A Sense of Honor* (New York: Prentice-Hall, 1981) is a fictional account—largely based on his own experiences as a midshipmen in the class of 1968—of the Naval Academy during the height of the Vietnam War. For how this period affected the Naval Academy, see Robert Timberg's *A Nightingale's Song* (New York: Simon and Schuster, 1995).

14. "They Do Not Speak Our Language," Special Collections Division, USNA archives, Folder-Language.

15. "Survey of Student Life at the U.S. Naval Academy 1946–76," Table 3 "What was your primary reason for accepting an appointment?," Table 9 "What did you consider your family's economic background to be?," and Table 11 "Did you intend upon a military career before you entered the academy?"

16. "Old Navy Line," *The Log,* 9 February 1945.

17. "Old Navy Line," *The Log,* 1 December 1944.

18. "Survey of Midshipmen Life at the U.S. Naval Academy 1946–76," summary of observations from question 17: "What did you consider the most challenging aspect of plebe indoctrination to be?"

19. Ibid.

20. "Survey of Midshipmen Life at the U.S. Naval Academy 1946–76," summary of observations from question 19: "How did plebe indoctrination prepare you for service with the fleet?"

21. Ibid.

22. "Survey of Midshipmen Life at the U.S. Naval Academy 1946–76," summary of observations from question 18: "What aspects of plebe indoctrination were counterproductive?"

23. Memory work for plebes could often splinter off into directions that had nothing to do with the academy but did satisfy the curiosity of their particular upperclassmen. During the war, plebes were often ordered to commit to memory the names of all the Japanese cruisers. And if they accomplished that task, they were to proceed next with learning all the Japanese destroyers. "Salty Sam," *The Log,* 9 February 1945 reported some of the information being required of plebes. One individual had to find out the name for a grasshopper's upper jaw. Another plebe was expected to know the song and verse of the Cuban National Anthem for a parade in honor of the Cuban president-elect. Finally, after guessing wrong as to the political office held by Harold Ickes, a plebe was punished by being forced to memorize the names of all the circuit judges of the Eastern Shore of Maryland.

24. "Survey of Midshipmen Life at the U.S. Naval Academy 1946–76," summary of observations from question 19: "How did plebe indoctrination prepare you for service with the fleet?"

25. "A Message to '50," *The Log,* 11 October 1946.

26. "Salty Sam," *The Log,* 23 January 1948. Plebes were generally held to higher standard in terms of their uniform and room appearance. In this case, an upperclassman was allowed to slide by with a uniform that no longer fit him. Such a case would have been a punishable offense for a plebe.

27. "Survey of Midshipmen Life at the U.S. Naval Academy 1946–76," summary of observations from question 17: "What did you consider the most challenging aspect of plebe indoctrination to be?"

28. Ibid.

29. "Survey of Midshipmen Life at the U.S. Naval Academy 1946–76," summary of observations from question 19: "How did plebe indoctrination prepare you for service with the fleet?"

30. Ibid.

31. Plebes generally learned about Bancroft Hall through *Reef Points*—an academy publication known as the "plebe's bible" because it contained all the information they were responsible for committing to memory each year.

32. Masland and Radway, *Soldiers and Scholars.*

33. "The Dope Sheet," *The Log,* 6 October 1944.

34. Midshipmen Administrative Conduct System detailed the regulations midshipmen were required to follow and the consequences for not doing so. USNA archives, Nimitz Library, Annapolis, MD.

35. "Salty Sam," *The Log,* 5 December 1947, talked about the pressure of living with random inspections by the executive department.

36. Goffman, *Asylums,* xiii.

37. "The Dark Ages," *The Log,* 1 February 1946; "Dragging thru the Ages," *The Log,* 2 May 1947; "Dragging thru the Ages," *The Log,* 19 April 1946.

38. *The Log,* 6 October 1944.

39. *The Lucky Bag 1947* has an excellent picture of a midshipman going over the wall in its introduction.

40. *The Lucky Bag 1947,* 194 gives a good description of how confusing induction day can be.

41. Goffman, *Asylums,* 50–55.

42. Historians have much work to do in understanding the plebe system as well as the indoctrination process throughout the American military. The value of many traditions and practices has often been assumed instead of substantiated by hard evidence. In some cases, this had led to tragedy. James Webb's *A Sense of Honor* is a fictional account of a plebe year at Annapolis in the late 1960s. An excellent study of the 1956 Ribbon Creek incident in which six Marine recruits died during a forced march to teach them discipline is John Stevens's *Court-Martial at Parris Island: The Ribbon Creek Incident* (Annapolis: Naval Institute Press, 1999).

43. Goffman, *Asylums,* 14.

44. Goffman, *Asylums,* 22 describes this as common at many such institutions.

45. *The Lucky Bag 1949,* "The Brigade was Waiting," 384–85.

46. "Survey of Midshipmen Life at the U.S. Naval Academy 1946–76," summary of observations for question 17: "What did you consider the most challenging aspect of plebe indoctrination to be?"

47. "Salty Sam," *The Log,* 10 October 1947 talks about how intimidating the first meal

after the return of the upperclassmen could be for plebes. Salty encouraged plebes that what's in store for them "won't hurt a bit, hardly."

48. "Survey of Midshipmen Life at the U.S. Naval Academy 1946–76," summary of observations for question 17: "What did you consider the most challenging aspect of plebe indoctrination to be?"

49. "Salty Sam," *The Log,* 5 February 1945.

50. See Sweetman and Cutler, *The United States Naval Academy,* for brief biographies of most academy superintendents.

51. Efforts by superintendents to upgrade the priority of the academy with regard to staffing are a topic often reflected in the annual reports to the *Board of Visitors of the United States Naval Academy.*

52. "Survey of Student Life at the U.S. Naval Academy 1946–76," Table 16 "What accounted most for any variations in the plebe system?"

53. For a discussion of this problem see *Reminiscences of RADM Draper Kauffmann* and *Reminiscences of VADM William Mack.*

54. "Salty Sam," *The Log,* 6 October 1944. Salty reported that officers had taken up using binoculars and walkie-talkies to locate and intercept midshipmen that were in the process of committing conduct violations.

55. "Survey of Student Life at the U.S. Naval Academy 1946–76," summary of observations for question 29: "How could the Executive Department have improved its relationship with the Brigade?"

56. "Salty Sam," *The Log,* 17 November 1944 and 23 January 1948.

57. "Salty Sam," *The Log,* 24 October 1947.

58. The character development of midshipmen has long been an important priority of the academy. The institution talks about this in its catalogs, reports of the superintendent, accreditation reports, etc. For example, see the comments of Captain Stuart Ingersoll, Commandant of Midshipmen in "To the Brigade," *The Log,* 20 April 1945.

59. "Survey of Student Life at the U.S. Naval Academy 1946–76," summary of observations for question 32: "What effect did the Executive Department have on your outlook on the fleet?"

60. "Salty Sam," *The Log,* 6 October 1944.

61. "Survey of Student Life at the U.S. Naval Academy 1946–76," summary of observations for question 29: "How could the Executive Department have improved its relationship with the Brigade?"; "Salty Sam," *The Log,* 6 October 1944.

62. "Salty Sam," *The Log,* 3 May 1946.

63. "Salty Sam," *The Log,* 18 January 1946.

64. "Survey of Student Life at the U.S. Naval Academy 1946–76," summary of observations for question 32: "What effect did the Executive Department have on your outlook on the fleet?"

65. "Salty Sam," *The Log,* 16 April 1948. Salty reported an incident where a commander not assigned to the Executive Department broke into his old room as a midshipman to retrieve contraband he had hidden there while at the academy. Incidents like these seemed to confirm for midshipman this whole idea of "cops and robbers." Many rules seemed to apply only to them because they were midshipmen.

66. Goffman, *Asylums,* 7.

67. Ibid., 79.

68. Various academy superintendents reiterated this point to organizations like the Board of Visitors in their annual reports.

69. Goffman, *Asylums,* 85.

70. Ibid., 96–99.

71. Ibid., 81.

72. "Salty Sam," *The Log,* 17 November 1944 used the adage "when the cat's away, the mice will play" to describe how midshipmen worked around the Executive Department's efforts to control them.

73. For an overview of issues related to student attrition see Office of the Super intendent—VADM James Calvert, Reference Files—box 3, folder 2 "Midshipmen Attrition Statistics, 1959–67, 1970–71"; box 3, folder 18 "Midshipmen Recruiting Letters"; and box 3 folder 19 "Midshipmen/Resignations Voluntary 1970–71," U.S. Naval Academy Archives, Nimitz Library, Annapolis, MD.

74. For an overview of the issues related to questionnaire design and survey polling, see Seymour Sudman and Norman Bradburn, *Asking Questions: A Practical Guide to Questionnaire Design* (San Francisco, Jossey-Bass, 1982); and Herbert Asher, *Polling and the Public: What Every Citizen Should Know* (Washington, D.C.: Congressional Quarterly Press, 1995).

75. "Survey of Midshipmen Life at the U.S. Naval Academy 1946–76," Tables 48–51.

76. Clifford Geertz, *The Interpretation of Cultures* (New York: Basic Books, 1973), 11.

77. For overview of the importance of military history and traditions to professional socialization, see Allan Millett, "The Study of Military History in the United States since World War II," in *Medelingen van de Sectie Militaire Geschiedenis* (The Hague, 1991); and "American Military History: Clio and Mars as 'Pards,'" in *Military History and the Military Profession,* ed. David Charters, Marc Milner, and J. Brent Wilson (Westport, CT: Praeger, 1992), 3–22.

78. "Old Navy Line," *The Log,* 20 April 1945.

79. "Survey of Student Life at the U.S. Naval Academy 1946–76," Table 60 "Overall ranking of Naval Academy experience," and Table 61 "Would you have attended another undergraduate institution?"

Chapter 1. The Naval Academy of the 1940s

1. The superintendent's reports to the Board of Visitors are indispensable in understanding World War II's effect on the Naval Academy. *The Log* and *The Lucky Bag* give a good glimpse of what concerned midshipmen at this time. The best secondary source on this period is Sweetman and Cutler's chapter "Men of Annapolis" in *The U.S. Naval Academy: An Illustrated History.*

2. For an analysis of officer education in the postwar era see Masland and Radway, *Soldiers and Scholars;* and Lovell, *Neither Athens Nor Sparta?*

3. For a summary of these changes, see *Superintendent's Statement to the Board of Visitors 1950.* Admiral Holloway frequently used the comparison of USNA to MIT in pushing for postwar academic reforms.

4. See "Class Policy of 1948B" and "The Superintendent's Open Letter to the First Class," in *Superintendent's Statement to the Board of Visitors 1950* and *Shipmate,* December 1947.

5. For the growing influence of naval aviation see Clark G. Reynolds, *Admiral John H. Towers: The Struggle for Naval Air Supremacy* (Annapolis: Naval Institute Press, 1991); and *The Fast Carriers: The Forging of an Air Navy* (New York: McGraw-Hill, 1968); Naval Institute Press, reprint 1992.

6. "Survey of Student Life at the U.S. Naval Academy 1946–76," Table 1 " How did you receive your appointment?"; and survey done on incoming plebe class by *The Log,* 6 October 1944 talk about changing demographics of the Brigade.

7. "Survey of Student Life at the U.S. Naval Academy 1946–76," Table 1 " How did

you receive your appointment?"; and survey done on incoming plebe class by *The Log,* 6 October 1944 talk about changing demographics of the Brigade.

8. See Sweetman and Cutler, *The U.S. Naval Academy,* for an overview of the pre–World War II academy.

9. *Reminiscences of Vice Admiral William Mack,* March 1980, U.S. Naval Institute Oral History Program, Naval Academy Archives, Annapolis, Maryland.

10. *Reminiscences of Vice Admiral William Smedberg III,* July 1979, U.S. Naval Institute Oral History Program, Naval Academy Archives, Annapolis, Maryland.

11. *Statement before the Board of Visitors of the Superintendent of the United States Naval Academy, Rear Admiral D. F. Sellars 1937,* Naval Academy Archives, Annapolis, Maryland.

12. Admiral Sellars made reference to this article in his remarks in *Statement Before The Board of Visitors 1937.* The article in question was a scathing attack on the educational system at Annapolis. While not addressing the merits of the author's argument specifically, the superintendent cautioned that this graduate, just like Dr. Angell, had little understanding of the academy's professional mission since he had never accepted a commission with the fleet.

13. John Brubacher and Willis Rudy, *Higher Education in Transition: A History of American Colleges and Universities, 1636–1976* (New York: Harper and Row,1976).

14. *Statement before the Board of Visitors 1937.* The same emphasis can be found in Admiral Sellars's other statements to the Board of Visitors in 1935 and 1936.

15. Ibid.

16. *Statement before the Board of Visitors of the Superintendent of the U.S. Naval Academy, Rear Admiral D .F. Sellars 1936.*

17. *Reminiscences of Vice Admiral William Mack.*

18. *Reminiscences of Hanson W. Baldwin,* 1976, U.S. Naval Institute Oral History Program, Naval Academy Archives, Annapolis, Maryland.

19. "Survey of Midshipmen Life at the U.S. Naval Academy 1946–76," summary of observations from question 19: "How did plebe indoctrination prepare you for service with the fleet?"

20. *Reminiscences of Hanson W. Baldwin,* 1976, U.S. Naval Institute Oral History Program, Naval Academy Archives, Annapolis, Maryland.

21. See either Masland and Radway, *Soldiers and Scholars,* or Lovell, *Neither Athens Nor Sparta?*

22. From this body of men come the following biographies, *The Lucky Bag 1948A* and "Survey of Student Life at the U.S. Naval Academy 1946–76," question 40: "Were there any other factors that affected your choice of service selection?"

23. Survey participants talked about the lottery process in their responses to question 40. The lottery method became a subject of some controversy in the early 1950s when midshipmen were still required to go to sea first before choosing either navy air or submarines. See "Salty Sam," *The Log,* 27 January 1950 and 3 March 1950 for a discussion of how the lottery worked.

24. "Salty Sam," *The Log,* 27 January 1950 and 3 March 1950.

25. "Survey of Midshipmen Life at the U.S. Naval Academy 1946–76," Table 3 "What was your primary reason for accepting an appointment?," and Table 9 "What did you consider your family's economic background to be?"

26. *Reminiscences of Vice Admiral William Mack;* and "Survey of Midshipmen Life at the U.S. Naval Academy 1946–76," Table 5 "Did your immediate family support your decision to come to the academy?," and Table 11 "Did you intend upon a military career before you entered the academy?"

27. *Statement Submitted to the Board of Visitors by the Superintendent of the U.S. Naval Academy, Rear Admiral Russell Wilson, 1941.*
28. Ibid.
29. "Salty Sam," *The Log,* 31 May 1946 and "Salty Sam," *The Log,* 2 May 1947.
30. *Superintendent's Statement to the Board of Visitors 1942;* and *Superintendent's Statement to the Board of Visitors, Rear Admiral John R. Beardall, 1943.*
31. "Survey of Midshipmen Life at the U.S. Naval Academy 1946–76," summary of observations for question 50: "In what ways did the Navy's experience in World War II filter over into the Naval Academy?"
32. *Superintendent's Statement to the Board of Visitors 1941;* and *Superintendent's Statement to the Board of Visitors 1942.*
33. *Superintendent's Statement to the Board of Visitors 1941;* and *Superintendent's Statement to the Board of Visitors 1942.*
34. Sweetman and Cutler, *The U.S. Naval Academy;* and Office of the Superintendent, Vice Admiral James Calvert, Reference Files, box 2, folder 7, "Faculty," Naval Academy Archives, Annapolis, Maryland.
35. "Survey of Student Life at the U.S. Naval Academy 1946–76," Table 18 "Did the academy strike an appropriate balance between academics and Bancroft Hall?"
36. *Statement of the Superintendent to the Board of Visitors 1942.*
37. Ibid.
38. During Rear Admiral Draper Kauffman's tenure as superintendent in the early 1960s, there was a turn back controversy involving a son of a former superintendent who had received an additional chance such as this.
39. Office of the Superintendent, Vice Admiral James Calvert, Reference Files, box 3, folder 2, "Midshipmen Attrition Statistics 1959–67, 1970–71," Naval Academy Archives, Annapolis, Maryland.
40. *Superintendent's Statement to the Board of Visitors 1941;* and *Superintendent's Statement to the Board of Visitors 1942.*
41. *Superintendent's Statement to the Board of Visitors 1943;* and *Superintendent's Statement to the Board of Visitors 1944.*
42. "Old Navy Line," *The Log,* 3 November 1944: "And it did come to pass that the power-that-be did come together, did decree that there was to be a *cruise.*" Note the italics as a sign of emphasis or disbelief.
43. *Superintendent's Statement to the Board of Visitors 1942;* and *Superintendent's Statement to the Board of Visitors 1943.*
44. "Survey of Student Life at the U.S. Naval Academy 1946–76," summary of observations to question 36: "Did your summer training adequately expose you to what life would be like in the fleet?"
45. "Salty Sam," *The Log,* 5 November 1948. Youngster cruise was also a midshipman's first extended break from the academy after plebe year. As such, it was not uncommon for some youngsters to get into some minor troubles in the fleet (missing ship's movement, oversleeping and missing watch, pulling some "cops and robbers" pranks on the ship's company). This sort of chicanery was expected of youngsters and an important part of that experience.
46. "Salty Sam," *The Log,* 11 October 1946 talks about the return of the normal cruise schedule and its importance to building professional character, "a man isn't a man till he's had a youngster cruise."
47. *Statement Submitted to the Board of Visitors by the Superintendent of the U.S. Naval Academy, Vice Admiral Aubrey W. Fitch 1946,* talks about the resumption of the normal cruise schedule.

48. "Survey of Midshipmen Life at the U.S. Naval Academy 1946–76," summary of observations for question 29: "What could the Executive Department and its officers have done to improve its relationship with the Brigade?"

49. "Salty Sam," *The Log,* 17 May 1946. Notorious watch officers became immortalized in this column for their exploits on duty. Midshipmen made it a point to see which officer had the watch because this gave them a good clue of how difficult the watch inspection might be, which regulations would be emphasized that day, and so forth.

50. *Superintendent's Statement to the Board of Visitors 1941;* and *Superintendent's Statement to the Board of Visitors 1942.*

51. In each annual report issued during the war, the academy's superintendent proudly announced that the current graduating class had become the largest in Naval Academy history.

52. "Survey of Midshipmen Life at the U.S. Naval Academy 1946–76," Table 32 "What functions did company officers perform best?"

53. *Superintendent's Statement to the Board of Visitors 1942;* and *Superintendent's Statement to the Board of Visitors 1943.*

54. "Class Policy of 1948B," *Report of the Board of Visitors 1948.* Admiral Holloway ordered that the policy carry the weight as other academy regulations, an important step to break away from what had happened during the war.

55. *Superintendent's Statement to the Board of Visitors 1946.*

56. "Survey of Midshipmen Life at the U.S. Naval Academy 1946–76," summary of observations to question 51: "How did the academy make midshipmen aware of the Navy's contributions in World War II?"

57. "Survey of Midshipmen Life at the U.S. Naval Academy 1946–76," Table 32 "What functions did company officers perform best?" and summary of observations to question 50: "In what ways, did the Navy's experience in World War II filter over into the Naval Academy?"

58. Reynold's *The Fast Carriers* is the best source on the expanded influence of naval aviation on the service culture of the post–World War II Navy.

59. "Wings of Gold," *The Log,* 15 February 1946.

60. *Superintendent's Statement to the Board of Visitors 1942.*

61. "Annapolis Looks to the Skies," *The Log,* 1 March 1946.

62. *Superintendent's Statement to the Board of Visitors 1946.*

63. *Reminiscences of Vice Admiral William Smedberg.*

64. "Annapolis Looks to the Skies."

65. "Midshipmen Get Air Training," *Shipmate,* February 1946; "Dunking Drills Prepare Midshipmen for Possible Emergency Plane Crashes," *Shipmate,* June 1948; and "Air Cruises and Summer Training," *Shipmate,* August–September 1949.

66. Gregory Mann, "The Relationship Between Athletic Participation and Non-Academic Adjustment at the U.S. Naval Academy" (Ph.D. dissertation, University of Maryland, 1957); and *Superintendent's Statement to the Board of Visitors 1942.*

67. "Survey of Midshipmen Life at the U.S. Naval Academy 1946–76," summary of observations for question 32: "In what ways, did the Executive Department affect your outlook on the fleet and your naval career?," and question 40b: "Did any warfare specialty have a particularly good or bad reputation in the Brigade?"

68. "Survey of Midshipmen Life at the U.S. Naval Academy 1946–76," summary of observations to question 52: "Did you perceive an unusual emphasis placed on naval aviation in your training and professional development at the Naval Academy?"

69. The lottery method became a subject of some controversy in the early 1950s when midshipmen were still required to go to sea first before choosing either navy air or sub-

marines. See "Salty Sam," *The Log,* 27 January 1950 and 3 March 1950 for a discussion of how the lottery worked.

70. "Enterprise Bell," *Shipmate,* June 1951.

71. *Statement to the Board of Visitors Submitted by the Superintendent of the U.S. Naval Academy, Rear Admiral James Holloway, April 1951.*

72. "Survey of Student Life at the U.S. Naval Academy 1946–76," summary of observations to question 51: "How did the academy make midshipmen aware of the Navy's contributions in World War II?"

73. "Memorial Plaques for Medal of Honor Winners," *Shipmate,* September 1950.

74. As an example see Admiral Chester Nimitz's commencement address to the class of 1947 contained in "Graduation Address by Fleet Admiral Nimitz," *Shipmate,* July 1946.

75. *Superintendent's Statement to the Board of Visitors 1944;* and *Superintendent's Statement to the Board of Visitors 1946.*

76. These ideas had circulated for some time. For a discussion of these proposals see "A West Coast Naval Academy?," *The Evening Capital,* 6 February 1941, Annapolis, Maryland.

77. A summary of the Holloway Plan is included as an appendix to the *Report of the Board of Visitors of the U.S. Naval Academy 1948* entitled "The Holloway Plan—A Summary View and Commentary." See also how the plan was presented to academy alumni in "The Holloway Plan," *Naval Institute Proceedings,* November 1948.

78. "The Holloway Plan," *Naval Institute Proceedings,* November 1948.

79. "Survey of Midshipmen Life at the U.S. Naval Academy 1946–76," Table 12 "Did this decision change while you were at the academy?"

80. "Survey of Midshipmen Life at the U.S. Naval Academy 1946–76," Table 3 "What was your primary reason for accepting an appointment?"

81. Opponents of the Holloway Plan contended that the emphasis on educational benefits was a critical flaw. Instead of attracting midshipmen who had a love of the Navy, the Holloway Plan appealed to those who had a more shallow commitment to the service. For a later critique of the Holloway Plan see "Demise of a Dream—Why the Holloway Plan Failed," *Shipmate,* January 1958.

82. Russell Weigley, *History of the United States Army* (New York: MacMillan Press, 1987).

83. "Salty Sam," *The Log,* 12 January 1945.

84. "The Plebe Goes Home," *The Log,* 18 January 1946.

85. *The Log,* 26 March 1947.

86. See Masland and Radway, *Soldiers and Scholars;* Lovell, *Neither Athens Nor Sparta?;* and Charles Sheppard, "An Analysis of Curricular Changes at the United States Naval Academy" (Ph.D. dissertation, George Washington University, 1974).

87. *Reminiscences of Vice Admiral William Smedberg III.*

88. *U.S. Naval Academy Report to the Middle States Association and Evaluation Report 26 November 1946.*

89. "Bachelor of Science Degree for Graduates of the Naval Academy," *Shipmate,* December 1947.

90. "An overview of curricular reforms can be seen in "Bachelor of Science Degree for Graduates of the Naval Academy" and "USNA—1948 Model," *Shipmate,* November 1948.

91. "Bachelor of Science Degree for Graduates of the Naval Academy" and "USNA—1948 Model," *Shipmate,* November 1948.

92. The change in tone at the academy can be seen from several sources. See "USNA—1947 Model," *Shipmate,* August 1947; and "An Open Letter to the First Class from the

Superintendent of the U.S. Naval Academy," *Shipmate,* December 1947, which detailed the new privileges and responsibilities.

93. *The Lucky Bag 1948B* paid tribute to Holloway's many accomplishments at the academy: "We will remember Admiral Holloway and his administration of the Naval Academy as a pleasing personal experience. The great good his planning will do for the professional officer will seem even more great to us . . . we will carry away from the academy a greater store of liberal knowledge . . . throughout our naval careers we will feel his influcnce."

94. "A Message to '50," *The Log,* 11 October 1946.

95. *The Log,* 3 November 1944 spotlighted the Bull Department (English, History and Government). The article suggested that this department was extremely popular with midshipmen because it never ordered a show of slide rules, meaning that it treated them as students first and did not use the classroom to reinforce standards of military behavior.

96. "Salty Sam," *The Log,* 19 November 1948.

97. "Salty Sam," *The Log,* 7 January 1949 talks about the dope system.

98. For a look at the academic climate see "Salty Sam," *The Log,* 1 February 1946 and 19 November 1948.

99. "Salty Sam," *The Log,* 3 November 1944.

100. "The Ballad of Slashin' Gish," *The Log,* 19 November 1948.

101. "Salty Sam," *The Log,* 19 November 1948 and 7 January 1949.

102. For a discussion of the academy's retention problems, see "Crossroads of the Navy," *Shipmate,* November 1947; "I Gave Up The Ship," *Shipmate,* January 1949; "President's Page," *Shipmate,* January 1949; and "Career Men," *Shipmate,* November 1949.

103. David Kennedy, *Freedom from Fear: The American People in Depression and War* (New York: Oxford University Press, 1999).

104. "Survey of Student Life at the U.S. Naval Academy 1946–76," Table 5 "Did your immediate family support your decision to come to the academy?"

105. "Survey of Midshipmen Life at the U.S. Naval Academy 1946–76," Table 6 "Did closest friends and peers support your decision?"

106. "Salty Sam," *The Log,* 7 December 1945. Midshipmen fretted that if their financial status did not improve they would be carrying a two-year debt with them into the fleet by graduation.

107. Congress eventually tied midshipmen salary increases to those of the fleet. Midshipmen were to be compensated at one-half the monthly salary of an ensign, whatever that sum might be. Although talked about since the end of the war, the plan stalled in Congress until 1956.

108. Memorandum from Commandant of Midshipmen to the Superintendent of the Naval Academy, 12 June 1945, subject—Superintendent's Annual Report for 1945, Office of the Superintendent, General Correspondence, Historical Matters 1845–1959, box 3, folder 5, Naval Academy Archives, Nimitz Library, Annapolis, Maryland.

109. "Letter of the Superintendent to Parents and Guardians of Midshipmen," June 1942, Vertical File—United States Naval Academy, Special Collections Division, Nimitz Library, Annapolis, Maryland.

110. "Salty Sam," *The Log,* 5 November 1948 and *The Log,* 7 February 1949 talked about how the additional expenses were causing them to fall into debt.

111. *Superintendent's Statement to the Board of Visitors 1946.*

112. *Superintendent's Statement to the Board of Visitors 1942;* and *Superintendent's Statement to the Board of Visitors 1943.*

113. "USNA 1947 Model," *Shipmate,* August 1947 talked about the most pressing needs of the academy.

114. Renovation of the academy's physical plant was a pressing issue in all of the superintendents' reports until the late 1950s.

115. "Salty Sam," *The Log*, 7 January 1949 and *The Log*, 21 January 1949 talked about how difficult the Maury Hall plan was to put into practice.

116. See especially *Superintendent's Statement to the Board of Visitors 1946;* and *Superintendent's Statement to the Board of Visitors 1951.*

117. Letter from the Head of the Department of Physical Training to the Superintendent of the Naval Academy, 30 June 1945, Office of the Superintendent, General Correspondence, Historical Matters 1845–1959, box 3, folder 5.

118. "Survey of Midshipmen Life at the U.S. Naval Academy 1946–76," Table 1 "How did you receive your appointment?"

119. *Shipmate*, December 1947.

120. "Survey of Midshipmen Life at the U.S. Naval Academy 1946–76," Table 9 "What did you consider your family's economic background to be?"

121. Peter Karsten, *The Naval Aristocracy* (New York: The Free Press, 1972).

122. "Survey of Midshipmen Life at the U.S. Naval Academy 1946–76," Table 7 "What was your religious preference when you entered the academy?"; and John Fitzgerald, "Changing Patterns of Officer Recruitment at the U.S. Naval Academy," *Armed Forces and Society* 8, no. 1 (fall 1981): 111–28.

123. "Survey of Midshipmen Life at the U.S. Naval Academy 1946–76," Table 7 "What was your religious preference when you entered the academy?"; and Vertical File, Religious Life of Midshipmen, Special Collections Division, Nimitz Library, Annapolis, MD.

124. James Patterson, *Grand Expectations: The United States, 1945–74* (New York: Oxford University Press, 1996).

125. Sweetman and Cutler, *The United States Naval Academy.* See the cartoon in *The Log*, 24 October 1946 as one example.

126. "Survey of Midshipmen Life at the U.S. Naval Academy 1946–76," Table 3 "What was your primary reason for accepting an appointment?"

127. "Survey of Midshipmen Life at the U.S. Naval Academy 1946–76," Table 62 "Reasons for appointment vs. economic class."

128. Ibid.

129. "Survey of Midshipmen Life at the U.S. Naval Academy 1946–76," Table 11 "Did you intend on a military career before you entered the academy?"; "Crossroads of the Navy," *Shipmate*, November 1947; "I Gave Up The Ship," *Shipmate*, January 1949; and "Career Men," *Shipmate*, November 1949.

130. "Unification vs. Merger," *Shipmate*, January 1946; "Can the Navy Ever Be Obsolete?," *Shipmate*, February 1946; and "Unification—A Blessing or a Curse?," *Shipmate*, November 1949.

131. "Survey of Midshipmen Life at the U.S. Naval Academy 1946–76," summary of observations to question 17: "What did you consider the most challenging aspect of plebe indoctrination to be?"

132. "Salty Sam," *The Log*, 5 February 1945; and *The Log*, 5 December 1947 talked about the demands of plebe year.

133. "Salty Sam," *The Log*, 7 January 1949; and *The Log*, 30 April 1948 talked about battles with the Executive Department.

134. "Salty Sam," *The Log*, 17 November 1944; and *The Log*, 1 December 1944 talked about how the game of "cops and robbers" was played and the punishments for being caught.

135. Goffman, *Asylums.*

136. *The Lucky Bag 1947.*

Chapter 2. The Naval Academy of the 1950s

1. "Salty Sam," *The Log,* 9 November 1951; *Superintendent's Statement to the Board of Visitors 1956; Superintendent's Statement to the Board of Visitors 1954.*
2. "Salty Sam," *The Log,* 21 December 1951, The academy was referred to as an "old dump."
3. "What can you expect in 15 years?," *The Log,* 3 December 1954 talked about career expectations, a declining standard of living, and chances of promotion. "Undesirable Attrition," *Shipmate,* January 1952; "So You Want Out," *Shipmate,* March 1954; "Resignation of Academy Men," *Shipmate,* September 1957.
4. Every year, the superintendent began giving an annual report on the status of the academy to *Shipmate.* The superintendent also fielded questions at an alumni forum during homecoming weekend.
5. *Superintendent's Statement to the Board of Visitors 1956.*
6. "Salty Sam," *The Log,* 12 April 1953 was the first report of a television being found in Bancroft Hall.
7. *Statement Submitted to the Board of Visitors by the Superintendent of the U.S. Naval Academy, Rear Admiral William Smedberg III, 1956.*
8. *The Middle States Association of Colleges and Secondary Schools Evaluation Report of the U.S. Naval Academy 1956.*
9. "Salty Sam," *The Log,* 18 January 1952 talked about the importance of gouge.
10. "Salty Sam," *The Log,* 3 February 1956.
11. "Salty Sam," *The Log,* 27 January 1950; "Salty Sam," *The Log,* 10 February 1950.
12. "The Academy Executive Department 1922–52," *Shipmate,* June 1952.
13. "To the Brigade," *The Log,* 8 October 1954.
14. "Salty Sam," *The Log,* 30 January 1953 talked about the desperate conditions in some of the academic buildings.
15. *Statement Submitted to the Board of Visitors by the Superintendent of the U.S. Naval Academy, Vice Admiral Turner Joy 1953.*
16. *Superintendent's Statement to the Board of Visitors, Rear Admiral Charles Melson 1959.*
17. *Statement Submitted to the Board of Visitors by the Superintendent of the U.S. Naval Academy, Vice Admiral Turner Joy 1953.*
18. "Salty Sam," *The Log,* 1 May 1950. "Most of them were awed by the bigness of it all and just a little depreciatory of our own Yard."
19. "Survey of Student Life at the U.S. Naval Academy 1946–76," Table 11 "Did you intend on a military career before you entered the academy?"; and Table 12 "Did this decision change while you were at the academy?"
20. *Superintendent's Statement to the Board of Visitors 1953.*
21. *Superintendent's Statement to the Board of Visitors 1956; Superintendent's Statement to the Board of Visitors 1955; Superintendent's Statement to the Board of Visitors 1954.*
22. *Superintendent's Statement to the Board of Visitors 1955.*
23. *Superintendent's Statement to the Board of Visitors 1953.*
24. *Report of the Board of Visitors of the U.S. Naval Academy 1959.*
25. Office of the Superintendent—Vice Admiral James Calvert, Reference Files, box 1, folder 13c, "Modernization and Expansion Program 1962–63," Naval Academy Archives, Annapolis, Maryland.
26. "The Superintendent Reports," *Shipmate,* August 1956, The last attempt to get the airfield described the project as a "Must. If we are to maintain a first-rate navy and attract

our share of the young men who would like to fly." *Superintendent's Statement to the Board of Visitors 1956; Superintendent's Statement to the Board of Visitors 1955; Superintendent's Statement to the Board of Visitors 1954.*

27. "Survey of Student Life at the U.S. Naval Academy 1946–76," Table 4 "What was your primary reason for accepting an appointment to the Naval Academy?"

28. Robert Timberg, *The Nightingale's Song* (New York: Simon and Schuster, 1995) talks about the mindset of this generation of midshipmen.

29. "Salty Sam," *The Log,* 27 January 1950.

30. "The Renaissance of Navy Sports," *The Log,* 7 November 1958.

31. "The Trend in Intercollegiate Athletics at the Naval Academy," *Shipmate,* February 1950.

32. "More on Navy Football," *Shipmate,* January 1951.

33. "An Open Letter to the Director of Athletics, USNA," *Shipmate,* February 1951.

34. "A Football Report," *Shipmate,* January 1948.

35. "Letter in Response to Open Letter," *Shipmate,* April 1951.

36. "Why a Naval Academy Athletic Association?," *Shipmate,* November 1957.

37. *Reminiscences of Rear Admiral Charles Loughlin,* Naval Institute Oral History Program. Rear Admiral Loughlin was a decorated submarine commander from World War II, best known for the controversial sinking of the Japanese cargo ship *Awa Maru*. He was the Director of Athletics at the academy during this critical period with the sports program.

38. "The Inside on Eddie," *The Log,* 2 October 1953.

39. *Reminiscences of Rear Admiral Charles Loughlin.*

40. Ibid.

41. "Survey of Student Life at the U.S. Naval Academy 1946–76," Tables 19–23, "Strongest relationships at the academy."

42. "Survey of Student Life at the U.S. Naval Academy 1946–76," Table 39 "Did varsity athletes get preferential treatment at the academy?"

43. There are a number of excellent primary group studies in recent military history. See S. L. A. Marshall, *Men Against Fire* (Washington, D.C.: Combat Forces Press, 1947); Omer Bartov, *Hitler's Army* (New York: Oxford University Press, 1991); and James McPherson, *For Cause and Comrades* (New York: Oxford University Press, 1997) as examples.

44. *Superintendent's Statement to the Board of Visitors 1956; Superintendent's Statement to the Board of Visitors 1954.*

45. "The Superintendent Reports," *Shipmate,* February 1957.

46. *Reminiscences of Vice Admiral William Smedberg.*

47. Ibid.

48. Ibid.

49. Ibid.

50. "The Superintendent Reports," *Shipmate,* September 1960.

51. "Where do we go from here?," *Shipmate,* June 1951. The alumni association is for "young and old alike to whom the navy is the common denominator."

52. "Survey of Student Life at the U.S. Naval Academy 1946–76," Table 52 "Alumni affiliation—joined academy alumni association."

53. "Will we need a navy to win?," *Shipmate,* August 1951.

54. "The Superintendent Reports," *Shipmate,* August 1956.

55. "To Naval Academy Alumni from the Superintendent," *Shipmate,* April 1951.

56. *Middle States Association of Colleges and Secondary Schools Evaluation Report of the U.S. Naval Academy, February 1956,* Naval Academy Archives, Annapolis, Maryland.

57. *Statement Submitted to the Board of Visitors by the Superintendent of the U.S. Naval Academy, Rear Admiral William Smedberg III, 1956; Statement Submitted to the Board of Visitors by the Superintendent of the U.S. Naval Academy, Rear Admiral Walter Boone,*

1955; Statement Submitted to the Board of Visitors by the Superintendent of the U.S. Naval Academy, Vice Admiral Turner Joy, 1954 and 1953.

58. *Statement Submitted to the Board of Visitors by the Superintendent of the U.S. Naval Academy, Rear Admiral Walter Boone, 1955.*
59. "To Naval Academy Alumni from the Superintendent," *Shipmate,* April 1951.
60. Ibid.
61. "How Many Admirals?," *The Log,* 12 January 1951 talks about the perceived correlation between athletic and military achievement.
62. "To Naval Academy Alumni from the Superintendent," *Shipmate,* April 1951.
63. *Middle States Association of Colleges and Universities Evaluation Report of the U.S. Naval Academy, February 1956,* Naval Academy Archives, Annapolis, Maryland.
64. *Statement to the Board of Visitors Submitted by the Superintendent of the U.S. Naval Academy, Rear Admiral William Smedberg III, 1956.*
65. Ibid.
66. "Salty Sam," *The Log,* 25 January 1957.
67. "Operation Propaganda," *The Log,* 13 December 1957.
68. "Survey of Midshipmen Life at the U.S. Naval Academy 1946–76," Table 2 "What region did you consider home before entering the academy?"
69. *Middle States Association of Colleges and Secondary Schools Evaluation Report of the U.S. Naval Academy, February 1956,* Naval Academy Archives, Annapolis, Maryland.
70. Ibid.
71. Ibid.
72. Ibid.
73. The best overview of the Sputnik education crisis is Clowse, *Brainpower for the Cold War.*
74. Hyman G. Rickover, *American Education: A National Failure* (New York: E. P. Dutton, 1963), and *Swiss Schools and Ours: Why Theirs Are Better* (New York: Little and Brown, 1962).
75. U.S. Congress, House, Committee on Appropriations, *Report on Russia by Vice Admiral Hyman Rickover,* 18 August 1959 (Washington, D.C.: Government Printing Office, 1959).
76. Ibid.
77. U.S. Congress, House, Committee on Appropriations, *Educational System at the Service Academies,* 18 August 1959 (Washington, D.C.: Government Printing Office, 1959).
78. "Rickover's Criticisms of the Naval Academy," *Shipmate,* August 1959. Rickover was not a favorite of other alumni because of his very public comments about the academy. This article did not disagree with Rickover's opinions but tried to downplay them by saying that the academy was already taking corrective action.
79. "American Higher Education 1958," *Shipmate,* February 1958. This article appeared shortly before the academy began tinkering with the curriculum again. It attempted to explain the education crisis to alumni and the opportunity it represented to the academy. "Down in Maryland with that Sailor Band," *Shipmate,* June 1958. This article was written by an army officer who had been an instructor at USNA. Again, this was an attempt to educate alumni about the importance of further curricular reform.
80. *Reminiscences of Vice Admiral William Smedberg; Reminiscences of Vice Admiral Charles Melson.*
81. "Superintendent's Report on the Use of the CEEB Test for Entrance to Naval Academy," *Shipmate,* September 1958. *Superintendent's Statement to the Board of Visitors, Rear Admiral Charles Melson 1959.*
82. *Report of the Board of Visitors of the U.S. Naval Academy 1959.*

83. *Reminiscences of Vice Admiral Charles Melson,* Naval Institute Oral History Program, Naval Academy Archives, Annapolis, Maryland.
84. *Report of the Board of Visitors of the U.S. Naval Academy 1959.*
85. *Superintendent's Statement to the Board of Visitors 1956; Superintendent's Statement to the Board of Visitors 1954.*
86. *Report of the Board of Visitors of the U.S. Naval Academy 1959.*
87. Ibid.
88. "Reorganization of Academic Departments," *Shipmate,* April 1959.
89. *Reminiscences of Vice Admiral Charles Melson,* Naval Institute Oral History Program, 1974, Naval Academy Archives, Annapolis, Maryland.
90. *Report of the Board of Visitors of the U.S. Naval Academy 1959.*
91. *Reminiscences of Vice Admiral William Smedberg.*
92. "Salty Sam," *The Log,* 3 March 1950. "Salty Sam," *The Log,* 30 January 1953 talked about the importance of WRNV.
93. "Salty Sam," *The Log,* 16 April 1954. Brand-new cars were a sign that first classmen were finally near the end of their struggle at the academy. "Salty Sam," *The Log,* 31 January 1952 talked about first classmen getting their cars. The academy had also begun installing vending machines in the basement of Bancroft Hall for the midshipmen's convenience.
94. "Salty Sam," *The Log,* 30 May 1952. Weekend privileges were being extended to second classmen.
95. *Reminiscences of Vice Admiral William Smedberg.*
96. "Salty Sam," *The Log,* 7 February 1958; "Salty Sam," *The Log,* 2 May 1958.
97. Patterson, *Grand Expectations,* is the best overview of post–World War II American society.
98. "Salty Sam," *The Log,* 12 April 1953; "Salty Sam," *The Log,* 4 March 1955. Television sets were making more of a regular appearance in Bancroft Hall.
99. "Salty Sam," *The Log,* 26 October 1951 talked about the tendency for academy alumni to reminisce about how hard they had it compared to today's midshipmen.
100. *Reminiscences of Vice Admiral William Smedberg.*
101. "Salty Sam," *The Log,* 31 January 1952.
102. "Salty Sam," *The Log,* 17 February 1956.
103. "With High Aspirations: Presently at the Top in the Academic Struggle," *The Log,* 7 December 1956; "All-American Boy," *The Log,* 20 March 1959.
104. "Survey of Student Life at the U.S. Naval Academy 1946–76," Table 3 "What was your primary reason for accepting an appointment?"
105. "Survey of Student Life at the U.S. Naval Academy 1946–76," summary of observations to question 54: "Why was the Air Force viewed as an attractive career choice by you or your classmates?"
106. "Salty Sam," *The Log,* 17 February 1956. Company officers began having first classmen in their homes for dinner with their families as part of this recruitment process, quite a change from the distant relationship of the past.
107. "Salty Sam," *The Log,* 12 May 1950. Midshipmen discovered on the air cruise that aviators had more fun than the surface navy. "Salty Sam," *The Log,* 1 November 1950 talked about the popularity of air orientation flights.
108. "Beyond the Call," *The Log,* 30 March 1951.
109. "We Chose Navy Line," *The Log,* 13 February 1953.
110. "Unification—A Blessing or a Curse?," *Shipmate,* November 1949; "Defense Reorganization—Why Not the Navy Way?," *Shipmate,* February 1958.
111. "Salty Sam," *The Log,* 1 June 1950. Midshipmen were not necessarily aware of the various reorganization plans, but they did understand that the crisis would affect their future.

112. Sweetman and Cutler, *The U.S. Naval Academy.*
113. "Salty Sam," *The Log,* 28 September 1956.
114. "Salty Sam," *The Log,* 14 May 1954; *Superintendent's Statement to the Board of Visitors 1954.*
115. "Salty Sam," *The Log,* 1 May 1950. Midshipmen learned that cadets could ride in cars and keep civilian clothes in their rooms—Pandora's box had been opened.
116. *Superintendent's Statement to the Board of Visitors 1955; Superintendent's Statement to the Board of Visitors 1953; Superintendent's Statement to the Board of Visitors 1952.*
117. Vertical File, USNA Honor Concept, Special Collections Division, Nimitz Library, Annapolis, Maryland.
118. "Salty Sam," *The Log,* 5 November 1954.
119. "Salty Sam," *The Log,* 1 December 1950; "Salty Sam," *The Log,* 15 December 1950 talked about midshipmen beating the system and enjoying its rewards. "Salty Sam," *The Log,* 18 October 1957 talked about squirreling food out of the mess hall against academy regulations.
120. Vertical File, USNA Honor Concept, Special Collections Division, Nimitz Library, Annapolis, Maryland.
121. "Salty Sam," *The Log,* 1 May 1950: "The things they did because they were honor we seemed to do anyway because we felt it was a part of our duty."
122. Vertical File, USNA Honor Concept, Special Collections Division, Nimitz Library, Annapolis, Maryland
123. "Salty Sam," *The Log,* 21 October 1955 talked about the new honor system but cautioned that it was something midshipmen had been essentially doing all the time.
124. "Salty Sam," *The Log,* 16 January 1953. An unpopular midshipman had his cruise box stolen and sent to the South Korean Naval Academy as a joke by his classmates.
125. "Salty Sam," *The Log,* 4 March 1955; "Salty Sam," *The Log,* 20 January 1956.
126. "Salty Sam," *The Log,* 15 December 1950.
127. *Statement to the Board of Visitors Submitted by the Superintendent of the U.S. Naval Academy, Rear Admiral Walter Boone, 1955.*
128. "The Annapolis Air Force," *Shipmate,* October 1999.
129. "By the services," *The Log,* 25 May 1951 spotlighted one room of four first classmen, each of whom chose a different military service (Army, Navy, Air Force, and Marine Corps) and the reasons for their choices.
130. "Salty Sam," *The Log,* 13 April 1951. Prior service returnees always had preference when it came to service selection. One midshipman was so desperate to select the Air Force that he claimed membership in the Civil Air Patrol as giving him that standing.
131. "I Chose the U.S. Air Force," *The Log,* 1 December 1952 examined the Air Force's popularity.
132. "Salty Sam," *The Log,* 23 November 1956.
133. "Salty Sam," *The Log,* 27 January 1950; "Salty Sam," *The Log,* 3 March 1950. This issue talked about how a first classman had selected duty aboard the Spanish prize, *Reina Mercedes,* as a way of short-circuiting the route to Pensacola. "Salty Sam," *The Log,* 18 December 1953. The lottery was still in effect and becoming more unpopular with each passing year.
134. "After Pensacola," *The Log,* 2 December 1955. At this point, the academy finally bent with the times. Midshipmen could elect naval aviation directly. The academy began educating them about a whole career path involving naval aviation.
135. "More Nuclear Power Trainees Wanted," *Shipmate,* February 1955.
136. "Clear the Bridge," *The Log,* 7 October 1955; "The New Fleet," *The Log,* 24 October 1958.

137. "Atomic Era Now Here," *The Log,* 8 October 1954; "Salty Sam," *The Log,* 23 November 1956. Midshipmen would show a growing interest in the nuclear submarine program but the academy blocked this as a first option until the early 1960s.

138. "Survey of Student Life at the U.S. Naval Academy 1946–76," Table 4 "What was your primary reason for accepting an appointment?," and Table 11 "Did you intend on a military career before you entered the academy?"

139. "News of Engineering," *The Log,* 3 May 1957. The Navy had its high tech programs, which more midshipmen wanted to join, but the academy would not break tradition here until the early 1960s.

140. "Career Men," *Shipmate,* November 1949.

141. "Salty Sam," *The Log,* 3 November 1950. After Admiral Holloway's relief, the new plebe policies largely disappeared too. "Salty Sam," *The Log,* 17 October 1951. Plebe indoctrination continued to vary substantially by company or battalion. "Salty Sam," *The Log,* 26 September 1958 described plebe indoctrination: "Plebes, I'm sure that they'll carefully guide and instruct you so that through precept and example YOU'LL BE RUN UNTIL YOU'RE RAGGED!"

142. "Salty Sam," *The Log,* 17 November 1950. Academics were being used to reinforce the character lessons of Bancroft Hall. "Salty Sam," *The Log,* 1 December 1952. "Cops and robbers" stories were a part of every issue of *The Log.*

143. "Salty Sam," *The Log,* 8 March 1957. The battle of "cops and robbers" took its toll on both parties. One first class midshipmen described the indoctrination process; "this may be interesting and informative but it's small consolation to those of us who have been indoctrinated half to death already."

144. "Salty Sam," *The Log,* 24 September 1954; "Salty Sam," *The Log,* 23 September 1955; "Salty Sam," *The Log,* 11 May 1956.

145. "Salty Sam," *The Log,* 12 January 1951; "Salty Sam," *The Log,* 16 February 1951. Midshipmen described themselves as inmates or shut-ins living in Bancroft Hall. "Salty Sam," *The Log,* 11 May 1951. Midshipmen described Bancroft Hall as a penitentiary. "Salty Sam," *The Log,* 1 November 1952. Bancroft Hall described as a monastery. "Salty Sam," *The Log,* 20 September 1957. This writer described life in Bancroft Hall: "Now we are safely back in the arms of Mother Bancroft and no longer have to worry about the wiles of women or worry how we will get the most out of the next day. Leave is at last over and we are once again in back in our sheltered haven called the Anne Arundel Country Club." "Salty Sam," *The Log,* 2 May 1958 described academy life: "it's that time of year when we all feel like inmates of the monkey house at the zoo."

146. "Salty Sam," *The Log,* 30 April 1953. Although they did not like it, midshipmen understood that character came through an application of severe discipline.

Chapter 3. The Early Years of the "Academic Revolution"

1. The best overview of the Sputnik educational crisis is Clowse, *Brainpower for the Cold War.* For issues relating to officer education and the service academies see Simons, *Liberal Education in the Service Academies.*

2. For an overview of curriculum changes during this period see Sheppard, "An Analysis of Curriculum Changes."

3. Ibid.

4. The best secondary source on the "academic revolution" and comparable developments at the other federal service academies is Lovell, *Neither Athens Nor Sparta?*

5. "Survey of Student Life at the U.S. Naval Academy 1946–76," summary of observations to question 56: "How were academic reforms received by the Brigade of Midshipmen?"

6. For an example of these differences in opinion see Sheppard's interview with Dr. Richard Folsom in "An Analysis of Curriculum Changes" and Vice Admiral Charles Melson's recollections of the same period in *Reminiscences of Vice Admiral Charles Melson,* U.S. Naval Institute Oral History Program, 1974, Naval Academy Archives, Nimitz Library, Annapolis, Maryland.

7. Sheppard, "An Analysis of Curriculum Changes"; *Reminiscences of Vice Admiral Charles Melson.*

8. For an overview of this period, see Sweetman and Cutler's chapter "Athens and Sparta" in *The U.S. Naval Academy.*

9. For the impact of this television show see "Men of Annapolis," *Shipmate* November 1999.

10. In an address given on 1 August 1963 to the incoming plebe class of 1967, President Kennedy gave an oft-quoted remark about his sentiments towards the navy: "I can imagine no more rewarding career, and any man who may be asked in this century what he did to make his life worthwhile, I think can respond with a good deal of pride and satisfaction—I served in the United States Navy." Special Collections Division, Nimitz Library, Annapolis, Maryland.

11. "Polaris—How Good?," *Shipmate,* June–July 1960; and "Midshipmen Serve on Submarines for the Summer," *Shipmate,* August 1961.

12. For an overview of the nuclear power program see Francis Duncan, *Rickover and the Nuclear Navy* (Annapolis: Naval Institute Press, 1990); and Theodore Rockwell, *The Rickover Effect: How One Man Made a Difference* (Annapolis: Naval Institute Press, 1992).

13. For an overview of the nuclear power program and the academic reforms at the academy, see Lovell's *Neither Athens Nor Sparta?*

14. "Survey of Student Life at the U.S. Naval Academy 1946–76," summary of observations to question 58: "In what ways did the Vietnam War affect life at the Naval Academy?"

15. See Sheppard's "An Analysis of Curriculum Changes" and *Reminiscences of Vice Admiral Horatio Rivera,* U.S. Naval Institute Oral History Project, May 1978, Naval Academy Archives, Nimitz Library, Annapolis, Maryland.

16. "USNA Still Needs a Library," *Shipmate,* April 1961.

17. Letter from the Chief of the Bureau of Naval Personnel to Dr. Richard Folsom, dated 31 March 1959. See also Folsom's interview in Sheppard's "An Analysis of Curriculum Changes."

18. Ibid.

19. *Reminiscences of Vice Admiral Charles Melson;* "The Superintendent Reports—Academic Reorganization," *Shipmate,* April 1959; and Lovell's *Neither Athens Nor Sparta?*

20. A good example of this sort of criticism is Admiral Rickover's report to Congress: U.S. Congress, House Committee on Appropriations, *Educational System at the Service Academies,* 18 August 1959 (Washington, D.C.: Government Printing Office, 1959).

21. *Reminiscences of Vice Admiral Charles Melson;* "The Superintendent Reports," *Shipmate,* June–July 1959; *Shipmate,* September-October 1959; *Superintendent's Statement to the Board of Visitors 1959;* and *Superintendent's Statement to the Board of Visitors 1960.*

22. Sheppard, "An Analysis of Curriculum Changes"; and *Reminiscences of Vice Admiral Horatio Rivera.*

23. Sheppard, "An Analysis of Curriculum Changes"; and *Reminiscences of Vice Admiral Horatio Rivera.*

24. "Survey of Student Life at the U.S. Naval Academy 1946–76," summary of observations to question 56: "How were academic reforms received by the Brigade of Midshipmen?"

25. *Report of the Board of Visitors of the U.S. Naval Academy 1959.*

26. *Superintendent's Statement to the Board of Visitors 1960.*

27. Sheppard, "An Analysis of Curriculum Changes"; Lovell's *Neither Athens Nor Sparta?; Reminiscences of Vice Admiral Horatio Rivera.*

28. Sheppard, "An Analysis of Curriculum Changes"; Lovell's *Neither Athens Nor Sparta?; Reminiscences of Vice Admiral Horatio Rivera.*

29. "Survey of Midshipmen Life at the U.S. Naval Academy 1946–76," Table 12 "Did this decision change while you were at the academy?"

30. Sheppard, "An Analysis of Curriculum Changes"; Lovell's *Neither Athens Nor Sparta?; Reminiscences of Vice Admiral Horatio Rivera.*

31. Sheppard, "An Analysis of Curriculum Changes."

32. "The Superintendent Reports," *Shipmate,* June–July 1960; and "Questions and Answers at the Alumni Assembly," *Shipmate,* November 1961.

33. "Rickover's Criticisms of Naval Academy," *Shipmate,* August 1959.

34. "Electives—Boon or Bane?," *Shipmate,* September–October 1960.

35. A description of this ceremony can be found in most *Lucky Bags* from this period.

36. "Electives—Boon or Bane?"

37. "The Bitter End," *The Log,* 17 April 1960; and "Logging," *The Log,* 17 November 1961.

38. *Supplemental Statement by Senators Saltonstall, Holland, Beall and Engle for Addition to the Report of the Naval Academy Board of Visitors 1959.*

39. *Educational System at the Service Academies;* and "Rickover's Criticisms of Naval Academy."

40. *Reminiscences of Vice Admiral Charles Melson;* and Lovell's *Neither Athens Nor Sparta?*

41. "The Superintendent Reports," *Shipmate,* June–July 1960.

42. Ibid.

43. *Reminiscences of Rear Admiral John Davidson,* U.S. Naval Institute Oral History Project, 1986, Naval Academy Archives, Nimitz Library, Annapolis, Maryland.

44. "New Directions in Naval Academy Education," *Proceedings,* May 1960 and "Questions and Answers at the Alumni Assembly," *Shipmate,* November 1961.

45. Superintendents talked about the professional socialization responsibilities of Bancroft Hall in their reports to the Board of Visitors.

46. The nature of what was being contested changed but the battleground between officers and midshipmen remained fixed in the early 1960s. See discussions of this in any issue of *The Log* from this period. "Salty Sam," *The Log,* 6 April 1962 talked about how one group of military instructors had midshipmen who had fallen asleep in their class stand before the class in their bare feet to keep them awake. "Salty Sam," *The Log,* 14 December 1962 talked about how the Weapons Department had deducted points from all students' final grades in anticipation of quizzes that were not given because of the Christmas leave period.

47. "Salty Sam," *The Log,* 17 November 1961 and 15 December 1961 talked about problems with midshipmen abusing civilian clothes and driving privileges. Television sets had become a popular item midshipmen were smuggling into Bancroft Hall. See "Salty Sam," *The Log,* 18 March 1960.

48. "Salty Sam," *The Log,* 30 September 1960.

49. "Salty Sam," *The Log,* 19 February 1960 and 4 March 1960 talked about first classmen's anticipation over having their term paper approved, the final academic barrier first classmen had to overcome before they could "coast" to graduation.

50. *Superintendent's Statement to the Board of Visitors 1961* and *Superintendent's Statement to the Board of Visitors 1962* talked about how requirements were being updated and changed.

51. "The Bitter End," *The Log,* 15 April 1960: "Perhaps we are the last of the old Navy, but essentially there is no difference at the Naval Academy. While the Navy changes, the system does not. The same common bonds that link us to the Midshipmen of 1845 will tie us to the Midshipmen of 2045."

52. "Logging," *The Log,* 17 November 1961: "the very idea of letting the plebes on the same YP's with us as we 'execute' tactics! Maybe they'll learn what not to do."

53. "Salty Sam," *The Log,* 5 October 1962; "Salty Sam," *The Log,* 16 November 1962; and "Salty Sam," *The Log,* 31 October 1963 talked about a gross violation of the formal plebe system; a first classmen was having his plebe do push-ups under the mess table and noticed the duty officer approaching the table. The officer expressed no concern about what was going on with the plebe but did want to know why the table was in disarray before the meal had formally commenced.

54. The plebe system would generate significant internal controversy during Admiral Kauffman's tenure as superintendent. Various members of the civilian faculty and one of the military department heads demanded significant reforms or else they would take their concerns public.

55. "Survey of Midshipmen Life at the U.S. Naval Academy 1946–76," Table 15 "To what degree did plebe indoctrination vary by company or battalion?"

56. "Survey of Midshipmen Life at the U.S. Naval Academy 1946–76," Table 13 "What part of your pre-academy background prepared you best for plebe year?"

57. Ibid.

58. "The Air Force Academy Honor Conference," *The Log,* 6 April 1962; "Logging," *The Log,* 4 May 1962.

59. See articles on academic freedom, the gouge, and honor in a two-part series in "Logging," *The Log,* 6 October 1961 and 20 October 1961.

60. "Logging," *The Log,* 6 October 1961 and 20 October 1961.

61. "Logging," *The Log,* 6 October 1961 and 20 October 1961. U.S. General Accounting Office, *DOD Service Academies: Comparison of Honor and Conduct Adjudicatory Processes,* April 1995.

62. Rumors were rampant at the academy up to the point the institution made the change. See "Logging," *The Log,* 17 November 1961; and "Salty Sam," *The Log,* 4 March 1960.

63. *Reminiscences of Rear Admiral John Davidson.*

64. Ibid.

65. The Executive Department's enforcement of proper marching etiquette was legendary at the academy. See "Salty Sam," *The Log,* 13 May 1960 and 28 October 1960 for recent examples.

66. "Survey of Student Life at the U.S. Naval Academy 1946–76," Tables 19–23 "strongest relationships at the academy," and Tables 24–29 "Unity building activities."

67. "Survey of Student Life at the U.S. Naval Academy 1946–76," Tables 19–23 "strongest relationships at the academy," and Tables 24–29 "Unity building activities."

68. "Survey of Student Life at the U.S. Naval Academy 1946–76," Question 24a: "Other groups in which midshipmen formed strong relationships?"

69. "New Swearing-In Ceremony," *Shipmate,* August 1962.

NOTES   371

70. "Logging," *The Log,* 12 May 1961; and "Questions and Answers at the Alumni Assembly," *Shipmate,* November 1961.
71. "New Directions in Academy Education," *Proceedings,* May 1960.
72. "Is the Versatile Line Officer Obsolete?," *Proceedings,* June 1959.
73. Ibid.
74. Ibid.
75. "Midshipmen Serve on Submarines for Summer," *Shipmate,* August 1961.
76. Duncan, *Rickover and the Nuclear Navy;* and Rockwell, *The Rickover Effect.*
77. Duncan, *Rickover and the Nuclear Navy;* and Rockwell, *The Rickover Effect.*
78. Duncan, *Rickover and the Nuclear Navy;* and Rockwell, *The Rickover Effect.*
79. U.S. Congress, House Committee on Appropriations, *Educational System at the Service Academies,* 18 August 1959 (Washington, D.C.: Government Printing Office, 1959).
80. Ibid.
81. "New Directions in Academy Education."
82. "Salty Sam," *The Log,* 22 February 1963.
83. "Letters to the Editor," *The Log,* 22 November 1960, 12 May 1961, and 6 October 1961.
84. "Letters to the Editor," *The Log,* 22 November 1960, 12 May 1961, and 6 October 1961.
85. "Letters to the Editor," *The Log,* 22 November 1960, 12 May 1961, and 6 October 1961.
86. "Letters to the Editor," *The Log,* 22 November 1960, 12 May 1961, and 6 October 1961.
87. "Letters to the Editor," *The Log,* 22 November 1960, 12 May 1961, and 6 October 1961.
88. "Survey of Student Life at the U.S. Naval Academy 1946–76," summary of observations to question 40b: "Did any warfare specialty have a particularly good or bad reputation with the Brigade?"
89. Ibid.

Chapter 4. The "Academic Revolution" Triumphant

1. The best overview of this period is Lovell's *Neither Athens Nor Sparta?* For background, see Sweetman and Cutler, *The U.S. Naval Academy.* The academy's reports to the Board of Visitors and relevant issues of *Shipmate* are invaluable for understanding this period.
2. Lovell, *Neither Athens Nor Sparta?*
3. "Rhodes Scholars? Yes! But Naval Officers First—A Century of Academic Achievements," *Shipmate,* September–October 1963; and "Education for Naval Officers—What Should It Be?," *Shipmate,* February 1963.
4. Lovell, *Neither Athens Nor Sparta?*
5. "Educational Policy Change at USNA," *Shipmate,* August 1962; *Report of the Board of Visitors 1963;* and *Superintendent's Statement to the Board of Visitors 1963.*
6. "A New Marking System at USNA," *Shipmate,* September–October 1963.
7. Ibid.
8. *Reminiscences of Vice Admiral Charles Minter,* U.S. Naval Institute Oral History

Project, October 1981; and "Superintendent's Report—Board of Trustees Meeting," *Shipmate,* January 1963.

9. *Reminiscences of Vice Admiral Charles Minter,* U.S. Naval Institute Oral History Project, October 1981; and "Superintendent's Report—Board of Trustees Meeting," *Shipmate,* January 1963.

10. *Reminiscences of Vice Admiral Charles Minter;* Office of the Superintendent, Vice Admiral James Calvert, Reference Files—box 3 folder 2, "Midshipmen Attrition Statistics 1959–67, 1970–71"; Naval Academy Archives, Vertical File—"Midshipmen Attrition and Turn backs," Special Collections Division, Naval Academy Archives.

11. Personal Papers of Captain Wayne Hoof, Captain Hoof was the head of the Department of English, Government, and History at this time. He had previously been the engineering department head. Hoof and a number of civilian faculty would raise questions about the plebe system and the academic reforms in 1966. Hoof's family provided these papers to the author for this project.

12. *Report of the Middle States Association Evaluation Team for the U.S. Naval Academy,* 20–23 March 1966.

13. Ibid.

14. Lovell, *Neither Athens Nor Sparta?*

15. "Educational Policy Change at USNA," *Shipmate,* August 1962; *Report of the Board of Visitors 1963;* and *Superintendent's Statement to the Board of Visitors 1963.*

16. Lovell, *Neither Athens Nor Sparta?;* and *Reminiscences of Vice Admiral Charles Minter.*

17. "Educational Policy Change at USNA," *Shipmate,* August 1962; and "USNA Faculty Reorganization," *Shipmate,* September 1962.

18. "Educational Policy Change at USNA," *Shipmate,* August 1962; and "USNA Faculty Reorganization," *Shipmate,* September 1962.

19. "Educational Policy Change at USNA," *Shipmate,* August 1962; and "USNA Faculty Reorganization," *Shipmate,* September 1962.

20. "Educational Policy Change at USNA," *Shipmate,* August 1962; and "USNA Faculty Reorganization," *Shipmate,* September 1962.

21. "Educational Policy Change at USNA," *Shipmate,* August 1962; and "USNA Faculty Reorganization," *Shipmate,* September 1962.

22. "Educational Policy Change at USNA," *Shipmate,* August 1962; and "USNA Faculty Reorganization," *Shipmate,* September 1962.

23. Letter from Secretary Korth to the Alumni Association, in "USNA Faculty Reorganization," *Shipmate,* September 1962.

24. Ibid.

25. Lovell, *Neither Athens Nor Sparta?;* Office of the Superintendent, Vice Admiral James Calvert Reference Files, box 2, folder 11, "Officer Faculty Assignment"; box 2, folder 8, "Faculty"; box 2, folder 7, "Faculty"; and "Educational Policy Change at USNA," *Shipmate,* August 1962.

26. Lovell, *Neither Athens Nor Sparta?;* Office of the Superintendent, Vice Admiral James Calvert Reference Files, box 2, folder 11, "Officer Faculty Assignment"; box 2, folder 8, "Faculty"; box 2, folder 7, "Faculty"; and "Educational Policy Change at USNA," *Shipmate,* August 1962.

27. "Educational Policy Change at USNA," *Shipmate,* August 1962; *Report of the Board of Visitors 1963;* and *Superintendent's Statement to the Board of Visitors 1963.*

28. *Report of the Board of Visitors 1963; Superintendent's Statement to the Board of Visitors 1963;* "Alumni Assembly—Questions and Answers, Homecoming 1962," *Shipmate,* November 1962; and "Superintendent's Report—Board of Trustees Meeting," *Shipmate,* January 1963.

29. *Report of the Board of Visitors 1963; Superintendent's Statement to the Board of Visitors 1963;* "Alumni Assembly—Questions and Answers, Homecoming 1962," *Shipmate,* November 1962; and "Superintendent's Report—Board of Trustees Meeting," *Shipmate,* January 1963.
30. *Report of the Board of Visitors 1963;* and *Superintendent's Statement to the Board of Visitors 1963.*
31. *Report of the Middle States Association Evaluation Team for the U.S. Naval Academy,* 20–23 March 1966.
32. Ibid.
33. Office of Superintendent, Vice Admiral James Calvert Reference Files, box 2, folder 5, "Faculty/Academic Dean Appointment 1965"; "Alumni Assembly—Questions and Answers, Homecoming 1962," *Shipmate,* November 1962; and "Superintendent's Report—Board of Trustees Meeting," *Shipmate,* January 1963.
34. Office of Superintendent, Vice Admiral James Calvert Reference Files, box 2, folder 5, "Faculty/Academic Dean Appointment 1965"; "Alumni Assembly—Questions and Answers, Homecoming 1962," *Shipmate,* November 1962; and "Superintendent's Report—Board of Trustees Meeting," *Shipmate,* January 1963.
35. *Report of the Board of Visitors 1963;* and *Superintendent's Statement to the Board of Visitors 1963.*
36. "Report on the Academic Dean," *The Log,* 31 October 1963.
37. Ibid.
38. Lovell, *Neither Athens Nor Sparta?;* J. Arthur Heise, *The Brass Factories: A Frank Appraisal of West Point, Annapolis, and Colorado Springs* (Washington, D.C.: Public Affairs Press, 1969); and David Boroff, "Teaching Young Sea Dogs Old Tricks," *Harper's Magazine,* January 1963.
39. *Report of the Board of Visitors 1964;* and *Superintendent's Statement to the Board of Visitors 1964.*
40. "Superintendent's Report—Board of Trustees Meeting," *Shipmate,* January 1963.
41. Ibid.
42. *Reminiscences of Vice Admiral Charles Minter.*
43. "Alumni Assembly 1964," *Shipmate,* November 1964; and *Reminiscences of Vice Admiral Charles Minter.*
44. *Reminiscences of Vice Admiral Charles Minter.*
45. *Reminiscences of Vice Admiral Charles Minter;* Office of the Superintendent, Vice Admiral James Calvert, Reference Files, box 3, folder 2, "Midshipmen Attrition Statistics 1959–67, 1970–71"; Vertical File, "Midshipmen Attrition and Turn backs," Special Collections Division, Naval Academy Archives.
46. "Alumni Assembly 1964," *Shipmate,* November 1964; and *Reminiscences of Vice Admiral Charles Minter.*
47. "Superintendent's Report—Board of Trustees Meeting," *Shipmate,* January 1963; and *Reminiscences of Vice Admiral Charles Minter.*
48. "Superintendent's Report—Board of Trustees Meeting," *Shipmate,* January 1963; and *Reminiscences of Vice Admiral Charles Minter.*
49. "Superintendent's Report—Board of Trustees Meeting," *Shipmate,* January 1963; and *Reminiscences of Vice Admiral Charles Minter.*
50. *Reminiscences of Vice Admiral Charles Minter.*
51. *Reminiscences of Vice Admiral Charles Minter; Report of the Board of Visitors 1964;* and *Superintendent's Statement to the Board of Visitors 1964.*
52. *Reminiscences of Vice Admiral Charles Minter.*
53. Ibid.
54. Ibid.

55. *Reminiscences of Vice Admiral Charles Minter;* and "Alumni Assembly 1964," *Shipmate,* November 1964.
56. *Reminiscences of Vice Admiral Charles Minter;* and "Alumni Assembly 1964," *Shipmate,* November 1964.
57. *Reminiscences of Vice Admiral Charles Minter;* and "Alumni Assembly 1964," *Shipmate,* November 1964.
58. *Reminiscences of Vice Admiral Charles Minter.*
59. Ibid.
60. "Rhodes Scholars? Yes! But Naval Officers First—A Century of Academic Achievements," *Shipmate,* September–October 1963.
61. Lovell, *Neither Athens Nor Sparta?*
62. David Boroff, "Teaching Young Sea Dogs Old Tricks," *Harper's Magazine,* January 1963.
63. James DeFrancia, "Annapolis—The Rebuttal of a Young Sea Dog," *Shipmate,* April 1963.
64. Ibid.
65. Ibid.
66. "Naval Academy Performance and Service Success," *Shipmate,* December 1964.
67. *Superintendent's Statement to the Board of Visitors 1964;* and *Reminiscences of Vice Admiral Charles Minter.*
68. "Ex Scientia Tridens—Navy's Trident Scholars Search for New Knowledge," *The Log,* 31 October 1963.
69. *Superintendent's Statement to the Board of Visitors 1964;* and "Ex Scientia Tridens—Navy's Trident Scholars Search for New Knowledge," *The Log,* 31 October 1963.
70. "Naval Academy Performance and Service Success," *Shipmate,* December 1964.
71. Ibid.
72. Ibid.
73. "New Marking System at USNA," *Shipmate,* September–October 1963.
74. Ibid.
75. Ibid.
76. Ibid.
77. Ibid.
78. "New Marking System at USNA," *Shipmate,* September–October 1963; and Lovell, *Neither Athens Nor Sparta?*
79. *Reminiscences of Vice Admiral Charles Minter;* and *Report of the Board of Visitors 1963.*
80. *Reminiscences of Vice Admiral Charles Minter;* and Office of the Superintendent, Vice Admiral James Calvert Reference Files, box 1, folder 13d, "Modernization and Expansion Program—Opposition to 1962–63"; box 1, folder 13c, "Modernization and Expansion Program—Support and Justification For, 1962–63"; box 1, folder 13b, "Modernization and Expansion Program—Superintendent's Response—February and March 1963."
81. "The Superintendent Reports—A New Administrative Organization," *Shipmate,* September–October 1964; and *Superintendent's Statement to the Board of Visitors 1964.*
82. "The Superintendent Reports—A New Administrative Organization," *Shipmate,* September–October 1964; and *Superintendent's Statement to the Board of Visitors 1964.*
83. "The Superintendent Reports on the Eve of Departure," *Shipmate,* June–July 1965.
84. *Report of the Board of Visitors 1964; Superintendent's Statement to the Board of Visitors 1964;* and *Reminiscences of Vice Admiral Charles Minter.*
85. *Report of the Board of Visitors 1964; Superintendent's Statement to the Board of Visitors 1964;* and *Reminiscences of Vice Admiral Charles Minter.*

86. *Report of the Board of Visitors 1964; Superintendent's Statement to the Board of Visitors 1964;* and *Reminiscences of Vice Admiral Charles Minter.*
87. *Superintendent's Statement to the Board of Visitors 1965.*
88. *Superintendent's Statement to the Board of Visitors 1964; Superintendent's Statement to the Board of Visitors 1965;* and Office of the Superintendent, Vice Admiral James Calvert Reference Files, box 3, folder 1, "Midshipmen At-Sea Training."
89. *Superintendent's Statement to the Board of Visitors 1964; Superintendent's Statement to the Board of Visitors 1965;* and Office of the Superintendent, Vice Admiral James Calvert Reference Files, box 3, folder 1, "Midshipmen At-Sea Training."
90. *Reminiscences of Vice Admiral Charles Minter; Superintendent's Statement to the Board of Visitors 1965;* and "The Superintendent Reports on the Eve of Departure," *Shipmate,* June–July 1965.
91. *Reminiscences of Vice Admiral Charles Minter; Superintendent's Statement to the Board of Visitors 1965;* and "The Superintendent Reports on the Eve of Departure," *Shipmate,* June–July 1965.

Chapter 5. "A Professional Revolution" at Annapolis

1. The best secondary sources on this period are John Lovell, *Neither Athens Nor Sparta?* and Heise, *The Brass Factories.*
2. *Reminiscences of Rear Admiral Draper Kauffman,* U.S. Naval Institute Oral History Project; *Report of the Middle States Association Evaluation Team for the U.S. Naval Academy,* 20–23 March 1966, and "Academic Controversy," *Shipmate,* May 1966, Naval Academy Archives, Nimitz Library, Annapolis, Maryland.
3. Captain Wayne Hoof, Head of the Department of English, History, and Government, 1965–67; Hoof's papers maintained by his family and in the temporary possession of the author.
4. Lovell, *Neither Athens Nor Sparta?*
5. *Superintendent's Statement to the Board of Visitors 1965; Superintendent's Statement to the Board of Visitors 1966; Superintendent's Statement to the Board of Visitors 1967;* and *Superintendent's Statement to the Board of Visitors 1968.*
6. *Report of the Middle States Association,* 20–23 March 1966; "Alumni Assembly," *Shipmate,* November 1965; "Alumni Assembly," *Shipmate,* December 1966; "Academic Program at USNA," *Shipmate,* May 1967; "Alumni Assembly," *Shipmate,* January 1968, "More Questions—1967 Alumni Assembly," *Shipmate,* February 1968, "The USNA and Its Curriculum—A Chronology of Changes and Some Problems," *Shipmate,* March 1968; and *Reminiscences of Rear Admiral Draper Kauffman.*
7. *Reminiscences of Rear Admiral Draper Kauffman; Superintendent's Statement to the Board of Visitors 1967;* and *Superintendent's Statement to the Board of Visitors 1968.*
8. Lovell, *Neither Athens Nor Sparta?;* Ben A. Franklin, "Rift at Annapolis Remains after Mediators Leave," *New York Times,* 20 November 1966.
9. "Survey of Student Life at the U.S. Naval Academy 1946–76", summary of responses to question 58: "In what ways did the Vietnam War affect life at the Naval Academy?" The first academy KIA was spotlighted in a feature article in *The Log,* 11 February 1966.
10. "Alumni Assembly," *Shipmate,* November 1965; "Alumni Assembly," *Shipmate,* December 1966; "Academic Program at USNA," *Shipmate,* May 1967; "Alumni Assembly," *Shipmate,* January 1968.
11. Captain Wayne Hoof. Several letters between the Executive Department and the

faculty question the need for scholarship when the midshipmen were preparing to go to Vietnam.

12. Office of the Superintendent, Vice Admiral James Calvert, Reference Files, box 1, folder 14, "Mobilization, 1968."

13. *Reminiscences of Rear Admiral Draper Kauffman; Superintendent's Statement to the Board of Visitors 1966; Superintendent's Statement to the Board of Visitors 1967;* and *Superintendent's Statement to the Board of Visitors 1968.*

14. "We Can't Let Them Be Forgotten," *The Log,* 20 November 1970; "Don't Let Them Be Forgotten," *The Lucky Bag 1971;* and "He Is Still Serving You," *The Lucky Bag 1972.*

15. *Report of the Middle States Association,* 20–23 March 1966; *Reminiscences of Rear Admiral Draper Kauffman;* Office of the Superintendent, Vice Admiral James Calvert, Reference Files, box 3, folder 21, "Midshipmen Separations, 1967–68"; box 3, folder 2, "Midshipmen Attrition Statistics, 1959–67, 1970–71."

16. *Report on the Meeting of Board of Visitors Committee on Academic and Professional Training,* 6 October 1967; *Superintendent's Statement to the Board of Visitors 1967;* and *Superintendent's Statement to the Board of Visitors 1968.*

17. "Attrition at the U.S. Naval Academy," *Shipmate,* September–October 1967; "A Serious and Growing Problem," *Shipmate,* April 1968.

18. Papers of Captain Wayne Hoof; *Reminiscences of Rear Admiral Draper Kauffman;* "Alumni Assembly 1967," *Shipmate,* January 1968; "On the Subject of Plebe Year," *Shipmate,* February 1967.

19. *Reminiscences of Rear Admiral Draper Kauffman; Superintendent's Statement to the Board of Visitors 1967; Superintendent's Statement to the Board of Visitors 1968;* "Drug Abuse," *The Lucky Bag 1971.*

20. *Reminiscences of Rear Admiral Draper Kauffman;* and Sweetman and Cutler, *The U.S. Naval Academy.*

21. *Reminiscences of Rear Admiral Draper Kauffman;* and Sweetman and Cutler, *The U.S. Naval Academy.*

22. *Reminiscences of Rear Admiral Draper Kauffman.*

23. *Reminiscences of Rear Admiral Draper Kauffman;* "The Superintendent Reports on the Eve of Departure," *Shipmate,* June–July 1965; "Alumni Assembly," *Shipmate,* November 1965.

24. "The Superintendent Reports on the Eve of Departure," *Shipmate,* June–July 1965.

25. *Report of the Middle States Association,* 20–23 March 1966; *Reminiscences of Rear Admiral Draper Kauffman;* Office of the Superintendent, Vice Admiral James Calvert, Reference Files, box 2, folder 5 "Faculty/Academic Dean Appointment, 1965"; box 2, folder 6, "Faculty-Civilian Affairs Committee;" box 2, folder 7, "Faculty"; box 2, folder 8, "Faculty"; Lovell, *Neither Athens Nor Sparta?*

26. *Report of the Middle States Association,* 20–23 March 1966.

27. Ibid.

28. *Reminiscences of Rear Admiral Draper Kauffman;* "Letter from Professor Vince Davis on USNA curriculum," *Shipmate,* March 1967; "The Naval Academy, Its Mission and Staff," *Shipmate,* September–October 1967; "Faculty Study," *Shipmate,* March 1968.

29. *Superintendent's Statement to the Board of Visitors 1966; Superintendent's Statement to the Board of Visitors 1967; Superintendent's Statement to the Board of Visitors 1968;* and *Reminiscences of Rear Admiral Draper Kauffman.*

30. *Reminiscences of Rear Admiral Draper Kauffman;* and Office of the Superintendent, Vice Admiral James Calvert, Reference Files, box 2, folder 11, "Officer Faculty Assignment."

31. *Report of the Middle States Association,* 20–23 March 1966; and *Reminiscences of Rear Admiral Draper Kauffman.*

32. *Report of the Middle States Association,* 20–23 March 1966; and *Reminiscences of Rear Admiral Draper Kauffman.*

33. Lovell, *Neither Athens Nor Sparta?; Reminiscences of Rear Admiral Draper Kauffman; Superintendent's Statement to the Board of Visitors 1967;* and Letter from the Committee on Grade Distribution and Control to the Academic Dean, 29 September 1965, Papers of Captain Wayne Hoof.

34. Letter from the Committee on Grade Distribution and Control to the Academic Dean.

35. "A New Marking System at USNA," *Shipmate,* September–October 1963; Letter from the Committee on Grade Distribution and Control to the Academic Dean; and *Reminiscences of Rear Admiral Draper Kauffman.*

36. *Report of the Middle States Association,* 20–23 March 1966; and Letter from the Committee on Grade Distribution and Control to the Academic Dean.

37. Lovell, *Neither Athens Nor Sparta?;* Ben A. Franklin, "Grades Inflated for Midshipmen," *New York Times,* 10 April 1966; and *Report of the Middle States Association,* 20–23 March 1966.

38. *Reminiscences of Rear Admiral Draper Kauffman.*

39. Letter from the Committee on Grade Distribution and Control to the Academic Dean.

40. *Reminiscences of Rear Admiral Draper Kauffman; Superintendent's Statement to the Board of Visitors 1966; Superintendent's Statement to the Board of Visitors 1967.*

41. Lovell, *Neither Athens Nor Sparta?;* and "Academic Controversy," *Shipmate,* May 1966.

42. *Reminiscences of Rear Admiral Draper Kauffman.*

43. Vertical File, "Midshipmen Attrition and Turn backs," Special Collections Division, Nimitz Library, U.S. Naval Academy.

44. *Report of the Middle States Association,* 20–23 March 1966.

45. *Reminiscences of Rear Admiral Draper Kauffman.*

46. "Academic Controversy," *Shipmate,* May 1966.

47. *Report to the Middle States Association of Colleges and Secondary Schools from the U.S. Naval Academy,* February 1966; and Office of the Superintendent, box 3, folder 17, "Middle States Association Preparation to Accreditation 1965."

48. *Superintendent's Statement to the Board of Visitors 1965;* and *Report of the Board of Visitors 1965.*

49. *Superintendent's Statement to the Board of Visitors 1965;* and *Report of the Board of Visitors 1965.*

50. *Report of the Middle States Association,* 20–23 March 1966.

51. Ibid.

52. Ibid.

53. *Report to the Middle States Association of Colleges and Secondary Schools from the U.S. Naval Academy;* and *Superintendent's Statement to the Board of Visitors 1965.*

54. *Report of the Middle States Association,* 20–23 March 1966.

55. *Report of the Middle States Association,* 20–23 March 1966; and *Reminiscences of Rear Admiral Draper Kauffman.*

56. *Report of the Middle States Association,* 20–23 March 1966.

57. *Report of the Middle States Association,* 20–23 March 1966; and *Reminiscences of Rear Admiral Draper Kauffman.*

58. *Report of the Middle States Association,* 20–23 March 1966; and *Reminiscences of Rear Admiral Draper Kauffman.*

59. *Report of the Middle States Association,* 20–23 March 1966; *Reminiscences of Rear Admiral Draper Kauffman;* and *Superintendent's Statement to the Board of Visitors 1965.*

60. *Report of the Middle States Association,* 20–23 March 1966; *Reminiscences of Rear Admiral Draper Kauffman;* and Lovell, *Neither Athens Nor Sparta?*
61. *Report of the Middle States Association,* 20–23 March 1966.
62. *Superintendent's Statement to the Board of Visitors 1966;* Office of the Superintendent, box 4, folder 8, "Progress Report—Middle States Association," 27 February 1967; "Progress Report—Middle States, 1967–69"; "Follow-up Report to the Middle States Association," 7 October 1969.
63. Office of the Superintendent, box 4, folder 8, "Progress Report—Middle States Association," 27 February 1967; "Progress Report—Middle States, 1967–69"; "Follow-up Report to the Middle States Association." 7 October 1969; and *Reminiscences of Rear Admiral Draper Kauffman.*
64. Office of the Superintendent, box 4, folder 8, "Progress Report—Middle States Association," 27 February 1967; "Progress Report—Middle States, 1967–69"; "Follow-up Report to the Middle States Association." 7 October 1969; and *Reminiscences of Rear Admiral Draper Kauffman.*
65. *Reminiscences of Rear Admiral Draper Kauffman;* Lovell, *Neither Athens Nor Sparta?;* Office of the Superintendent, Vice Admiral James Calvert, Reference Files, box 2, folder 6, "Faculty—Civilian Faculty Affairs Committee."
66. *Reminiscences of Rear Admiral Draper Kauffman;* Lovell, *Neither Athens Nor Sparta?;* Office of the Superintendent, Vice Admiral James Calvert, Reference Files, box 2, folder 6, "Faculty—Civilian Faculty Affairs Committee."
67. *Reminiscences of Rear Admiral Draper Kauffman;* and Lovell, *Neither Athens Nor Sparta?*
68. *Reminiscences of Rear Admiral Draper Kauffman;* and Lovell, *Neither Athens Nor Sparta?*
69. "Academic Controversy," *Shipmate,* May 1966.
70. Letter from Vice Admiral William Smedberg to the *Washington Post, Shipmate,* May 1966.
71. *Report of the Middle States Association,* 20–23 March 1966.
72. "Survey of Midshipmen Life at the U.S. Naval Academy 1946–76," summary of observations for questions 17: "What did you consider the most challenging aspect of the plebe indoctrination system to be?" and 18: "What aspects, if any, of plebe indoctrination did you feel were counterproductive?"; and Commandant of Midshipmen Instruction 1531.2C, 10 August 1966, "Plebe Indoctrination."
73. "Survey of Midshipmen Life at the U.S. Naval Academy 1946–76," summary of observations for questions 17: "What did you consider the most challenging aspect of the plebe indoctrination system to be?" and 18: "What aspects, if any, of plebe indoctrination did you feel were counterproductive?"; and Commandant of Midshipmen Instruction 1531.2C, 10 August 1966, "Plebe Indoctrination."
74. *Superintendent's Statement to the Board of Visitors 1965; Superintendent's Statement to the Board of Visitors 1966; Superintendent's Statement to the Board of Visitors 1967;* and *Reminiscences of Rear Admiral Draper Kauffman.*
75. "Survey of Midshipmen Life at the U.S. Naval Academy 1946–76," Table 15 "To what degree, did the plebe system vary by company or battalion?" and Table 21 "What accounted most for any variations in the plebe system?"
76. "Survey of Midshipmen Life at the U.S. Naval Academy 1946–76," Table 31 "Who controlled the Brigade on a day to day basis?" and Table 32 "What functions did company officers perform best?"; and "Salty Sam," *The Log,* 17 November 1967 talks about just such an incident—a company officer was more concerned about the condition of a first classman's uniform than his physical hazing of a plebe.

77. "Survey of Midshipmen Life at the U.S. Naval Academy 1946–76," summary of observations to question 19: "In what ways did plebe indoctrination prepare you for your service with the fleet?"; and "On the Subject of Plebe Year," *Shipmate,* February 1967.

78. Papers of Captain Wayne Hoof; Heise, *The Brass Factories.*

79. Letter from Captain Wayne Hoof to Chief of Naval Personnel, dated 2 November 1966, "Plebe Indoctrination System at U.S. Naval Academy"; and Letter from Captain Wayne Hoof to the Secretary of the Navy, dated 21 November 1966, "Constructive Criticism and Suggestion pertaining to Improvements in Naval Efficiency."

80. Memorandum of Telephone Conversation between Captain Wayne Hoof and Captain Kenneth Brown concerning Brown's testimony made during the Randolph Investigation, dated 18 January 1967.

81. Papers of Captain Wayne Hoof; Heise, *The Brass Factories.*

82. Letter from Professor Robert Seager to Rear Admiral Draper Kauffman, dated 19 October 1966; Letter from Professor Robert Seager to Rear Admiral Draper Kauffman, dated 14 November 1966; and Letter from Professor Robert Seager to Rear Admiral Draper Kauffman, dated 28 November 1966.

83. Letter from Professor Robert Seager to Rear Admiral Draper Kauffman, dated 19 October 1966.

84. Ibid.

85. Letter from Professor E. B. Potter to Head of the English, History, and Government Department, dated 21 October 1966, "Plebe Indoctrination at the U.S. Naval Academy."

86. Ibid.

87. Ibid.

88. Letter from Chairman, Fourth Class Committee (Professor A. S. Pitt) to Head of English, History, and Government Department, dated 21 October 1966, "Plebe Indoctrination System."

89. Letter from Professor Douglas R. Lacey to Head of English, History, and Government Department, dated 24 October 1966, "Plebe Indoctrination."

90. Letter from Head of English, History, and Government Department to Superintendent, U.S. Naval Academy, dated 10 October 1966, explaining reasons for request of change of duty orders.

91. Letter from Captain Wayne Hoof to Chief of Naval Personnel, dated 2 November 1966, "Plebe Indoctrination System at U.S. Naval Academy."

92. Ibid.

93. "Salty Sam," *The Log,* 6 October 1967, 3 November 1967, and 15 December 1967.

94. "Superintendent's goals for upcoming academic year," *The Log,* 30 September 1966.

95. Letter from Head of English, History and Government Department to Superintendent, dated 13 October 1966, "Plebe Indoctrination Program."

96. Ibid.

97. Letter from Head of English, History, and Government Department to Superintendent, dated 10 October 1966, "Midshipman L. A. Panza, Fourth Class."

98. Letter from Midshipmen Leonard Panza to Superintendent, dated 10 October 1966, discussing reasons for resignation.

99. Letter from Midshipmen Jeffrey Leppert to Secretary of the Navy, dated 11 December 1966, discussing reasons for resignation.

100. Letter from Captain Wayne Hoof to Chief of Naval Personnel, dated 2 November 1966, "Plebe Indoctrination System at U.S. Naval Academy"; and Letter from Captain Wayne Hoof to the Secretary of the Navy, dated 21 November 1966, "Constructive Criticism and Suggestion Pertaining to Improvements in Naval Efficiency."

101. Letter from Professor Robert Seager to Superintendent, dated 14 November 1966, discussing the case of Midshipman Anthony Jackson.
102. Letter from Midshipman Anthony Jackson to Professor Robert Seager, dated 7 November 1966, discussing reasons for resignation.
103. Letter from Head of English, History and Government Department to Superintendent, dated 13 October 1966, "Plebe Indoctrination Program."
104. Letter from Captain Wayne Hoof to Chief of Naval Personnel, dated 2 November 1966, "Plebe Indoctrination System at U.S. Naval Academy."
105. Ibid.
106. Ibid.
107. Letter from Captain Wayne Hoof to the Secretary of the Navy, dated 21 November 1966, "Constructive Criticism and Suggestion Pertaining to Improvements in Naval Efficiency."
108. Letter from Superintendent to Captain Wayne Hoof, dated 7 November 1966; and Letter from Superintendent to Captain Wayne Hoof, dated 15 November 1966, both on the subject "Investigation of Plebe Indoctrination System."
109. Letter from Superintendent to Captain Wayne Hoof, dated 15 November 1966.
110. Letter from Commander Donald Smith to Superintendent, dated 22 November 1966, "Investigation of Allegations Concerning Plebe Indoctrination System at U.S. Naval Academy."
111. Letter from Captain Wayne Hoof to Chief of Naval Personnel, dated 18 November 1966, "Plebe Indoctrination System"; Letter from Captain Wayne Hoof to the Secretary of the Navy, dated 21 November 1966, "Constructive Criticism and Suggestion Pertaining to Improvements in Naval Efficiency"; and Letter from Captain Wayne Hoof to Chief of Naval Operations, dated 21 November 1966, "Plebe Indoctrination System."
112. Memorandum from Public Affairs Officer to Superintendent, dated 21 November 1966, "Discussion with *New York Times* Reporter Ben Franklin."
113. Papers of Captain Wayne Hoof; and Heise, *The Brass Factories.*
114. Superintendent Memorandum, dated 18 November 1966, "Midshipmen Time and Effort Board"; Letter from Midshipmen Time and Effort Working Committee to Chairman, Midshipmen Time and Effort Board, dated 12 December 1966, "Impact of Plebe Indoctrination."
115. Superintendent Memorandum, dated 18 November 1966, "Midshipmen Time and Effort Board"; Letter from Midshipmen Time and Effort Working Committee to Chairman, Midshipmen Time and Effort Board, dated 12 December 1966, "Impact of Plebe Indoctrination."
116. "Plebe Year," *Shipmate,* February 1967.
117. Correspondence between Captain Hoof and Professor Seager after crisis was over; Captain Hoof's obituary in *Shipmate,* May 1990; and *Reminiscences of Rear Admiral Draper Kauffman.*
118. *Superintendent's Statement to the Board of Visitors 1967; Superintendent's Statement to the Board of Visitors 1968;* and *Reminiscences of Rear Admiral Draper Kauffman.*
119. *Superintendent's Statement to the Board of Visitors 1967; Superintendent's Statement to the Board of Visitors 1968;* and *Reminiscences of Rear Admiral Draper Kauffman.*
120. *Superintendent's Statement to the Board of Visitors 1967; Superintendent's Statement to the Board of Visitors 1968;* and *Reminiscences of Rear Admiral Draper Kauffman.*
121. *Reminiscences of Rear Admiral Draper Kauffman.*
122. *Superintendent's Statement to the Board of Visitors 1967; Superintendent's Statement to the Board of Visitors 1968;* and *Reminiscences of Rear Admiral Draper Kauffman.*
123. *Superintendent's Statement to the Board of Visitors 1967; Superintendent's Statement to the Board of Visitors 1968;* and *Reminiscences of Rear Admiral Draper Kauffman.*

124. *Superintendent's Statement to the Board of Visitors 1967; Superintendent's Statement to the Board of Visitors 1968;* and *Reminiscences of Rear Admiral Draper Kauffman.*
125. *Superintendent's Statement to the Board of Visitors 1967; Superintendent's Statement to the Board of Visitors 1968;* and *Reminiscences of Rear Admiral Draper Kauffman.*
126. *Reminiscences of Rear Admiral Draper Kauffman.*

CHAPTER 6. THE FINE LINE BETWEEN ATHENS AND SPARTA

1. For Calvert's biography, see "And Calvert Personified Innovation," *Baltimore Sun,* 4 June 1973; John Lovell, *Neither Athens Nor Sparta?;* and Sweetman and Cutler, *The U.S. Naval Academy.*
2. James Calvert, *Surface at the Pole; the Extraordinary Voyages of the USS Skate* (New York: McGraw-Hill, 1960); and James Calvert, *The Naval Profession* (New York: McGraw-Hill, 1971).
3. James Calvert, "The Fine Line at the Naval Academy," *Proceedings,* October 1970.
4. James, Calvert, "Thoughts Upon Conclusion of a Four Year Tour," *Shipmate,* April 1972.
5. Office of the Superintendent, Vice Admiral James Calvert, Reference Files, box 1, folder 10, "Grooming and Uniform Standards, 1970–72."
6. The chapel court case was covered extensively in the major newspapers. See "Seven Service Academy Students Sue On Chapel Attendance Regulation," *Washington Post,* 21 January 1970; "Compulsory Worship," *The Washington Post,* 26 January 1970; "Chapel Suit," *The Evening Capital,* 28 January 1970; "Is Compulsory Chapel Unconstitutional?," *Washington Post,* 7 February 1970; and "Calvert Says Compulsory Worship Vital," *The Evening Capital,* 10 February 1970. See also *Reminiscences of Captain Roland Faulk,* U.S. Naval Institute Oral History Program, 10 November 1974. Faulk was the command chaplain at Annapolis during the court case. He opposed the continuance of mandatory chapel.
7. Interview with the author and Captain Eugene G. Anderson, 30 August 1998. Anderson served as the 6th Battalion Officer under Admiral Calvert. He was also the officer in charge of the Fourth Class Regiment during Calvert's substantial changes to the plebe system.
8. James Calvert, "The Fine Line at the Naval Academy," *Proceedings,* October 1970; and "Thoughts upon Conclusion of a Four Year Tour," *Shipmate,* April 1972.
9. "The Plebe Indoctrination System," *Shipmate,* June 1970; "Homecoming 1971," *Shipmate,* January 1972; "A Youngster Looks Back at Plebe Year," *Shipmate,* December 1971; *Superintendent's Statement to the Board of Visitors, April 1969; Superintendent's Statement to the Board of Visitors, May 1970; Superintendent's Statement to the Board of Visitors, April 1971;* and *Report of the Board of Visitors, December 1971.*
10. "A Few Inches from the Yard," *Shipmate,* March 1972
11. "Homecoming 1971," *Shipmate,* January 1972; "A Word from Today," *Shipmate,* September–October 1970; and *Superintendent's Statement to the Board of Visitors, April 1969.*
12. *U.S. Naval Academy Command History II 1970–71,* volume 1, Naval Academy Archives, Nimitz Library, Annapolis, Maryland; and "Homecoming 1971," *Shipmate,* January 1972.
13. Office of the Superintendent, Vice Admiral James Calvert, Reference Files, box 3, folder 17, "Midshipmen Publications—The Log 1970"; "Letters to the Editor," *The Log,* 19 November 1971; and "Sound Off '73," *The Log,* 19 November 1971.

14. "Homecoming 1971," *Shipmate,* January 1972. Admiral Calvert talked about the drug problem to parents in a personal letter dated 26 May 1971. The letter can be found in Office of the Superintendent, Vice Admiral James Calvert, Reference Files, box 3, folder 15, "Miscellaneous, 1968–71."

15. Hanson Baldwin, "Where Have All the Flowers Gone," *Shipmate,* September–October 1970; "Homecoming 1970," *Shipmate,* December 1970; and "Thoughts upon Conclusion of a Four Year Tour," *Shipmate,* April 1972.

16. "The Fine Line at the Naval Academy," *Proceedings,* October 1970; and "Thoughts upon Conclusion of a Four Year Tour," *Shipmate,* April 1972.

17. "The Fine Line at the Naval Academy," *Proceedings,* October 1970, and "Thoughts upon Conclusion of a Four Year Tour," *Shipmate,* April 1972.

18. Hanson Baldwin, "Where Have All the Flowers Gone"; and Paul Schratz, "And in 25 More Years," *Shipmate,* September–October 1970.

19. "A Last Word on Hair," *The Log,* 15 December 1971.

20. "Challenge and Change: The Naval Academy, 1959–68," *Shipmate,* April 1972.

21. "The Fine Line at the Naval Academy," *Proceedings,* October 1970.

22. Ibid.

23. *Superintendent's Statement to the Board of Visitors, November 1968;* and "Homecoming 1968," *Shipmate,* December 1968.

24. "The Fine Line at the Naval Academy," *Proceedings,* October 1970.

25. "Homecoming 1969," *Shipmate,* December 1969; "Homecoming 1970," *Shipmate,* December 1970; "Homecoming 1971," *Shipmate,* January 1972; and *Superintendent's Statement to the Board of Visitors, May 1970.*

26. "The Fine Line at the Naval Academy," *Proceedings,* October 1970; and "Thoughts upon Conclusion of a Four Year Tour," *Shipmate,* April 1972.

27. "The Fine Line at the Naval Academy," *Proceedings,* October 1970.

28. Ibid.

29. "The Fine Line at the Naval Academy," *Proceedings,* October 1970; and "The Naval Academy," *Army-Navy Football Program 1970,* Special Collections Division, Naval Academy Archives.

30. "The Naval Academy," *Army-Navy Football Program 1970,* Special Collections Division, Naval Academy Archives.

31. "Progress Report, Middle States Association, 1967–69"; Office of the Superintendent, box 4, folder 8, "Follow-up report to the Middle States Association, October 7, 1969"; and Office of the Superintendent, box 4, folder 99, "Middle States Association 1970–76."

32. Personal Letter from Admiral Calvert to Paul Schratz, 11 March 1970. Schratz was an analyst in naval affairs who wrote for *Shipmate* and other defense publications. The letter can be found in Office of the Superintendent, box 4, folder 99, "Middle States Association 1970–76."

33. "Distribution of Enrollment in Majors," *U.S. Naval Academy Command History 1972–73,* Naval Academy Archives, Nimitz Library.

34. Ibid.

35. Ibid.

36. "Distribution of Enrollment in Majors," *U.S. Naval Academy Command History 1972–73;* "Homecoming 1970," *Shipmate,* December 1970; *Superintendent's Statement to the Board of Visitors, May 1970;* and *Superintendent's Statement to the Board of Visitors, April 1971.*

37. "Distribution of Enrollment in Majors," *U.S. Naval Academy Command History 1972–73;* "Homecoming 1970," *Shipmate,* December 1970; *Superintendent's Statement to the Board of Visitors May 1970;* and *Superintendent's Statement to the Board of Visitors, April 1971.*

NOTES 383

38. Letter from Admiral Calvert to Parents of Midshipmen, 14 May 1971, *U.S. Naval Academy Command History II 1970–71.*
39. "Distribution of enrollment in majors," *U.S. Naval Academy Command History 1972–73.*
40. *Superintendent's Statement to the Board of Visitors, April 1971.*
41. *Superintendent's Statement to the Board of Visitors, April 1971;* and Letter from Admiral Calvert to Parents of Midshipmen, 14 May 1971.
42. "Reorganization of Academic Departments," *U.S. Naval Academy Command History 1972–73.*
43. Office of the Superintendent, Vice Admiral James Calvert, Reference Files, box 1, folder 17, "Organization, USNA, 1968, 70–71."
44. "Reorganization of Academic Departments," *U.S. Naval Academy Command History 1972–73.*
45. "Professional Training for Graduates of U.S. Naval Academy and NROTC," CNO memorandum for Secretary of the Navy, 24 February 1971, Office of the Superintendent, Vice Admiral James Calvert, Reference Files, box 3, folder 8, "Excess Leave (Law) Program 1971."
46. "Homecoming 1971," *Shipmate,* January 1972.
47. "Professional Training for Graduates of U.S. Naval Academy and NROTC," CNO memorandum for Secretary of the Navy, 24 February 1971.
48. "Naval Academy Excess Leave Program," Memorandum for Superintendent, USNA from BUPERS, 19 April 1971, Office of the Superintendent, Vice Admiral James Calvert, Reference Files, box 3, folder 8, "Excess Leave (Law) Program 1971."
49. Ibid.
50. "Naval Academy Excess Leave Program," Memorandum to BUPERS from Superintendent, USNA, 17 September 1971, Office of the Superintendent, Vice Admiral James Calvert, Reference Files, box 3, folder 8, "Excess Leave (Law) Program 1971."
51. "USNA Position Paper on Excess Leave Program," Office of the Superintendent, Vice Admiral James Calvert, Reference Files, box 3, folder 8, "Excess Leave (Law) Program 1971."
52. *Superintendent's Statement to the Board of Visitors, November 1968;* and "A Program for the Best—Find Them," *Shipmate,* January 1970.
53. "And in 25 More Years," *Shipmate,* September–October 1970.
54. "Thoughts upon Conclusion of a Four Year Tour," *Shipmate,* April 1972.
55. Personal Letter from Admiral Calvert to Paul Schratz, 11 March 1970.
56. *Board of Visitors Report, December 1968;* "Homecoming 1969," *Shipmate,* December 1969; and "Homecoming 1970," *Shipmate,* December 1970.
57. *Superintendent's Statement to the Board of Visitors, November 1968; Board of Visitors Report, May 1970.*
58. *Superintendent's Statement to the Board of Visitors, April 1971; Board of Visitors Report, December 1971;* and "Homecoming 1969," *Shipmate,* December 1969.
59. *Superintendent's Statement to the Board of Visitors, April 1971; Board of Visitors Report, December 1971.*
60. "Homecoming 1968," *Shipmate,* December 1968; "Homecoming 1969," *Shipmate,* December 1969; and "Homecoming 1970," *Shipmate,* December 1970.
61. *Board of Visitors Report, December 1971;* and *Board of Visitors Report, May 1972.*
62. *Board of Visitors Report, December 1971;* and *Board of Visitors Report, May 1972.*
63. "Survey of Midshipmen Life at the U.S. Naval Academy 1946–76," Table 40 "Did minority midshipmen get preferential treatment at the academy?"
64. "Do You Know Him?," *The Log,* 9 May 1969; "Midshipmen Resignations," Memorandum from Commandant of Midshipmen to Superintendent, 17 March 1971, Office of

Superintendent, Vice Admiral James Calvert, Reference Files, box 3, folder 19, "Midshipmen Resignations Voluntary, 1970–71."

65. "Homecoming 1969," *Shipmate,* December 1969; and "Homecoming 1970," *Shipmate,* December 1970.

66. Office of Superintendent, Vice Admiral James Calvert, Reference Files, box 3, folder 19, "Midshipmen Resignations Voluntary, 1970–71."

67. "The Fine Line at the Naval Academy," *Proceedings,* October 1970; "Homecoming 1970," *Shipmate,* December 1970; and "Distribution of enrollment in majors," *U.S. Naval Academy Command History 1972–73.*

68. "Survey of Midshipmen Life at the U.S. Naval Academy 1946–76," Table 27 "Unity building activities—common classes."

69. "Survey of Midshipmen Life at the U.S. Naval Academy 1946–76," Question 24: "Which groups did you forge your strongest relationships?"

70. "Comments on Report of Recruitment Research Study Group of 4 November 1970," Memorandum from Dean of Admissions to Superintendent, 23 November 1970, Office of Superintendent, Vice Admiral James Calvert, Reference Files, box 3, folder 19, "Midshipmen Resignations Voluntary, 1970–71."

71. Ibid.

72. "Questions and Answers," *Shipmate,* January 1969.

73. Office of the Superintendent, Vice Admiral James Calvert, Reference Files, box 3, folder 21, "Midshipmen Separations, 1967–68."

74. "Comments on Report of Recruitment Research Study Group of 4 November 1970," Memorandum from Dean of Admissions to Superintendent, 23 November 1970, Office of Superintendent, Vice Admiral James Calvert, Reference Files, box 3, folder 19, "Midshipmen Resignations Voluntary, 1970–71."

75. *Superintendent's Statement to the Board of Visitors, April 1971.*

76. "Thoughts upon Conclusion of a Four Year Tour," *Shipmate,* April 1972.

77. *U.S. Naval Academy Command History II 1970–71,* volume 1; *Board of Visitors Report December 1971; Superintendent's Statement to the Board of Visitors, April 1971;* and *Superintendent's Statement to the Board of Visitors, May 1970.*

78. *U.S. Naval Academy Command History II 1970–71,* volume 1; *Board of Visitors Report December 1971; Superintendent's Statement to the Board of Visitors, April 1971;* and *Superintendent's Statement to the Board of Visitors, May 1970.*

79. *Superintendent's Statement to the Board of Visitors, April 1971;* and *Superintendent's Statement to the Board of Visitors,* May 1970.

80. Office of the Superintendent, Vice Admiral James Calvert, Reference Files, box 3, folder 1, "Midshipmen At-Sea Training, 1967–71."

81. Letter from Superintendent USNA to Commander, Cruiser-Destroyer Force Atlantic, Office of the Superintendent, Vice Admiral James Calvert, Reference Files, box 3, folder 1, "Midshipmen At-Sea Training, 1967–71."

82. Letter from Commander, Submarine Force Atlantic to Superintendent, USNA, Office of the Superintendent, Vice Admiral James Calvert, Reference Files, box 3, folder 1, "Midshipmen At-Sea Training, 1967–71."

83. *Superintendent's Statement to the Board of Visitors, May 1970.*

84. USNA Instruction 1531.30, "USNA Professional Competency Objectives," 14 April 1972.

85. USNA Instruction 1531.30, "Competency Expected of a U.S. Naval Academy Graduate in the Naval Profession," 14 April 1972.

86. See Memorandum for the Classes of 1973 and 1974, "Professional Readiness Objectives and Examination," 24 May 1972; and "The Log Advisor," *The Log,* 28 April 1972 for the midshipmen's reaction to the exam.

87. *Board of Visitors Report, April 1971.*
88. "Thoughts upon Conclusion of a Four Year Tour," *Shipmate,* April 1972; and "Salty Sam," *The Log,* 30 October 1972 for midshipmen's reaction to this policy.
89. Interview with the author and Captain Eugene G. Anderson, 30 August 1998.
90. *Superintendent's Statement to the Board of Visitors, November 1968;* and *Superintendent's Statement to the Board of Visitors, April 1969.*
91. To illustrate the quality of company officers being assigned at this time, three of Anderson's officers eventually went on to flag rank in the late 1980s: Gary Roughead, Albert Koneztni, and future Marine commandant, Charles Krulak.
92. *Superintendent's Statement to the Board of Visitors, April 1969.*
93. "Homecoming 1969," *Shipmate,* December 1969; and "Homecoming 1971," *Shipmate,* January 1972.
94. *Superintendent's Statement to the Board of Visitors, April 1969.*
95. Ibid.
96. *Superintendent's Statement to the Board of Visitors, May 1970; Superintendent's Statement to the Board of Visitors, April 1971; Board of Visitors Report, December 1971.*
97. "A Word from Today," *Shipmate,* September–October 1970.
98. "Letters to the Editor," *The Log,* 21 November 1969.
99. "Editorial on Plebe System," *The Log,* 3 October 1969; and "Speaking Out," *The Log,* 17 October 1969.
100. "Homecoming 1971," *Shipmate,* January 1972; and "A Few Inches from the Yard," *Shipmate,* March 1972.
101. "Homecoming 1971," *Shipmate,* January 1972; and "A Few Inches from the Yard," *Shipmate,* March 1972.
102. "Homecoming 1971," *Shipmate,* January 1972; and "A Few Inches from the Yard," *Shipmate,* March 1972.
103. "Analyzing the New USNA," *The Log,* 9 October 1970.
104. "Salty Sam," *The Log,* 18 February 1972; and "Salty Sam," *The Log,* 21 November 1969.
105. "Letters to the Editor," *The Log,* 19 November 1971.
106. "Letters to the Editor," *The Log,* 20 February 1970.
107. "Letters to the Editor," *The Log,* 19 November 1971.
108. "It's That Time Again: Gold Stripe Fever," *The Log,* 21 November 1969.
109. "Letters to the Editor," *The Log,* 20 February 1970.
110. "Survey of Midshipmen Life at the U.S. Naval Academy, 1946–76," summary of observations to question 58: "In what ways did the Vietnam War affect life at the Naval Academy?"
111. "Logging" and "In Memoriam," *The Log,* 11 February 1966; and "Salty Sam," *The Log,* 22 April 1966.
112. "Looking Back On Four Years," *The Log,* 31 May 1967; and "A Time to Think, A Time to Remember," *The Log,* 8 November 1968.
113. "An Officer's Moral Obligation," *The Log,* 23 April 1971; and "Letters to the Editor," *The Log,* 10 April 1970.
114. "We Can't Let Them Be Forgotten," *The Log,* 20 November 1970; "Just 1600 Men" and "The SECNAV Speaks Out on POWs," *Shipmate,* April 1971.
115. "Ecology is Real," *The Log,* 10 April 1970.
116. "Politics and the (Single) Mid," *The Log,* 19 November 1971.
117. "A Mids-eye View of Woodstock," *The Log,* 3 October 1969.
118. Office of the Superintendent, Vice Admiral James Calvert, Reference Files, box 3, folder 17, "Midshipmen Publications—The Log 1970."
119. Ibid.

120. "Seven Service Academy Students Sue On Chapel Attendance Regulation," *Washington Post,* 21 January 1970; "Compulsory Worship," *Washington Post,* 26 January 1970; "Chapel Suit," *The Evening Capital,* 28 January 1970; "Is Compulsory Chapel Unconstitutional?," *Washington Post,* 7 February 1970; and "Calvert Says Compulsory Worship Vital," *The Evening Capital,* 10 February 1970. See also *Reminiscences of Captain Roland Faulk,* U.S. Naval Institute Oral History Program, 10 November 1974.
121. "Salty Sam," *The Log,* 30 January 1970.
122. "Editorial," *The Log,* 30 January 1970.
123. "Letters to the Editor," *The Log,* 10 April 1970.
124. Office of the Superintendent, Vice Admiral James Calvert, Reference Files, box 3, folder 17, "Midshipmen Publications—The Log 1970."
125. Office of the Superintendent, Vice Admiral James Calvert, Reference Files, box 1, folder 10, "Grooming Standards."
126. "Letters to the Editor," *The Log,* 17 October 1969.
127. "Letters to the Editor," *The Log,* 28 March 1972.
128. "A Last Word On Hair," *The Log,* 15 December 1971.
129. "Dear John," *The Log,* 17 November 1967, 19 January 1968, 1 March 1968, 3 May 1968, and 20 November 1970.
130. "Where to Live—Or How to Entertain and Play on $7.16 a Month," *The Log,* 15 December 1971.
131. "Survey of Midshipmen Life at the U.S. Naval Academy, 1946–76," Table 11 "Did you intend on a military career before you entered the academy?"
132. "Is the Grass Greener?," *The Log,* 15 December 1971.
133. "73 Sounds Off," *The Log,* 19 November 1971.
134. "Survey of Midshipmen Life at the U.S. Naval Academy 1946–76," Table 60 "Overall ranking of academy experience," and Table 61 "Would you have attended another undergraduate institution?"
135. "73 Sounds Off," *The Log,* 19 November 1971.
136. "Different—Sure We're Different," *The Lucky Bag 1970.*

Chapter 7. Steering a Sensible Course

1. Lovell, *Neither Athens Nor Sparta?*
2. "Worlds Apart?," *Proceedings,* April 1973.
3. *Reminiscences of Vice Admiral William Mack,* U.S. Naval Institute Oral History Program, March 1980.
4. Ibid.
5. Ibid.
6. *U.S. Naval Academy Command History, Volume 6, 1974–75,* Naval Academy Archives, Nimitz Library, Annapolis, Maryland.
7. Ibid.
8. "Review of Faculty Mix at U.S. Service Academies and the Senior and Intermediate Colleges, 16 March 1977," Naval Academy Archives, Nimitz Library, Annapolis, Maryland.
9. *Reminiscences of Vice Admiral William Mack.* "Alumni Assembly 1974," *Shipmate,* January 1975.
10. "Alumni Assembly 1974," *Shipmate,* January 1975.
11. *U.S. Naval Academy Command History, Volume 6, 1974–75;* and *Report to the U.S. Naval Academy by the Middle States Association, 14–17 March 1976.*

NOTES 387

12. *Board of Visitors Report, December 1972; Board of Visitors Report, April 1973; Superintendent's Statement to the Board of Visitors, December 1973;* and *Reminiscences of Vice Admiral William Mack.* "Rickover on USNA," *The Log,* 26 April 1974.
13. "Rickover on USNA," *The Log,* 26 April 1974.
14. "Questions and Answers Alumni Assembly 1976," *Shipmate* December 1976; *U.S. Naval Academy Command History, Volume 6, 1974–75;* and *Reminiscences of Vice Admiral William Mack.*
15. *U.S. Naval Academy Command History, Volume 6, 1974–75; Superintendent's Statement to the Board of Visitors, December 1973;* and *Superintendent's Statement to the Board of Visitors, November 1975.*
16. *Board of Visitors Report, April 1974; Superintendent's Statement to the Board of Visitors, December 1973;* and *Board of Visitors Report, December 1973.*
17. *Superintendent's Statement to the Board of Visitors, April 1974.*
18. *Superintendent's Statement to the Board of Visitors, November 1975;* and *Reminiscences of Vice Admiral William Mack.*
19. *U.S. Naval Academy Command History, Volume 6, 1974–75.*
20. "Mailboat," *Shipmate,* June 1973.
21. Ibid.
22. *Report to the U.S. Naval Academy by the Middle States Association, 14–17 March 1976; Reminiscences of Vice Admiral William Mack; Superintendent's Statement to the Board of Visitors, November 1975;* and *Superintendent's Statement to the Board of Visitors, December 1973.*
23. *Reminiscences of Vice Admiral William Mack.*
24. Ibid.
25. "Changes in the Making," *The Log,* 6 February 1976.
26. Memorandum from the Chief of Naval Operations to Deputy Chief of Naval Operations (Manpower), Director, Naval Education and Training; and Superintendent, U.S. Naval Academy, "Naval Academy Education and Training Policy," 3 November 1975.
27. "Minutes of the Spring 1977 Meeting of the Academic Advisory Board," *U.S. Naval Academy Command History, Volume 7, 1976–77.*
28. *Board of Visitors Report, December 1972; Board of Visitors Report, April 1973; Superintendent's Statement to the Board of Visitors, December 1973.*
29. *U.S. Naval Academy Command History, Volume 6, 1974–75.*
30. *Board of Visitors Report, December 1972; Superintendent's Statement to the Board of Visitors, December 1973;* and *Superintendent's Statement to the Board of Visitors, July 1975.*
31. *Board of Visitors Report, December 1972; Superintendent's Statement to the Board of Visitors, December 1973;* and *Superintendent's Statement to the Board of Visitors, July 1975.*
32. *Board of Visitors Report, December 1972; Superintendent's Statement to the Board of Visitors, December 1973;* and *Superintendent's Statement to the Board of Visitors, July 1975.*
33. *Reminiscences of Vice Admiral William Mack.*
34. "Alumni Assembly," *Shipmate,* December 1972; and "Alumni Assembly 1974," *Shipmate,* January 1975.
35. *Superintendent's Statement to the Board of Visitors, December 1974;* and *Superintendent's Statement to the Board of Visitors, November 1975.*
36. *Superintendent's Statement to the Board of Visitors, December 1974;* and *Superintendent's Statement to the Board of Visitors, November 1975.*
37. "Over Rate Academics at USNA?," *Shipmate,* March 1976.

38. *Reminiscences of Vice Admiral William Mack; U.S. Naval Academy Command History, Volume 5, 1973–74;* and "Alumni Assembly 1974," *Shipmate,* January 1975.

39. *Reminiscences of Vice Admiral William Mack;* "Interview with Rear Admiral Max Morris," *The Log,* 1 June 1973; and "New 'dant Discusses Goals," *The Log,* 5 October 1973.

40. *Board of Visitors Report, December 1972.*

41. Commandant of Midshipmen Notice 1531, "Sunday Morning Activities," 5 January 1973; and *Reminiscences of Vice Admiral William Mack.*

42. "The Big Mack," *The Log,* 17 November 1972.

43. Commandant of Midshipmen Notice 1000, "Advance Change No. 5–1 to Midshipmen Regulations Hair and Beards," 31 October 1972.

44. "Salty Sam," *The Log,* 17 November 1972; and "Letters to the Editor," *The Log,* 13 December 1972.

45. "Alumni Assembly 1974," *Shipmate* March 1975.

46. "Letters to the Editor," *The Log,* 17 November 1972.

47. "Editorial," *The Log,* 17 November 1972.

48. "Alumni Assembly 1974," *Shipmate* March 1975; and Midshipmen Regulations Advance Change 6–2, Rule 0402 "Use of Alcoholic Beverages," *U.S. Naval Academy Command History 1972–73.*

49. "Alumni Assembly 1974," *Shipmate* March 1975; and Midshipmen Regulations Advance Change 6–2, Rule 0402 "Use of Alcoholic Beverages," *U.S. Naval Academy Command History 1972–73.*

50. *Reminiscences of Vice Admiral William Mack;* "Interview with Rear Admiral Max Morris," *The Log,* 1 June 1973; and "New 'dant Discusses Goals," *The Log,* 5 October 1973.

51. "Has the academy gone to hell?," *Shipmate* January–February 1976; and "Re. Has the academy gone to hell?," *Shipmate,* May 1976.

52. "Has the academy gone to hell?," *Shipmate* January–February 1976; and "Re. Has the academy gone to hell?," *Shipmate,* May 1976.

53. "A Few Inches from the Yard," *Shipmate,* January 1975.

54. Ibid.

55. Ibid.

56. *Reminiscences of Vice Admiral William Mack;* and "Letters to the Editor," *The Log,* 23 March 1973.

57. "Interview with Rear Admiral Max Morris," *The Log,* 1 June 1973; and "New 'dant Discusses Goals," *The Log,* 5 October 1973.

58. "Mailboat," *Shipmate,* June 1976.

59. *Superintendent's Statement to the Board of Visitors, July 1975.*

60. "4–1's Finest," *The Log,* 4 October 1974, and "Interview with Jim Fitzsimonds," *The Log,* 26 April 1974.

61. *U.S. Naval Academy Report to the Middle States Association 26 November 1946; Evaluation Report for the Middle States Association 26 February 1956;* and *Report of the Middle States Association Evaluation of the U.S. Naval Academy, 20 March 1966.*

62. *Report to the U.S. Naval Academy by the Middle States Association, 14–17 March 1976.*

63. Ibid.

64. Ibid.

65. Ibid.

66. Ibid.

Bibliography

Contemporary Works on the Naval Academy

"Academic Program at USNA." *Shipmate,* May 1967.
"The Academy Executive Department." *Shipmate,* June 1952.
"Air Cruises and Summer Training." *Shipmate,* August–September 1949.
"Alumni Assembly—Questions and Answers, Homecoming 1962." *Shipmate,* November 1962.
"Alumni Assembly 1964." *Shipmate,* November 1964.
"Alumni Assembly." *Shipmate,* November 1965.
"Alumni Assembly." *Shipmate,* December 1966.
"Alumni Assembly." *Shipmate,* January 1968.
"Alumni Assembly." *Shipmate,* December 1972.
"Alumni Assembly 1974." *Shipmate,* January 1975.
"American Higher Education 1958." *Shipmate,* February 1958.
"An Open Letter to the Director of Athletics, USNA." *Shipmate,* February 1950.
"Attrition at the U.S. Naval Academy." *Shipmate,* September–October 1967.
"Bachelor of Science Degree for Graduates of the Naval Academy." *Shipmate,* December 1947.
Baldwin, Hanson. "Where Have All the Flowers Gone." *Shipmate,* September–October 1970.
Boroff, David. "Teaching Young Sea Dogs Old Tricks." *Harper's Magazine,* January 1963.
Brinckloe, William. "Is the Versatile Line Officer Obsolete?" *Proceedings,* June 1959.
Calvert, James. "The Fine Line at the Naval Academy." *Proceedings,* October 1970.
———. *The Naval Profession.* New York: McGraw-Hill, 1971.
———. "A Program for the Best—Find Them." *Shipmate,* January 1970.
———. *Surface at the Pole; the Extraordinary Voyages of the USS Skate.* New York: McGraw-Hill, 1960.
———. "Thoughts upon Conclusion of a Four Year Tour." *Shipmate,* April 1972.
"Can the Navy Ever Be Obsolete?" *Shipmate,* February 1946.
"Calvert Says Compulsory Worship Vital." *The Evening Capital,* 10 February 1970.
"Career Men." *Shipmate,* November 1949.
Chafee, John. "The SECNAV Speaks Out on POWs." *Shipmate,* April 1971.
"Challenge and Change, The Naval Academy, 1959–68." *Shipmate,* April 1972.
"Chapel Suit." *The Evening Capital,* 28 January 1970.
Coleman, Sam. "Midshipmen Get Air Training." *Shipmate,* February 1946.
"Compulsory Worship." *Washington Post,* 26 January 1970.

389

"Crossroads of the Navy." *Shipmate,* November 1947.
Defrancia, James. "Annapolis—The Rebuttal of a Young Sea Dog." *Shipmate,* April 1963.
"Distribution of Enrollment in Majors." *Shipmate,* December 1070.
"Dunking Drills Prepare Midshipmen for Possible Emergency Plane Crashes." *Shipmate,* June 1948.
Edelstein, Daniel. "Worlds Apart." *Proceedings,* April 1973.
"Education for Naval Officers—What Should It Be?" *Shipmate,* February 1963.
"Electives—Boon or Bane?" *Shipmate,* August 1959.
Eller, E. M. "Will We Need a Navy to Win?" *Shipmate,* August 1951.
"Enterprise Bell." *Shipmate,* June 1951.
"Faculty Study." *Shipmate,* March 1968.
"A Few Inches From The Yard." *Shipmate,* March 1972.
"A Few Inches from the Yard." *Shipmate,* January 1975.
Finos, V. P. "Regarding Has the Academy Gone to Hell." *Shipmate,* May 1976.
Fitzgerald, W. F. "Academic Controversy." *Shipmate,* May 1966.
Franklin, Ben. "Grades Inflated for Midshipmen." *New York Times,* 10 April 1966.
—. "Rift Remains at Annapolis after Mediators Leave." *New York Times,* 20 November 1966.
Hawkins. Ernest. "The Naval Academy, Its Mission and Staff." *Shipmate,* September–October 1967.
Hayes, John. "Defense Reorganization—Why Not the Navy Way?" *Shipmate,* February 1958.
Heise, J. Arthur. *The Brass Factories: A Frank Appraisal of West Point, Annapolis, and the Air Force Academy.* Washington, D.C.: Public Affairs Press, 1969.
Higbee, John. "A Youngster Looks Back at Plebe Year." *Shipmate,* December 1971.
"The Holloway Plan." *Proceedings,* November 1948.
"Homecoming 1968." *Shipmate,* December 1968.
"Homecoming 1969." *Shipmate,* December 1969.
"Homecoming 1970." *Shipmate,* December 1970.
"Homecoming 1971." *Shipmate,* January 1972.
Howe, F. N. "The Plebe Indoctrination System." *Shipmate,* June 1970.
Hughes, Wayne. "New Directions in Naval Academy Education." *Proceedings,* May 1960.
Huntington, Samuel. "Educational Policy Change at USNA." *Shipmate,* August 1962.
"Is Compulsory Chapel Unconstitutional?" *Washington Post,* 7 February 1970.
Kalisch, Bertram. "Unification—A Blessing or a Curse?" *Shipmate,* November 1949.
Lautermilch, P. A. "Where Do We Go from Here?" *Shipmate,* June 1951.
"Letter from Professor Vince Davis on USNA Curriculum." *Shipmate,* March 1967.
"Letter from Vice Admiral William Smedberg to *The Washington Post,*" *Shipmate,* May 1966.
"Letter in Response to Open Letter." *Shipmate,* April 1951.
"Mailboat." *Shipmate,* June 1973.
———. *Shipmate,* June 1976.
Mann, Gregory. "The Relationship Between Athletic Participation and Non-Academic Adjustment at the U.S. Naval Academy." Ph.D. dissertation, University of Maryland, 1957.

McDonough, Joseph. "Down in Maryland with that Sailor Band." *Shipmate*, June 1958.
McKean, William. "Demise of a Dream—Why the Holloway Plan Failed." *Shipmate*, January 1958.
McNitt, Robert. "A New Marking System at USNA." *Shipmate*, September–October 1963.
"Memorial Plaques for Medal of Honor Winners." *Shipmate*, September 1950.
"Midshipmen Serve on Submarines for the Summer." *Shipmate*, August 1961.
"More Nuclear Power Trainees Wanted." *Shipmate*, February 1955.
"More on Navy Football." *Shipmate*, January 1951.
"More Questions—1967 Alumni Assembly." *Shipmate*, February 1968.
National Alumni Public Relations Committee. "Polaris—How Good?" *Shipmate*, June–July 1960.
"Naval Academy Performance and Career Success." *Shipmate*, December 1964.
"New Swearing-In Ceremony." *Shipmate*, August 1962.
Nimitz, Chester. "Graduation Address by Fleet Admiral Nimitz." *Shipmate*, July 1946.
"On the Subject of Plebe Year." *Shipmate*, February 1967.
Perot, H. Ross. "Just 1600 Men." *Shipmate*, April 1971.
"Plebe Year." *Shipmate*, February 1967.
"President's Page." *Shipmate*, January 1949.
"Questions and Answers at the Alumni Assembly." *Shipmate*, November 1961.
"Questions and Answers." *Shipmate*, January 1969.
"Questions and Answers Alumni Assembly 1976." *Shipmate*, December 1976.
"Reorganization of Academic Departments." *Shipmate*, April 1959.
"A Reserve Looks at Regulars." *Shipmate*, July 1946.
"Resignation of Academy Men." *Shipmate*, September 1957.
"Rhodes Scholars? Yes! But Naval Officers First—A Century of Academic Achievements." *Shipmate*, September–October 1963.
Rickover, Hyman. *American Education: A National Failure*. New York: E. P. Dutton, 1963.
———. *Swiss Schools and Ours: Why Theirs Are Better*. New York: Little and Brown, 1962.
"Rickover's Criticisms of the Naval Academy." *Shipmate*, August 1959.
Schlosser, Frank. "The Trend in Intercollegiate Athletics." *Shipmate*, February 1950.
Schratz, Paul. "And in 25 More Years." *Shipmate*, September–October 1970.
"A Serious and Growing Problem." *Shipmate*, April 1968.
"Seven Service Academy Students Sue on Chapel Attendance Regulation." *Washington Post*, 21 January 1970.
Sher, Tom. "A Word from Today." *Shipmate*, September–October 1970.
Sima, F. F. "Has the Academy Gone to Hell?" *Shipmate*, January-February 1976.
Simons, William. *Liberal Education in the Service Academies*. New York: Teacher's College, Columbia University, 1965.
"So You Want Out." *Shipmate*, March 1954.
Speer, Talbot. "A West Coast Naval Academy?" *The Evening Capital*, 6 February 1941.
"Superintendent's Report—Board of Trustees Meeting." *Shipmate*, January 1963.
"Superintendent's Report on the Use of the CEEB Test for Entrance to the Naval Academy." *Shipmate*, September 1958.
"The Superintendent Reports." *Shipmate*, August 1956.

"The Superintendent Reports." *Shipmate*, February 1957.
"The Superintendent Reports." *Shipmate*, June–July 1959.
"The Superintendent Reports." *Shipmate*, September—October 1959.
"The Superintendent Reports." *Shipmate*, June–July 1960.
"The Superintendent Reports." *Shipmate*, September 1960.
"The Superintendent Reports—A New Administrative Organization." *Shipmate*, September–October 1964.
"The Superintendent Reports on the Eve of Departure." *Shipmate*, June–July 1965.
Taylor, E. B. "A Football Report." *Shipmate*, January 1948.
Thomas, Philip. "USNA—1947 Model." *Shipmate*, August 1947.
Timberg, Robert. "And Calvert Personified Innovation." *Baltimore Sun*, 4 June 1973.
"To Naval Academy Alumni from the Superintendent." *Shipmate*, April 1951.
"Undesirable Attrition." *Shipmate*, January 1952.
"Unification vs. Merger." *Shipmate*, January 1946.
"USNA—1948 Model." *Shipmate*, November 1948.
"The USNA and Its Curriculum—A Chronology of Changes and Some Problems." *Shipmate*, March 1968.
"USNA Still Needs a Library." *Shipmate*, April 1961.
Weise, Steve. "Over Rate Academics at USNA?" *Shipmate*, March 1976.
"Why a Naval Academy Athletic Association?" *Shipmate*, November 1957.
"Why Not a Navy Gray Line?" *Shipmate*, January 1946.
Williams, Winston. "I Gave Up the Ship." *Shipmate*, January 1949.
Wright, Jerauld. "USNA Faculty Reorganization." *Shipmate*, September 1962.

Government Sources

United States General Accounting Office Report to Congressional Committees. "DOD Service Academies—Comparison of Honor and Adjudicatory Processes." April 1995.

United States General Accounting Office Report to Congressional Committees. "Review of Faculty Mix at U.S. Service Academies and the Senior and Intermediate Colleges." 16 March 1977.

U.S. Congress, House Committee on Appropriations. *Report on Russia by Vice Admiral Hyman Rickover.* Washington, D.C.: Government Printing Office, 1959.

U.S. Congress, House Committee on Appropriations. *Educational System at the Service Academies.* Washington, D.C.: Government Printing Office, 1959.

Investigations and Inspections of the Naval Academy

The Middle States Association of Colleges and Secondary Schools Evaluation Report of the U.S. Naval Academy, 1956.

Report of the Middle States Association Evaluation Team for the U.S. Naval Academy, March 1966.

Report to the U.S. Naval Academy by the Middle States Association, March 1976.

U.S. *Naval Academy Report to the Middle States Association and Evaluation Report,* November 1946.

Midshipmen Periodicals

The 1940s

"The Ballad of Slashin' Gish." *The Log,* 19 November 1948.
"The Brigade was Waiting." *The Lucky Bag 1949.*
"The Bull Department." *The Log,* 3 November 1944.
Child, Danny. "The Dope Sheet." *The Log,* 6 October 1944.
"The Dark Ages." *The Log,* 1 February 1946.
"Dragging thru the Ages." *The Log,* 2 May 1947.
Ingersoll, Stuart. "To the Brigade." *The Log,* 20 April 1945.
Kay, H. N. "The Plebe Goes Home." *The Log,* 18 January 1946.
Leyerle, J. F. "Wings of Gold." *The Log,* 15 February 1946.
The Lucky Bag 1947.
The Lucky Bag 1948A.
The Lucky Bag 1948B.
Monaghan, W. F. "A Message to '50." *The Log,* 11 October 1946.
"Old Navy Line." *The Log,* 3 November 1944.
———. *The Log,* 9 February 1945.
———. *The Log,* 20 April 1945.
"Salty Sam." *The Log,* 6 October 1944.
———. *The Log,* 3 November 1944.
———. *The Log,* 17 November 1944.
———. *The Log,* 1 December 1944.
———. *The Log,* 5 February 1945.
———. *The Log,* 9 February 1945.
———. *The Log,* 20 April 1945.
———. *The Log,* 7 December 1945.
———. *The Log,* 18 January 1946.
———. *The Log,* 1 February 1946.
———. *The Log,* 1 March 1946.
———. *The Log,* 3 May 1946.
———. *The Log,* 17 May 1946.
———. *The Log,* 31 May 1946.
———. *The Log,* 11 October 1946.
———. *The Log,* 26 March 1947.
———. *The Log,* 2 May 1947.
———. *The Log,* 10 October 1947.
———. *The Log,* 24 October 1947.
———. *The Log,* 5 December 1947.

———. *The Log,* 23 January 1948.
———. *The Log,* 16 April 1948.
———. *The Log,* 30 April 1948.
———. *The Log,* 5 November 1948.
———. *The Log,* 19 November 1948.
———. *The Log,* 7 January 1949.
———. *The Log,* 21 January 1949.
———. *The Log,* 7 February 1949.
Reavis, W. A. "Washday Blues." *The Log,* 1 March 1946.
Reef Points
"Spring." *The Log,* 3 May 1946.
Tolk, D. R. "Annapolis Looks to the Skies." *The Log,* 1 March 1946.

1950s

"All-American Boy." *The Log,* 20 March 1959.
"Beyond the Call." *The Log,* 30 March 1951.
"By the Services." *The Log,* 25 May 1951.
Cutter, Slade. "The Renaissance of Navy Sports." *The Log,* 7 November 1958.
Ellis, Don. "I Chose the Air Force." *The Log,* 1 December 1952.
———. "We Chose Navy Line." *The Log,* 13 February 1953.
Gerson, Gordy. "News of Engineering." *The Log,* 3 May 1957.
"The Inside on Eddie." *The Log,* 2 October 1953.
The Lucky Bag 1957.
Middleton, Johnny. "Clear the Bridge." *The Log,* 7 October 1955.
Oppenheimer, Phil. "The New Fleet." *The Log,* 24 October 1958.
Poole, Jim. "He Leads Us All." *The Log,* 24 January 1958.
———. "With High Aspirations: Presently at the Top in the Academic Struggle." *The Log,* 7 December 1956.
"Salty Sam." *The Log,* 27 January 1950.
———. *The Log,* 10 February 1950.
———. *The Log,* 3 March 1950.
———. *The Log,* 1 May 1950.
———. *The Log,* 12 May 1950.
———. *The Log,* 1 June 1950.
———. *The Log,* 1 November 1950.
———. *The Log,* 17 November 1950.
———. *The Log,* 1 December 1950.
———. *The Log,* 15 December 1950.
———. *The Log,* 12 January 1951.
———. *The Log,* 16 February 1951.
———. *The Log,* 13 April 1951.
———. *The Log,* 11 May 1951.

———. *The Log*, 17 October 1951.
———. *The Log*, 26 October 1951.
———. *The Log*, 9 November 1951.
———. *The Log*, 12 December 1951.
———. *The Log*, 18 January 1952.
———. *The Log*, 31 January 1952.
———. *The Log*, 30 May 1952.
———. *The Log*, 1 November 1952.
———. *The Log*, 1 December 1952.
———. *The Log*, 16 January 1953.
———. *The Log*, 30 January 1953.
———. *The Log*, 12 April 1953.
———. *The Log*, 30 April 1953.
———. *The Log*, 18 December 1953.
———. *The Log*, 16 April 1954.
———. *The Log*, 14 May 1954.
———. *The Log*, 24 September 1954.
———. *The Log*, 5 November 1954.
———. *The Log*, 4 March 1955.
———. *The Log*, 23 September 1955.
———. *The Log*, 21 October 1955.
———. *The Log*, 20 January 1956.
———. *The Log*, 3 February 1956.
———. *The Log*, 17 February 1956.
———. *The Log*, 11 May 1956.
———. *The Log*, 28 September 1956.
———. *The Log*, 23 November 1956.
———. *The Log*, 25 January 1957.
———. *The Log*, 8 March 1957.
———. *The Log*, 20 September 1957.
———. *The Log*, 18 October 1957.
———. *The Log*, 7 February 1958.
———. *The Log*, 2 May 1958.
———. *The Log*, 26 September 1958.
Schwer, Fred. "Top Man in the Brigade." *The Log*, 20 September 1957.
Silbey, Dave. "After Pensacola." *The Log*, 2 December 1955.
"To the Brigade." *The Log*, 8 October 1954.
"What Can You Expect in 15 Years?" *The Log*, 3 December 1954.
Williams, Jimmy, and Banana Oil Henderson. "Operation Propaganda." *The Log*, 13 December 1957.
Winnefeld, J. A. "How Many Admirals." *The Log*, 12 January 1951.
Wright, J. A. "Atomic Era Now Here." *The Log*, 8 October 1954.

The 1960s

"Dear John." *The Log*, 17 November 1967.

———. *The Log*, 19 January 1968.
———. *The Log*, 1 March 1968.
"Editorial on Plebe System." *The Log*, 3 October 1969.
"Ex Scientia Tridens—Navy's Trident Scholars Search for New Knowledge." *The Log*, 31 October 1963.
Johnson, J. T. "Report on the Academic Dean." *The Log*, 31 October 1963.
Kauffman, Draper. "Superintendent's Goals for Upcoming Academic Year." *The Log*, 30 September 1966.
Kirchberg, Mike. "Looking Back on Four Years." *The Log*, 31 May 1967.
"Letters to the Editor." *The Log*, 22 November 1960.
———. *The Log*, 12 May 1961.
———. *The Log*, 6 October 1961.
———. *The Log*, 17 October 1969.
———. *The Log*, 21 November 1969.
"Logging." *The Log*, 12 May 1961.
———. *The Log*, 6 October 1961.
———. *The Log*, 20 October 1961.
———. *The Log*, 17 November 1961.
———. *The Log*, 11 February 1966.
The Lucky Bag 1960.
Riles, C. E. "Do You Know Him?" *The Log*, 9 May 1969.
Sage, Jud. "The Air Force Academy Honor Conference." *The Log*, 6 April 1962.
"Salty Sam." *The Log*, 19 February 1960.
———. *The Log*, 4 March 1960.
———. *The Log*, 18 March 1960.
———. *The Log*, 17 April 1960.
———. *The Log*, 13 May 1960.
———. *The Log*, 30 September 1960.
———. *The Log*, 28 October 1960.
———. *The Log*, 17 November 1961.
———. *The Log*, 6 April 1962.
———. *The Log*, 5 October 1962.
———. *The Log*, 16 November 1962.
———. *The Log*, 14 December 1962.
———. *The Log*, 22 February 1963.
———. *The Log*, 22 April 1966.
———. *The Log*, 3 November 1967.
———. *The Log*, 17 November 1967.
———. *The Log*, 15 December 1967.
———. *The Log*, 21 November 1969.
Scheffer, Steve. "The Bitter End." *The Log*, 15 April 1960.
"Speaking Out." *The Log*, 17 October 1969.
Taylor, Bill. "In Memoriam." *The Log*, 11 February 1966.
Unhjem, Mark. "A Time To Think, A Time To Remember." *The Log*, 8 November 1968.

The 1970s

Akers, Carl. "Where to Live—Or How to Entertain and Play on $7.16 a Month." *The Log*, 15 December 1971.
"Changes in the Making." *The Log*, 6 February 1976.
"Different—Sure We're Different." *The Lucky Bag 1970*.
"Dear John." *The Log*, 20 November 1970.
Dean, Steve. "The Big Mack." *The Log*, 17 November 1972.
"Don't Let Them Be Forgotten." *The Lucky Bag 1971*.
"Drug Abuse." *The Lucky Bag 1971*.
"Ecology Is Real." *The Log*, 10 April 1970.
"Editorial." *The Log*, 30 January 1970.
———. *The Log*, 17 November 1972.
Erkenbrack, Steve. "A Last Word on Hair." *The Log*, 15 December 1971.
Fitzsimonds, Jim. "Rickover on USNA." *The Log*, 26 April 1974.
Foster, Brad. "Analyzing the New USNA." *The Log*, 9 October 1970.
"It's That Time Again: Gold Stripe Fever." *The Log*, 21 November 1969.
Kerekes, Bill. "Politics and the (Single) Mid." *The Log*, 19 November 1971.
Klein, Gary. " '73 Sounds Off." *The Log*, 19 November 1971.
"Letters to the Editor." *The Log*, 20 February 1970.
———. *The Log*, 10 April 1970.
———. *The Log*, 28 March 1972.
———. *The Log*, 17 November 1972.
———. *The Log*, 13 December 1972.
———. *The Log*, 23 March 1973.
"The Log Advisor." *The Log*, 28 April 1972.
The Lucky Bag 1970.
The Lucky Bag 1971.
The Lucky Bag 1972.
McKlesky, Kevin. "Sound Off '73." *The Log*, 19 November 1971.
Montor, Karel. "Is the Grass Greener?" *The Log*, 15 December 1971.
"An Officer's Moral Obligation." *The Log*, 23 April 1971.
"Salty Sam." *The Log*, 30 January 1970.
———. *The Log*, 10 April 1970.
———. *The Log*, 19 November 1971.
———. *The Log*, 18 February 1972.
———. *The Log*, 30 October 1972.
———. *The Log*, 17 November 1972.
———. *The Log*, 19 December 1973.
Stavridis, Jim. "Interview with Jim Fitzsimonds." *The Log*, 26 April 1974.
———. "Interview with Rear Admiral Max Morris." *The Log*, 1 June 1973.
———. "New 'dant Discusses Goals." *The Log*, 5 October 1973.
———. "4–1's Finest." *The Log*, 4 October 1974.
Trant, Mike. "A Mids-eye View of Woodstock." *The Log*, 3 October 1969.

"We Can't Let Them Be Forgotten." *The Log,* 20 November 1970.

NAVAL ACADEMY SOURCES

"Class Policy of 1948B." *Superintendent's Statement to the Board of Visitors 1950* and *Shipmate,* December 1947.
Commandant of Midshipmen Notice 1000, "Advance Change No. 5–1 to Midshipmen Regulations Hair and Beards." 31 October 1972.
Commandant of Midshipmen Notice 1531. "Sunday Morning Activities." 5 January 1973.
Holloway, James Jr. "The Holloway Plan—A Summary View and Commentary." *Report of the Board of Visitors of the U.S. Naval Academy, 1948.*
"Letter of the Superintendent to Parents and Guardians of Midshipmen June 1942." Vertical File, "U.S. Naval Academy."
Letter from the Chief of Naval Personnel to Dr. Richard Folsom, 31 March 1959.
Letter from Vice Admiral James Calvert to Parents of Midshipmen, 14 May 1971.
Memorandum for the Classes of 1973 and 1974. "Professional Readiness Objectives and Examination." 24 May 1972.
"Midshipmen Attrition and Turn Backs." Vertical File, Special Collections Division.
Midshipmen Regulations Advance Change 6–2 Rule 0402. "Use of Alcoholic Beverages."
Office of the Superintendent, General Correspondence, Historical Matters 1845–1959, Box 3, Folder 5.
Office of the Superintendent, Vice Admiral James Calvert, Reference Files. "Excess Leave (Law) Program 1971." Box 3, Folder 8.
———. "Faculty—Civilian Affairs Committee." Box 2, Folder 7.
———. "Faculty." Box 2, Folder 7.
———. "Faculty." Box 2, Folder 8.
———. "Faculty/Academic Dean Appointment 1965." Box 2, Folder 5.
———. "Grooming and Uniform Standards, 1970–72." Box 1, Folder 10.
———. "Middle States Association Preparation to Accreditation, 1965." Box 3, Folder 17.
———. "Middle Sates Association 1970–76." Box 4, Folder 8.
———. "Midshipmen At-Sea Training." Box 3, Folder 1.
———. "Midshipmen Attrition Statistics, 1959–67, 1970–71." Box 3, Folder 2.
———. "Midshipmen Publications—The Log 1970." Box 3, Folder 17.
———. "Midshipmen Recruiting Letters." Box 3, Folder 18.
———. "Midshipmen Resignations Voluntary, 1970–71." Box 3, Folder 19.
———. "Midshipmen Separations, 1967–68." Box 3, Folder 21.
———. "Miscellaneous, 1968–71." Box 3, Folder 15.
———. "Mobilization, 1968." Box 1, Folder 14.
———. "Modernization and Expansion Program, Superintendent's Response, February and March 1963." Box 1, Folder 13b.
———. "Modernization and Expansion Program—Support and Justification For, 1962–63." Box 1, Folder 13c.
———. "Modernization and Expansion Program—Opposition to, 1962–63." Box 1, Folder 13d.

"The Naval Academy." *Army-Navy Football Program 1970.*
———. "Officer Faculty Assignment." Box 2, Folder 11.
———. "Organization, USNA, 1968, 70–71." Box 1, Folder 17.
———. "Progress Report—Middle States Association, February 1967"; "Progress Report—Middle States—1967–69"; "Follow Up Report to the Middle States Association, October 1969." Box 4, Folder 8.
"Religious Life of Midshipmen." Vertical File, Special Collections Division.
Report of the Board of Visitors 1948.
Report of the Board of Visitors 1959.
Report of the Board of Visitors 1963.
Report of the Board of Visitors 1964.
Report of the Board of Visitors 1965.
Report of the Board of Visitors 1968.
Report of the Board of Visitors 1970.
Report of the Board of Visitors 1971.
Report of the Board of Visitors 1972.
Report of the Board of Visitors 1973.
Report of the Board of Visitors 1974.
Report on the Meeting of Board of Visitors Committee on Academic and Professional Training. October 1967.
Report to the Middle States Association of Colleges and Secondary Schools from the U.S. Naval Academy, February 1966.
Superintendent's Statement to the Board of Visitors 1936.
Superintendent's Statement to the Board of Visitors 1937.
Superintendent's Statement to the Board of Visitors 1941.
Superintendent's Statement to the Board of Visitors 1942.
Superintendent's Statement to the Board of Visitors 1943.
Superintendent's Statement to the Board of Visitors 1944.
Superintendent's Statement to the Board of Visitors 1946.
Superintendent's Statement to the Board of Visitors 1951.
Superintendent's Statement to the Board of Visitors 1952.
Superintendent's Statement to the Board of Visitors 1953.
Superintendent's Statement to the Board of Visitors 1954.
Superintendent's Statement to the Board of Visitors 1955.
Superintendent's Statement to the Board of Visitors 1956.
Superintendent's Statement to the Board of Visitors 1959.
Superintendent's Statement to the Board of Visitors 1960.
Superintendent's Statement to the Board of Visitors 1961.
Superintendent's Statement to the Board of Visitors 1962.
Superintendent's Statement to the Board of Visitors 1963.
Superintendent's Statement to the Board of Visitors 1964.
Superintendent's Statement to the Board of Visitors 1965.
Superintendent's Statement to the Board of Visitors 1966.
Superintendent's Statement to the Board of Visitors 1967.

Superintendent's Statement to the Board of Visitors 1968.
Superintendent's Statement to the Board of Visitors 1969.
Superintendent's Statement to the Board of Visitors 1970.
Superintendent's Statement to the Board of Visitors 1971.
Superintendent's Statement to the Board of Visitors 1973.
Superintendent's Statement to the Board of Visitors 1974.
Superintendent's Statement to the Board of Visitors 1975.
Supplemental Statement by Senators Saltonstall, Holland, Beall, and Engle for addition to the Report of the Board of Visitors 1959.
"The Superintendent's Open Letter to the First Class." *Superintendent's Statement to the Board of Visitors 1950* and *Shipmate,* December 1947.
"They Don't Speak Our Language." Language, Vertical File, Special Collections Division.
U.S. Naval Academy Command History 1970–71.
U.S. Naval Academy Command History 1972–73.
U.S. Naval Academy Command History 1973–74.
U.S. Naval Academy Command History 1974–75.
U.S. Naval Academy Command History 1976–77.
"USNA Honor Concept." Vertical File, Special Collections Division.
USNA Instruction 1531.30, "USNA Professional Competency Objectives." 14 April 1972.

Oral Histories

Reminiscences of Hanson W. Baldwin. U.S. Naval Institute Oral History Program.
Reminiscences of Rear Admiral John Davidson. U.S. Naval Institute Oral History Program.
Reminiscences of Captain Roland Faulk. U.S. Naval Institute Oral History Program.
Reminiscences of Rear Admiral Draper Kauffman. U.S. Naval Institute Oral History Program.
Reminiscences of Rear Admiral Charles Loughlin. U.S. Naval Institute Oral History Program.
Reminiscences of Vice Admiral William Mack. U.S. Naval Institute Oral History Program.
Reminiscences of Vice Admiral Charles Melson. U.S. Naval Institute Oral History Program.
Reminiscences of Vice Admiral Charles Minter. U.S. Naval Institute Oral History Program.
Reminiscences of Vice Admiral Horatio Rivera. U.S. Naval Institute Oral History Program.
Reminiscences of Vice Admiral William Smedberg. U.S. Naval Institute Oral History Program.

Papers of Captain Wayne Hoof

Letter from Captain Wayne Hoof to Chief of Naval Personnel. "Plebe Indoctrination System at the U.S. Naval Academy." 2 November 1966.
Letter from Captain Wayne Hoof to Chief of Naval Personnel. "Plebe Indoctrination System." 21 November 1966.
Letter from Captain Wayne Hoof to the Secretary of the Navy. "Constructive Criticism and Suggestions Pertaining to Improvements in Naval Efficiency." 21 November 1966.

Letter from Captain Wayne Hoof to Superintendent. "Investigation of Plebe Indoctrination System." 15 November 1966.
Letter of Commander Donald Smith to Superintendent. "Investigation of Allegations Concerning Plebe Indoctrination System at U.S. Naval Academy." 22 November 1966.
Letter from Head of English, History and Government Department to Superintendent, U.S. Naval Academy. "Plebe Indoctrination Program." 13 October 1966.
Letter from Head of English, History and Government Department to Superintendent, U.S. Naval Academy. "Midshipman L. A. Panza, Fourth Class." 10 October 1966.
Letter from Head of English, History and Government Department to Superintendent, U.S. Naval Academy. "Request for Change of Duty Orders." 10 October 1966.
Letter from Midshipman Anthony Jackson to Professor Robert Seager. "Reasons for Resignation." 7 November 1966.
Letter from Midshipman Jeffrey Leppert to Secretary of the Navy. "Reasons for Resignation." 11 December 1966.
Letter from Midshipman Leonard Panza to Superintendent. "Reasons for Resignation." 10 October 1966.
Letter from Midshipmen Time and Effort Working Committee to Chairman, Midshipmen Time and Effort Board. "Impact of Plebe Indoctrination." 12 December 1966.
Letter from Professor A. S. Pitt to Head of English, History, and Government Department. "Plebe Indoctrination System." 21 October 1966.
Letter from Professor Douglas Lacey to Head of English, History, and Government Department. "Plebe Indoctrination." 24 October 1966.
Letter from Professor E. B. Potter to Head of English, History, and Government Department. "Plebe Indoctrination at U.S. Naval Academy." 21 October 1966.
Letter from Professor Robert Seager to Rear Admiral Draper Kauffman. "Plebe Indoctrination System." 19 October 1966.
———. 14 November 1966.
———. 28 November 1966.
Letter from Professor Robert Seager to Superintendent. "Case of Midshipman Anthony Jackson." 14 November 1966.
Letter from Superintendent to Captain Wayne Hoof. "Investigation of Plebe Indoctrination System." 7 November 1966.
"Letter from the Committee on Grade Distribution and Control to the Academic Dean." 29 September 1965.
Memorandum from Public Affairs Officer to Superintendent. "Discussion with *New York Times* Reporter Ben Franklin." 21 November 1966.
Memorandum from Superintendent to Midshipmen Time and Effort Board. "Midshipmen Time and Effort Board." 18 November 1966.
"Memorandum of Telephone Conversation between Captain Wayne Hoof and Captain Kenneth Brown." 18 January 1967.
Obituary of Captain Wayne Hoof. *Shipmate,* May 1990.

Secondary Sources

Asher, Herbert. *Polling and the Public: What Every Citizen Should Know.* Washington, D.C.: Congressional Quarterly Press, 1995.

Brubacher, John, and Willis Rudy. *Higher Education in Transition: A History of American Colleges and Universities, 1636–1976.* New York: Harper and Row, 1976.

Clowse, Barbara Barksdale. *Brainpower for the Cold War.* Westport, CT: Greenwood Press, 1981.

Duncan, Francis. *Rickover and the Nuclear Navy.* Annapolis: Naval Institute Press, 1990.

Fitzgerald, John. "Changing Patterns of Officer Recruitment at the U.S. Naval Academy." *Armed Forces and Society* 8, 1 (fall 1981).

Forney, Todd. "Charting Institutional Change: The U.S. Naval Academy during the 1960s." In *New Interpretations in Naval History: Selected Papers from the Thirteenth Naval History Symposium,* edited by William McBride and Eric Reed. Annapolis: Naval Institute Press, 1998.

Geertz, Clifford. *An Interpretation of Cultures.* New York: Basic Books, 1973.

Goffman, Erving. *Asylums: Essays on the Social Situation of Mental Patients and Other Inmates.* Chicago: Aldine University Press, 1961.

Huntington, Samuel. *The Soldier and the State.* Cambridge: Harvard University Press, 1957.

Karsten, Peter. *The Naval Aristocracy.* New York: Free Press, 1972.

Kennedy, David. *Freedom from Fear: The American People in Depression and War.* New York: Oxford University Press, 1999.

Lovell, John. *Neither Athens Nor Sparta?* Bloomington: Indiana University Press, 1979.

Masland, John, and Lawrence Radway. *Soldiers and Scholars Military Education and National Policy.* Princeton: Princeton University Press, 1957.

"Men of Annapolis." *Shipmate,* November 1999.

Millett, Allan. *Military Professionalism and Officership in America.* Columbus, OH: Mershon Center Press, 1977.

———. *The American Political System and Civilian Control of the Military: A Historical Perspective.* Columbus, OH: Mershon Center Press, 1979.

———. "The Study of Military History Since World War II." *Medlingen van de Sectie Militaire Geschiedenis.* The Hague, 1991.

———. "American Military History: Clio and Mars as 'Pards.'" In *Military History and the Military Profession,* edited by David Charters, Marc Milner, and J. Brent Wilson. Westport, CT: Praeger, 1992.

Nassr, Michael. "The Annapolis Air Force." *Shipmate,* October 1999.

Patterson, James. *Grand Expectations: The United States 1945–74.* New York: Oxford University Press, 1996.

Reynolds, Clark G. *The Fast Carriers: The Forging of an Air Navy.* Annapolis: Naval Institute Press, 1992.

———. *Admiral John H. Towers: The Struggle for Naval Air Supremacy.* Annapolis: Naval Institute Press, 1991.

Rockwell, Theodore. *The Rickover Effect: How One Man Made A Difference.* Annapolis: Naval Institute Press, 1992.

Roush, Paul. "A Tangled Webb." *Proceedings,* August 1997.

Sheppard, Charles. "An Analysis of Curriculum Changes at the U.S. Naval Academy during the Period 1959 through 1974." Ph.D. dissertation, George Washington University, 1974.

Sudman, Seymour, and Norman Bradburn. *Asking Questions: A Practical Guide to Questionnaire Design.* San Francisco: Jossey-Bass, 1982.

Sweetman, Jack, and Thomas Cutler. *The U.S. Naval Academy: An Illustrated History.* Annapolis: Naval Institute Press, 1995.

Timberg, Robert. *A Nightingale's Song.* New York: Simon and Schuster, 1995.

Webb, James. *A Sense of Honor.* Englewood Cliffs, NJ: Prentice-Hall, 1981.

———. "Women Can't Fight." *The Washingtonian,* November 1979.

Weigley, Russell. *History of the U.S. Army.* New York: MacMillan Press, 1987.

Whitfield, Stephen. *The Culture of the Cold War.* Baltimore: Johns Hopkins University Press, 1996.

Index

Academic Advisory Board, 181–83, 252
Academic Board, 41, 47, 98, 115, 145, 157, 161–62, 174, 214, 222–23
Academic Dean, 110, 137–39, 142, 144–46, 154, 162, 167, 174, 182–83, 222
Academic Department Heads, 28, 62, 88, 174, 181, 183, 214, 263
Academic Failures, 98, 166, 170, 176, 220, 274
Academic Forum, 183
Academic Minor, 110, 116, 122, 162–63, 272
Academic Major, 16, 18, 35, 87, 110, 116, 146, 162–63, 204, 211–12, 220, 222, 246, 249, 272
"Academic Revolution," 16–18, 33–35, 41, 62, 65, 81, 87, 93, 98–99, 107, 111–13, 121, 123, 125, 130, 135–37, 139, 141–42, 145, 156, 158, 160, 166–67, 172, 174–75, 178, 187, 199, 203, 206, 208, 210, 217, 222, 246–47, 249, 253–54, 262, 268, 272
Accelerated Curriculum, 34, 44–51, 168
Accreditation, 62, 95, 183, 270
Adams, Jim, 262
African Americans, 71, 218–19, 250–51
Air Cruises, 52
Aircraft Carrier, 39, 48, 52, 102, 132, 134
Airfield, 52, 82, 84
Air Force, 15, 35, 54, 82, 102, 104, 107–8, 112, 131–32, 135, 154, 271
Air Force Academy (Colorado Springs), 82, 97, 107, 154, 176, 272
Alcohol, 16, 35, 99, 253, 257–58
Alumni, 14–18, 36, 80–81, 88–89, 99, 111, 121–22, 125, 127–28, 130, 136–37, 139, 142, 145, 148, 166, 179, 195, 220, 272

Alumni Association, 37, 70, 80, 89–91, 178–79, 184
American Civil Liberties Union (ACLU), 204
American Council on Education, 39, 62
American Association of University Professors (AAUP), 181, 187, 273
Angell, James, 41–42
Anchormen, 156, 159, 176, 274
Appointment Process, 80, 92
Aptitude for Service Boards, 227
Army, 81, 103–4
Army-Navy Game, 25, 32, 196, 229
Association of American Colleges, 39, 62
Atomic Bomb, 60
Attrition, 97–98, 176–77, 180, 184, 216, 219–20, 250–51, 274
Automobile Privileges, 16, 35, 80, 99–100, 123, 152, 206, 229, 259–60
Aviation Program, 52–54

Baldwin, Hanson, 42–44, 140
Bancroft Hall, 14, 16, 18, 23–29, 33–34, 39, 42, 44, 49, 56–57, 60, 63, 65, 69, 73–74, 80, 82–83, 86, 95–96, 100, 102, 107, 111, 114, 119, 122–23, 126, 137, 147–48, 164, 166, 182, 185, 193, 197, 204, 207, 212–13, 217, 221, 226, 229, 231, 250, 253, 260, 263
Battalion, 20, 125, 185
Battalion Officers, 29–30, 32, 49–51, 122, 135, 226, 260
Bellino, Joe, 89
Blue and Gold Program, 146–47, 179, 222, 273
Board of Visitors, 33, 117, 120, 141, 181–82, 251
Boroff, David, 154–55

405

Brigade Commander, 229
Brigade of Midshipmen, 33, 56, 67, 82–83, 93, 111, 119, 124–25, 150, 185, 205–6, 213, 226, 228, 230, 236, 261, 267
Brinckloe, William, 130
Bringle, Bush, 51
Brown, Kenneth, 186–87, 190
Brown, Wesley, 71
Bulkeley, John, 51
Bureau of Naval Personnel (BUPERS), 41, 60, 62, 99, 114, 140, 143, 151, 195–96, 217, 251–52
Cadets, 81, 83, 104–6
Calvert, James, 164, 198–99, 203–6, 208–11, 213–14, 216, 219, 222–23, 228, 230, 236, 239, 246–48, 267, 274
Candidates, 92, 147–48, 159, 170, 216
Candidate Guidance Office, 93, 218, 250–51
Cannon, Clarence, 96
Casualty Lists, 168
Chauvenet Hall, 161
Chief of Naval Education and Training (CNET), 251–52
Chief of Naval Operations (CNO), 196, 203
Civilian Faculty, 41, 46–47, 64, 98, 110, 116, 143–44, 146, 154, 168, 173–74, 177, 183, 186, 263, 272
Class Privileges, 24, 63
Classmates, 42, 107, 119, 127–28, 149, 28
Classmate Loyalty, 65, 105–6, 136–27, 269
Cold War, 15, 66, 71, 81–82, 95–96, 103, 113
College Entrance Examination Board (CEEB), 80, 97, 115, 162, 170, 218
Color Company, 128
Combat Preparation, 20, 22, 26, 42, 46, 48–49, 55, 167, 186, 265–66
Commandant of Midshipmen, 28–29, 95, 110, 122, 180, 183, 229, 263
Company Culture, 18, 20, 42, 87, 128–29
Company Officers, 29–30, 32, 39, 49–51, 73, 116, 122, 135, 137–38, 148, 150, 168, 187–88, 196–97, 226, 253, 260
Company Section, 21, 35, 127–28, 135
Come Around, 42–43, 150, 185
Congress, 67, 96, 107, 111, 154, 217

Congressional Liaison Office, 217
"Cops and Robbers," 30–32, 105, 124, 229, 231, 260, 272
Curving Grades, 41, 81, 137, 159, 167, 176, 270

Daily Quiz, 41, 64–65, 159–60
Dark Ages, 22
Davidson, John, 122, 127, 139
"Dear John" Letters, 241
Defense Department Reorganization, 34–35, 72, 89, 102–3, 271
Defrancia, James, 154–55
Demerits, 31–32, 73, 205, 261
Dewey and Santee Basin Project (Landfill Project), 83–84
Demobilization, 55–56, 66–67, 82–85, 242, 252
Dope System, 64–65, 81, 100, 105–6, 126, 148, 156, 26
Drought, A. Bernard, 145–46, 162–63, 175, 199, 211
Drugs, 170, 206, 253

Education, 38–39, 94–95, 111, 114–15, 117, 167, 179, 201, 204, 265
Electives, 35, 115–16, 118–19, 122, 124, 127–28, 133, 143, 149, 156, 163, 167, 174, 210
Engineer's Council for Professional Development (ECPD), 211
English, History & Government Department (E,H&G), 186–90
Erdelatz, Eddie, 86, 105
Excess Leave (Law) Program, 215–16
Exchange Officers, 104, 107
Exchange Visits, 83, 104–5
Executive Department, 28–33, 35, 63, 73, 95, 107, 139, 151, 157, 185–86, 191, 197, 200–201, 205, 230–31, 253, 258, 261, 267
Expansion, 35
Extra Duty, 24, 31–32, 73, 123, 229

Faculty Education Program, 143, 173
Faculty Senate, 181, 183, 273
Fallback Majors, 213–14
Fields of Concentration, 163, 210–11, 213
Fitch, Aubrey, 67
Fitzsimonds, Jim, 261–62
Fluckey, Eugene, 88

INDEX

Folsom Board (Curriculum Review Board), 98–99, 111, 113–18, 121, 136, 141, 172, 178, 266, 272
Folsom, Richard, 98–99, 113–14, 118, 159, 182
Football Players, 80, 85–86
Forbes, Donald, 259, 261
Foreign Affairs Conference, 117
French Battalions, 42
Fulbright Program, 187–88, 249

Gates, Thomas, 88
G. I. Bill, 40
Grade Controls, 159, 166, 172, 174–76, 187, 263
Graduate Performance Evaluation System (GRAPES), 224
Great Depression, 45
Grooming Standards, 16, 237–41, 257
Gouge, 106, 259

Haig, Alexander, 104
Haircut, 207, 237–41, 257
Halsey, William, 51, 55
Halsey Field House, 83
Hazing, 17, 42–43, 63, 72, 185, 197
Herndon Monument, 22, 129
Hill, Harry, 79, 94, 105–6, 115
Holloway, James Jr., 39, 56, 79, 81, 88, 99–100, 103, 114–15, 151, 204, 209, 263, 267
Holloway, James III, 252
Holloway Board, 56–60, 69, 85
Holloway Reforms, 35, 60–65, 95
Hoof, Wayne, 189–98, 226, 266
Honor Concept, 27, 34, 81, 105–6, 126–27
Human Goals Program, 253
Huntington, Samuel, 14, 141

Immediate Master's Program, 198
Induction Day, 25–26, 227
Inspection, 23–24, 30–31
Interservice Training, 104

Jackson, Anthony, 193–94
Johnson, Louis, 103–4
Joy, Turner, 94
June Week, 199

Kauffman, Draper, 170–72, 176–77, 183, 187–88, 194, 196–200, 203–4, 222

King, Ernest, 55
Kinney, Sheldon, 164–65, 185, 190, 194
Kirkpatrick, Charles, 139, 147–54, 156–57, 161–62, 175, 273
Korean War, 35, 94
Korth, Fred, 139–42, 172–73, 267, 273

Lacey, Douglas, 189
Larson, Charles, 100–102
Late Lights Privileges, 151–52
Lawrence, William, 106
Leppert, Jeffrey, 193
Letter Grading Scale, 137, 159–61, 166, 174–76
Liberty Privileges, 16, 24, 63, 99, 123, 206, 229, 258, 260
Library, 62, 114, 178
Lockstep Curriculum, 18, 40, 60, 62, 96–97, 105, 110, 114–16, 119, 122, 136, 156, 159, 161, 199, 210–11, 220, 271
Log, The, 19, 30, 33, 71, 100, 145, 191, 206, 228, 230, 235–37, 241, 260–61
Lucky Bag, The, 33, 74, 243

Mack, William, 40, 42, 45, 246–48, 250–51, 255–56, 258, 261
Mandatory Chapel, 16, 35, 204, 236–37, 256–57
Mandatory Sea Tour, 39, 41, 54, 82, 102, 107
Manning Board, 79, 82
Marine Corps, 19, 28, 44, 154, 168, 193, 212
Maury Hall, 69
McDonald, David, 172
McNamara, Robert, 172
Medal of Honor Rooms, 55
Melson, Charles, 115, 121–22, 162, 214
Memorial Hall, 55
"Men of Annapolis," 93, 112
Mentor Relationship (Plebe System), 42, 164, 190
Mess Hall Routine, 27, 42, 69, 82, 105
Michelson Hall, 161
"Mickey Mouse" Regulations, 18, 30–32, 64, 259–60
Middle States Association, 39, 62, 81, 94, 111, 114, 138, 173, 178, 181–83, 185, 262, 264, 266
Midshipmen Time and Effort Board, 197
Military Academy (West Point), 81, 83, 97, 99, 104–7, 154, 164, 176

408 INDEX

Military Faculty, 41, 46–47, 64, 111, 118, 123, 137–38, 141, 144, 168, 173–74, 189
Military Specialization, 15, 63, 130–31, 135, 207, 210–11, 222, 224, 231, 270
Minimum Service Obligation, 217, 255, 263–64
Minority Affairs Officer, 251
Minter, Charles, 147–54, 161–66, 177, 184–85, 273
Mission Statement, 36
"MIT on the Severn," 39, 64, 79, 94, 172, 195, 206
Moreell Plan, 141
Morris, Max, 259–60

National Defense Education Act of 1958, 96
Naval Academy Athletic Association (NAAA), 86–88
Naval Academy Foundation, 86
Naval Academy Preparatory School (NAPS), 221
Naval Academy Training Squadron (NATRON), 223
Naval Aviation, 39, 51–54, 81, 84, 102, 131, 135, 168, 198, 211, 225, 253
Naval Aviators, 39, 52–54, 141, 225
Naval Research Laboratory, 117
Naval Reserve Officer Training Commission (NROTC), 15, 23, 58–60, 66, 85, 109, 118, 140, 144, 158, 216, 249, 254, 257, 269–70
Navy Juniors, 45, 271
Navy-Marine Corps Memorial Stadium, 79, 87–89, 179
Navy Science Symposium, 117
Nimitz, Chester, 51, 55
Nimitz Library, 263
Nitze, Paul, 196
Nuclear Power Program, 96, 102, 112, 116, 131–35, 156, 198, 212, 220, 249

Office of Naval Research, 117
Ogden, Bruce, 261
Operation Information, 80, 93, 218, 251, 273

Qualified Alternate Rule (Public Law 586), 92, 217, 274

Panza, Leonard, 192–93
Patton, George Jr., 104

Performance Boards, 227
Perot, H. Ross, 106
Physical Plant, 28, 40, 67–69, 79, 82–83, 116, 162, 168, 271
Pirie, Robert, 52
Pitt, A. S., 189
Plebe, 59, 63, 69, 86, 111, 115–16, 119, 124, 129, 137, 149–50, 152, 164–65, 170, 176, 185–86, 190, 192, 198, 205, 213, 226–28
Plebe Indoctrination, 16–17, 19–23, 33, 39, 42, 86, 121, 124–26, 128, 134, 137, 149, 166, 184–86, 188–90, 194, 196–97, 207, 226–27, 235, 246, 265, 268–69
Plebe Rates, 21, 26–27, 149, 185, 191
Plebe Servitude, 21, 27, 44, 73, 185
Plebe Year, 14, 22, 72, 149–50, 167, 170, 185–86, 191, 197, 205, 227–28
Poindexter, John, 102
Polaris Program, 112, 132
Potter, E. B., 188–89
Pre-Med Program (Bioscience Major), 215–16, 248
Prior Enlisted Midshipmen, 70, 193, 221
Professional Development Board, 223–24
Professional Military Order of Merit (PMOOM), 255
"Professional Officer and the Human Person, The," 253
Professional Readiness Exam, 224–25, 255
Professional Revolution, 168, 199, 222
Professional Socialization, 14–15, 21, 24–26, 28–30, 36, 39–40, 48–49, 51, 55–57, 67, 69, 84–85, 87, 100, 104, 107, 116, 119, 121, 127–29, 140, 142, 158, 172, 174, 186, 220, 223, 231, 242, 246, 264–66, 270, 275
Professional Training and Education Board (PT&E Board), 200–201
Prospective Nominees, 249–50

Radios, 81, 99
Randolph, Jennings, 186
"Realistic Military Environment," 256, 258–60
Retention Rates (Academy Graduates), 40, 57–58, 66–67, 117–18, 140, 158, 221, 242

INDEX

Rickover, Hyman, 15, 96–97, 109, 112, 115, 119, 121, 129, 131, 133–34, 136, 138–40, 143, 154, 165, 203, 210, 212, 225, 249, 266, 271
Rickover Hall, 209
Rivero, Horatio, 113, 182
Roman Catholic Midshipmen, 70–71, 271

"Salty Sam," 30–31, 64, 230, 236
Scholars of the House Program (Yale University), 156
Seager, Robert, 187–89, 193, 198
Secretary of the Navy's Board on Educational Requirements (SABER), 113
Sellars, David, 42, 58, 79
Service Selection Lottery, 41, 44, 64, 99, 108
Seven-Mile Limit, 81, 99, 257–58
Shadow Command, 205, 229–31, 235, 260–62
Sideburns, 257
"Slash" Midshipmen, 17, 64–65, 100, 124, 129, 148, 156, 270
Smedberg, William, 41, 62, 88–89, 99, 115, 142–43, 182, 184
Smith, Donald, 196
Spanish Battalions, 42
Sputnik Educational Crisis, 15, 81, 95–96, 110, 132, 271
Squad System, 164–65, 185, 190–91
Staubach, Roger, 89
Stearns-Eisenhower Board, 81, 103–4
Strategic Nuclear Deterrence, 131–32, 271
Stripers, 39, 100–101, 156–58, 165, 177, 205–6, 218, 227–31, 259–61
Submarines, 84, 96, 108–9, 112, 131–34, 224, 254, 271
Summer Cruises, 21, 48–49, 51, 164, 200, 223–24, 252
Superintendents, 28–29, 33, 63, 67, 69, 79, 88, 91, 97–98, 122, 138, 145, 180, 183, 263
Superintendent's List, 81, 100–102
Surface Line, 39, 44, 54, 73, 81, 102, 104, 135, 223–24, 254–55
Surface Warfare Officer School (SWOS), 254–55

Television Sets, 80
Thirty-Six Company Expansion, 150–51, 185–86

Total Institutions, 14, 24, 32, 73–74, 109, 155, 268
"Trade School" Academy, 38, 70, 166, 168, 195, 198–99, 207, 231
Training, 15, 17, 38–39, 48–52, 94–95, 111, 115, 167, 179, 204, 265
Trident Scholars, 110, 156–57, 273
Turnbacks, 47–48, 159, 177, 263

Unification Controversy, 103–4
"Unity of Suffering" Experience, 18, 119, 127, 159, 220, 268
Upperclassmen, 20, 23–24, 39, 69, 82, 99, 111, 115–16, 119, 124–25, 137, 148–50, 152, 167, 185, 190–92, 205, 213, 221, 226–28, 267–68, 272

Validation, 110, 115–16, 122, 133, 156, 163, 199
Versatility (Versatile Line Officer), 130–31, 133, 135
Vietnam War, 16, 34–35, 112–13, 143, 151, 168–69, 173–74, 178, 184, 187–88, 192, 199, 202, 205, 207, 209, 214, 216, 219, 221, 223, 232–34, 242
Vietnam Prisoners of War, 170, 233–34
Vision Waivers, 218, 250
Voluntary Resignations, 98, 137, 148–49, 170, 176, 180, 192, 219, 221, 226, 274

Warfare Communities, 72, 87, 109, 164, 210, 224
Warnecke Plan, 161
Wigs, 237–39
Woodstock, 235
Working Class Midshipmen, 18, 40, 70, 72
World War II, 15, 17, 18, 35, 38–40, 44–51, 54, 65, 74, 79, 85, 94, 102, 112, 129, 145, 168, 171, 188, 203, 262, 269–70

Zumwalt, Elmo, 16, 216, 239, 246–47, 251, 257
1946 Middle States Report, 62
1956 Middle States Report, 94–95, 98
1966 Middle States Report, 138, 144, 165–66, 173, 176–77, 179–82, 222, 260
1976 Middle States Report, 262, 264